ABOUT THE AUTHOR

Danny Wallace is the author of several books, including *Join Me* and *Friends Like These*. His TV work includes his own BBC2 series, *How To Start Your Own Country*, as well as *Horizon*, *Test the Nation* and *School's Out*. He writes an award-nominated column in *ShortList* magazine, and hosts *The Danny Wallace Radio Show* each week on XFM, both of which keep him busy, but not too busy that he can't go to the pub or play on his Xbox. He lives in London, in a little house, with a little wife.

www.dannywallace.com

*For my mum and dad
And for Sammy*

**THE AMAZING TALE OF WHAT HAPPENS
WHEN YOU DECIDE TO SAY ... YES**

DANNY WALLACE

EBURY
PRESS

1 3 5 7 9 10 8 6 4 2

Published in 2008 by Ebury Press, an imprint of Ebury Publishing
A Random House Group Company
First Published in Great Britain in 2005
This edition published 2008

Copyright © Danny Wallace 2008

Danny Wallace has asserted his right to be identified as the author of this Work in
accordance with the Copyright, Designs and Patents Act 1988

The Random House Group Limited Reg. No. 954009

Addresses for companies within the Random House Group can be found at
www.randomhouse.co.uk

A CIP catalogue record for this book is available from the British Library

The Random House Group Limited supports The Forest Stewardship Council
(FSC), the leading international forest certification organisation. All our titles that
are printed on Greenpeace approved FSC certified paper carry the FSC logo. Our
paper procurement policy can be found at www.rbooks.co.uk/environment

Printed in the UK by CPI Cox & Wyman, Reading, Berkshire

ISBN 9780091927905

All photography © Danny Wallace unless otherwise credited

To buy books by your favourite authors and register for offers visit
www.rbooks.co.uk

Danny would like to thank

Ian, Hanne, Wag and Lizzie, Jake Lingwood and all at Ebury, Simon Trewin, Sophie Laurimore, Jago Irwin and everyone at PFD, Ryan Fischer-Harbage and all at Simon & Schuster, Daniel Greenberg, Sarah Bennie, the award-winning Stine Smemo, Di Riley, Claire Kingston, Dawn Burnett and Little Hannah Telfer, Bob Glanville, Dr Frank Cottrell Boyce (who wishes he was Swiss), Mike Gayle (for being Mike Gayle), Howie and Liz at UTA, Andrew Collins, Espen Tarnesvik, Dominant Joly, Marc Gehring, Ricky the sound man and his colleague Jeff, Jonathan Davies, Karl Pilkington (keep existing), Paul Lewis (who I must point out for legal reasons has not bullied since 1995), Xavier McMahon and family, cheeky Kieran Harte, Gareth Jones, Dan Glew and everyone at Cactus TV (thanks for giving me a break), Daisy Gates, Lisa Thomas and all at Karushi, Lee Phillips and LeafStorm, James @ Two Associates, Charlie, Matt and James from Busted (!), my wonderful joinees (making the world a better place, one Friday at a time!), the Venerable Samten Kelsang and everyone at the excellent and very good value Losang Dragpa Centre, Hypnotist Hugh Lennon and Murphy the Hypnodog, Arlene for the won-ton, Dean the soldier, Ian Critchley, Myfanwy Moore, Graham Smith, John Pidgeon and all at the BBC (still the best place to work in the world).

Special thanks to my mum and dad, and to Greta Elizabeth McMahon, for between them making everything brilliant.

'The wise man can pick up a grain of sand and envision a whole universe.

But the stupid man will just lay down on some seaweed

and roll around until he's completely draped in it.

Then he'll stand up and go, "Hey, I'm Vine Man!"'

— Jack Handey

Prologue

In which we set the scene

In twenty minutes it would be midnight. I was standing in the rain outside the house of a rich banker in Las Vegas.

I checked my pockets. I had everything I needed. The photos. The keys to the car. The silver pocket watch.

Most importantly, I had the gun.

Because I had been asked to kill a man.

And I had said 'Yes'.

Ahem.

I wasn't really. And I hadn't, really.

I mean, when was the last time *you* were asked to kill a man? It happens to me very rarely. And I'm not sure I could even do it, to be honest. If you asked me today whether I would kill a man for you, I'd most likely refuse flat out, and even if I asked for more details, my decision would still most likely be not to do it.

'No,' I'd say. 'Surely you can resolve your issues with this man another way?'

And you'd see my point, and say Yes, and I'd suggest you beat him at chess instead, and you'd walk away shamefaced yet impressed by my wisdom.

Nope. I can honestly say I have never killed a man. Not on purpose, anyway. And the only reason I forced you to imagine me on the verge of undertaking a messy assassination in Las Vegas was to give you an idea of how my life *could* have gone. How this story *could* have started. Me, standing in the rain, charged with a terrible and sinister mission, gun in hand. I mean, I *hate* rain. And I'd look *rubbish* with a gun. I wouldn't *dare* be out on my own after midnight in Las Vegas. I rather frown upon murder. And I really don't know *where* a silver pocket watch comes into all this.

So thankfully, the real story doesn't start this way. But the real story did take me to some strange places, meeting some strange people, doing some strange things. And the real story takes place over several months, not so long ago. Several months which changed not just my life, but my entire *way* of life, and my entire *attitude* to life.

I should just say thanks to all those people I've written about in the next few hundred pages. Their names are real, apart from those few cases where I've changed a name or detail to save anyone any obvious embarrassment, or – in one rather central and vital person's case – just because they thought it would be cool and so asked. There is also, I'm afraid, the odd occasion where I've moved an event to a slightly different time or place … but this is for your own good. I don't want you falling asleep on me. I've got some very important things to say.

I wrote this book after keeping a diary. Some of that diary I have written more on than other bits, some I didn't include at all, and some has made it in word for word. I recommend keeping a diary. Diaries are cool.

And lastly: do me a favour. While you read this book – however long it takes you, and wherever you end up doing it – make a note of all the times you could have said Yes to something. And think about where that Yes could have led you. It might come in handy one day.

You look lovely today, by the way.

Danny Wallace
St Petersburg, June 2005

January 12th

I have started this diary to record all that is going on in my life. All that one day I will be pleased I had recorded for posterity. If you are a historian from the future, please – save your thanks. Your time will be better spent reading up on my thoughts and philosophies.

So, with pen in hand, I say to you, Life: I am ready! Throw at me what you will!

January 19th

Nothing yet.

Buddha! I'd love to meet Buddha. He looks like a right laugh. What did this bloke look like? If he had a beard it was probably Jesus, and if he had a belly it was probably Buddha.'

'He had a beard, but it wasn't a Jesus beard.'

'A belly, then?' he said, with what looked like real hope in his eyes. 'Did he have a Buddha belly?'

'I'm fairly sure he wasn't Buddha, either. This was an Indian bloke. His name was Medhi, or something.'

'"Medhi" sounds a bit like "Jesus".'

'No it doesn't. And it wasn't Jesus. What would Jesus be doing in Bethnal Green?'

'There are some nice discount shops in Bethnal Green.'

'Jesus is the son of God, Ian, he doesn't need discount shops.'

'Cor. Imagine the pocket money you'd get if you were the son of God.'

'Ian … I'm trying to tell you about my life-changing moment and you're going on about Jesus in a pound shop.'

'Sorry, go on. So there was this bloke on a bus last week, who wasn't a deity or a son of a God, and then there was also your diary?'

Yes. There was also my diary. High up on the list, right under the bus, was my diary. A diary I had only started because I was afraid I would forget all the wonderful things I was doing. All the dazzling, crazy, hazy times. The important times, the carefree times, the times I'd look back on as the times of my life.

Only when I flicked through it did I realise there was nothing to forget. Or, rather, nothing worth remembering.

Things had been different last year. Last year was a year of adventure. Of fun. Of friends. But I'd slowly begun to realise, six months into a new year, that all my stories were about last year. All my memories, too. I'd been cruising on past glories, dining out on better times. Well, that's not strictly true. Not true at all. I'd been dining *in* on them.

For a number of months I'd been labouring under the impression that everything in my life was fine. I was a single man, in his mid-twenties, living in one of the most exciting cities in the world. Turns out I was a single man, in his pants, sitting in his flat.

It had happened to me once before, this strange sense of mid-twenties crisis, but it had happened when I'd lacked direction. These days I *had* direction. Plenty of it. But the direction was down.

In my mind, I was one of London's young, thrusting urbanites. In my mind, I was always on the go, always had somewhere to be, always in the thick of things. I thought I was like something out of an advert. I probably even thought I had a moped.

I couldn't have been more wrong. About the moped, especially.

And this is what I would finally realise for sure after I got home from talking to the man on the bus.

I'd ended up talking to the man on the bus quite by chance.

It was, until that moment, just another day working in the West End, followed by just another dash to the tube station, in what was just another hopeless attempt to beat the rush hour and get home without spending an hour on a crowded train with my cheeks pressed up against a stranger's nipples, receiving severe paper cuts every time they turned a page of their book.

We'd been standing, me and this man, waiting for the Central Line train to take us from Holborn to the East End when the announcement had spluttered and stuttered its way over the tannoy. It was a security alert. We were being asked to leave. Our journeys home had just gained an hour. We'd be shunted and squeezed on to buses outside and driven home, very slowly, during rush hour, on a rainy, rainy London night.

The man and I had raised our eyebrows at each other and smiled in a what's-the-world-coming-to way, but other than that we didn't say a word to one another. We'd simply started to walk up the stairs and out of the station, like the good, old-fashioned, obedient British citizens we were.

'Nice weather for this!' said the man, as we jogged through a slanting rain and flashed our travelcards at the bus driver. I ha-ha'd, probably a little too ha-hard, and we joined the seething masses on board the bus.

After ten minutes and three stops, we found seats for ourselves, and after another ten, we had begun to chat.

'Where are you headed?' I'd asked.

'Aldgate,' he'd replied.

The man, as it turned out, was a teacher.

And he was about to teach me.

'So what did he teach you?' said Ian.

'I'll tell you in a minute.'

'Tell me now. I want to know what kind of wisdom he imparted on you that's caused you to summon me here.'

'I didn't "summon" you here.'

'You sent me an e-mail saying your entire life had changed and that you wanted to meet up more.'

'That's hardly summoning. I was more saying "do you fancy a pint?"'

'Great. I do. Thanks.'

I sighed, stood up, and went to get a round in.

Now that I think about it, my downward spiral had probably started after I'd been dumped by my girlfriend in the late autumn. It was a shock to the system; a body blow that had really changed things.

But don't go thinking I'm all hung up on an ex-girlfriend. This isn't one of those stories of obsession, and regret, and of trying-to-get-back-together. I've never been someone who would have made an effective stalker, for one thing, lacking as I do both the necessary energies, and a decent pair of binoculars.

It's just that being dumped suddenly puts time into perspective. I'm not saying my three years with Hanne were wasted, because they weren't; they were great and warm and loving. I'm just saying that at the end of any relationship you take a long hard look at the years that have gone and say 'what now?'

So I did three years of growing up in two weeks. I returned to the world of freelance employment as a radio producer at the BBC. I got a mortgage. And a pension. I started to shop at Habitat and IKEA. I experimented with new and exciting pastas. I bought a colander, and some air freshener, and a fountain pen. I learnt how to iron. I even bought a plant.

Most of these were small changes. But soon, quite without my knowing, I developed a certain satisfaction for staying in. For pottering about, and tinkering with things. For slouching, and napping, and channel-hopping. Soon, that was all I wanted to do. And so I became the man who could wriggle out of any prior engagement. Who could spot an invitation coming a mile off and head it off at the pass. The man who'd gladly swap a night down the pub for just one whiff of an episode of *EastEnders*. The man who'd send an e-mail instead of attend a birthday. Who'd text instead of call, and call instead of visit. I became the man who'd white-lie. The man who always had an excuse. The man who always said no.

And I was perfectly happy. Perfectly happy to be me, myself, and ironing. Perfectly happy until that night, on that bus, next to that man.

* * *

4

'Okay. So there was a man,' said Ian. 'And you sat next to him. So far this isn't really what you'd call a classic anecdote.'

'But it's what he told me that was important, Ian.'

'Yes, it sounds it. But *what* did he say? What was it that he actually said that changed things? Because right now, all I know is that a man said something to you.'

'Have patience.'

'He said "have patience"?'

'No, that's what I said, just then. What *he* said was more important.'

'But what *was* it?'

It was my friends who'd noticed it first. They'd noticed I'd changed, or that I just wasn't around as much as I used to be, or that I was just saying 'no' a lot more.

There were the odd nights down the pub, of course, and I always agreed that we should do it more often, but it just never seemed to be the right night. I was too tired, or there was something I wanted to watch, or I just felt like being alone. I couldn't put my finger on it. But it didn't make me sad – that was the weird thing. Not while it was happening, anyway. It only made me sad when I finally realised the effect it was having on my friendships; on the friends I was letting down, or annoying, or disappointing, or even losing.

But at the time, I just didn't notice it. The sad fact is, saying no had become a habit.

'Aha! I knew it!' said Ian, pointing his finger slightly too close to my face. 'I *knew* you were always making excuses!'

'I know. And I'm sorry.'

'That night when you said you couldn't come out because you'd won a competition to meet Lionel Richie, was that an excuse?'

'Yes.'

'How about that time you couldn't come out because you said you'd accidentally reversed all your leg joints?'

'That was quite obviously a lie. And I'm sorry. But there will be no more excuses. Honestly, Ian, I'm a changed man.'

'Jesus, Dan … that night I sent Hanne round your house you acted all offended when she even *suggested* you were making up excuses!'

* * *

Ian had become concerned that I wasn't going out enough any more. And so he'd decided to take matters into his own hands. Every couple of days there'd be another idea, or invitation, or suggestion for a night out. He'd send me e-mails, and text me, and leave grumpy messages on my answerphone.

'Danny,' they'd say. 'I know you're there. How do I know you're there? Because you're *always* there. You're not picking up because you're scared I'll invite you out, which I'm going to do anyway. We'll be at the pub from eight. I look forward to receiving your standard text message saying you can't make it and you're sorry and we should have fun. Bye.'

And then I'd get all hoity-toity and text him, and say I'M NOT IN ACTUALLY. I'M OUT. BUT I CAN'T MAKE IT SO I'M SORRY AND HAVE FUN. And then I'd realise that he'd left the message on my home phone, and that to have heard it I would have to have been in. And then I'd blush and he'd text back and call me a wanker.

But then one evening Ian had bumped into Hanne, and shared his concerns. That Friday night, she'd turned up at nine or ten o'clock, unannounced, and carrying a bottle of wine.

'So what's going on?' she said, using her hand to brush some stale rice off the sofa and taking a seat.

'How do you mean?'

'You. What's happened to you?'

Hanne filled some glasses while I considered her question. I didn't know what she meant. I checked myself in the mirror to see what could possibly have happened to me. Maybe someone had painted a tiger on my face, or tied balloons to my ears.

'Nothing's happened to me, Hanne.'

'Well, I suppose that's true.'

'Eh?'

'What I mean, Dan, is that *nothing's* happened to you. Nothing does, any more, apparently. Your friends are worried. Where have you been for the past six months?'

'Here,' I said, confused. 'I've been right here!'

'Precisely. You've been here. Where were you on Steve's birthday?'

'I was … busy!' I lied, trying desperately to remember what excuse I'd used that time. 'I went to a Women and War exhibition.'

I never said they were good excuses.

'Okay. And where were you when everyone else was at Tom's stag night?'

'Again – busy. I'm very busy, Hanne. Look at me.'

I don't know why I asked Hanne to look at me. It's not as if I looked particularly busy. I was just a man standing up.

'You're no more busy than your friends. We've all got jobs, Dan, but we all find time to do other things, too. You've cut yourself off, and we're concerned. You don't have fun any more.'

'I do! I have loads of fun! And I have loads of fun new hobbies!'

'Like what?'

I struggled to find an answer. Of course I had fun! Surely I did! I just couldn't think of any examples right now. Hanne had put me on the spot, that was all. But there must be *something* I enjoy doing.

'I … enjoy toast.' I said.

'You enjoy toast,' said Hanne, who, because she is Norwegian, likes to be matter-of-fact about things.

'Yes, but not just toast,' I said, defensively. 'Other things, too.'

'Like what?'

My mind raced. What else was fun?

'Theme parks.'

'Right,' said Hanne. 'So you've been eating toast and going to theme parks, have you?'

'Yes.'

'For six months.'

'On and off.'

'You hate theme parks,' she said. 'So which theme parks?'

'What?'

'Which theme parks have you been going to?'

I think she may have been on to me. I looked around the room, desperate for inspiration.

'Shelf … Adventure.'

'Sorry?'

I cleared my throat.

'Shelf Adventure.'

'*Shelf Adventure*?'

'Yup.'

Hanne took a sip of her wine. So did I. Of *my* wine, I mean, not hers. Taking a sip of *her* wine would have spoilt the atmosphere.

'Any others?' she said, finally. I could tell she thought she was going to enjoy catching me out. 'Or was it just Shelf Adventure?'

* * *

'So you were making Shelf Adventure up too! I *knew* it!' said Ian.

'Of *course* I was making Shelf Adventure up! How many adventures can you have with a shelf?'

'I couldn't find a *thing* about it on the Internet. Hanne knew you were lying too, you know.'

'I guessed that she probably had,' I said.

'And then what happened?'

'Is this about us, Dan?' said Hanne, getting her stuff together in the hall-way. 'Because we split up?'

I didn't know what to say. So I didn't say anything at all.

'It just seems like you're doing all the things that I would once have loved you to do … the job, the mortgage, the staying in more … you're not doing this … for *me*, are you?'

I smiled, gently.

'No, Hanne. Don't worry.'

'Because you know that now we've split up you can do all the things that used to annoy me? You can come home drunk whenever you like, and you can do as many stupid boy-projects as you want.'

'It's not about us, Hanne …'

'Because you know that just because you've changed doesn't mean we're going to get back together, don't you?'

'I know.'

'Even if you *did* buy handwash for the bathroom.'

'I know,' I said.

'And you can't mend a relationship with a garlic crusher.'

'Is that a Norwegian proverb?'

'No. I'm referring to the new garlic crusher in your kitchen.'

'I didn't even know it was a garlic crusher. And no, I know you can't mend a relationship with a garlic crusher. To be honest, I don't even know how you crush a garlic with one.'

'Okay, then,' said Hanne, opening the door to leave. 'But listen. You should make more of an effort. It's time you got back out there. It's time you stopped making excuses, and saying no to everyone. Because you're not just saying no to your friends – you're saying no to yourself.'

I paused for a second to place the quote.

'*Dawson's Creek*?'

'Yep,' said Hanne.

'Bye.'
'Bye.'

'Look, Dan,' said Ian. 'Will you just tell me what this fucking bloke on the bus said to you, or should I make another appointment?'

'Okay, I'll tell you.'

I put my pint down on the table and looked Ian in the eye.

'He said: "Say Yes more".'

I picked my pint up again and took a sip. I raised my eyebrows to show Ian he should be impressed, but for some reason he still appeared to be waiting for more. That's the problem with the MTV generation. Never satisfied.

'Is that it?' he said. '"Say Yes more"?'

'Yep,' I said, smiling. 'That's it.'

The sentence had tripped off the man on the bus's tongue like he'd been saying it all his life.

'Say Yes more,' he'd said.

'Say Yes more,' I'd repeated. Three little words of such power.

'The people without passion are the ones who always say no,' he'd said, moments before, and I'd turned, stunned, to listen.

'But the happiest people are the ones who understand that good things occur when one *allows* them to.'

And that was that.

That was all it took to turn my life on its head. A few choice sentences from a complete and utter stranger. A stranger on a bus. And a bearded stranger, at that. This went against everything I held as true. If there was one lesson that had been drummed into me as a kid, it was never listen to a bearded stranger.

I'll be honest; it was a fairly odd moment for me. I felt like the Karate Kid sitting next to Mr Miyage. One minute we'd been idly chatting about this, about that, and about what we'd done with our weeks, and the next, this thin and bearded man had dropped a philosophical bombshell.

I couldn't work out whether it was just coincidence. Whether his words were really intended for me, whether they truly reflected on our conversation, or whether they were just the throwaway ramblings of some bloke on a bus. If I'd been in another mood, I might just have laughed them off, or buried my head in my newspaper, or politely

9

ignored them. But with my friends' concerns, and everything that had happened – or, in a way, everything that *hadn't* happened – the words took on a strange and important resonance.

Say Yes more.

And that was when I had my revelatory moment.

'That is the stupidest bloody thing I have ever bloody heard,' said Ian, ever the diplomat. 'Some drunk bloke on a bus mutters something oblique and you claim it's changed your life? Bollocks. How come you never listen to me when I'm drunk?'

'Because when you're drunk you usually talk about us buying a caravan and moving to Dorset.'

'Oh, we should, though, just think of the …'

'And anyway, he wasn't drunk. We'd been talking about what we'd been up to in the week. He seemed very interested.'

'And what did you tell him?'

'I told him I'd been staying in a lot. Not doing much. Having early nights.'

'And that was all?'

'Pretty much.'

And it was. The simple fact of the matter was that this man would probably have had no idea of the impact of his words. I was surely just someone who wanted to make a decision; who deep down *wanted* to make a change. His words were just the catalyst that kickstarted me into action. I wish I could claim that he was a shaman, or some kind of spiritual figure sent into my life at that time to push me over the edge. And as much as I'd like to believe that, the fact is, he was probably just a bloke on a bus. Just like the next bloke *you'll* sit next to on a bus. But chatty. And wise.

'He doesn't sound much like Jesus to me,' said Ian. 'Apart from the beard.'

'I never said he was Jesus!'

'Or Buddha, for that matter. Buddha would've probably just smiled a lot. Or taken you to a nice restaurant. That's the thing about Buddha, he knows how to have a good time.'

'Ian, listen. It wasn't Jesus. Or Buddha. It was just some bloke on a bus.'

'So why are you taking him so seriously?'

'Because he was right. And *you* were right. And Hanne was right. But the thing is, none of you knows *how* right you were!'

'So what are you saying? Just that you're going to start saying Yes more? That's hardly an announcement.'

'I'm going to say Yes to *everything*.'

'Everything? What do you mean, everything?'

'I mean, I'm going to say Yes to everything from now on.'

Ian looked shocked.

'When do you start?'

'That's just the thing,' I said, finishing my pint and looking him dead in the eye. 'I already have.'

2

In which Daniel becomes Increasingly Excited

This was it.

This was bloody *it*.

I didn't know what 'it' was yet but by God it was this and that was enough for me.

It had been just ten minutes since the man on the bus had uttered his words of wisdom, and I was excited. And inspired. And slightly out of breath, because sometimes when I'm excited and inspired I tend to try and leap up staircases, when really I should realise that I live on the fourth floor and such exertions do not become me.

But my red face and now dampened forehead didn't matter, because the thing is, what the man on the bus had said to me had struck a chord. No, more than that. It made complete and utter sense. I know it sounds odd, and I know it might seem meaningless to you, but to me those three words had … *done* something. *Triggered* something. *Meant* something. It was like the man had known about me, in a way I hadn't even known about myself. Which is quite a disquieting idea, unless it turns out that the thing you didn't know about yourself was quite glamorous, like you were a matador, or you once freed some slaves, in which case you'd be quite grateful to whoever pointed it out.

But what he'd shown me about myself wasn't glamorous. It was worrying. It was something I had to change. And luckily, he'd shown me the way. He'd provided me with a moment of pure and happy clarity.

I was smiling, now. Grinning, as I walked through the door of my flat, and flicked the kettle on, and reached for a mug. Had I been a more feminine man I dare say I'd have probably skipped about a bit as well, although as I suspect I'd make quite a *sensible* feminine man, I would not have done this around boiling water, and I would certainly have put the mug down first.

I paced the kitchen, thinking and rethinking the night's events, and then, just before the click of the kettle, I realised something.

I could see.

Not just what was around me.

But what I'd been doing wrong.

And how I could turn it around.

I could see exactly how my life should be.

I was on the verge of something. But sometimes, to look forward, you have to look back. So I went and got my diary. And, even though I suspected it would be the case, I was nevertheless shocked at what I saw.

I saw nothing.

Well, virtually nothing.

Nothing, apart from missed opportunities. And blank spaces. And things I'd scribbled out, or hadn't gone to, or said I couldn't make. Acres of white. Acres of white lies.

I'd missed birthdays. I'd missed barbecues. I'd missed various and assorted parties. I'd missed dinner with friends, I'd missed nights down the pub, I'd missed Tom's stag do. God, Tom's stag do. I bet that had been *legendary*. I bet they'd all got together and painted his privates blue and handcuffed him to the buffet car of a train. Suddenly, *I* wanted to do that. *I* wanted to paint men's privates blue and handcuff them to buffet cars!

But not just that … I wanted to do *all* the things I'd missed out on. I wanted to turn the clock back and shout Yes to all the things I'd mumbled no to. Not just the big nights, or the main events, or the frantic celebrations … but to the little things. The normal things. The things that sometimes matter the most.

I scanned and rescanned my diary. Hanne had been right. Ian had been right. Everyone had been right except me. As I flicked my way through the months that had flown by, I realised with horror that probably the most excitement I'd had was on 18 April, when I'd gone to PC World to buy a new printer cartridge. Suddenly, that didn't seem like enough. I mean, yeah, at a push I could probably scrape a short anecdote out of it, but still … it was hardly one to save for the grandchildren, was it?

And hang about – *what* grandchildren? I was already 26, and there wasn't even a *hint* of a grandchild in the pipeline! Who was I going to tell all my stories to when I was old? Who was I going to impress with my tales of short uneventful walks to PC World and me worrying that there wasn't going to be the right kind of printer cartridge in stock, but it being all right because in the end there actually was?

And who was going to *give* me grandchildren? Well, my kid, obviously – but who was going to give me one of *those*? Maybe I'd already missed out on the woman of my dreams! Maybe she'd been out there, waiting for me all this time, but she'd got bored, and moved on. Maybe she'd been working in the buffet car the night they painted Tom's privates blue! She certainly hadn't been in PC World!

My inspiration had turned to panic. Who knew what I had already missed out on in life? Now I would never know what *might* have happened, who I *might* have met, what I *might* have done, where I *might* have ended up, how different life *could* have been. And my friends … how many connections had I lost? How many people would simply have got used to me not being there and given up on me?

I was angry at myself. I had wasted half my year. Half a year *gone*. Thrown away. Swapped for toast, and evenings in front of the telly. It was all here – or, rather, it *wasn't* – in black and white, and blue and red. Every dull non-entry was a sharp slap in the face.

I had to get back out there. I had to start living life, rather than just living.

And it was obvious how.

Say Yes more.

I would say Yes more. Saying Yes more would get me out of this rut. It would rekindle my love for life. It would bring back the old me. The me that had died a little the day I'd been dumped. I just needed a little kickstart. A little fun. A chance to live in a completely different way. I could treat it like an experiment. A study in my own behaviour. A study in positivity, and opportunity, and chance.

This was serious. This went beyond what Hanne would have called a 'Stupid Boy Project', because now … now I was dealing with a whole new *Way of Life*.

My mind was racing. This could work. But how should I approach it? How would I say Yes more?

I decided I needed to tackle the problem quickly and efficiently. If I could spend just a day on this, surely that would be all I'd need? I'd go out to whatever was happening, hang out with whoever wanted to, and let life just lead the way. I'd surrender myself for twenty-four hours, answer everything with a Yes, and let opportunity and chance boot me out of this mid-twenties crisis.

I started to get ready for bed.

A day. Yes. A day. A day of relentless positivity. What harm could that do? A day of saying Yes. Yes to anything. Anything and everything.

A day of being a Yes Man.

Yes.

'Hello, can I speak to Mr Wallace, please?'

'Yes!'

'Hello, Mr Wallace, I'm phoning from Mark 1 double glazing in London, would you have a moment to talk about double glazing, sir?'

'Yes!'

'Have you ever thought about having your house or apartment double-glazed at all?'

'Yes!'

'And have you been put off in the past by high prices at all?'

'Yes, I have, Yes.'

'Can I ask you, would you be interested in a free, no-obligation quote for double glazing on your property, Mr Wallace?'

'Yes!'

'Okay ... well, what we can do is, we can certainly send one of our representatives round to your place of residence. Is there a particular time or day that's good for you?'

'Yes.'

'Uh-huh ... and ... when would that be?'

'You suggest a time.'

'Right. How are you fixed for Tuesday, Mr Wallace?'

'Yes, Tuesday. Yes.'

'2 pm?'

'Yes.'

'Okay, let me just make a note ... so, that's Tuesday, at—'

'Um ... I should warn you, though ... I am already fully double-glazed.'

'You're what, sorry?'

'I already have double glazing throughout my flat.'

'Right ... so ... sorry, I don't—'

'I'm just saying, I've already got plenty of double glazing, but you shouldn't let that put you off. Life should be all about taking opportunities, you know? The best things that ever happened to us happened because we said Yes, just like the man on the bus told me. I realise that now.'

'Well, wait a second ... why would you want a quote?'

'Sorry?'

'Why would you want a quote on double glazing when you're already fully double glazed?'

'Well, you asked, and—'

'Just seems like a bit of a waste of everyone's time, Mr Wallace—'

'I just thought it might be nice. Maybe you could come round and tell me what you think of the double glazing I've already got. We could have some tea. You could still give me a quote if you like.'

'I have to go now, Mister Wallace, okay?'

'Yes.'

And that is how my Yes experiment started – confusing a cold-caller with my unnerving desire to discuss all aspects of double glazing and the double-glazed.

I'd woken up only minutes before and was now lying in bed with a grin on my face and a head full of thoughts. What should I do? Where should I go? How should I begin?

But that wasn't up to me. None of it was. I had to see how things went. I had to go with the flow. I got up and switched my computer on, willing it to provide me with all the opportunities I'd been batting away only a day before. I had a few e-mails, and quickly scanned through them.

One was from Hanne. Could we have a chat? Yes.

Another was from my good friend Wag. Did I fancy a pint some time? Yes.

Another was from a complete stranger. Would I like a bigger penis? Ye— hang on. Who was this from?

Would you like a bigger penis? New Penis Patch Technology now means thousands of men just like you can ...

Oh. Spam. Still, I'd rather it was a piece of spam than a suggestion from an ex-girlfriend. My mouse pointer hovered over the delete button, an instant reaction formed by thousands of similar unsolicited e-mails in the past, but then I realised ... that wasn't the spirit. Or the attitude. Or the game.

So I said 'Yes'. And I laughed. And then I clicked on the link, added my credit card details and ordered the Amazing Penis Patch. Well, it couldn't hurt, could it? Not unless you put it on wrong.

I filled the kettle and scratched around in the cupboard, looking for something to eat. I found a small box of Coco Pops that I didn't know I had, and was absolutely delighted.

I walked back to the computer, hoping that in the five minutes since I'd written back to Hanne and Wag, they'd replied with suggested times and places. But they hadn't. So I decided to take matters into my own hands. I sat down at my computer and drafted an e-mail. And when I'd done that, I sent it to every friend I felt I'd let down, or said no to, or hadn't seen in too long.

This is what I wrote:

>To: Mates
>From: Danny
>Subject: Me, you and us

Hey there
Listen. It's been too long. That's my fault, and I'm sorry. But
I've changed. I'm going to be more like the old me now. So,
if you fancy meeting up ... let me know.
Your pal (I hope)
Danny

I felt oddly cleansed. But then I decided to up the ante. I phoned Hanne.

'Hey Hanne, it's Danny.'

'Hey, Dan. You got my e-mail?'

'I did. And Yes, I would *love* to meet up for a chat.'

'Okay ... in town for a coffee? Today?'

'Yes.'

'Four-ish?'

'Fine.'

'I'll meet you by Covent Garden tube. Is that okay?'

'Yes, absolutely. I'll see you there.'

Great! That was easy! I had just successfully organised a meeting with my ex-girlfriend. If there were such a thing as the grown-up Scouts, I'd probably get a badge for that.

Next, I phoned Wag.

'Wag! Waggle! Wagamama!'

Sadly, this is not me saying that. This is how Wag chooses to answer the phone sometimes.

'Hey Wag ... I got your e-mail. I do indeed fancy a pint sometime. When and where do you recommend?'

'Coool ... you about today?'

'Yes.'

Ooh, hang on, though. I started to realise that blindly saying Yes to everything could well have its complications. What would I do if he suggested 4 pm for a coffee at Covent Garden?

'How about seven for a pint at the Horse and Groom?'

Thank God Wag was a bloke.

'Done,' I said.

This was all going very well. Very well indeed.

Arrangements for the day made, I pootled down to the corner shop to buy milk and a newspaper or two. I was already starting to feel like a new man, which probably explains why I also bought a pot of natural yoghurt and some freshly squeezed orange juice. It was the kind of feeling that usually ends up with me considering going to the gym, or getting a dog and walking it a bit, and doing all the things that blokes in catalogues do. It was a feeling I hadn't had in quite some time.

Back upstairs, I sat down with my tea and my newspapers and looked up at the clock. Midday. Just four short hours before I had to be anywhere. I could relax.

Trouble was, I didn't want to relax. I wanted to get on with things. I wanted to say Yes more. But there would be time.

I started to leaf through the *Guardian* before realising that I was kidding myself and so picked up the *Sun* instead. I wish I was the type of person who could read their *Guardian* before reading the *Sun*, but even as a kid I'd want to eat the chocolate mousse before I attempted the healthy stuff.

I amused myself with a piece about a young Scottish man who'd tried to take his kite out in a storm and ended up flying for three-quarters of a mile, before I turned the page and saw, in a small box at the top of the page …

DO YOU HAVE AN INVENTION?

I bristled with excitement. Now, technically, no, I didn't have an invention. I had no invention at all. But this tiny advert was an opportunity. An opportunity to try my hand at something new. I could invent something! Maybe that's why I was put here on earth! To be an inventor!

I tore the ad out and read it again. It had been placed by the Patents and Trademarks Institute of America, and it was offering to help new inventors get their brilliant inventions off the ground. Ace! All I had to do was phone them up and ask for an information pack. Five minutes later, I'd done just that, and had been assured my information pack was on its way to me. I could relax again.

I finished off my copy of the *Sun*, picked up the *Guardian*, put it down again and decided to head into town a little earlier than I'd planned.

I could always buy the *Mirror* on the way.

It was a sunny day and it felt like a different city.

London was bright and full of colour. Even my walk to the tube station, under deafening railway arches and down sparse streets, pavements broken up by tufts of dying grass and puddles of spit, had a certain beauty about it.

But now here I was, walking from Leicester Square up to Covent Garden, and feeling quite proud to be a Londoner. No more Yes Moments had presented themselves since I'd left the flat, but one was just around the corner.

'Cup of tea, please,' I said to the man in the café.

'Sugar?' he said.

'No thanks.'

'50p, please,' he said, putting my polystyrene cup in front of me.

I reached for my change and realised I'd made a huge error. An error which I hope you will find excusable, based as it is on twenty years of habitual tea drinking.

'Sorry, you asked me if I wanted sugar …'

'Yeah,' he said. 'You said no.'

'I know. But … could you ask me again?' I slid the tea back towards him.

'Eh?'

'Could you ask me if I want sugar again please?'

The man frowned slightly, but then obliged. He picked up the cup and said: 'Sugar?'

I cleared my throat.

'Yes please,' I said.

'How many?'

Now it was my turn to frown.

'I don't know. I don't take sugar.'

Now we were both frowning at the same time.

'Just give me whatever you think's reasonable,' I shrugged.

20

The man took a spoon and, without even breaking eye contact, slowly and carefully put three heaped teaspoons of sugar into my tiny cup.

'Okay?' he said.

'Yes,' I said. 'Thank you very much.'

Now, I realise that this sugar-based story probably reaches new lows in terms of contemporary European storytelling, and that as you read this, half of you is probably tempted to turn back a few pages in order to enjoy a winner like the PC World story once more, but to me, this really meant something. I've been drinking tea for a long time. A lot of it. And this was the first time I have ever consciously asked for it with sugar. It represented a lot to me – it represented that I was willing to change even the most basic, ground-in aspects of my daily routine. It was a discovery which excited me.

I left the shop, sugared tea in hand, and wandered further towards Covent Garden, pausing only to watch a juggler drop his balls and a small child nearly run off with one of them. It was this that was distracting me when I was pounced upon.

'Excuse me, sir, do you have two minutes?'

'Yes,' I said, instantly and with joy in my heart. I turned to see a short woman with curly ginger hair and a bright green bib on. She was carrying a clipboard and she looked very bubbly.

'Great! Can I tell you a little bit about Help the Aged?'

Ten minutes later and we'd had a lovely and informative chat about the elderly. I'd agreed to sign up to their Adopt-a-Granny scheme and had directed a few quid of my monthly earnings towards some deserving old woman's upkeep. Mainly because she kept beginning her sentences with the words 'would you be interested in …' and I kept saying 'Yes'. But I didn't mind. After all, thanks to me, some old granny would now never have to worry about where the next mint was coming from. I said goodbye to the little bubbly ginger lady and walked on, towards the tube station. It'd be time to meet Hanne soon, and I wanted to have a look in some of the fancy shops before we hooked up. But then I heard a voice to my right.

'Excuse me, sir, do you have two minutes?'

I was certain I'd heard those words before. Not too long before, either.

I turned to see a tallish man, with a long nose, and a green bib. A green bib with the words 'Adopt-a-Granny' on it.

'Er, well, Yes, but—'

'Great! Can I tell you a little bit about Help the Aged?'

And he did.

'So you're late because …'

'I was adopting some grannies.'

'I should have guessed,' said Hanne, and we started to walk to a nearby café. 'It is, after all, why *most* people are late these days. Anyway. It's good to see you. It's been too long.'

Since we'd split – which is my nice way of saying 'since she'd dumped me' – Hanne and I had remained very good friends. We'd started off having lunch every week, and sometimes we'd catch a quick drink if we could, but lately we'd been seeing a lot less of each other. That was fair enough, I'd reasoned. After all, Hanne had been concentrating on making great waves in her career and I, of course, had been eating toast.

'How's Lizzie?' asked Hanne, and I smiled.

Since the break-up, neither Hanne nor myself had been in another relationship. I'd come close, with a girl called Lizzie. A *fantastic* girl called Lizzie. But Lizzie, of course, had left. Not because we'd split up. But because ten days after we'd met she'd had to go back to where she'd come from. Australia. About as far away as it's possible to get. We were still in e-mail contact, and there was even the odd phone call, but we both knew, as much as we liked each other, it was an impossible situation.

'You liked her, didn't you?' said Hanne.

'Yeah,' I said. 'I did. She was cool.'

Hanne had been a great girlfriend. And an even better ex-girlfriend. She was supportive of the whole Lizzie thing when I'd told her. And, even better, she'd never put me in a similar position. There's a time after every split-up when you genuinely hope the other person will find it so hard to get over you that they'll book themselves straight into the nearest nunnery … Hanne hadn't gone quite that far. But as yet, neither had she brought out the jealous ex-boyfriend in me.

'I know things never really got off the ground with you and Lizzie,' she said. 'But you'd have *liked* them to, wouldn't you?'

'Well … yeah,' I said. 'I would.'

It was nice of Hanne to care, I thought.

'And you and I have been apart for quite a while now, haven't we …'

'Yes … I mean … I suppose we have.'

Suddenly, it felt like Hanne had brought this up out of more than concern. It was like she was building up to something. I could tell she was, in fact, because she'd started to play with her napkin and she wasn't looking me in the eye. If you're ever having dinner with Hanne, look out for this, because it may mean you won't make it to dessert. But what was on her mind?

'I know there's no need to ask you this, Dan … but the thing is … we were together for quite a while and I'd just feel better if I said this to you now, to get it out in the open, you know …'

Oh. Oh my. Suddenly I realised. Hanne was about to ask if we could get back together!

'And … well, God, this is stupid … I don't know why I'm so nervous asking you this …'

Blimey! She was! She was about to ask to get back together! What was I going to say? How did I feel?

'I know your answer already, Dan, but I just want to hear it from you …'

She had real love in her eyes, now … Yes, it was fairly well hidden, but that's probably what she loved about me most – that I just knew these things.

'… and you must be completely honest with me about this …'

God, this must be hard for her; realising she'd made the biggest mistake of her young life, knowing she'd have to plead with me to get me back … I had to play this with great care …

'It's okay, Hanne,' I said. 'You can talk to me about anything.'

She squeezed my hand.

'Would you mind,' she said, 'if I started seeing someone else?'

Oh.

'There. Said it,' she said, and sat back in her chair with a smile.

I didn't quite know what to say. She'd met someone else. Jesus. What should I say? I had to smile and say well done, clearly. But oh, God – she was asking me for my blessing. The girl I'd been out with for three years who'd dumped me was asking for my blessing. This was it! The end of an era!

Who had she met? Or had it gone further? Oh, no. Hanne was engaged, wasn't she? And she was probably pregnant, too. And he was probably an *amazing* bloke. He was probably a baron, or something! I bet he was a millionaire. I always knew Hanne would end up with a millionaire. A millionaire who was dashing, and had a castle, and who when offered an Amazing Penis Patch at a party would just laugh heartily, as if the very idea was the silliest thing he'd ever heard. I hated him. He was a twat.

'Danny?' said Hanne. 'What are you thinking?'

I snapped back into reality.

'I was just wondering if he was a baron.'

Hanne smiled.

'No, he's not a baron.'

It sounds odd, but this was a genuine relief.

'But I like him. He reminds me of you a little. Just less … work.'

'Well … that's …'

'I know, I know. You're cool with it. I mean, of course you are.'

And I was. I *was* cool with it. In fact, the more Hanne talked about him, the more cool with it I began to feel. If this whole Yes thing had been about starting again, then surely this was one of the best things that could have happened. It was significant. It represented something. It was out with the old, in with the new.

'Danny? You're not saying much.' She looked concerned. 'Do you *mind* that I want to start seeing someone else?'

I was about to shake my head, and smile, and say, Hanne, that's the best thing ever. Go forth and make this bloke yours.

But suddenly I realised what she'd just said – or, rather, the *way* in which she'd said it – and my stomach churned slightly.

'Sorry?' I said, playing for time, but it was already too late.

'I said, you don't mind that I want to start seeing someone else, do you?'

Hanne smiled sweetly. It was short-lived.

'Yes.'

Her eyes narrowed.

'Yes what?'

'Yes to what you just said.'

'Yes you don't mind, or yes you do?'

I think I looked a bit scared now.

'Yes.'

Hanne's mouth dropped open.

'Yes, you mind? You *mind* that I want to start seeing someone else?'

Oh, God.

'Yes.'

Now, clearly, this was a *stupid* thing to be saying. And the fact that Hanne kept repeating the question and I kept saying Yes to it wasn't helping matters much either.

She looked shocked. Utterly shocked.

'I'm shocked,' she said. Which just adds extra weight to my previous statement.

'I'm just trying to be more *positive*, you see,' I tried.

'But this isn't positive! It's negative! *Very* negative! How can you say that? How can you say you mind when I was so cool about you and Lizzie? Because I was *so* cool about you and Lizzie!'

'Well … it depends on *how* you ask me, you see … if you said, "will you give me your blessing to start seeing this bloke?", then I would *definitely* say Yes …'

'Oh, so I need your blessing, do I? Oh, I see. So it's a power thing? I need your blessing before I can start seeing this guy? Is that what you're saying, Danny?'

'Hanne, please, stop asking me questions …'

'I don't need your blessing for *anything*! Do you understand?'

Aha! A way out!

'Yes! Yes, I understand!'

'And you accept that?'

'Yes! Absolutely! Yes to that.'

'Good. So. I'll ask you again,' said Hanne. 'Do you have any objections to me seeing this man?'

I took a deep breath.

'Yes.'

I'll be honest. The meeting with Hanne hadn't gone quite as well as it could've. I imagine that if the Man Scouts *did* exist, they'd have asked for their badge back. Although I would doubtless have secured first prize if ever someone had thought to invent an award for Britain's Reddest Woman.

I started to wish that I'd refined my scheme somewhat. Saying Yes to everything anyone asked me was suddenly starting to feel like asking for trouble. And not telling anyone what I was up to could also bring its own problems – not as bad as the problems I'd face if word *did* get out, but still …

I started to feel like maybe a drink would be a good idea.

I phoned Wag.

'Listen,' I said. 'Do you fancy meeting up a bit earlier?'

'When?' said Wag.

'An hour?'

'See you there.'

* * *

'So,' said Wag, putting his pint down, 'you're late.'

'Sorry,' I said, slightly out of breath, and sitting myself down.

I was twenty minutes late for meeting Wag because, on my way out of the tube, a man sitting on the steps had asked me if I could spare any change at all. I'd said Yes, and handed him what I could spare. Five minutes later, another man I was walking past asked me whether I could spare any change. But I'd given all my spare change to the first man, so I had to go to a cashpoint to get some money out, and then find a shop to buy something from so that I would have some change which I could adequately call 'spare' to give to the second man. And after I'd done that I'd bumped into the first man again, who didn't recognise me and asked me whether or not I had any spare change at all.

Wag just looked at me.

'Why didn't you just say "no"?'

Good question. I tried to change the subject.

'Nice tie,' I said.

'I'm not wearing a tie.'

There was an awkward silence.

'So did you get me a pint?' I asked.

'Yes,' said Wag. 'But I drank it.'

'Oh.'

'Your round.'

'Right.'

I went to get the beers in.

Wag and I sat in the corner of the Horse and Groom and quietly supped at our pints. He's a good friend of mine, who shares a love of table football and intellectual chit-chat. I'd met him a couple of years previously at a wedding, and we'd been hanging out solidly ever since. We'd discussed this and that already; his burgeoning musical career, for one thing. He was about to set off for Germany to do some complicated technical work with the boyband Busted, and had just returned from a tour of the same country with Right Said Fred (though for some reason he always forgets to tell people about this). We'd also touched upon some of his odd ideas about life. For one thing, he is a firm believer that his haircut – the mullet – will one day be regarded as the height of style and cool, and all he has to do is wait. For another, he truly and deeply believes that one day, men too will bear children, despite the widely hailed success of the current system. He was perhaps not, with hindsight, the best person with which to discuss my troubles with Hanne …

'What you've got to understand, Danny,' he said, 'is that you obviously have a problem with moving on. You nearly managed it, with that Lizzie girl, but it didn't work out. And because of that, you resent Hanne trying to move on with her own life. Am I getting close?'

He was getting nowhere near, to be honest, but I played the game and nodded. Wag looked delighted.

'I'm good!' he said. 'Aren't I good?'

I nodded again, and said, 'Yes.'

'Deep down, this is all to do with Lizzie,' he said. 'Let me break it down for you …'

And this is where I started to drift off …

It sounds like a cliché, but I started to fall for Lizzie the moment she got her purse out and showed me a picture of a big prawn.

'This one's my favourite,' she'd said. 'Look at the size of it.'

It was the day after Boxing Day and we were with mutual friends in a small pub just off Brick Lane.

'It certainly does look like a very big prawn,' I said.

'Show him that other one you've got,' said Rohan, the man who'd brought us all there. 'The one of the big egg.'

'Aw, Danny doesn't want to see that,' said Lizzie. 'It's just a picture of a big egg.'

But I did. I really did want to see a picture of a big egg.

So Lizzie delved deeper into her bag and produced a photo she'd taken herself, of a big egg.

'This big egg isn't actually there any more,' she said. 'It used to be in Geelong, near where I'm from, but protestors had it removed.'

I had a look at the big egg. Just like the prawn, it was pretty big. Only a bit more eggy, and less obviously prawn-like.

'You probably think it's a bit weird, me having photos of big prawns and big eggs in my bag,' she said.

But I didn't. I thought it was the coolest thing on earth.

'And that, my friend, is why you will never get married. Not to a woman, anyway.'

'Sorry, what?'

'Were you listening to a thing I just said?'

'Yes.'

'So what did I say?'

I had absolutely no idea.

'Something to do with a woman?'

Wag made a tsk noise and raised his eyebrows.

'Sorry,' I said. 'It was just … you know. I was thinking of Lizzie.'

'Oh,' said Wag. 'Right.'

'I suppose today with Hanne reminded me. I'm at this crossroads, though, Wag. I can feel it. I'm changing, and it's a good thing. When Lizzie left, it was just another reason to stay in and lay low. Dumped by my girlfriend, left by a fantastic girl I hadn't even had the chance to date properly.'

'At this rate they'll be ditching you before you've even met them,' said Wag, helpfully. 'They probably already are. Right this moment, all around the country, dozens of girls are probably dumping you left right and centre, and not even having the good grace to tell you about it. They're probably keeping your favourite CDs, too, and badmouthing you to mutual friends you didn't know you had.'

'Thanks for that, Wag.'

He smiled a that's-okay smile. Wag was in high spirits tonight, and so we drank and laughed and drank some more. Mainly because he kept saying 'd'you fancy another pint?' and I kept saying 'Yes'.

And, with each sip, I felt a little bit better.

'So … do you have pictures of any other big things?' I asked, as we left the pub and walked up Brick Lane. 'Or is it just prawns and eggs?'

'Not with me,' said Lizzie. 'But I can get you some, if you like. There's a picture I've got of a big pineapple …'

'That sounds perfect,' I'd said. 'A big pineapple picture would be perfect.'

Lizzie smiled.

'Okay. Are you around tomorrow? Are you coming to Rohan's for New Year's?'

'Yes. I definitely am.'

I made a mental note to ask Rohan where and when it was, and whether it was all right if I turned up after all, having already said no to the invite. As usual.

'Cool. Well, I'll bring a picture of a big pineapple,' said Lizzie, climbing into her taxi.

'And if you're lucky,' she said, just before closing the door, 'I'll bring a picture of a big cow, as well …'

I think it's fair to say that I'd never looked forward to seeing a picture of a big cow quite as much.

'Right,' said Wag, when the bell finally sounded for last orders. 'Let's go to a club, yeah?'

'Yes,' I said, with all the assurance of a man quite certain of his decision.

Wag balked.

'What?'

'Yes. Let's go to a club. Yes.'

'A club?'

'Yeah.'

Wag looked confused. The pints had taken their toll, but my faith and enthusiasm in what I was doing had grown. It is quite amazing what several pints of lager can do for your confidence.

'What club?'

'Eh?'

'What club are you on about?'

'It was *your* idea,' I said. 'You said "let's go to a club".'

'Did I?'

'Yes! You always do!'

'Well … only because I don't expect you to agree! Since when have you wanted to go to a club? Why do you want to go to a club?'

'Because you asked, Wag. Come on. It's Saturday night. We're in the middle of London. This is what we're *supposed* to do at 26.'

'But … it's nearly eleven at night! What's got into you?'

'I told you! Life is for living! Strangers are just friends you haven't met yet! Sometimes the biggest risk is never taking one!'

'You've changed your tune!'

'Yes. I have.'

Wag looked worried.

'You said let's go to a club, mate. I said Yes. You know what we have to do now,' I said.

And with that, we went in search of a club.

'So… all these pictures of big things,' I said, tentatively. 'Is that … like… a hobby of yours?'

'No, no,' said Lizzie, smiling. 'My brothers send them to me. As a joke. And it's not "big things". It's "Big Things". Capital "b", capital "t".'

'How do you know I didn't use capitals?' I said.

'I just do,' she said.

'Big Things,' I said, trying somehow to make sure I'd said a capital 't'.

'My brothers sent them to me. To remind me of home. They think it's funny. I think it's geeky.'

'I think it's ... cool,' I said, and immediately wished I hadn't.

'Big Things are dotted all around Australia. For some reason, it's quite an Australian thing.'

'To build huge concrete representations of ...'

Lizzie handed me another picture.

'Rolling pins?' I said.

'Yep. Rolling pins, bananas, barrels, lobsters, koalas...'

'Ah,' I said. 'Now a big koala makes sense. I mean, that's Australian.'

'Yeah, the Big Koala,' she laughed. 'Imagine how proud that makes us feel. There's even a Giant Ned Kelly.'

'Wow,' I said. 'A Giant Ned Kelly. I would love to see a Giant Ned Kelly.'

'You should get yourself an Aussie girl, then,' she said, and she smiled in a way that made me feel a bit ... well ... fizzy.

Yes. Fizzy. Shut up.

'I suppose I should,' I said, suddenly slightly flushed.

I've just realised I'm making it sound like Lizzie and I have only just met. But the fact is, that's how it felt. In reality, we'd known each other for a number of months, but only in the way that friends of friends usually do. Lizzie had gone out with a friend of mine for a while, but we'd never hung out, never got to know each other. We always had to be somewhere else, with other people, doing other things, and suddenly I realised that I didn't really know her at all. And suddenly, I really wanted to.

'So what would you build, then?' she said. 'If you had to build a Big Thing for me to take a picture of?'

I thought about it. Whatever I said had to be good. This was the kind of thing girls asked you when they were checking you out. It was a sort of basic psychology test. If I said something like 'a lovely big puppy', then that would be good. Saying something along the lines of 'a really huge knife' or 'a giant smiling knocker' ... well ... that would clearly be quite bad.

What do girls like? And what do girls like that I like?

'I ... would have to say ...' I said, reaching desperately for girl-friendly ideas, 'a baby.'

Lizzie just looked at me.

'A baby?' she said, flatly.

I'd clearly just made my answer too obvious. She knew instantly why I'd chosen a baby. Because that, in my mind, is what a girl would want to hear. I had to do something. I had to change my answer.

'Hang on, though, because it's not just a baby.'

'What is it, then? A 2-in-1 thing? Both a baby and a bottle opener?'

'No. It's a ... special kind of baby.'

Lizzie raised her eyebrows, waiting for my elaboration.

I had it!

'It's a Chinese one.'

Lizzie somehow managed to raise her eyebrows even further than they were already. I wouldn't have thought it possible, because Lizzie, as far as I could tell, wasn't made of cartoons.

'A Chinese baby?' she said.

'A massive Chinese baby,' I corrected her.

'Sorry,' she replied, but I'm not sure that she was. 'A massive Chinese baby?'

She was right. I did indeed seem to have specified a massive Chinese baby. Why the hell had I specified a massive Chinese baby?

'That's correct,' I said, firmly, like I'd thought it through. 'A massive Chinese baby.'

'And why would you build a massive Chinese baby?' she said, in a tone which I hoped was gentle amusement but could just as easily have been the way experienced therapists talk to disturbed children.

'Well ... there's nothing cuter than a Chinese baby,' I said, which I thought was fair enough. 'I mean, that's not to say other Chinese people aren't cute, too. Well, no, that sounds patronising ...'

Lizzie folded her arms.

'... what I mean is, Chinese babies are cute, and so are ... well ... Chinese pensioners, now that I think about it. But ... you know ... anything in between, I can take or leave, to be honest ...'

Suddenly, this wasn't going so well. But I was sure I could rescue it.

'Let's face it,' I said. 'People would come from miles around to see my massive Chinese baby.'

PEOPLE WOULD COME FROM MILES AROUND TO SEE MY MASSIVE CHINESE BABY? What the hell was I saying?!

I stopped speaking immediately and stared into my drink.

Lizzie spoke next.

'Um ... well, I think that if there ...'

But I wouldn't find out what Lizzie thought. Because suddenly Rohan was there, with fresh cans of lager and a bowl of little carrots, and he sat down next to us, and we started to talk about London and Australia and how much Lizzie was looking forward to going back, and not one more word was said about massive Chinese babies for the rest of the evening.

The rest of the year, in fact.

It was twenty past three in the morning, and Wag and I were as drunk as we'd ever been.

We'd ended up, somehow, sitting in the corner of a club in Soho talking to three Australian lads, in town on holiday. I was using all the Australian knowledge I had to impress them.

'So you've got Big Pineapples, haven't you?' I said. 'And a Big Prawn. And you've got that Giant Ned Kelly, too.'

But the men were looking at me blankly.

'You know ... those sculptures you've got all over the place? You must've seen them. The Big Barrel, and The Big Mosquito? The Big Worm? The Big Orange? I've never been over there, but I've seen pictures that this girl I was sort of seeing showed me, and it sounds *amazing*.'

I was still getting blank looks. I decided I probably just hadn't said enough Big Things. So I continued.

'The Big Can. The Big Cod. The Big Carrot. The—'

'—Big Boring Bastard,' said Wag, and everyone laughed.

'I am talking about Australian culture here, Wag.' He was annoying me now, so I'll tell you his real name is actually Wayne. 'It is important that these gentlemen know that we in the United Kingdom are taking an interest.'

'But they're Austrian,' said Wag.

I looked at the three men.

'Are you Austrian?' I slurred.

They nodded.

'I'm terribly sorry. I thought you were Australian. Why did I think you were Australian?'

Everyone just sort of shrugged.

'But I've been talking to you about Australia and being Australian for about—'

'Twenty minutes,' said one of them. In an Austrian accent. It was then that I noticed his AUSTRIA t-shirt.

'Yes. Twenty minutes,' I said. 'Well, I hope you've at least learnt a little something about Australia from our conversations. Good day to you, and welcome to our country.'

Wag and I sauntered gracefully away from the Austrians, or as gracefully as it's possible to saunter while still swaying quite a lot and bumping into people, and stood at the edge of the dance floor.

'Drink?' said Wag.

'Yes!' I nearly shouted, correctly identifying a Yes Moment. 'Yes, Yes, Yes!'

I was pointing in the air and jabbing my finger with every 'Yes', and continued doing so long after Wag had gone to the bar.

It was probably this that attracted the man wearing the sombrero.

At first I assumed he was a Mexican, but slowly began to realise that a real Mexican probably wouldn't be wearing a sombrero in a London nightclub. And he'd probably have a real moustache, not a stick-on one. A Mexican with a stick-on moustache would be like a Super-Mexican, because he'd have two moustaches, and that'd be cool, because a Super-Mexican could probably use his poncho as a cape, and then I realised I was saying all this to the man's face.

'Tequila?' he said, by way of a response, revealing himself to be a novelty tequila seller. He revealed what at first glance appeared to be a gun holster but was actually holding a whole bottle of the stuff. 'It's one pound a shot.'

Now, I have developed, over the years, an amazing ability to avoid tequila. A number of unfortunate escapades have happened to me as a result of drinking it, and as a result I have an almost subconscious ability to say 'no' whenever the word is mentioned.

So I said …

'Yes!'

The man poured me a shot and I downed it.

'Another?'

I looked a lot less keen this time.

'Yes,' I said, without the previous exclamation mark, and with a slightly sickly feeling in my stomach. To be perfectly honest, I'm fairly sure I'd had more than enough to drink already. But that wasn't the game. I downed my second shot and smiled at the Mexican, willing him to walk away. Either he got the gist or he thought I was coming on to him, because he walked away very quickly indeed.

I tried to focus my eyes on the dance floor. Ah, that looked like fun. I was suddenly convinced I was a very good dancer indeed, certainly as good as that lady in the blue top, or that one in the green. And they were *very* good. Especially the one in the blue top. She was brilliant! But she'd be no match for me. Maybe I should instigate a dance-off with her. Sure, she looked like she knew what she was doing, with her arms and legs and head and stuff, but mere physical fitness and co-ordination and probable classical training was no match for my artistic flailings. I could do what she was doing, I was convinced of it. But unlike the classically trained my dancing had no respect for so-called 'boundaries'; I wasn't afraid to break the rules. I'd probably scare the blue-top lady, or her mate in the green, or even that big friend of theirs – the one staring me straight in the eyes and now walking right up to me. That was probably why he was coming towards me, in actual fact. To tell me they all knew what I was thinking, and that I was right – I *was* the rightful Lord of the Dance! Then we'd probably all go back to theirs, and I'd show them some of my moves, and we'd all be great mates, and …

'Are you looking at my girlfriend?' said the man, suddenly inches away from me, and not looking like the happiest bloke in the world.

'Uh?' I said, brilliantly.

'Are you looking at my girlfriend?'

I smiled, and tried to stifle a little tequila-burp.

'Am I looking at your girlfriend?' I said, in what I hoped was a *very* amusing voice.

The man wasn't amused.

I suddenly realised he was serious. My instinct told me to say no. No to whatever he was suggesting. It was a definite No Moment.

'Who's your girlfriend?' I asked, as if showing a willingess to under-take detailed research was going to make things better.

'Blue top,' he said.

Oh. Her.

'You make a lovely couple,' I tried.

'So are you looking at her?'

This was awkward. Every part of my being was screaming at me to make peace with this man, to say 'no' and walk away, but it was *obvious* I had been looking at her, and anyway, I already knew what I had to say … what I'd decided I'd *have* to say …

'Yes,' I said.

The man looked a little shocked by this. He looked back at his girl-friend, and then at me again.

'Right,' he said. 'So … you're looking at my girlfriend.'

'Yup,' I said, trying a little half-smile.

He smiled back. This wasn't going too badly, I suppose. Maybe he was still going to hail me as the Lord of the Dance.

But then, slowly …

'Do I look like the sort of idiot who'd let you look at my girlfriend?'

Uh-oh. He was upping the stakes. Quite considerably. He was asking me to call him an idiot. To his face. To his big, manly face. What do you say to a question like that?

Well, you don't say …

'Yes.'

I was now cringing slightly, and trying my hardest to make my answer sound like a question rather than a statement.

The man smiled again. I was hoping it was a smile of acceptance and gratitude, like I'd told him exactly what he'd always wanted to hear. It was a long shot, to be honest.

He took another small step towards me. I could smell him.

'Are you looking for a fucking smack in the mouth?' he said.

It's about now that I should have feigned a heart attack, or fainted, or run away, or broken down in tears, or renounced my position as the Yes Man. I should have shouted for Wag, or pretended I was in the FBI, or begged for forgiveness. But I didn't. I saw this as a challenge. A challenge to who I was, and what I wanted to achieve. How serious was I about this? How much did I care? I tensed up, closed my eyes, and said …

'Yes.'

Jesus. I had just said, Yes, I am looking for a fucking smack in the mouth. And I wasn't. I rarely am.

I was now bracing myself for the impact. I could already feel the punch, before it even happened. I turned my head slightly, hoping he'd miss my nose, and not smash my glasses, or my cheekbone, or anything else he could possibly smash, or crack, or bruise, or burst.

But nothing happened.

I opened my eyes.

He was just standing there, looking at me, watching me flinch.

I watched him, watching me flinch.

And then he spoke.

'You fucking psycho.'

I blinked a couple of times.

And then he pushed my shoulder, turned and walked away.

My God.

I had survived. I had survived a punch-up in a nightclub! Fair enough, there hadn't been any actual punches. But I had survived nonetheless! I had been the Yes Man, and I had stared death in the face, and I had come out of it unscathed!

Wag was suddenly by my side. He'd clearly been watching from some distance away.

'Do you want to leave, right now?' he said.

'Yes I do,' I said, and we left, right then.

'I'm sorry for what I was saying earlier,' I said. 'You know ... about massive Chinese babies.'

I'd managed to catch up with Lizzie a little after midnight, in the first few minutes of a brand new year.

'What – that? Well, as a matter of fact, I agree. There's almost nothing cuter than a Chinese baby.'

'You agree?' I said, like I'd have walked away if she'd said she preferred German ones.

'Of course I do. Listen, if I'm not married with kids by the time I'm thirty-five, just get me drunk and take me down Chinatown.'

I laughed, more out of shock than anything.

'So what've you been up to lately?' she said.

'Not much, if I'm honest,' I said. 'I've kind of been keeping myself to myself.'

Lizzie made a concerned face.

'Why?' she said, but I didn't want to talk about it. So I changed the subject.

'So, listen ... is that true, what you were saying to Rohan earlier? About going back to Australia?'

'Yep. In ten days. I'm starting a new job. So, it's back to the Aussie summer. Beats the British rain. What happened to white Christmases? I'd wanted to see my first snow.'

'You haven't seen snow?' I said.

'Terrible, isn't it? I've never seen snow, and you've never seen a Giant Ned Kelly,' she said. 'And people complain about wars, eh?'

And we laughed, and an hour later, and I still don't know how, we had kissed.

* * *

Outside the club, I started to laugh.

And laugh, and laugh, and laugh.

I was utterly exhilarated. I am not, by nature, a fighter. And yet I'd nearly got into a fight. A fight! Me! And I'd *won*!

'I just won a fight, Wag! With a man twice my size!'

'You *didn't* win a fight. And he *wasn't* twice your size. He was about an inch taller than you.'

'He was massive! And I won!'

'You did not win. He just decided not to hit you, that's all. What did you say to him, anyway?'

'I told him I was looking at his girlfriend and that he was an idiot and then I dared him to punch me!'

'You did what?'

'That's right! I said, "Yes, I am looking at your girlfriend. Punch me if you dare, you big idiot!"'

'You *said* that?'

'Kind of, Yes! Well, no, not really. But I was taken with the moment, Wag! It was brilliant! I was taken with the moment and look at me – I'm still here!'

Wag did as I asked and looked at me.

'You're a drunk man who escaped a beating.'

'I know! It's great!'

It sounds stupid, and I know it must be difficult to understand, but I felt … well … I felt on top of the world.

We walked to where we'd find a nightbus but a dodgy old Volvo pulled up alongside us.

'Minicab?' said the man inside.

'Do I *look* like a minicab?' I said, and nearly wet myself laughing. Neither Wag nor the driver seemed to find it quite as amusing as I did.

'I'm going to take this cab,' I said to Wag.

'You sure?'

I shrugged.

'He asked.'

'What are you doing later in the week?' he said.

'Whatever you want.'

As the cab raced alongside the Thames, I was excited. And enthralled. And I felt like a little kid on the verge of something thrilling. At one point we overtook a night bus and I found myself craning round to take a look at the passengers inside. Part of me was hoping I might catch a glimpse of the man who'd unwittingly kickstarted all of this, and if I did, I'd stop the cab, and get out, and jump on the bus to tell him how I was changing, and what I'd already done, and how I'd had the best day ever. And all thanks to him! Him and his three, simple words.

I got home, made a cup of tea, and switched my computer on. I was happy, and tired, and ready for bed.

I brushed my teeth while I checked my e-mails.

There was one from my friend Matt.

Danny! Nice to hear from you! How's about breakfast tomorrow? 9.30? Camden?

I looked at my watch. Tomorrow was now today. It was getting on for 6 am. To get to Camden I'd have to be up again in just a couple of hours, and I suspected I might be in line for quite a hangover.

I started to write back to Matt …

Matt,
Had a bit of a late one, mate. Can we raincheck? Maybe we can meet next week, or how abou

But then I stopped in my tracks. Writing those words felt empty. Hollow. Like I'd learnt *nothing*. Sure, my day of Yes was over, but … *one* more Yes couldn't hurt, could it?

So one by one I deleted each of the letters I'd written … and I replaced them, slowly, drunkenly, with the letters …

Y

e

s

By lunchtime I was certain I'd made the right decision.

Here I was, among friends, in a light and breezy café, my hangover nursed by reading the papers and drinking coffee and sharing jokes and laughing. For the first time in months, I felt warm, and cosy, and like I was *part of* something.

I'd made one small change in my life, and already, things were improving. And all I'd had to do was let them happen.

And that was when I'd phoned Ian and told him to meet me at the pub that night so I could tell him all about the decision that had revolutionised my life...

Because I could feel it.

I was the Yes Man.

3

*In which Daniel lifts up his Head,
and beholds the Sun*

—

Not much had been said for the past minute or two. We were just sitting there – two men, staring into space, considering it all. The events of the past few days were obviously a lot for Ian to take in. This was pretty philosophical stuff.

'Ian?' I said.

Nothing. Just a blank stare.

'Ian, did you hear all that?'

I tried to steal one of his peanuts, and he seemed to stir.

'Right … two things,' he said, pointing his finger in the air. 'Number one … at the end of that little tirade, you just called yourself the Yes Man.'

'Yeah.'

'Well, you can't. It's entirely wanky. What were you going to do, make yourself a little cape?'

'It was just a figure of—'

'Or did you see yourself as some kind of Dice Man for the day? Eh? Which is it? Superman, or Dice Man?'

'Well …'

'Because you can't go about being a Dice Man. What if you'd got asked to murder someone? The Dice Man was asked to murder someone.'

'That was a novel. And anyway, he wasn't *asked* to murder someone. He *chose* to, or, at least he chose to let his dice choose to. He had *millions* of options – I only had *one*. To say Yes.'

Ian waved my explanation away and continued.

'The second thing … I hope that after nearly getting your face

41

bashed in by a stranger in a club, you put an end to all this. Yes, so you had a lovely breakfast in Camden with Matt and the others. But I know you, Danny, and a lovely breakfast in Camden with Matt and the others will never be enough for you. You'll decide that it *meant* something.'

'It did! It represents a whole new way of life!'

'Oh, God. Look, Danny, this is to do with Lizzie, isn't it?'

'It's got nothing to do with Lizzie!' I said.

'Before she left, she said, "Come and visit me in Australia some-time," and you said no.'

'I didn't say no! I said, Yes, definitely.'

'But you *meant* no, didn't you? You had no intention of going!'

'It'd be punishing myself,' I said, sulkily. 'Why fall for someone who lives 18,000 miles away?'

'That's academic,' said Ian, who had a habit of using words like 'academic' in order to sound wise. 'You already *had* fallen for her.'

'Ian, this is about all manner of things. You know how I was living my life. And you know how I *should* live my life. *That's* what this is about. And that's why I've decided to continue with it.'

'*Continue* with it? You can't! Fair enough, be a bit more open, say Yes a bit more, but don't just do it blindly. Use some discretion!'

'I need to see where else it takes me, Ian. Just for a bit. Just for a week.'

'A week? No! You've done it for a day! Don't do it for a week! I guarantee you, you *will* end up murdering someone. And nobody likes a murderer.'

'One week is all I'm talking about.'

'Starting when?'

'Starting now.'

Ian stared at me.

'Okay … so will you buy me a pint?'

I stood up and got my wallet out.

Ian smiled broadly.

'Actually,' he said, 'I like this quite a lot.'

The thing that Ian just didn't understand – could probably *never* under-stand – was just how good saying Yes had made me feel. It was utterly liberating. My life was in the hands of everyone but me. Where would I be tomorrow? Where would I be the day after that? Who would I meet? What would we do? I had given up control.

I told Ian that we would meet in one week's time, back in the Yorkshire Grey, and I would prove to him I was taking this seriously. I would go back to my diary. I would make a note of everything I'd done. And I would present him with the evidence.

'Is a diary truly evidence?' he'd said.

'If it's admissible in court,' I'd said, 'it's admissible to *you*.'

Ian thought about it, and nodded, and said, 'Fair enough.'

I left the pub and began my week of Yes.

Now, conventional storytelling dictates that, if I were doing this properly, I would now tell you everything that happened over the course of the next few days, in the correct order, and one at a time. I'd tell you what happened on Monday (which was great) and then on Tuesday (similarly great) and then I'd tell you what happened on Wednesday (which I really rather enjoyed).

But this *isn't* a conventional story. And if we were down the pub, you and me, and you asked me to tell you what happened next, it would take all my concentration and willpower not to skip straight to this next bit, tell you it, then grab your shoulders, and shake you, and say 'so what d'you think of *that*?!' I know I shouldn't do it, but believe me, I've told the story in pubs to friends who bear more than a passing resemblance to you since this happened, and this is the way a story like this *should* be told. So I want to skip forward slightly. Only to the end of my week of Yes. To Friday. Because what happened on Friday was *incredible*.

It was Friday.

I'd been saying Yes to everything for four whole days, now, and it had been going well. Yes was proving to be an interesting companion, constantly urging me to enjoy myself a little bit more.

I woke around nine and wondered whether today would be the day I'd go into BBC Broadcasting House – the place where I am loosely employed as a freelance radio producer – and decided that no, it probably wasn't. Not while there were Yeses running free in the wild, begging to be captured.

I got up, made a cup of tea and checked my e-mails, eager to see what this day could hold as the experiment eased to its conclusion.

I'd noticed that since I'd replied to the kind and generous offer from the *Amazing Penis Patch* people, the amount of spam I was receiving had increased somewhat … it was like my computer had started shouting at me…

Discount drugs! No prescription needed! Click here!
Cheap softwares for you! All are Original Genuine!
Viagra at $0.95 a dose! Excellent value! Click here!

It was funny. It seemed that just because I was the kind of person who would respond to the offer of an *Amazing Penis Patch*, the world had suddenly decided that I might also like weight gain supplements, acne pills, books on how to succeed with girls, revolutionary hair transplants and Viagra. I just couldn't work it out. What was it about a man who'd buy a penis patch that screamed 'help!'?

Nevertheless, seeing each missive as an instruction and understanding my duty to stick rigorously to the word Yes until the week was out, I did as they asked, and clicked where they wanted me to, and studied the relevant websites. Incredibly, only one led to an actual purchase, posing, as it did, a yesable question and then following it up with an achievable instruction …

WANT TO BE A LEGALLY ORDAINED MINISTER?

Yes!

BUY OUR MINISTRY IN A BOX!

All right then!

Ten minutes later and I'd filled in the online application and purchased my very own ministry in a box. I would now, apparently, be legally allowed to set up my own church and then marry couples and baptise small children. Or large children. Hell, I could baptise anything I wanted, whatever its size! I was a bloody minister! And within 28 days, I would have the small plastic card which proved it – and all for a mere $119! And they say spam is bad.

I was excited. Who'd have thought, a week before, that I, Danny Wallace, would be one step closer to founding his own church?

As well as spam, I'd also started to get more e-mails from my friends. The first I found my way to was from Matt.

Danny,

Up for a kickabout? I've got a new ball! We're meeting in Hyde Park at twelve.

Was I up for a kickabout? Of *course* I was up for a kickabout! I wrote back and said I'd be there, shorts 'n' all.

An hour or two later, freshly showered and wearing odd socks, I made my way to the tube. It was a sunny day; perfect for football and friends. But as I got to the station a few minutes later, I noticed a man with a white stick and a slightly concerned look on his face. He wasn't really moving, just standing there, and I wondered for a second what the etiquette was in a situation like this. Should I be politically correct, and ignore a blind man, as I would anyone else looking lost outside a tube station, or should I take the fact that he was blind into account? But then I thought … what if this was an opportunity? What if we struck up a conversation, and became instant friends, and ended up going on a wonderful adventure together, like the kid and that bloke from *Scent of a Woman*? It was unlikely … but surely it was an opportunity?

In the end, I took a breath, and took the plunge.

'Hi. Are you okay?'

The man seemed a little startled by my intrusion, and I instantly regretted my decision.

'Yes. Yes, I'm fine. I'm just … waiting for someone.'

Of course he was. I was an idiot. A patronising idiot. But then he added a gracious 'Thank you, though,' and I felt less awkward. I started to walk away, the promise of a marvellous adventure with the man fading fast. But as I was nearly up the little steps, he said, 'Actually … could you help me?' and I walked back to him.

He had two 50p pieces in his hand and he held them up.

'Do you have a one pound coin?'

He opened his other palm, ready for me to place a quid there.

'Oh, right … sure … hang on …'

I searched my pockets and gave a slightly unnecessary running commentary as I did so. But I didn't have a pound coin. Just a fiver.

'Hang on … I'll go and get some change.'

I jogged over to the little newspaper stall outside Bow Road station and bought the cheapest paper they had: the *Sun*.

I returned to the man moments later.

'Got one,' I said.

45

'Great,' said the man, and I popped the pound coin in his hand.

And then I waited for him to give me my two 50p pieces in exchange.

But he didn't.

He just said, 'That's brilliant, thanks.'

And I just stood there.

'That's okay,' I said.

And I stood there some more.

'I was just a bit short,' he said. But still there were no 50ps to be seen.

'Oh,' I said.

And I waited another couple of seconds for him to give me my money. I didn't really know what to do. I mean, he'd shown me those 50ps. That was clearly part of the bargain. And yet the moment I'd given him my pound, they'd disappeared. But what could I do? He was a blind man! I couldn't demand a blind man give me two 50ps! There was probably a law, or something!

'Thanks, then,' he said, clearly bored of my presence and willing me away.

'That's okay,' I said, rather pathetically, and drifted away, confused by my encounter and slightly dirtied by it, too.

I walked down the stairs, and found my way to the train. Ah well. At least I now had a newspaper to while away the journey. I suppose some good had come out of it.

I started to flick through it, determined to make full use of it, taking in the day's news and humming a happy tune. So engrossed was I that I didn't even look up when something fell out of the middle pages and into my lap. It took me another two stops to realise that whatever had fallen out was, on first glance, some kind of advertisement. I very nearly went straight back to reading the paper, but then something about it caught my eye. It was a competition of some kind. A sheet of scratchcards. With an instruction.

An invitation.

An *opportunity*!

PLAY SCRATCH-A-MILLION!

Okay!

But hang on. What was Scratch-a-Million?

I immediately scanned the rules on the back of the sheet. Inside the newspaper, it said, were six numbers. All you had to do was check your free scratchcard for those numbers and then rub them off. If you got three matching amounts, that was the amount that you would win. Simple!

I set about finding the numbers and discovered, to my delight, that my scratchcard had all six of that day's numbers. I felt a bit silly all of a sudden. I scanned left and right just to make sure no one was watching me. I, like you, am all too aware of what a rip-off the scratchcards that fall out of newspapers and magazines are. I used to fall for them all the time as a kid. 'Well done!' they'd tell you. 'You've won a star prize!' And then you'd run to the phone and dial the number and spend £14 of your parents' money in order to find out you hadn't won one of the star prizes on the front of the card, like a boat, or one of only three brand new widescreen TVs. No. You'd won one of six millions hairclips.

But this was no time for embarrassment. Not any more.

So I rubbed the first panel away.

25,000.

Cor! A great start! £25,000!

I looked up, proud of my latest accomplishment, but no one was there to congratulate me, so I continued.

I rubbed the next panel away.

25,000.

Brilliant! Another £25,000! All I needed now was a third '25,000' and then a world of unthinkable riches would be mine. But as you and I both know, that's not how scratchcards work. They give you a thrill, a moment of escapism in which you're happily tricked into thinking you might have a chance of winning a new life, and then they dash your hopes just as quickly as they got them up. Oh, yeah. I knew how it worked, all right. I knew what to expect. I was one step ahead of those scratchcard boys, and one step ahead of the rest of the *Sun*-reading public, too, as I scratched off a third box and saw …

25,000.

Hang about.

What were those numbers again?

Oh …

Oh. My. Lord.

25,000. 25,000. 25,000.

I couldn't breathe.

I had just won £25,000.

I told you it was incredible.

4

In which Daniel makes an Unfortunate Error

I was happy. Maybe a little too happy. But winning £25,000 on a scratch-card you never would've normally scratched can do that to a man. Evidently, it was rather suspicious.

'Why are you smiling so much?' asked Hanne. I'd phoned her up and we'd agreed to meet up again, in a café not far from Holborn. She wanted me to apologise for my behaviour; I wanted to tell her all about my scratchcard win.

'Danny? What's with the smile? Really?'

'I'm just really happy,' I said, building up to my moment.

Hanne just looked at me.

'You're scaring me, Danny.'

'I'm just happy, honestly. Happy for so many reasons. Happy to be here. With you. Hanne. My ex-girlfriend.'

Hanne's eyes got a little wider.

'And I just wanted to say how fantastic – how really *fantastic* – it is that you've found this new man. I think it's fantastic. I think it's really fantastic.'

I smiled, broadly, to show just how *fantastic* I really thought it was. And I did. It was fantastic. *Everything* was.

'Danny … are you … *high*?'

I considered the question, and conceded.

'A little.'

I was, in fact, and to quote our American friends, high on *life*. My bumper jackpot win had put me in a rather generous frame of mind.

'First of all,' I said, 'I *insist* on paying for your latte.'

I held both my hands up to show that there would be no arguing with me on this one. This was on me.

'Thanks,' said Hanne, brightly (although some might say a little too quickly). 'Why are you in such a jolly mood?'

'A jolly mood? I suppose I *am* in a jolly mood. Wouldn't *you* be, after winning …' I paused for dramatic effect '… £25,000?'

Hanne looked stunned. Absolutely *stunned*. I laughed.

'You won £25,000?' she said. 'You *really* won £25,000? *How*?'

'Well …'

I thought about it. Do I tell Hanne exactly how? Do I tell her I owe it all to what she'd call a 'stupid boy-project'? The very thing that had split us up? Maybe it would finally convince her that these are *good* things! But that would also confirm everything she thinks she knows about me … so do I project a new me? A new, smarter, grown-up, career-minded, pasta-making, garlic-crushing me?

'All I had to do was scratch …'

She looked impressed.

'You're good at that,' she said. 'You were *always* scratching when we went out. But my God, Danny! It's incredible! £25,000!'

'I know!'

'So … when do you get the money?'

Ah.

Now, that was the problem.

One hour later. The Yorkshire Grey, with Ian.

'Ian, I am going to tell you something. Something *brilliant*.'

'You've written a poem.'

'No. Better. This …'

I pulled my diary out of my bag.

'… is my diary. I want you to read it. It will tell you all the things I've said Yes to over the past week, and give you some idea of my dedication and commitment to the cause.

Ian started to flick through it, found a page, and stopped.

'"Bought some new printer cartridges."'

'Ignore that,' I said, taking it from him and finding the correct week. 'Here …'

Ian started to read out loud.

Monday

Passed the Scientology centre on Tottenham Court Road. A lady asked me if I wanted to undertake a free personality test. I said Yes. It took forty minutes and it turns out I am quite nice.

'Are you sure she did it properly?'

'Read on.'

The mad preacher on Oxford Street who walks around with a loudhaler telling people 'Don't be a sinner! Be a winner!' shouted at me as I passed him today. He said, 'You! Are you ready to take the Jesus Test?' I walked up to him and said that Yes, I was ready to take the Jesus Test, and asked him what it was and would Jesus be doing it himself. He didn't seem to know what to do next, and ignored me, and just carried on shouting about how we shouldn't be sinners, but winners instead. I wonder how many people have taken the Jesus Test, and whether if they passed, they were actually allowed to be Jesus for a bit.

'Danny, what's all this leading—'

'You'll find out. Read on.'

And I stood up to go to the bar.

When I came back, pint in hand, Ian had made good headway.

'So … you attended a golf sale, yes?'

'Yes.'

'And you said Yes to a waiter's recommendation of the fish, even though you don't eat fish and you never have?'

'Yes. I was wrong about them. I always thought they were looking at me strangely – even the ones without heads. Turns out they were just being tasty.'

'Okay …'

Ian retraced with his finger what he'd already read.

'And you went to a gig … you bought a new type of shower gel and a sandwich from Boots, "thanks to clever phrasing on their in-store marketing" …'

'Yep.'

'You took a leaflet for an English language school and did as it said by checking out the website … you tried a new type of chocolate bar … you sent off for a brochure about Turkey …'

'"*Turkey: Land of Great Wonder*".'

'You said Yes when someone asked if you'd mind lending them a tenner.'

'I did.'

'You bought some stamps off an old woman. You said Yes to going out for a drink with a boring colleague. You made good use of a money-off voucher. And you attended the leaving do of a man you'd never met and consequently weren't all that sorry to see go.'

'All that and more. Where are you up to?'

'Thursday.'

Thursday

A heart-stopping moment on the tube today. I saw an advertisement which read can you really afford not to buy in Spain?

For a second I knew one thing: I was going to have to invest in a villa.

And then I reread the ad, and realised that, actually, Yes, I really could afford not to buy in Spain. The only people who can't, I think, are probably Spanish.

Ian rolled his eyes, which I thought was a little unfair, because that's actually quite an important social comment, and he scanned on.

Said Yes to giving a bloke some change. Said Yes to a market researcher.

He started to speed-read.

Yes to meeting with Wag next week. Yes to applying for a new type of credit card. Yes to going for coffee with Hanne. Yes to man obsessed with saving the whales.

He got to Friday.

Friday

I bought a ministry in a box.

'What's a ministry in a box?'

'I can do weddings and stuff. Read on.'

'What do you mean you can do weddings and stuff?'

'I'm a minister. I can do weddings and christenings and stuff. Read on.'

'You're a *minister*?!'

'Read on!'

He did as I said but then stopped, dead. He didn't look up. He read, and reread the sentence in front of him. And then he said it out loud.

He looked up at me, slowly.

'You're bloody kidding me.'

I shook my head.

'You're bloody *kidding* me!'

I had prepared for this. I reached into my pocket and brought out my winning scratchcard – the same scratchcard that had stunned Hanne into silence just an hour earlier. I slid it across the table to him.

He picked it up, and took in the numbers.

25,000. 25,000. 25,000.

He shook his head, bewildered.

'How did—'

'I said Yes to going to play football, right?'

He nodded.

'If I hadn't, I wouldn't have left the flat when I did. I bumped into a man who I otherwise wouldn't have met, and he needed a pound. I said Yes. But I had to get change. So I bought a newspaper, which I wouldn't have done if I hadn't said Yes, and in the newspaper, which I wouldn't have bought if I hadn't needed change for a man I wouldn't have met if I hadn't said Yes in the first place, was a scratchcard. And it said I should play it, and I did. And I won.'

Ian laughed.

'Wow …' he said.

'It was a chain reaction, Ian. Each Yes took me closer to that £25,000. Yes *wanted* me to win.'

Ian slid the scratchcard back across the table to me.

'God … so … when do you get the money?'

Ah.

Now, that was the problem.

What I now had to tell Ian, and what I'd had to tell Hanne before, was a little difficult for me to go through with.

It's something that, until *you've* won £25,000 while sitting on a tube train dozens of metres underground and surrounded by complete and utter strangers, you may find a little difficult to relate to. But this is what happened, and there's not a part of me that wishes it hadn't.

Ten minutes after winning £25,000 …

… I lost £25,000.

The very second I'd won the money I'd wanted to tell someone. Anyone. But phones don't work underground, and it wasn't as if I could just run up and down the carriage screaming and dancing, as this is London, and even sneezing in public is illegal if you make eye contact. So I just had to bite my lip, and sit there, and try somehow to suppress my giggles and smiles.

£25,000!

I'd get off at the next stop. I'd get out of the train, head for the streets, and then phone the claim line. And then I'd go to Rio, or Cuba, or wherever the travel agent recommended this time of year, and I'd smoke elaborate cigars offered to me by dusty street urchins, and I'd … I dunno … I'd buy a panda. Yes! I'd buy a panda! For my mum! And a top hat for my dad! A top hat of solid gold!

But as the train lurched and rocked its way through the tunnels, I suddenly started to feel a little paranoid. What if I'd done this wrong? What if I was mistaken? What if I *hadn't* won £25,000 after all?

I rechecked the numbers. My fears were unfounded. I'd *definitely* won. They were the same.

But what if it was an old card? From another day?

Nope. It was today. Absolutely.

I rescanned the rules.

Scratch off the six numbers …

The six numbers? Well, I'd only scratched off *three*. So, quietly and secretly, I found the other three numbers and matched them, too.

5000.

Next one …

5000.

Blimey! What if I got another 5000!

I scratched the next one …

2.

Gah! Nearly another 5000 there! How cool would that have been? To have landed the only multi-winning scratchcard ever produced! And it made me wonder … what was under the other squares? If there was another 5000, would that mean I could claim for *£30,000*?

Quickly, I scratched away …

1.

1! Pah! I laugh in the face of 1! I had 25,000 of those now!

5.

Gah. Not good enough.

But the next one …

5000.

5000!

My God! That can't be right! What did *that* mean?

I struggled to maintain my composure but failed, and let an odd, slightly feminine yelp sneak out. Could they count? I know that only the first six really counted, but what if there was a loophole of some kind? What if I'd now won *£30,000*?

I tore through the pages once more to find the rules. There was one box with big bold letters telling you what to do and how to do it. And there was another box, which seemed to stretch out over half the page, and had some of the smallest print known to mankind …

I squinted to read it.

Minimum age … fine … *claim line* … fine … *three like amounts* … fine … *late claims will not be accepted* … *cards containing printing errors will be void* … *limited prize pool* … fine fine fine …

But what about the extra bonus money? Was there anything about that?

Numbers will be published all week … I scanned on …

Claims must be … I kept scanning …

Residents of … I scanned on …

And then I saw it.

Only scratch the silver panels which match your numbers …

Hang about … *what* was that?

Scratching silver panels which do not match your numbers will void your card.

I read it again.

I looked at my card.

I thought about what I'd done.

And then I said the word 'SHIT' so loudly that the entire row of people opposite looked up at me.

I hadn't really known how Hanne would take it at the time. I suspected she might think it was – you know – 'typical'. She'd gone bright red for a moment or two, and I thought I might be in line for a lecture, so I'd said, 'I'll still pay for your latte.'

Ian's reaction had been more instant. He had taken it very badly. To begin with he too had gone bright red, and then he took a breath so deep I was momentarily concerned he was going to get some balloons out and start crafting model animals.

And then he let rip.

'You … *stupid* … bloody … *idiot*!' he said, teeth gritted and eyes angry.

'What?' I said, slightly offended.

'You had 25 grand, Danny! 25 *grand*! And you threw it away!'

He seemed unnecessarily vocal. Perhaps he thought I owed him 25 grand, or something.

'I can't believe what you did! How do you lose 25 grand?'

'I didn't read the small print.'

'You didn't read the small print,' he said, matter-of-factly, with his hands in the air.

'No,' I said. 'The small print telling me to only scratch the numbers that I had.'

He crossed his arms and shook his head.

'*Why* didn't you only scratch the numbers that you had? Why do you think they had numbers?'

'I don't know. There was another panel there, which said VOID IF REMOVED. I figured that so long as I left that one untouched, I could scratch whatever I liked! I was just too tempted. I was sitting on a tube train and I couldn't get off or tell anyone I'd won, and I just did it!'

'But even though you scratched too many panels, you still had the winning numbers?'

'Yes, and I tried to explain that to the lady on the claim line, but she didn't want to know! She told me that the rules were there, in black and white. I told her that the rules were also in the tiniest writing known to man and tucked away where I couldn't see them! To be honest, I don't know why they'd introduce such a pointless rule.'

'To stop people like you from winning their money! Oh my God, man … you *threw it away*!'

'I didn't throw it away, I just made a mistake – but look, that's not the point, because—'

'What do you mean, that's not the point? What other point *is* there? You had £25,000 in your hands, and you threw it away! So much for saying Yes to stuff. Well, I hope you've learnt your lesson …'

But Ian was wrong. There *was* a lesson to be learnt, but not the one he thought. And it was a valuable one. I tried to explain it to him.

'The point is, mate, I *won* that money. I won £25,000!'

He looked confused.

'No, you didn't.'

'Yes, I did. I *won* it!'

'But you lost it again!'

'Forget that bit.'

Ian looked like he was about to burst.

'No! That's ludicrous! How am I supposed to forget that bit? You're saying all this like there's a lesson to be learnt! There's no lesson here! There's no *advantage* in not having won that money! There's just a tit called Danny Wallace!'

But I'd already rationalised the whole thing in my head. And I knew I was right.

'Listen to me – it doesn't *matter* that I lost the money, Ian. Not in the least! The point is, if I hadn't said Yes, I wouldn't have won it. It's what it *signifies* that matters! I said Yes to playing football, right? If I hadn't, I wouldn't have met the bloke, bought the paper, sat on the train and played the scratchcard. I would still be sitting here in the pub with you but we'd be talking about how this whole Yes thing had ended, rather than ... how it *begins* ...'

Ian looked more confused than ever.

'So it begins with you losing £25,000?'

'No – it begins with me *winning* it ... *that's* the point! Yes made me *win*!'

I was determined. Perhaps, psychologically, it was a survival thing. Perhaps the decision I then made was one of self-preservation. And perhaps the spin I put on the whole thing was there to stop me from sinking back into a world of negativity. But losing that £25,000 just as quickly as I'd won it really didn't bother me. If anything, it excited me *even more*.

I'd told myself that I'd got *on* that tube train without the money, so I shouldn't be bothered if I got *off* it in the same way. Yes had won me that money. Saying Yes had *made me rich*. Fair enough, being an utter *twat* had made me poor again – but that wasn't the fault of Yes. Yes *wanted* me to have that money. It *wanted* me to do well. And it surely couldn't be long before Yes gave me another, similar opportunity. If only I gave it *time*.

'I've got something here,' I said. 'Something I want you to look after.'

I opened my diary again, at the back this time, and pulled out a paper napkin.

'You want me to look after a *napkin*?'

'It's not a napkin. Not any more. It's all I could find to write on. Read it. It's a manifesto. A *Yes Man*ifesto.'

Ian sighed, and read out loud – something he was getting better and better at today.

57

YES MANIFESTO

I, Danny Wallace, being of sound mind and body, do hereby write this manifesto for my life.

'Oh, you complete and utter—'
    'Read it! It's important! This is about my life!'

I swear I will be more open to opportunity. I swear I will live my life taking every available chance. I swear I will say Yes to every favour, request, suggestion and invitation – the little things that come our way every day.

I SWEAR THAT HENCEFORTH, I WILL SAY YES WHERE ONCE I WOULD HAVE SAID NO.

I will do whatever I can to achieve a Yes. But people who know I'm the Yes Man are not allowed to tell other people, or take advantage of my situation. That means you, Ian.

'I don't need to take advantage of your situation! You're doomed!'
    I waved him on, determined for him to understand the significance of the moment.

This will continue until New Year's Eve, this year.

PS. This is not a Stupid Boy Project. This is a Way Of Life.

'Oh, for God's sake,' said Ian. 'The end of the *year*?! That's months away! You'll *die*!'
    'I'll be *fine*!'
    'What if you get asked to be in two places at once?' he said.
    'Then I'll do my best to make it happen.'
    'People will notice! They'll notice all you ever say is Yes!'
    'I've refined the scheme. I won't say Yes, Berlin is in Scotland, or Yes, I am a pregnant mother of two. I will essentially remove the element of dishonesty. But I *will* say Yes to opportunities. To favours. To requests. To suggestions. And to invitations. People will just think I'm … happy.'

'They'll think you're *simple*!'

Ian was getting very agitated.

'And … oh, my God! … what if you *do* get asked to kill a man?'

Ian's face flashed a look of fearful concern. I tried to calm him.

'That doesn't happen in real life, Ian.'

'Him!' said Ian, pointing at an old man in the corner. 'Kill that fella there!'

'Ian, that doesn't count,' I said, glancing at a now rather worried-looking pensioner. 'You know what I'm doing – you don't count – you are automatically ruled out from giving me … "opportunities". And you can tell no one. Okay? *No one.* I want this to be a learning experience. A genuine human experiment in happiness and positivity.'

'I can't believe you've thought this through.'

'This is important to me.'

'And what happens when you fail?'

'What do you mean, *when* I fail? How can I fail? It's only saying Yes to stuff! How can you fail at that?'

'It's saying Yes to *everything*. How can you *not* fail?'

'Nonsense. I'll keep showing you my diary. I'll keep you updated on everything I do.'

'But you'll never do it!'

'I will!'

'If ever there was a time for a drunken bet, it was now.'

'No. No bets. This is more important than that.'

'Fine. But if I find out you've been saying no, then …'

He looked at me with steely determination.

'Then what?'

'Then I'll think of something. And you'll take your punishment like a man.'

'Fine,' I said.

'Fine,' he said.

'Fine,' I said.

We both sat back in our chairs. I thought about what a pity it was that we didn't have American accents, because that would all have been a lot more dramatic if we had. I think Ian was probably thinking the same.

And then he said, 'Pint?'

And I said, 'Yes.'

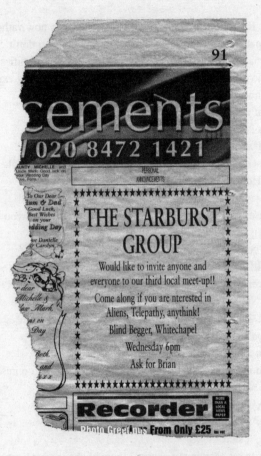

cements

020 8472 1421

PERSONAL
ANNOUNCEMENTS

THE STARBURST GROUP

Would like to invite anyone and everyone to our third local meet-up!!

Come along if you are nterested in Aliens, Telepathy, anythink!

Blind Begger, Whitechapel

Wednesday 6pm

Ask for Brian

Recorder MORE THAN A LOCAL NEWS PAPER

Photo Greetings From Only £25

5

*In which Daniel receives Word
from the Sultanate of Oman*

Let there be no doubt about this whatsoever.

By carefully crafting my Yes Manifesto, I knew I'd just made the most important decision of my young life.

This was big. Bigger than A levels. Bigger than university. Bigger than leaving Argos when I was 15. And, just like leaving Argos, it was exciting; I had no idea where it could lead. There was no discernible target to speak of. What was I aiming for? What did I hope to achieve? There was no one else involved; no bet, no rival, no one to impress or beat but me. Yeah, so Ian had talked vaguely of a punishment – but that was just macho posturing. This was the ultimate in self-help. A key to getting out more. To random meetings with random people doing random things … I was no longer in control. I could no longer make things happen. I could only agree to them. I could *literally* only agree to them. Some people will claim to be the type of person who just can't say no. Now, so could I.

I awoke, a day into my life of Yes, at about nine, and wondered whether today would be the day I'd pop into BBC Broadcasting House and try and get some work done. I decided it probably wouldn't. I still had too much to do. Too much to say Yes to. Once the novelty had worn off, and I'd got into the swing of Yes, *then* I'd pop into work. For now, I'd claim to be 'working from home'. You can do that when you're freelance.

I flicked my computer on, made a cup of tea, and checked my e-mails. There was the now usual array of spam messages, urging me to look at their website, or yelling at me about mortgage deals and cut-price (thankfully, none of them had resorted to just *asking* me to buy their stuff). But then … as I clicked on to the next one … I was startled and confused.

Because the next thing I read was a desperate call for help. A desperate call for help …

> **To: danny@dannywallace.com**
> **From: SULTAN QABOOS**
> **Subject: URGENT BUSINESS TRANSACTION**
>
> **THE PALACE–MUSCAT**
> **P.O.BOX 632 MUSCAT PC 113 OMAN.**
>
> **ATTENTION PLEASE,**
>
> **I TAKE THE PLEASURE TO GET ASSOCIATED WITH YOU AND DESIRE TO INTRODUCE MYSELF, REQUESTING FOR YOUR EXPERT ADVISES AND IMMEDIATE LINE OF ACTION.**
>
> **I AM OMAR, SON OF THE MURDERED SULTAN, SULTAN OF THE SULTANATE OF OMAN.**

Jesus! I had just received an e-mail from the son of a Sultan! I didn't know whether to curtsey or bow! What was the son of a Sultan doing e-mailing me? How did that happen? And how did he hear of me?

> **I CAME TO KNOW YOUR EXPERTISE AND PROFESSIONALLISM IN BUSINESS FROM MY FATHER, AND AM THUS CONFIDENTLY WRITING, THAT YOU WILL ACCEPT MY REQUEST TO PROVIDE YOUR EXPERTISE PROFESSIONALLISM IN BUSINESS.**

My professionallism in business? *What* professionallism in business? And is that really how you spell professionallism?

> **I ASK YOU TO KEEP THIS CONFIDENTIAL.I AM TO TRUST YOU WITH MY LIFE, AS MY FATHER DID.**

What?

> **MY FATHER WAS LAST NIGHT MURDERED BY HIS POLITICAL ENEMIES.**

What?!

**NOW THOSE SAME ENEMIES ARE ATTEMPTING TO TAKE CONTROL
OF HIS FINANCES. I HAVE BEEN ABLE TO SECRETLY TAKE $40
MILLION AND INTEND TO FLEE THE COUNTRY.**

How do you *secretly* take 40 million dollars? Do you nick a dollar a
week for 40 million weeks?

**I WILL LIKE YOU TO USE YOUR EXPERTISE AND PROFESSIONAL-
ISM IN BUSINESS TO HELP ME ESCAPE MY MONEY AND INVEST
FOR ME.**

What professionalism in business!?

**ON YOUR CONFIRMING ACCEPTING MY REQUEST IN TOTALITY YOU
WILL RECEIVE 25% OF THE MONEY ($10 MILLION).**

Okay, say no more, that's fine, when do we do it?

**PLEASE KEEP THIS TOTALLY CONFIDENTIAL. PLEASE I HOPE YOU
WILL SAY YOU WILL HELP ME. PLEASE ACT SOON, WE MUST
PREPARE. IT IS GOD'S WILL.**

OMAR

Good God!

But hang on … let's get this into perspective.

The son of a murdered Sultan was asking for my help. Me! And he
was offering me $10 million. $10 million if I said Yes! That beats
£25,000 any day! Already, Yes was planning to make me rich again!

Now, usually, of course, I'd be a little sceptical. This kind of thing
rarely, if ever, happens to me. In fact, now that I think about it, I can't
remember the last time I helped a Sultan. Even a little. I'm not proud
about that. It's just that I'm not sure I'd even know how to do it, or what
they'd need help with. I'm ashamed to say I know very little about magic
carpets as it is, and if you gave me a big curly sword I'd probably give
it straight back to you.

But here was a man in need … so I wrote back …

To: Sultan Qaboos
From: Danny Wallace
Subject: RE: URGENT BUSINESS TRANSACTION

Dear Omar, son of the murdered Sultan Qaboos,

Yes, of course I will help you!

Danny

PS. Sorry about your dad.

And that was that.

So right now, somewhere in the middle of cyberspace, my agreement and best wishes were winging their way to a troubled son of a Sultan – a man probably cowering under a table in some ornate mansion somewhere, with a chair forced up against the door and only a big bald genie for protection. Or maybe he was already on the run. Maybe he was sneaking from village to village, under cover of darkness, dressed as a peasant woman and fearing for his life! How happy he would be when he read that I, Danny Wallace, a specky bloke with toothpaste round his mouth, would indeed lend him some of his professionalism in business!

I sat by my computer, eagerly clicking the Get Mail button, hoping each time that the next click would bring a response from Omar. But time after time, all I heard was the mocking dull thud that whoever designed my computer decided would represent the sound of 'no mail'. The dull thud of a punch in the paunch. The dull thud of 'no messages, why do you bother?, not even *other* nerds want to write to you'.

But I wasn't giving up on Omar. I made another cup of tea, found a biscuit at the back of my cupboard, and sat, staring intently at my screen, willing him to write back – willing him to know that it was all going to be okay – willing him to *just hang on*.

And then I got bored and got on with my day.

I was doing the washing-up when I heard a bing-bong. New mail!

I ran to my computer, fearing Omar was in danger.

It was Hanne.

Danny,
Just checking you're not too depressed about losing that 25
grand.
Hanne

I replied.

Hanne,
Not to worry. I just agreed to help the son of a murdered
sultan and he said he'd give me ten million dollars.
Danny

I waited around for a bit, but Hanne didn't reply. She was probably busy.

Aside from Omar, there didn't seem to be too much happening today. Not much to say Yes to. So I decided that today *would* be the day I'd go into work, after all.

I was sure I'd find plenty to do.

The first of Australia's Big Things, since you ask, was The Big Banana.

Erected in 1963 by an American immigrant named John Landi, it was a personal and heartfelt tribute to the banana and was intended to attract visitors from miles and miles around.

It worked.

From all over Australia, banana lovers flocked to The Big Banana to celebrate the world of bananas and immerse themselves in the adjoining banana plantation. It became a symbol of all that was right with the humble banana, and somewhere for dedicated banana fans to centre their energies and focus their banana-based efforts.

And it also meant that from 1963 onwards, John Landi sold a *lot* more bananas.

Perhaps for that reason, the idea took off.

Almost immediately, Australians of the North, South, East and West realised that they could draw major national attention to their farms, their businesses and even their hobbies, just by building huge, colourful statues in honour of whatever was at the core of their obsession. From Sydney to the Sunshine Coast, just like Lizzie had told me, these Big Things began to line the highways and byways of Australia. Naturally, some garnered more praise and plaudits than others ... The Big Pineapple of 1972, experts agree, is probably the most successful of all

The Big Things, and in the 1970s and early '80s really brought pineapples and pineapple-related issues to the fore. But The Big Oyster, a towering testament to the vast oyster beds of the Manning River region, is something that few Australians like to talk about. It plays, they will tell you with their eyes fixed to the floor, a sad second fiddle to The Big Prawn, only a few miles to the north.

I was beginning to really love Big Things. And right now, sitting in an office at the BBC, I was clicking my way around the Web, finding out all about them. I was fascinated. And I was slowly finding my favourites, too. The Big Rock, for example (imagine that!), or The Big Avocado, to be found at Duranbah's popular theme park, Tropical Fruit World (formerly known as Avocado Adventureland … an experience which sounds only marginally more appealing than an afternoon at my very own Shelf Adventure).

'Dan, can I have a word?'

It was my boss's voice, and I span round in my chair, deftly quitting the Internet as I did so in order to hide the words 'Tropical Fruit World' from my screen. Sadly, all it did was bring up the game of MineSweeper I'd been playing earlier, but my boss politely ignored it.

'Listen, say no if you don't want to, but there's a meeting over at TV Centre later this week – some kind of development thing – and they want someone from radio to attend. Everyone I've asked seems very busy all of a sudden. Funny how everyone gets busy when there's something they don't want to say Yes to. So how about you? Can you make it?'

'Yes!' I said, proud that I was bucking the trend. 'Definitely. What kind of meeting is it again?'

'Development. The usual thing. People sitting around coming up with ideas. But you're up for it?'

'Yes.'

'Okay. Great. I'll tell them. Thanks, Dan. And enjoy Tropical Fruit World.'

He closed the door and I decided I'd better get on and do some work.

Working from home is a great thing, but so is working from BBC Broadcasting House – home to a thousand scruffy, cardiganed radio producers. Part of my freelance contract demanded that I spend a couple of days a week sitting in one of the offices here, working up ideas, and that was just dandy by me.

I'd worked for the BBC ever since leaving university, when I'd somehow talked my way into a six-month traineeship in the Light Entertainment department, and now here I was, a bona-fide Light Entertainment producer, a few years shy of thirty and my first-ever cardigan. Quite what qualifies as Light Entertainment I've never been sure, though you and I both now know that cardigans are involved, and I'm fairly sure it also has something to do with Nicholas Parsons.

But Broadcasting House is a fantastic place to work, steeped as it is in glorious radio history – from Churchill's wartime addresses to the comedy of the Goons – and it was always with a sense of genuine pride that I walked through the huge brass doors with my special BBC pass clipped to my jeans. Fair enough, it's not as if I was the man charged with making the type of quality journalism that the world has come to rely on as the most trustworthy and respected on the planet. It's not as if I was one of those who were bringing down governments, or exposing corruption, or staying up all night poring through secret dossiers and turning them into the next day's global headlines. But I *was* one of the ones making silly and obscure little programmes that might pass the time on the commute home, or be heard by a lonely shepherd tuning in to the World Service somewhere on the Savannah plains, or confuse a prisoner in some jail somewhere with a topical joke they blatantly wouldn't understand because they'd been inside on arson charges since 1987. It's a strange job, but the way I think of it is, *someone* has to bewilder the shepherds and confuse the prisoners.

So anyway, I was trying to get some work done. I really was. But there were a couple of things against me. The first was the growing realisation and excitement that my life was in the hands of just about everyone else in the world, but not me, and that just one well-placed Yes to one well-placed opportunity could change or improve or, if Ian was to be believed, destroy my life for ever. And the second thing that was against me getting any work done today was that there was very little work to be done. I was between projects. Sure, I could start a new one. But that would just be making work for myself. Who does that? And anyway – who wanted to work, when they could dance and play outside, in the sunshine, saying Yes to people willy-nilly, instead? I started to stride out of the office, looking for all the world like someone who was on his way to a meeting at which he'd say lots of important things, involving words like 'merger' or 'hierarchy'; the kind of meeting normal men would faint in, and women would avoid for fear of leaving the room impregnated by the sheer weight of the testosterone in the air.

Testosterone that probably smelt like quality aftershave. Real men sweat that stuff.

'Hi Danny,' said a voice to my left, all of a sudden.

'Hello!' I boomed, still imagining myself to be quite important.

'How are you?'

It was Robert, a technician I'd worked with on a rather intense week-long edit. An edit which had actually seemed like it was closer to a month – mainly because Robert was cramming for a pub quiz final and kept stopping every five minutes to tell me a little-known fact about the animal kingdom, or ask me to test him on what was number one in the charts in specific weeks in the 1990s.

'I'm fine, thanks, Robert.'

'Waiting for the lift?'

'Yep. Are you?'

'Nope,' he said.

And then the lift arrived and he got in with me.

'I'm going to have a little party next week, Danny. Nothing fancy, just a few friends from "the industry".'

He used his hands to signify the speech marks, and then laughed and shook his head as he enjoyed what he'd done.

'I was wondering whether you might like to come along?'

Ordinarily, this would have been a tricky one to answer. It's not because Robert is a boring man – he's not, and I'll always defend him on that – it's just that he's terribly dull.

'Of course I would, Robert,' I said, pleased at least that I'd have another thing to pop in the diary. 'I'd be delighted, in fact.'

'Oh, cool. Ace. You're the only one from the BBC who can make it! Everyone else is really busy at the moment.'

'I've been hearing that, yes.'

'Okay. Well. I'll e-mail you?'

'Great.'

And with that, Robert and I stepped out of the lift, we shook hands, and he stepped back in and went all the way back up to the fifth floor again.

It was still sunny as I walked down Regent Street, and I was smiling. Since my scratchcard win, I'd started to wonder something … what if, potentially, every single moment I was awake could lead to somewhere wonderful? What if all I had to do was keep my eyes wide open and welcoming? After all, the man on the bus had made me realise that some-times those little negatives of daily life don't have to be negatives at all. The crush of the tube, or the bus that doesn't stop for you, or the night-club that won't let you in ... before, I'd thought of those as self-contained little moments. I'd never really considered that they might be beginnings; that they might lead somewhere; that they might be for the best.

And this was precisely the attitude I needed when I headed for the underground, and saw something that, only days before, would have made my heart sink and my body weary. A huge, seven-wide queue of people, spilling out of Oxford Circus station and on to the street. Once again, the tube was at a standstill. I joined the back of the queue and looked around me. Perhaps a hundred people were here, with more on the other side of the street, all of them waiting for the station to reopen, all of them cursing their luck, or shouting into their phones, or kicking their heels in the sun. It was a tired, frustrated mob, and for a moment I was nearly one of them ... until I remembered that the last time this kind of thing had happened to me was the night I'd met the man on the bus ... and then I *realised*. This was *perfect*. This was another opportunity to see what life would throw at me! Did I want to stand here, by a busy road with its dust and horns and smoke, or did I want to treat this as a *chance*? Did I want to stand here, with an angry mob of commuters and tourists, or did I want to *do* something? What if I just walked away? What if I just walked past the tube, and just took life as it came? What would happen?

So I walked.

I walked, that night, wherever the wind seemed to take me. Down Oxford Street, into Soho, towards Piccadilly Circus, and then Leicester Square. I was walking slowly, willing opportunities to come my way, but gradually noticing things I'd never noticed about London before. Just little things. Like the statue of Charlie Chaplin in the centre of Leicester Square. Or the telephone boxes in Chinatown that have been crafted to look like pagodas. Or the tiny dance put on by the little wooden peasants hidden inside the clock on the Swiss Centre, which they perform faith-fully once an hour, on the hour, to the delight of tourists and tourists alone. I was starting to discover that for someone who lived in this city, I really didn't know it very well.

I walked towards Holborn, past Chancery Lane, and explored Fleet Street, stopping to study a plaque in honour of someone called Wallace, and sat on a bench in the City of London, while I watched a man in a suit silently fit an entire bagel into his mouth. I sauntered, and I meandered, and I ambled along … and before too long I realised I was most of the way home. It was strange. I'd always rushed my way around my city before. London was just the collective term for lots of different places I'd had to get to, quickly. But tonight … I'd *walked* home. Slowly. And taken everything in. And enjoyed it. I had gradually rediscovered, and then quickly fallen back in love with, my own city.

I arrived back at my flat late, but relaxed and happy. I shoved a curry into the microwave, flicked on the kettle, and sat down at my computer to check my e-mails.

Hi! I'm Sandi! Would you like to see me get hot and wild with my college roommates?

Now, I didn't know who Sandi was, but she seemed friendly enough, and it was a lovely offer, but it could wait.

Another e-mail came from Robert the technician, with full details of his party. 'Bring a fact!' it said. 'Stump a stranger and break the ice!'

And that was about it.

I got my diary out, added the date of Robert's party, and added all the other things I'd said Yes to today. But I was disappointed. My walk around London had enthused me – surely I could find *something* else to say Yes to?

I sat on the sofa with my cup of tea and started to idly flick through the *Tower Hamlets Recorder* – a newspaper I tend to hide when being visited by my mum, seeing as how every other story tends to feature heavily one or more of the words 'stabbing', 'robbed' or 'police believe the muggers are targeting the bespectacled' – trying to find something of interest.

There was the usual array of crime. A fete. An article about a historic bench.

But there, on the opposite page … tucked away, next to a birthday advert and a picture of a very old cat, was the following important announcement …

THE STARBURST GROUP Would like to invite anyone and everyone to our third local meet-up! Come along if you are nterested in aliens, telepathy, anythink! Blind Beggar, Whitechapel, Wednesday, 6 pm. Ask for Brian.

An invitation! To anyone and everyone! Including me!

Granted, it looked a bit strange … and usually, I'd go to great lengths to avoid hanging around with *anyone* who says 'anythink' instead of 'anything' … but not this time.

I smiled. Wednesday was tomorrow. I made a note of the address, I switched the computer off, and I went to bed.

Well, no, hang on.

I smiled, I made a note of the address, I clicked on a link and looked at a colourful picture of Sandi getting hot and wild with her college roommates, I smiled again, I switched the computer off, and *then* I went to bed.

Smiling.

The Blind Beggar pub, not too far from my own home, is a piece of East End legend.

It was there that Ronnie Kray, one of London's celebrated gangster twins, the Krays, shot and killed a burly ex-con named George Cornwell. Every cab driver in London will tell you that they were there the night it happened, and it's best to just keep quiet when they say this. According to police reports, the only two other people who *were* there that night were a couple of rent boys, and I can tell you from experience that cab drivers don't like it if you ask them what it was like to be a 1960s male prostitute.

The Krays, of course, did *something* almost *everywhere* in East London. Grab a pensioner in the East End and point at whatever you like.

'Yes,' they'll say. 'That is the very wall that the Kray Twins probably once saw on their way somewhere. Are you a tourist? Can I have five pounds?'

Of course, some landmarks are more famous than others. There's Pellicci's café, in which the Krays used to do their business and drink their tea. There's Turnmills nightclub, where Mad Frankie Fraser got shot in the head and lived to tell the tale. There's the house on Evering Road in Stoke Newington, where Reggie Kray stabbed Jack 'The Hat' McVitie. Who, before you ask, was a man and not a hat, and will doubt-less remain that way until *The Animated Adventures of the Kray Twins* finally gets the green light.

The Blind Beggar, though, is the true East London Krays experience, and a bit of an odd choice for the Starburst Group to hold one of their meetings in, to be honest.

'Of course,' said James, one of the people I'd correctly identified as a Starburster, 'I know someone who was here the night it happened. Saw the whole thing.'

The others – Laura, Bob and Brian himself – all looked fairly impressed.

'Is he a cab driver?' I asked.

James looked at me, shocked.

'Why, do you know him?' he said.

I decided it would probably be better for me not to introduce myself to the group with lighthearted tales of male prostitution, so I shook my head and said 'no'.

The Starburst Group, it turns out, meets once a month in various pubs around London and is essentially made up of these four people, the odd guest, and one other regular, who was currently on holiday in Malaga.

'There are others, though,' said Brian. 'Plenty of others. Many in the States, a couple in France, and of course there are hundreds on the mailing list who we've never met. Though I doubt we'll ever truly meet *them* …'

Brian looked knowingly at the others and they chuckled.

'How come?' I asked.

'Let's just say they know a little more about us than we do about *them*,' said Brian, and Laura, I *think*, mouthed the word 'Government'.

I was excited to be here. Saying Yes had introduced me to my first bunch of strangers. Strangers with some rather strange ideas …

'So,' said Brian. 'Bob's got some things to run past us on his pyramid theories. Bob's our resident Egyptologist, Danny.'

'Right!' I said, enthusiastically. 'Brilliant!'

'Do you know much about the pyramids, Danny?' asked Bob, who was bald, with a silver-grey goatee and a waistcoat with little moons on it.

'Er … well, I know that they're in Egypt.'

'That's right, very good,' he said, sincerely. 'But who built them?'

I thought it over.

'Egyptians?' I tried.

Bob smiled.

'That would certainly conform to popular opinion,' he said. 'While it may be true that some Egyptians *were* involved in the process, I think they may have had a little help.'

At this point, Laura, who was still wearing a hat even though she was indoors and there was central heating, made a little mm-hmm sound, as if to confirm what Bob was saying.

'Who do you reckon helped them?' I asked.

Everyone looked at me, ready to gauge my reaction.

'Aliens,' said Bob.

My reaction was to blink a couple of times and then say, 'Aliens?'

'Think about it,' said Bob.

I thought about it. It didn't help.

'Are you completely sure about this?' I said.

'Actually, Danny, it's not all that far-fetched,' said Laura. 'Studies of ancient hieroglyphics show that the Egyptians often talked of beings from the sky who would impart great wisdom and bestow wondrous new technologies upon them. If you look at ancient Egyptian art you will see many unusual shapes, some of which do bear an uncanny resemblance to spacecraft.'

James nodded and looked enigmatic. Brian sipped at his lemonade. Bob continued.

'Moreover, the pyramids at Giza are built in the exact layout of the stars in Orion's Belt. And when you divide the circumference of the Great Pyramid by twice its height, you get the figure 3.141.'

'Pi,' said Brian, with a wink.

'But ... do aliens *have* pi?' I said. 'Why couldn't it just have been some Egyptians who ... you know ... were good at building?'

'A possibility! Certainly a possibility!' said Bob. 'But there is absolutely no record of who built them. And the Egyptians recorded *everything*. Wars, kings, pharaoh worship, everything that went on. But not the building of the pyramids. Odd, eh?'

Brian let out a sudden and short burst of totally inexplicable laughter.

I tried to work out how simply not knowing who built the pyramids meant that aliens did it. I mean, I don't know who nicked my bike from outside Loughborough Leisure Centre when I was nine, but it seems unfair to lay the blame at the feet of our extraterrestrial cousins. If they have feet.

'But anyway, to the new stuff,' said Bob, and James and Laura leaned in slightly. 'An American Starburster put this to me this week over MSN Messenger and I promised I'd share it with the group.'

He looked to me and I suddenly realised I was considered one of the group. I was a *Starburster*! Brilliant!

'Now, I hadn't heard this before, but the Cydonia site on Mars provides us with better evidence than ever that the pyramids were indeed built by aliens. Early pictures of Mars – and I have checked this out on the Internet – do show what appears to be a face and some pyramidical monuments located side by side.'

James got a pad out and made a note of something, urgently.

'Closer inspection of the face shows it to be humanoid in structure ...'

This was the first time I had ever heard the word 'humanoid' used by any humanoid, ever, and I enjoyed it greatly. I nodded along, fascinated.

'... and in many ways very similar in form to that of the Sphinx.'

Everyone just sort of looked at each other, and then at me. I looked back at them and stuck my bottom lip out, nodded and raised my eyebrows, as if to give the impression that I had been won over by the weight of their evidence, which was only polite. 'Yep,' I seemed to be saying, 'it appears that the pyramids were indeed built by aliens.'

'Fascinating,' said Laura. 'That is fascinating. You have to wonder how pyramids got up there, on Mars.'

James looked up at the ceiling, probably for clues.

'Maybe it was some Egyptians,' I tried, and immediately regretted it.

But then Bob laughed. And James laughed. And everyone laughed. And then Bob spoilt it by saying 'No. It was *definitely* aliens.'

'So what made you decide to come to one of our meetings?' said Brian, half an hour later.

'You invited me,' I said. 'Well, you invited *everyone*. I saw your ad.'

We were standing by the bar, away from Bob, Laura and James.

'I was a little annoyed by that advert, I'll be honest.'

'Why?'

'Well, I phoned it in, and they put a little border of stars around it, for a start, which I did *not* ask for, and which just makes us look *mad*. And then they played with what I'd written. I said, "Come along if you are interested in aliens, telepathy – anything at all." And they changed that to "Come along if you are interested in aliens, telepathy – any*think*!" And on top of that, they missed the "i" on "interested", and they capitalised the "w" on "would". The woman on the end of the phone even added her own exclamation marks. Still. I suppose it worked. You came. You just thought "I'll go to that", did you?'

'I ... um ... I don't know,' I started. 'I guess it just felt right. I just thought I'd be open to it and say Yes.'

'Well, that's good. The closed mind is a disease. You need to have an open mind otherwise life will just pass you by. You'll be an observer, rather than a participant. Does that make sense?'

It did.

'I'm trying to say Yes more in general,' I said. 'As a person, I mean.'

You'll notice I glossed over the part about 'in general' meaning 'all the time, to everything, ever'.

'Are you? That's a good idea. Be open to experience. Why did you decide to do that?'

'Something someone said to me. A bloke on a bus. I'd ended up chatting to him after our tube home got cancelled, and there we were on this bus when he came out with it. "Say Yes more," he said. Out of virtually nowhere. So that's what I'm doing.'

Brian pulled an overly intrigued face.

'Wow,' he said. 'And you're taking him seriously?'

'Well, yes,' I said.

'Who was he?'

'I dunno. He was an Asian guy – a teacher, he said. From around here, actually. Aldgate.'

Brian stuck his bottom lip out and raised his eyebrows.

'A teacher,' he said. 'Makes sense. So he struck a chord, did he? When he said that?'

'Could be my traya!' said Laura, who had now joined us, and Brian laughed at her.

'Your what?' I said.

'No, no … *Maitreya*,' said Brian. 'The World Teacher.'

'What's a World Teacher?' I said.

'I shouldn't worry,' said Brian. 'He doesn't exist.'

'He *could* exist,' said Laura. 'We just don't *know* he exists. Same goes for most deities or enlightened beings.'

I was intrigued. This sounded interesting. I mean, not as interesting as aliens building the pyramids, but fairly interesting all the same.

'Enlightened beings?'

'Beings who walk among us, and help us with our daily lives. You could say Maitreya is in charge of them. He's supposed to live around here.'

This was getting a bit weird.

'You know where an enlightened being lives?'

'Well, not exactly. But he's in the East End somewhere. Brian knows more about it than I do.'

I looked towards Brian, but he was back at the bar, and although I made a mental note to ask more about Maitreya the God of the East End, the conversation soon moved on.

Despite the slightly strange undertones, I'd enjoyed hanging out with the Starburst Group. Brian (specialist chosen subject: 'Them', what 'They' are up to, and how 'They' achieve it) had a mysterious past and was the most intense of the four. Laura (specialist chosen subject: angels, the afterlife, and 'hidden helpers') was a former social worker and had a quick and quiet laugh. James (conspiracies, conspirators and the conspired-against) liked motorbikes, and had chosen tonight's venue because it was 'biker friendly'. And Bob (aliens, Egyptology, and the TV series *Stargate*) used to teach woodwork but saw a UFO while driving through the Lake District in 1982 and decided woodwork seemed a bit pointless in comparison.

'We're having another meeting in six weeks or so, in Willesden Green,' said Laura. 'It's near my house. Will you be coming to that one? We'd love to have you there.'

'Yes,' I said, reaching into my pocket for my diary. 'Yes, I'll be there. Definitely.'

I caught Brian's eye. He smiled at me.

'We haven't decided what we'll be talking about yet,' she said.

'Perhaps we could talk about Maitreya,' joked Brian. 'Seeing as you've met him.'

I laughed. But Laura was insistent.

'We could if you like,' she said. 'Or if you've any other unusual interests?'

It was clear what she was getting at. She wanted to know if I liked angels. Or UFOs. Or if I had a poster of Spock on my wall.

'I'm pretty … open-minded,' I said. 'There are lots of things that interest me.'

'Like …?'

Well, what was I going to say? I couldn't exactly say 'badminton', could I? What was … you know … *paranormal*?

'Ghostbusters.'

Clearly, I had failed to impress them.

'Hey – my friend Wag reckons that men can have babies … they just haven't worked out how yet. He says it makes perfect sense. What do you think of that?'

'Oh,' said Laura. 'I have actually heard that before.'

Of course she had.

'A man named Linton ... I *think* that was his name ... proposed an interesting theory of fatherhood ... he had worked out that the man needs to be around forty, and sexually active. The man and the lady lie side by side and use their forefingers only and I won't say too much more if that's all right, and anyway, if they are successful then around a year later the man will find he is able to have a baby.'

'Oh!' said James. 'On his own?'

'No,' said Laura. 'By another man. But the interesting thing about all this is that men can actually nurse babies using their breast, but after birth they will have to cork their birth canal.'

I saw Brian shift slightly uncomfortably at the thought of corking his birth canal.

'Some people say that this was the way man got life before woman was created,' said Laura. 'Though obviously I have my own theories about that.'

Obviously.

As I trudged towards the Mile End road, I smiled. That had been a good, solid Yes. I'd had a fine time with the Starburst Group – against all the odds, in a way. Or, at least, against my preconceptions. I liked the fact that those four key members had found each other. I liked the fact that while their beliefs were slightly off-kilter, they'd created their own club in which anything could be discussed, considered, thrown about and shared. And that they were so welcoming. Each had the confidence that being around a good friend brings ... and they were obviously good friends.

'Whenever I'm down in the dumps,' Laura had said, at one point. 'I get myself a hat.'

'I *wondered* where you'd been getting them ...' said James, and the table had erupted with laughter. It had been warm, and cosy, and if it hadn't been mainly to do with aliens and pyramids, it would've been like any night down the pub with four friends.

On my return, I was pleased to see I had received a reply from Omar, my endangered Sultan friend.

To: danny@dannywallace.com
From: SULTAN QABOOS
Subject: RE: URGENT BUSINESS TRANSACTION

DEAR danny

MAY GOD BLESS YOU danny FOR TAKING MY OPPORTUNITY. MAY ALL YOU DO AND MEET BE SUCCESS. I MUST HAVE YOUR COMPLETE FAITH AND TRUST danny. I FEEL I CAN TRUST YOU 100%.

MY FATHER'S ENEMIES ARE MOVING QUICKLY AND SOON WE WILL HAVE NO TIME. I MUST ESCAPE THE $40 MILLION URGENTLY. WE MUST WASTE NO TIME.

I REQUEST YOU TO KINDLY TAKE THE MONEY INTO A BANK ACCOUNT IN AN APPROPRIATE BANK, WHERE THE MONEY IS SAFE.

AFTER THE SUCCESSFUL COMPLETION OF THIS VENTURE I WILL INVITE YOU TO MY SULTANATE SO AS TO TO KNOW YOU ON A PERSONAL LEVEL.

LOOKING FORWARD TO YOUR IMMEDIATE RESPONSE. ARE YOU STILL WILLING TO HELP. SEND ME YOU BANK ACCOUNT DETAIL AND PHONE NUMBER danny.

OMAR

Thank God Omar was all right. He'd had me a little worried there, but I suppose you get busy when you're trying to sneak out of the country with forty million dollars.

Tonight had taught me it was important to grab my Yeses, wherever they come from. So I thought about what to write back to Omar. It was lovely of him to make this personal; to invite me to his sultanate after we'd done our business. Clearly, he thought of me as a friend now. Just look at the gentle way he was writing my name. He wasn't writing in that scary, shouty, all-capitals way when he said my name. No. I wasn't DANNY. I was danny. It was almost as if the letter was already written, and he'd gone back in and added my name in afterwards.

My reply was swift and, I would hope, helpful.

Dear Omar,

How exciting! I would love to come and visit you in your sultanate so you can know me on a personal level. And hey – maybe you can come and stay in my flat in Bow afterwards. I can only offer you a futon, but it's 'KING SIZE' – is a King bigger than a Sultan? I suppose if he was a fat king like Henry the Eighth then Yes, but there are probably loads of fat sultans, too.

I am sorry if that is offensive.

Moving on, Yes, I am still willing to help you. I will look into opening a bank account asap.

Cheers!

Danny

I updated my diary, and I went to bed, happy.

This was all working out beautifully.

Selected extracts from the diary of a Yes Man: 1

June 22nd

What a lovely day!

Not only is it sunny and bright, but I am pleased to announce I have been contacted by the people at CapitalOne – I have been 'specially selected' to be invited to apply for 'a new type of credit card'! I sent off my application immediately, enclosing a friendly note of thanks.

June 23rd

Saw an advert in the *Sun*. It said DO YOU LOOK LIKE SOMEONE FAMOUS? DO YOU WANT TO MAKE SOME MONEY? FILL IN OUR ONLINE APPLICATION, SEND US A PHOTO, AND EARN YOURSELF SOME SERIOUS CASH!

I decided that the answers to their questions were Yes and Yes. And then I tried to work out who I looked like. I decided I could probably either pass myself off as Harry Potter's older brother, or as one of The Proclaimers. They were one of my favourite bands when I was a little boy, and I suppose it's just blind luck I ended up looking like one of them. Or looking like both of them, in fact, seeing as how they're twins and everything.

I sent my photo off with the heading: 'Meet Britain's only one-man Proclaimers tribute act!' I don't see how they can turn me down. Two twins for the price of one!

June 24th

Joy!

I accepted an invitation from American Express to apply for a 'new *type* of credit card'. How many new types can there be? Maybe I can start to classify them, like some kind of plastic-obsessed Darwin. 'Look, that's a Wallace credit card,' people of the future will say. 'How do you know?' other people will say. 'You can tell by the markings,' the first people will say. 'And also by the fact that there's no money left on it.'

June 26th

A woman sitting opposite me on the tube had her newspaper folded in an odd way this morning. Virtually screaming out at me on one side were 'Want to get clean?' and 'Clean your whole house – experience the magnificent power of steam cleaning!' on the other. Next to a picture of the new Light 'n' Easy Steam Cleaner was a picture of a smiling Su Pollard, who was hailing it as 'Brilliantly simple – simply brilliant!' She must really love it. The manufacturers were proud to be able to offer it to me at the new low price of just £24.95. I have ordered one. I am going to experience the magnificent power of steam cleaning. I will let you know how I get on once it arrives. Hopefully it will be both brilliantly simple and simply brilliant.

June 28th

Today, I accepted an invitation from Morgan Stanley to apply for 'a new type of credit card'. I also received my new type of credit card from the CapitalOne people. It's shiny.

I also bought two copies of the *Big Issue*.

July 1st

Worked all day, then had a pint with Wag. Turned into many pints. He has a remarkable knack of saying 'd'ya fancy another?' I invited him to both the parties I was invited to tonight. Sadly, one was deep in West London, so we could only stay for twenty minutes, because we had to go to one in the far reaches of East London, which was just finishing as we arrived. Wag wasn't very pleased.

July 2nd

While walking through Hackney a few days ago, I noticed a piece of yellow paper stuck to a lamppost saying 'WANT TO GET RICH QUICK?' I decided that Yes, I did, and I read further. All I had to do was send off a cheque for £12 and I would receive a whole book, free, in the post. It arrived today. It is called '501 Ways To Make Easy Money When You're Skint'. It is brilliant. Among its suggestions for simple moneymaking schemes are goatkeeping, glamour photography, and inventing a game, 'such as Monopoly, or the Rubik's Cube'.

It also says, 'A small piece of land is all you need to start a go-kart centre!'

It would seem they've forgotten that it's quite important to have go-karts, too. And qualified instructors. And insurance. And protective headgear. And a licence.

Nevertheless, I have decided that if they're offering me the opportunity to earn lots of money, I cannot turn it down. I have chosen to try and earn some money by having a letter published in a newspaper.

July 4th

I have experienced the magnificent power of steam cleaning. It was both brilliantly simple, *and* simply brilliant – though due to a slippery step I did at one point very nearly scorch my gentleman's agreements.

July 5th

In my efforts to 'Get rich quick' by writing to newspapers and magazines, I noticed that the *Sun* says on its letters page that it pays £20 for letters it publishes, as well as handy hints and tips. I sent this one in today.

A handy hint or tip for quick moneymaking is to send a letter to the Sun *– according to its letters page, they pay £20 for letters they publish, as well as handy hints or tips!*
   D. Wallace, London

I await my £20. But just on the off-chance, I also sent this one in.
A small piece of land is all you need to start a go-kart centre!
Easy money.

July 6th

I have had word from the lookalike people. They have decided 'upon careful consideration' that I do not look like *either* of The Proclaimers. *Either* of them! I am a little upset at how frankly they put this. Couldn't they have had a little sensitivity? Maybe written to me one week to say that I don't look like *one* of the twins, left it a bit, and then written to me a week later to say that I don't look like the *other* one, either? All I'm asking is that they let me down gently.

If I ever start a lookalike agency for people who think they look like one or more twins, it will definitely be one that cares.

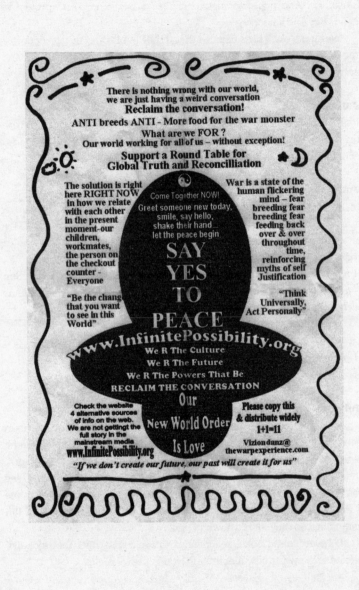

6

In which Daniel Breaks the Law

I awoke, in the morning, to find a most exciting surprise in the post.

A letter from the Patent and Trademark Institute of America! Finally, the DO YOU HAVE AN INVENTION? people had written back to me.

How important I felt! Strangely, though, the Patent and Trademark Institute of America seemed not to be based in Los Angeles, or New York, or San Francisco. No. It was based in Blackpool. On a very normal-sounding street.

Encouragingly, however, they appeared to be taking me very seriously already. They even started their letter to me 'Dear Inventor'. Immediately, I knew I was in safe hands. These people knew what they were doing. They clearly recognised in me the ability to create life-changing and practical inventions, and had decided, after careful consideration, to offer me a 'Free New Product Analysis'.

'There is no cost for this initial analysis,' they wrote. 'Why not invest a few minutes today to properly document an idea and our experience will be available within a week.'

Good God! I had the ear of the Patent and Trademark Institute of America! And they wanted me to submit my idea! All I needed now was to have one!

I was excited. I wish I could say I came from a long family line of inventors, but I don't. Unless you consider the fact that I was born and bred in Scotland – the country responsible for anaesthetics, golf, quinine, marmalade, the steam engine, the adhesive postage stamp, the microwave oven, the fridge and – yes – hollow pipe drainage. And which of us hasn't got a few stories about what hollow pipe drainage means to us?

I had my own inventions, of course – mostly based around the game Twister. There was Travel Twister, for starters, but later I'd taken this on a step and invented the Twister bedspread. I was sure that this would be a surefire hit with male students, at last giving them a valid excuse to invite girls back to their rooms … but I was heartbroken when, a year later, I discovered in a Sunday supplement that someone else had had not only the exact same idea but had actually gone to the trouble of patenting and marketing it. Damn the organised and resourceful! Well, I wasn't going to get caught out like that again. Not now I had the ear of the Patent and Trademark Institute of America.

But I did still have one little trick left up my sleeve: *the electric toilet seat lifter*! Never again would men have to stoop down to lift the toilet seat up. Never again would men have to ask themselves that universal and age-old question – why *do* women always leave the toilet seat down?

Now, thanks to me, couples up and down the country would have one less thing to argue about. Divorces would decrease, families would stay together, toilet seats would have to be rinsed less. Because I, Danny Wallace, was an inventor!

I threw some cereal into a bowl and began to devour the information pack sent to me by my new friends at the Institute, looking for more hints and tips on what they were after, just in case my fallback idea somehow wasn't right.

But that was the thing – there were no hints on what they *were* after. Just what they *weren't* …

RESTRICTED IDEAS *NOT* TO BE SUBMITTED

Perpetual motion devices
Military weapons

Bollocks. My first two obvious ports of call, ripped from my hands by the invention fascists. I *love* inventing perpetual motion devices.

Pornographic devices

A pornographic *device*? How many pornographic *devices* were they getting? And what *is* a pornographic device, anyway?

Untested or unproved chemical formulas, or cures for illnesses.

Well, that wasn't fair. Now I couldn't send them untested or unproved cures for illnesses. I had *loads* of them! I'd have to actually test them out on my mates first.

Products based on unrealistic levels of technology

Bang goes the time machine. This was getting harder by the minute.

Literary or musical works

Right. So I couldn't invent a poem or a new musical note. Which, if you've ever heard me sing, is all I seem to do.

Toilet seat lifters

What?!

But mine's *electric*!

Well, that was fine, I suppose. This would obviously just take a little more work on my part. I sat down to think about what I should invent.

I looked around the flat for inspiration.

The mug. Invented.

The chair. Invented.

Shoes. Done.

Blimey. How do you go about inventing things?

The door. Invented.

Stairs. Invented.

The telly. Invented.

It was all very frustrating. Why was everything in my flat already invented? I was severely vexed, I don't mind telling you. I had to admit that maybe development just wasn't my thing.

I put my jacket on, and grumpily prepared myself for the development meeting at the BBC.

I walked into BBC Television Centre to be met by a man named Tom.

'So you've worked in television before, haven't you, Danny?'

'Well, Yes,' I said. 'But not very much. I prefer radio.'

'Ah, why's that? Because the pictures are better on the radio? Because there are less people involved, and your vision can become a reality?'

'Um … Yes. And also, the radio department is a lot closer to my flat.'

We walked through the vast, shiny corridors of power towards the lifts that would take us to our meeting. Television Centre is rather different from Broadcasting House. The latter is rather tatty, on the whole, with musty carpets and light bulbs that have needed changing since the Second World War. Television Centre, on the other hand, is a vision of the future; with huge, glass newsrooms, and reception areas that look like they've been hit by some kind of pastelbomb, and even areas for producer-relaxation that have been dubbed 'ThinkPods'. I'd love to work somewhere that had a ThinkPod. I'd probably get a lot more thinking done. And I've *always* liked pods.

We arrived at the development meeting and I took a seat.

'Okay, everyone, this is Danny, he's joining us today from the radio department in order to give us a different perspective on things.'

I smiled eagerly and waved to my TV colleagues. One of them waved back. Another managed a weary smile. Two of them hardly looked up from their pads.

'Danny, do you want to just tell us a couple of the things that you're working on right now?'

Hmm. Tricky. Should I mention the inventions?

'I'm working on some new radio show ideas,' I said, before adding, by way of taking up a bit more time, 'which I am working on.'

This seemed enough for everyone, and we cracked on with the meeting.

'Right then,' said Tom, cheerily. 'The first thing we need to do is decide whether or not to continue developing this chat show format.'

'No,' said a man opposite me, dismissively. He was wearing designer spectacles and an ironic t-shirt, so he certainly looked like he knew what he was doing.

'I agree,' said the girl next to him. 'Kill it. It's going nowhere.'

'Danny? What do you think?'

'Well, I don't really know anything about it,' I said.

And so they filled me in.

And to be honest, it didn't sound like a bad show. I'm not allowed to tell you much about it, but it involved a pretty big concept, a host like Johnny Vaughan and a guest like Delia Smith. I didn't know that much about development work, but I was sure they could probably get *something* out of it.

'So bin it or keep it?' said Tom, and there were a few murmurs of 'bin it'.

'Danny? Would you watch that show if it was on?'

I thought about it. Was that an invitation? A suggestion?

'Yes, probably,' I said. 'I suppose it depends upon the trailer.'

Someone said 'hmm' quite loudly.

'Really?' said the man in the ironic t-shirt, smirking. 'The trailer?'

'Well … Yes,' I said, standing my ground. 'I mean, you know … if it looked … inviting.'

'I see what you're saying, Danny,' said Tom. 'It's crucial that this show feels inclusive.'

Phew.

'That is definitely what I was saying just then,' I said.

'Good,' said Tom. 'I think it's got potential, too.'

Wahey!

The man in the t-shirt was quick to backtrack.

'Yes, well, obviously, with a bit of development, and the right kind of—'

'So,' said Tom, cutting him off, 'who wants to take the idea on? Do a bit more work on it?'

No one said anything.

'Danny? How about you?'

'Me?'

'Well, I mean, there's no pressure. Just see how you get on?'

'I'll do it,' the t-shirt man said, immediately.

Tom ignored him.

'Danny?'

'Yes. Sure.'

'Good.'

No, not good. Bad. What the hell was I doing? I knew nothing about this idea except that it had Delia Smith in it. And now here I was taking responsibility for it! What was I supposed to do with it? And now Tom was moving his way through the agenda, and everyone was saying no, we should drop this idea, or no, that idea is going nowhere, and here I am saying Yes, I'll do a little work on that idea, or Yes, I don't mind doing a bit of development on this one. I watched in horror as more and more documents and show outlines and pieces of paper were put in front of me. All this work! I was actively volunteering for all this work! This wasn't like me at all!

'Arse,' said Tom. 'Look at the time. I'm late. Right, so … who's doing what for the next meeting?'

Everyone looked at me.

'I think Danny's doing ... well ... *everything*,' said Sam.

'Oh. Right. Well. Danny ...' said Tom. 'Do you want to come to the next meeting on Friday and let us know how you got on? I'll clear it with your radio people.'

'Yes,' I said, slightly heavily. 'That would be excellent.'

'And in the meantime, I'd like everyone to come up with three new ideas for Saturday night entertainment shows. Okay? Good. See you Friday.'

'This is terrible, Ian,' I said, walking away from TV Centre, mobile in hand. 'I'm in over my head. I just kept saying Yes every time they asked me to do something.'

'Oh, come on! You're a producer! You can produce!'

'No ... I'm a *radio* producer. In Light Entertainment. We are unique. We are a different breed. We were born to get to work a bit late, and spend the morning eating bananas and surfing the Internet, and then head for the pub in the afternoon. We are not like television producers. Television producers are hungry for success, and they get up early, and they eat cocaine, and they dress like people out of magazines, and they know people like David Beckham and Ant 'n' Dec. Who do I know? Brian Perkins.'

'Well, so what? You've said Yes to the work so do it and then just forget about it. I've a feeling that once they see what you're capable of, you won't have to worry about being asked back.'

'But they're expecting success! And Tom wants another three ideas on his desk by Friday.'

'What kind of ideas?'

'Just ... ideas. Ideas for entertainment shows.'

'Oh ...' said Ian.

'What?'

'Nothing. It's just that ... well ...'

'What?'

'*I've* got some ideas.'

'Meet me in the pub in half an hour ...'

'No, Ian.'

'Why not? It's a perfectly good idea.'

'*How To Get Fat* is not a perfectly good idea. Who's going to want to watch a show which tells them how to get fat?'

'Skinny people.'

'No.'

'This one, then,' he said, sliding another piece of paper over the pub table.

'*What Do Moles Mean …?*'

'You know … what does it mean if you've got a mole on your cheek? Is it different from having one on your ear?'

'No.'

'How do you know?'

'I *don't* know, I'm saying no to the idea. It's rubbish.'

'There is no such thing as a bad idea, Dan!'

'What?'

'I saw a lady on telly saying that. "There's no such thing as a bad idea," she said. "And even a bad idea can lead to a good one."'

'But I thought that *no* idea was a bad idea,' I said, confused.

'Exactly. No idea is a bad idea. Exactly.'

'But if there are no bad ideas, how can we get from a bad idea to a good one?'

'Exactly, my friend. No idea is a bad idea. There are only … ideas. How about *A Toddler's Guide To War*?'

'That's a bad idea.'

'Yes, true enough. *My Philosophies and Beliefs*?'

'What's that?'

'It's just a show about my philosophies and beliefs. Each week, Ian Collins takes a sideways glance at …'

'No.'

Ian looked at me, coldly.

'You don't half say no a lot these days …'

I left the pub, and, with a slightly grumpy face, headed off to do my homework.

Once home, I flicked my computer on and prepared to come up with some Saturday night entertainment brilliance.

How to Get Fat.

Maybe there was something in it.

I typed the title on to an otherwise blank document and stared at it for a little while.

But then I was distracted.

By Omar.

DEAR BROTHER danny

THANK YOU FOR YOUR LAST NOTE YOU SENT ME. BUT WE MUST MOVE QUICKLY. I MUST HAVE YOUR BANK DETAILS RIGHT NOW. SEND THEM TO ME.

ARE YOU ALSO FREE TO TRAVEL TO HOLLAND, NETHERLAND. YOU NEED TO BRING CASH GIFTS TO ASSOCIATES OF MY FATHER, WHO HELP US MOVE THE MILLIONS OF DOLLAR.

Eh?! He'd never mentioned that I'd have to travel to Holland before! And what was all this about bringing cash gifts?

I KNOW IT IS MUCH TO ASK, I AM TAKING A BIG RISK IN CONTACTING YOU.

PLEASE SIR WE MUST MOVE NOW. IT IS GOD'S WILL. SEND ME YOU DETAILS.

OMAR

I'll be honest: in the two days since I'd last heard from Omar, my feelings towards him had cooled slightly. And paranoia had set in. What if he wasn't *really* the son of a murdered Sultan? What if he was just after my bank account details? Neither did I like this fresh talk of international travel and gifts for mysterious strangers. Omar was moving a bit too quickly for my liking. It felt like next he'd be telling me I had pretty hair and could I please look into marriage visas.

Dear Omar,

Is it really necessary for me to travel to Holland with cash gifts for your father's associates? I mean, I'm essentially saying Yes, but could you perhaps loan me a million or so for the time being, and take it out of my final cut? I'll pay for the flight and stuff, and keep the receipts in a special envelope.

Cheers!
Danny

I pressed Send and hoped that my e-mail would at least find Omar well. He was probably just excited, poor chap. After all, he'd be moving house soon, and that's quite an exciting thing. I suppose if the worst came to the worst, I could stump up for the cash gifts. I had a few grand I'd managed to save up due to basically never leaving the house, and I could always use that. So long as it didn't turn out to be one of those Nigerian e-mail scams you hear so much about.

Nah. I was just being cynical. And Yes was about losing that.

The following morning there was no word from Omar. I decided not to worry about it. I had a few chores to do in town and so set off for the shops.

Now, you'd think that this would be quite a risky business, when you've decided to say Yes to invitations, offers and suggestions … but I'm pleased to tell you that the modern-day advertiser has missed a vital trick. It seems the more 'sophisticated' they think they've got, the less direct questions they ask, and the fewer direct suggestions they make. In the old days, of course, I'd have been utterly surrounded by easy-to-follow instructions, such as DRINK MILK or BUY BREAD, and would have spent my days both drinking milk and buying bread, but nowadays, with their aspirational photoshoots and subliminal messaging, they were missing out on the simpleton market – the people like me, who'd do as they say, if only they said it.

Ha. They'd never get me now, I thought, as I walked out of the Virgin Megastore with my BUY 2 GET 1 FREE bag of DVDs, and started to cross the road towards Piccadilly Circus.

I fancied another walk around London today, seeing where the wind took me and letting life lead the way. I crossed the road as a stiff wind cleaned the streets and battered the tourists, and noticed that up ahead of me there appeared to be a small group of leafleters. I suddenly felt a little wary; I'd already adopted two grannies, I didn't need any more – unless I was thinking of starting up some kind of pensioner crèche facility. But nevertheless, I continued to walk towards them, and, once I noted a total absence of green bibs or clipboards, took a leaflet from a girl in a summery dress and auburn hair.

SAY YES TO PEACE

I read it again. It still said SAY YES TO PEACE. It seemed oddly appropriate.

Like it was a sign of some kind. A sign that Saying Yes was the Way Ahead.

Come together NOW! Greet someone new today – smile, say
hello, shake their hand … and let the peace begin …

Well, that was nice. And so I did what it said. I walked straight up to the person who had given it to me, I smiled, I said hello, I shook their hand, and I waited for the peace to begin.

'I'm Katherine,' she said.

'Danny,' I said.

And then I let life lead the way.

Katherine, Josh and Mike are three people who share a love of peace.

'It's all about making connections with people,' said Katherine. 'If you can make people understand peace, you are quite literally giving them the world.'

Katherine is also someone who says 'literally' quite a lot.

'It literally gets up my nose, that people just walk around when they could be making a difference.'

If they were literally getting up her nose when they were walking around, then I would suggest she's probably standing a little too close to them.

'We believe in something called Social Acupuncture,' said Mike, the tallest of the three, and the man who'd printed out the leaflets. 'You can make a difference with a single act of conversation.'

'It's all about spreading a message,' added Josh, who was wearing quite a smart baseball cap and a Nike top, and didn't really look like he belonged there. 'You can give people hope if they know you can create peace.'

Katherine nodded. I got the sense that she was the driving force behind the team. We were standing near the Eros statue in the middle of Piccadilly Circus and I didn't really know where things were heading. But I liked the three of them. They seemed genuinely committed to spreading peace through the considered use of leaflets.

'What do you think of the Iraq war?' said Josh, clearly testing me.

'Well … war is bad,' I said, and he and Mike nodded.

'Sometimes a simple message like that can be the most powerful,' said Katherine.

'Feel free to use it,' I said, hoping perhaps that 'WAR IS BAD' might be the next 'in' slogan.

'Thanks,' said Josh, and I realised that maybe it could.

'Would you be interested in helping us spread that message?'

It had all happened rather quickly, but now here I was standing in the middle of Piccadilly Circus with a Virgin Megastore bag in one hand and my very own bunch of SAY YES TO PEACE leaflets in the other. Bloody hell! I had left the house a normal man. I would return as a *peace activist*!

Katherine, Josh and Mike were clearly very pleased that their numbers had increased to the tune of one, and were enthusiastically showing me how it was done.

'Do you like peace, sir?' said Katherine, to one middle-aged man who simply strode past her, putting one hand up to bat away her leaflet.

'Say Yes to peace,' said Josh, to a lady holding a phone in one hand and a shopping bag in the other, and who didn't really look like she wanted to stop and chat about bringing about world peace. I imagine that kind of attitude literally wound Katherine right up.

I managed to give a man a leaflet. I was quite pleased with myself and watched him walk away reading it, but then he stopped and turned around.

'What does this bit mean?' he said. He pointed it out to me, and I read it.

War is a state of the human flickering mind – fear breeding fear breeding fear, feeding back over and over throughout time, reinforcing myths of self-justification.

I hmm'd. The man looked at me. It wasn't the snappiest of slogans. I read it again.

'To be honest, I'm not really sure *what* that means,' I said. 'I think it essentially means that … war is bad.'

He handed the leaflet back to me.

'Deep,' he said, with more than a hint of sarcasm in his voice, and I felt terrible for letting Katherine and the others down. My slogan was obviously rubbish. So I looked at the leaflet, and said, 'Be the change that you want to see in this world!' and smiled. I wasn't sure if I was doing this social acupuncture thing very well. Judging by the look on the back of the man's head, he wasn't, either.

* * *

'We're going to chalk for peace in a bit,' said Katherine, after ten minutes or so. 'Up for it?'

'Yes!' I said. 'What's chalking for peace?'

'We get some chalk and write anti-war slogans all over the place,' said Josh.

'Like where?'

'Pavements, mainly,' said Katherine.

'Does it work?' I asked.

'Yes,' said Katherine, matter-of-factly. 'Of course it does.'

'Got the chalk,' said Mike, striding purposefully into the group. 'Here you go …'

He handed out three pieces of chalk each. I got a red one, a white one, and a blue one. Perfect, I thought. The colours of the Union Jack *and* the Stars and Stripes. Now I could *really* let those governments know how I felt.

But what to write?

Katherine, Mike and Josh were already hunched over, or squatting, or sitting down, letting the world have it.

'Katherine, what should I write?' I said, genuinely lost for inspiration.

'Write what you said earlier.'

'War Is Bad? I think it might be a bit *too* simple,' I said.

'Well … I like writing OUR NEW WORLD ORDER IS LOVE.'

'Yes, that's nice,' I said, and then looked to see what the others were writing.

Mike was writing ANTI BREEDS ANTI, which sounded a bit too close to incest for my liking, and Josh was writing WE ARE ALL RESPONSIBLE.

'Just write what you feel,' said Katherine. 'Look at the leaflet, or something. We get a lot of our stuff from the website. We share our consciousness.'

'That's quite good,' I said. '"Share Your Consciousness!"'

Katherine didn't look too sure.

I thought about it some more. Write what you feel? What did I *feel*?

I decided to write MAKE TEA, NOT WAR.

It'd been *hours* since my last cup.

Katherine crept up behind me.

'That's good,' she said. 'Make Tea, Not War. Tea is a conduit to conversation. It is a peaceful action. When we make tea, we make conversation, and through conversation, we can stop war. Guys! Look what Danny's written!'

Mike and Josh jogged over.

'Make Tea, Not War,' said Mike.

'Tea …' said Josh. 'War.' And then he smiled and nodded. 'It's a bit like "Make Love, Not War", but with tea.'

'Yes,' I said. 'It's a more British version. A little less rude.'

'What made you think of that?' asked Mike.

'I … like making tea,' I shrugged. 'And I don't like … making war.'

I don't think I'd been quite meaningful enough for them, so I tried harder.

'And also … tea is a conduit to conversation. And conversation … can stop wars.'

'Tea *is* a conduit to conversation,' said Josh. 'Hence the tea ceremonies of ancient Japan, or the tea gardens of seventeenth-century Holland.'

I nodded and pointed at him, like that was *exactly* what I'd meant.

Mike clapped his hands together a couple of times, and said 'brilliant', and went straight off to write MAKE TEA, NOT WAR on the side of a wall. Katherine looked at me, proudly. I suddenly felt like I was Doing My Bit.

'"Make Tea, Not War,"' said Katherine. 'You're good.'

'I'm quite good with social campaigning,' I admitted. 'I intend one day to write a song entitled "Stop The Mugging – Start The Hugging"'.

'That's really *nice*,' said Katherine, who I think may have been falling in love with me slightly. 'Could I take your details?'

Yep. She *definitely* was.

'Because my girlfriend and I run regular songwriting workshops.'

Oh.

Katherine had been very thorough when she'd taken my details. She'd wanted to know my home address, home telephone number, e-mail address, mobile number and whether or not I had access to a fax machine. I told her what she wanted to know. I trusted her, and Mike and Josh. They seemed good sorts. Out to change the world, but doing it quietly, and with chalk. And anyway, it wasn't as if she was likely to try and use my details to burgle me. She'd be more likely to break in and replace all my vegetables with organic ones.

'Thank you for your help today, Danny,' said Katherine.

'That's okay. I enjoyed it.'

'You took to it very well. I suppose you're always helping with things, are you?'

'Not really,' I said, shrugging. 'But you asked, and so I thought I would. Oh … hang on, though. There's another man I'm helping at the moment. A Sultan. Well, the son of a Sultan.'

The others looked impressed, and they were right to be.

'He wrote to me to ask for my help. He needs to get $40 million out of Oman before he is murdered by his late father's political enemies.'

'… Oh,' said Katherine, slowly.

'Internet scam, is it?' said Josh, and Mike elbowed him in the ribs.

'You're always so bloody negative,' said Mike.

'It's not an Internet scam, actually,' I said. 'It is a cry for help.'

Mike put his hand on my shoulder, and nodded, sincerely.

We were in a pub called the Goose, now, a moment away from Brixton tube station, having taken the Say Yes To Peace campaign as far as it could go in Piccadilly. Both Katherine and Josh (who, as it turned out, were flatmates) lived not far from here, and Mike, who'd only met them a couple of months before in this very pub, was thinking of relocating.

'It's too easy to say that the people in charge are morons,' he said, directing the conversation at me now. 'Too easy to say get out of government. Instead, we say Yes. To peace.'

Mike got out a packet of fags and offered them around. Both Katherine and Josh took one.

'It's just the best way to do things,' said Katherine, topping up our glasses with a bottle of rather rough red wine.

'Changing the world one person at a time.'

Mike offered me a cigarette. Instantly, my hand went up to indicate I was fine. It was force of habit. But then I remembered who I was and what I was doing, and I said thanks and took one.

'And positivity is the stronger message. It works. It's the only way to fight a battle, if you …'

She paused while Mike lit her cigarette, then Josh's, and then mine.

I sucked hard at it. I'd seen enough smokers to know the drill.

'… anyway,' said Josh, cutting her off. 'No is the most negative word you can say.'

'Literally,' said Katherine, happy for him to take over.

'And Yes is the most *positive* word you can say. So we go from the double-negative 'No To War' to the double-positive 'Yes To Peace', and you can see how much better that sounds.'

I was trying to, but my throat was burning. I had, up until this point in my life, largely attempted to avoid cigarettes. I coughed and passed it off as an energetic nod.

'Yes, No … Yes, No … I know which one *I* prefer,' said Josh.

'"No", probably,' said Mike, and Josh told him to shut it.

I pressed on with my cigarette, although I now wasn't really inhaling the smoke. I was just sucking it in, holding it in my mouth, and blowing it straight out again. Straight *at* people. As such, I was creating an oddly smoky atmosphere. But I'll tell you what – I felt strangely cool and grown-up. I probably looked a bit like James Dean, only with glasses and watery, weeping eyes.

'But it's so hard to interest the media,' said Katherine. 'It's a *positive* message, you'd think they'd be up for that.'

'I put in a call to BBC Bristol the other night,' said Josh. 'They said if we can assemble a large group there, and chalk for peace, they'd probably cover it.'

'That's good,' said Mike.

'Have you ever thought that maybe … you just need to simplify your message?' I said, and the attention of the group was mine. 'I mean … I know "War Is Bad" is too simple, but I think maybe saying things like … you know … "War is the state of the flickering human mind" might put a few people off.'

'We got that leaflet from the Infinite Possibility website,' said Katherine. 'I actually think that's a great message.'

'It is, it is,' I said. 'It's just that I don't really understand it.'

'Well …' said Josh. 'Can you come up with something better?'

I now had my challenge for the evening.

Mike had bought another bottle of rough red wine, and was now off playing the trivia machine. Katherine and Josh had been debating the ethics of the US using oil as a wedge to gain political control over other countries – a debate I had tried to join in with until I realised that they'd both done some background reading while I'd only seen an episode of *Dead Ringers*.

I'd been doing my best to come up with a punchy new media campaign to help this brave group of peace campaigners to victory. But inspiration just wasn't coming.

'Have a go?' said Mike, back from the machine and holding out what looked like a rubbish cigarette. It was a joint.

'In *here*?' I said, looking around the pub.

'Outside,' he said. 'Not in here.'

My God. This was a watershed moment. Could I really allow Yes to make me break the law?

I took it.

'Right,' I said. 'I've got it. I've absolutely got it this time. This is brilliant.'

I assembled my notes. Which came in the form of a beermat and, as such, didn't really require much assembling.

'Okay … what are we aiming for?'

'Peace,' said Katherine.

'Yes, peace,' I said. 'But what else beforehand?'

'Media coverage,' said Josh.

'Precisely. I have devised a new and original media campaign which will lead directly to the governments of this world laying down their weapons and picking up … I dunno … chalk, instead.'

I had been outside the Goose breaking the law with Mike when it had happened. I'd looked up, seen a beautiful painting hanging from the front of the pub, and been transfixed. Utterly transfixed. The smoke had framed the painting for a moment and it was then that the idea had struck me.

'That's it!' I'd said. 'That's the message!'

'So what is it?' said Katherine.

'This has to be catchy, yes? And it has to communicate a real, social message?'

'Yes.'

'Well … how about we use …'

I looked from person to person, anticipating their reaction.

'Geese.'

I didn't get quite the reaction I'd hoped for.

'Geese?' said Josh.

'Geese,' I confirmed. 'Geese For Peace.'

I let the words hang in the air. No one said much.

'Oh, come on, *Geese For Peace*, it's brilliant!'

Still no one said anything. I decided this might require further explanation. And, despite the room appearing to spin slightly, I gave it a go.

'What we do, right?' I began. 'Is we make tiny little signs saying GEESE FOR PEACE. And then we stick them outside geese farms and near geese in general. We then tip the media off that the geese are getting agitated about this whole war business and have started, against all the odds, to stage their own animal peace protests.'

Katherine and Josh just nodded at me, open-mouthed – clearly they were impressed. This was going well.

'We get some photographers down there. We secretly tell people up and down the country to make their own GEESE FOR PEACE signs, and quietly stick them in the ground in farms and zoos. The media will have a field day. People *literally* won't believe it, Katherine! It will be like mother nature herself is rising up and saying *no* to *war*!'

Katherine put her hand up to correct me.

'*Yes* to *peace.*'

'Sorry. But it will be like the geese themselves are making a stand. Imagine it! Geese, the world over, saying Yes to Peace!'

'I like it,' said Mike, who was clearly on my level, although I couldn't help but suspect he was a little stoned. Lucky *I* wasn't, or we wouldn't have Geese For Peace.

'But why geese?' said Josh.

'It rhymes with peace!' Mike and I said, in near-unison.

'Ohh,' said Katherine, obviously finally realising the brilliance of my scheme.

And then – quite out of the blue – I had *another* excellent idea.

'Hey Mike,' I said. 'Imagine this … what if there was a shop called *Pizza Hat* … and all it sold was *hats* shaped like *pizzas*?!'

And then Mike started to giggle, and so did I, and we couldn't stop ourselves, and we laughed like mentals, and I hit my hand down on the table and nearly knocked over the wine, and Mike laughed even more, and we both started to virtually cry with laughter at the thought of hats shaped like pizzas.

'Pizza *Hat*!' Mike exclaimed. 'Hit the Hat!'

Yep. He was definitely stoned.

And then we talked about my brilliant Geese For Peace idea a bit more.

An hour or so later, as I stumbled home, I realised that maybe the effects of the little disco cigarette I'd had with Mike had affected me in more ways than I'd previously thought. Fair enough, it'd had nothing to do with Geese For Peace, because that was blatantly a very strong concept, but it was what happened next that concerned me.

I'd made it home and decided that a nice cup of tea was what I needed most in this world. So I started to make one. It took a lot longer than it usually did, and I found the plume of steam that rose from the kettle so fascinating and beautiful that I must've watched it boil three times before even trying to find a teabag.

When eventually I did, I got the milk out the fridge and found a spoon, which I promptly dropped. It clattered on the floor.

As I stooped to pick it up … I suddenly realised … this was it. *This* was my invention.

A spoon you couldn't drop!

A spoon … that hovers!

That'd be amazing!

But how would I make it hover?

Tiny fans, maybe?

Yes, that's it! Dozens of tiny fans attached to the underside of a spoon.

I ran to my desk and started to make some rudimentary sketches. I was buzzing. I had just invented the hover spoon! Oh, how the offices of the Patent and Trademark Institute of America would stop and applaud when news of the hover spoon spread! And best of all, we could do spin-off spoons … teaspoons, tablespoons … even a huge, hovering ladle!

I phoned Ian.

'Hello?'

'Ian, it's Danny!'

'How's it going?'

'Not bad – listen. What would you say if I told you you could have a spoon …' I paused to allow him time to picture a spoon '… that could *hover*!'

Ian didn't say anything. Well, clearly, he had some pretty big thinking to do. Ian always thought he knew where he was with spoons, but I'd just messed with his preconceptions. The boundaries of cutlery had been given a severe kick into the future, and I think Ian knew that. I was a revolutionary, passing on my insight and vision to … well … a *normal* person. I mean, *you're* a normal person. What would *you* do if a visionary like me phoned you up and told you he'd invented the hover spoon?

And then I realised Ian had hung up.

I decided that my so-called equal Ian was just too caught up in convention. He was still living with a very 1990s view of spoons (and cutlery in general to be honest), and if you ever meet him I'd like you to promise me that you'll point that out to him.

Moodily, I switched my computer on and checked my e-mails.

Omar had written to me again. And he sounded tetchy.

DEAR danny

**BUT WHAT IS THE ACCOUNT DETAILS. I MUST HAVE THE DETAIL SO
I CAN GIVE YOU THE MONEY. WHAT ARE THE ACCOUNT DETAILS.
GIVE THEM TO ME.**

IT IS GOD'S WILL!

OMAR

I made a 'harumph' sound, I drank my tea, I ate an inexplicably large amount of toast, and I went to bed.

'You're going to do *what*?' said Ian, slamming his pint down on the table.

It was the next day and I was seeking his advice.

'I'm going to give Omar my bank account details.'

'You're going to give him your details! Oh, brilliant! First the hover spoon, now this. Two of the worst ideas in the world, in just 24 short hours ...'

I thought it best not to mention the peace-geese, which, for some odd reason, had lost some of its power overnight.

'Well, what if I don't give him my savings account details? What if I started a brand new account, into which he can deposit his many millions of dollars? I have to help him.'

'But *why*?'

'He seems very insistent. The poor lad is about to be murdered by his late father's political enemies, Ian!'

'It's a scam, Dan!'

'Oh, not *you*, as well,' I said, wisely, and with some degree of pity in my voice. 'I have experience of scammers, my friend. And if this is a scam, then it's a bloody clever one.'

'Danny, of *course* it's a scam! I've seen stuff like this on *Watchdog*! They send out thousands of e-mails and if you respond, they know the e-mail address is real, and then you get loads more of them. All they need is one person like you – a person who says Yes when they should blatantly say no! They're going to try and rip you off!'

'Listen here, Mr Cynical. I was like you once. Not so long ago, I would have *definitely* thought it was a scam, too. But this whole Yes Man thing has started to teach me the benefits of thinking positively. I should trust my fellow man. Approach things with optimism. Treat people like they're already friends. And is it *really* too far-fetched to suggest that the murdered Sultan of Oman, who I never met, used to speak of me with such affection that his son, facing a possible murder plot by the same men who killed his father, might want to get in touch with me, Danny Wallace, in order to secure the safety of forty million dollars?'

I hoped Ian was considering what I was saying carefully. But I'm disappointed to say he really jumped the gun.

'Of *course* it's too far-fetched, you fucking idiot!'

Sometimes I pity the cynical.

'He's invited me to his house, Ian. I hardly think he'd invite me to his house if he were planning on scamming me before I even got there. It'd make dinnertime a little awkward, don't you think? He just wants a little of my professionalism in business.'

'*What* professionalism in business? You can't even use a stapler properly! This was all done by e-mail, wasn't it?'

'Of course. Omar is lying low at the moment. He had to set up a free e-mail account so that he was in no way traceable. You know. By his enemies, and that.'

'And he's asked you for your bank account details?'

'Yes. And to travel to Holland with cash gifts for his late father's business associates.'

'Anything else?'

'My phone number.'

'And I suppose you gave that to him, as well, did you?'

'Ian, it is God's will! And anyway, this is incredibly liberating. I feel like I don't have to make any choices, any more. Everything's done for me.'

'Look … I forbid you from giving this man your bank account details. Okay?'

'You can't forbid me from stuff! What are you going to do? Tell my mum and dad?'

'If I have to.'

'*Please* don't tell my mum and dad.'

'This Yes thing is a little dangerous, Dan. I thought all you'd be saying Yes to would be nights down the pub and perhaps lending me a tenner now and then. I didn't realise you'd be doing things like this. This is dangerous. And it could get out of hand – these e-mails things often do. You're lucky Omar is the only one who's asked for your details …'

I didn't say anything.

It dawned on Ian.

'Other people have asked you, haven't they? Oh, Danny, no … who else has asked you for your bank account details?'

The fact of the matter was, *loads* of people had suddenly asked me for my bank account details. And word of my willingness to help Omar, son of the murdered Sultan of Oman, must have spread in some pretty royal circles.

In the days that had followed our initial exchange, I was contacted by people like His Highness Shaik Isa Bin Sulman al Khalifa, Emir of the State of Bahrain, who had apparently heard some pretty good things about me and wanted me to be his property manager abroad in return for a share of $120 million.

And let's not forget King Asiam Okofonachi, of the Aziam village deep down in the Accra native clans and the great-great-grandson of the mighty warrior legend Okofonachi. King Asiam had just been told he had one month left to live and while he was dealing with that just fine, he was nevertheless determined not to leave his huge gold fortune to his two sons, because 'they are involved with drug sniffings and harlot doings'. He was happy, however, for a random stranger like me to have his money – provided I promised not to spend it on drug sniffings and harlot doings. Oh, and PS: could I please pop over to Ghana and bring lots of money for, you know, set-up costs and that.

Actually, hang on, these were *definitely* scams, weren't they.

No. Wait. *Trust in Yes*.

'Right. Okay,' said Ian, rubbing the bridge of his nose in the way that slightly weary teachers who wear glasses often do, just to show you that they care and they're a lot more intelligent than you. 'And you didn't find it suspicious at all that Kings and Emirs and bloody Dukes of Hazzard were all suddenly e-mailing you out of the blue and claiming you're their saviour and then asking for your bank account details?'

'I thought it was unusual, yes, but optimism is—'

'*Unusual*? Danny, they're all claiming to be billionaires, and yet they write their own bloody e-mails and they use bloody hotmail!'

I made a grumpy face. What was it about me that Ian thought Sultans, Emirs and Kings wouldn't want a part of?

'Listen,' I said. 'When Omar, son of the murdered Sultan, comes good and hands me my share of $40 million—'

'Who have you sent your details to?'

'No one yet – I'm thinking of doing a mass-mailing—'

'You're not!'

'I am! But Omar was first. He should—'

'Dan. Just tell me. What's this Omar's e-mail address?'

He was looking at me, sternly. I tried to say something but he raised his finger at me and for some reason I found it a bit frightening.

'If you're saying you can't get out of this, Dan, then maybe I should – before you get beaten up by a couple of Sultans in a Dutch hotel room …'

I nodded, silently. Ian put his finger back down again.

'So … what's the address?'

>TO: Omar
>FROM: Ian
>Subject: Bad News

Dear Omar,

I take the pleasure to get associated with you and desire to introduce myself, requesting for your expert advises and immediate line of action.

I am Ian, friend of Danny.

This morning Danny was arrested for a crime he did not commit and is now in a big jail. Before they took him away, he talked of you with great affection and trust.

He has entrusted me with his affairs and I have noticed that he has over £1000 in his bank account. It is my opinion that his mum will try and take this off him as she has access to his bank account details too.

I wish to flee the country and move to somewhere like Oman, where I could live with you in your Sultanate.

If you help me move this £1000 into a safe foreign bank account then for your troubles I am prepared to give you 25% (£250).

It may be necessary for you to travel to Holland to present gifts to some of Danny's mates. They're not fussy, buy them a Toblerone at the airport or something. It is God's will, etc.

Please my brother we must move quickly. His mum is closing in.

Send me your bank details. I trust you 100%.

Ian.

PS. This is not an e-mail scam.

And that, my friend, is how Ian bloody Collins lost me ten million dollars.

And not just $10 million. But the share of $120 million that the Shaik had offered me. And the $87 million of gold that the King had waved my way. And nearly $200 million more from other assorted dignitaries in apparent need of a little of the Wallace magic.

Ian had come around that night and, after e-mailing Omar (who I hope wasn't too annoyed and was indeed fibbing about the whole murder plot thing) set me up with a powerful junk mail filter. Now, he said, I wouldn't have to worry about spam any more. I could concentrate on the *proper* Yes opportunities, he said. Like going to the pub and lending him tenners.

Omar never wrote back. But I was grateful to Ian. Grateful that he'd been willing to turn a blind eye to an opportunity to see me go bankrupt. And grateful to him for saving me an airfare to Holland. Because that's where he'd proved to me they operate from.

'Look at these,' he said, clicking from website to website. 'These show you the stories behind the scams. People fall for them every day. Some of them are lucky and just lose a few grand after paying ridiculous "set-up" costs that don't exist. Others are unluckier. Some of them end up heading off to Holland where they're told they'll be able to pick up their money. They're met by a representative of the King, or the Emir, or the bloody Sultan, fleeced for all their money, and in some cases beaten to a pulp.'

'But I thought Holland was so laid-back!' I said. 'Why are they beating people to a pulp? It doesn't seem right, somehow.'

'It's the European capital of scams, Dan. And of big men who beat you up.'

'But who are they?'

'Thugs, mainly. I mean, many of them are harmless. But some are gangs. Drugs gangs, linked to organised crime.'

I shuddered.

'That could have happened to me! Omar asked me if going to Holland would have been possible! I would've gone! I would've been beaten up by a burly drugs gang!'

'That's why I'm saying, Dan … look, maybe this Yes thing has gone far enough already. You know? Maybe it's time to call it off? It all seems a little … pointless. What are you learning, here? What have you done so far of worth?'

I was confused. But I shook my head.

'No, Ian. That Yes happened for a reason. And you were there to ward it off. You saved me. And anyway, it won't happen again, will it?'

'It shouldn't. The junk mail filter is on maximum. Just avoid the bloody Internet, Danny. You'll get stuck in a rut. You'll be falling for scams and buying penis patches and saying Yes to any old nutjob who can find your address. Avoid your bloody e-mails.'

I nodded.

'Fine.'

'And remember, one No is all I need to unleash the full and terrifying power of … the punishment!' he said.

I looked him in the eye.

'You haven't thought of a punishment yet, have you?' I said.

He shook his head.

'No.'

Ian was right. I had to avoid my computer. It was nothing but a world of risky Yeses in a neat little box. That wasn't what I wanted. I wanted safety. Security. Comfort. A world without risk or challenge.

So I drank my tea, and I stayed in the kitchen, and I vowed to look not once at my computer.

And then I walked into the living room, switched it on, and checked my e-mails. There were two: one from Tom at the BBC, reminding me of the next day's development meeting, for which I should bring plenty of ideas and energy. And the other from Brian, the Starburster:

Danny,
I have some interesting information for you … are you free to meet me at the New Clifton Bengali Restaurant on

Whitechapel Road tomorrow night at 6 pm? Just next to Aldgate tube. Do say yes ...

Brian

Oh, bollocks. Ian had been right. Now I'd have to spend another entire evening talking about aliens and pyramids again. Maybe all this *was* pointless.

I thought about what to write back. But then I noticed that Brian hadn't quite finished his e-mail.

I scrolled down.

And I was intrigued.

PS. It concerns your man on the bus.

7

In which Daniel proposes a Theory,
attends a Party, and Vexes a Rival

I didn't know precisely what Brian wanted to tell me about the man on
the bus. It seemed strange to me that he had anything to tell at all. The
man on the bus was, after all, just a man on a bus. But I'd written back
to Brian almost immediately, and told him that, Yes, I would meet him at
the curryhouse in order to hear his very important information. It was an
odd Yes to be saying, but that was fine by me. Odd Yeses still counted –
they all did, whatever their level.

Because Yes, Yeses come in levels. There are, in fact, several levels
of Yes. Perhaps you yourself have unwittingly been at the mercy of one
of them today. Perhaps that's how you ended up at the shops, or treated
yourself to that elaborate coffee – maybe that's even how you ended up
holding this book. The Yes levels (yevels) are everywhere (yeverywhere),
and they do their best to help us along in our everyday lives. And if, as I
suspect is the case, you have bought this book as some kind of rudimentary self-help manual, you may wish to take note of the following.

THE FIVE LEVELS OF YES

Level One: *The easy level.* This is saying Yes to questions such as
'Would you like some free money?', 'How about one for the road?',
'Would you like to see a picture of a pony?' and 'Why don't you take the
rest of the day off?'

Level Two: *The still-quite-easy level.* Level Two is only slightly trickier.
It's saying Yes to doing that hilarious impression you do. Saying yeah,
okay, I'll video that thing for you on BBC2 tonight. It's saying Yes, of

course I'll make you a coffee, and what's more, I don't necessarily expect a coffee back one day, either.

Level Three: *The making-an-effort level.* It's Level Three, and things are getting harder. But not so hard that you'd want to make a fuss about them – that's the beauty of Level Three. It's saying Yes to the party you don't really want to go to – and then actually going to it. It's saying Yes to going for a drink after work, when really, what you want to do is watch *The Weakest Link* and eat a samosa. It's saying Yes to anything that requires a journey of more than forty minutes, and/or more than one change of bus. It's agreeing to accompany an elderly aunt to the toilet and not running off when she shouts, 'I'm finished!'

Level Four: *The too-much-effort level.* Ah, Level Four. Our old enemy. This is saying Yes to attending a christening – *any* christening. Yes to anything that involves modern dance, or having to make and bring your own canapes. It's saying Yes to something you know will be awkward; it's saying Yes when what you really want to say is absolutely not.

Level Five: *The forget-it level.* Most of us never attain Level Five status. This is saying Yes to attending a wedding. In Mozambique. It's saying Yes to going to a terrible dinner party on the other side of town that you know you're not welcome at because the last time you were there you insulted someone's wife and were sick in the host's shoes. And it's fancy dress. And Claire Sweeney will be there. It's anything involving planes. Anything involving pains. Anything that you totally, utterly, wholeheartedly can't, won't or mustn't say Yes to. *That*, my friend, is Level Five.

I reasoned that so far in my adventure I'd been hovering pretty much around Level Three ... and that was fine by me. Like I'd said to Ian, this was still early days. 31 December was still months away. But things were chugging along quite nicely. I was making an effort. Getting back out there. Saying Yes to things I usually just couldn't be arsed to do. It was all pretty much Level Three stuff, but Level Three was where I was happiest. It just felt right, and I felt better. Other people, too, were remarking upon the sudden change they'd seen in me.

Wag was delighted that I was out and about more now. He'd begun to realise that all he'd have to do was pick up the phone and I'd be there, in a flash and a jiffy, unless, of course, I'd said Yes to being somewhere else … but rules is rules: a little bit of effort and I'd usually be able to swing both. Wag was touched, and I wasn't going to disillusion him. I'd also been able to catch up with friends I hadn't seen in ages – just because I was now usually in town of an evening and could get pretty much anywhere, quickly. And so I caught up with Carl, and Stefan, and Nerys, and Nathan, and Dara, and Nina, and Noel, and more.

Things were good. Things were fine. Everything was under control.

It was 4 pm and I was walking out of BBC Television Centre with something of a spring in my step. My second development meeting had gone incredibly well.

I mean, *ridiculously* well.

Fair enough, most of my ideas had been poo-poohed before I'd even finished saying the titles, and after a couple of them I'd sensed a few people in the room actually struggling not to boo, but as far as I was concerned, I'd managed to say Yes to almost everything I was asked about, and as such, I deemed the meeting an outright success. Plus, quite a few mediocre ideas and at least three awful ones had been saved from the dustbin thanks to a little bit of blind positivity. If you pay your licence fee you should be quite grateful to me at this point.

I'm paraphrasing, but Tom had told me he liked me, after the meeting. I was fresh, he said. And not cynical and jaundiced like most of the people who came to these things. I wasn't dismissive. In fact – and I'm still paraphrasing here – I was the opposite! I was a *nurturer* of ideas. I was *positive*.

'You *understand*,' he said. 'That no idea is a bad idea. And even bad ones can lead to a good one. That's what development is all about.'

I was smiling rather widely. All I'd done was approach things in an incredibly positive manner, and look what was happening: I was being lavished with praise by an authority figure!

'Just out of interest,' said Tom, 'what kind of contract have you got with the radio department?'

'A couple of days a week at the moment … just while I'm looking for new projects, so—'

'And what do you do the rest of the week?'

I drink tea, Tom, and I write to Sultans.

'Oh, you know … this and that.'

'Have you ever thought about working over here for a while?'

'Sorry?'

'We've got a space on one of our teams. We need someone like you, I think. Someone who can come in and bring a sense of positive energy to the room.'

Wow! Positive energy!

'Can you send me your CV?'

'Yes,' I said.

'Good. You've proved you're a natural developer. You can take an idea and run with it. I mean, okay, you ran in a pretty weird direction with that *How To Get Fat* idea, and what you got out of it wasn't brilliant, but—'

'Hey,' I said, raising my finger. 'There's no such thing as a bad idea!'

'Precisely, Danny. Apart maybe from that one case. But all I'm saying is, consider coming on board.'

'Okay,' I said. 'I will.'

'So where are you off to now?' said Tom.

'I'm off to meet a man about a bus,' I said.

The New Clifton Bengali Restaurant is in Whitechapel Road, just a stone's throw from the Blind Beggar pub – the place I'd last met Brian and learnt all about how aliens had built the pyramids while those lazy Egyptians just sat there worshipping cats and drawing on the walls.

I wasn't sure what information Brian had managed to glean about my man on the bus, but he was local to the East End, as, I assume, was the man I met that night, so I was hoping for some positive identification at the very least.

Brian was already there when I arrived.

'Hello!' I said, happily taking a seat.

'Danny, hello,' he said, 'thanks for coming. I assume it's because you're still saying Yes more?'

'No, no,' I said, because I didn't want to be rude and make him think that was the only reason I'd shown up. 'Well … Yes.'

'That's fine. Because it would appear you are doing the right thing.'

'Am I?'

He nodded.

There was a brief silence. I wasn't sure whose turn it was to speak next. But Brian didn't say anything so I decided it was probably mine.

'So … what's up? Shall we order something?'

Brian caught the eye of a waiter, and we ordered some curry.

When the waiter disappeared, Brian tapped his fingers on the table and then, slightly coyly I thought, said:

114

'Danny, over the weekend I did a little research … just a few Internet sites and so on, but I thought it was worth sharing the information with you.'

'What kind of research?' I said, knowing all too well that when grown men use the words 'research' and 'Internet' in the same sentence, a court case usually follows soon after.

'I was reminded of something, that was all. When you told me – us – about the man you met on the bus that night, Laura made reference to the Maitreya … and I followed it up.'

'Yeah, but that's not real, though … I mean, you said it yourself—'

'Yes, but I also said it is good to keep an open mind on things. So … could you just run what happened by me again?'

This was all a bit odd. What I'd told them about the man on the bus seemed pretty clear. A man on a bus said something to me. And that was it. But nevertheless, I obliged …

'Um … well, I was sitting on a bus, next to this man, and—'

'What did he look like?'

'He was an Asian guy. And he had a beard.'

Brian turned over a small piece of paper that had been face down on the table and held it up to me.

'Is this him?'

I couldn't really tell. The picture had been printed from the Internet, and was black-and-white and rather blurry. It was of an Asian-looking man with a beard, wearing a white robe and standing in a large crowd of people. It was subtitled 'Kenya, 1988'. I was amazed. Brian had brought props!

'I'm not sure …' I said, and I could see faint disappointment in Brian's face, so I took another look, keen to be as helpful as possible. 'I suppose the *beard* looks quite similar.'

Brian closed his eyes and signalled for me to continue.

'Anyway … we were talking about this and that, and about what we'd done with our weeks, and I mentioned how I was basically staying in all the time and turning things down, and he said, "So say Yes more", or words to that effect, and that was that, really.'

Brian frowned.

'And that was that? You just started saying Yes more after that?'

'Yes.'

'And is it working? What's happened?'

'Well … I've been having fun. I've been out a lot more, and I've met new people, and I'm off to a party later, and I nearly won £25,000. I bought a steam cleaner, and my career seems to be benefiting, too, so … Yes.'

Brian folded his arms and leaned forward in his chair.

'This may sound a little outlandish to you, Danny, but what if I were to tell you that there is a school of thought which suggests that Jesus himself is alive and well and living not five minutes from here in Brick Lane?'

There. He'd said it.

To be honest, I didn't know quite how to react. I decided that the best way to react was to just sit there, with my mouth slightly open, and a general look of bewilderment about me. I hadn't had Brian down as a religious activist before now, and this seemed a slightly eccentric and ineffectual way for him to be spreading the good word – particularly as I was struggling to see the relevance of that particular statement to what we'd just been talking about.

'Er … I don't know *what* I'd say to that,' I said. 'I suppose I'd say: "Is he?"'

Brian sat back in his chair.

'Jesus. The Christ. Bodhisattva. The Iman Madhi. Krishna. Maitreya. Call him what you will. But yes, he is. According to some, anyway.'

'And … what's this got to do with me?' I said, as politely as I could, because it suddenly appeared you never knew *where* Jesus might be sitting.

'Maitreya, as we shall call him, has been living among the Pakistani-Indian community of Brick Lane since the 19th of July 1977, according to my research. He is what they call a Master of Wisdom, come here to oversee and to teach. He is a spokesman for justice and sharing.'

I considered what Brian was telling me.

'He's been quite quiet,' I said. 'For a spokesman, I mean.'

'No, Danny, he hasn't. Apparently, he has been actively working among us in those 25 years and lives in the world today along with several other Masters of Wisdom. And those masters are training people, and touching their lives, and changing the world.'

'And … how do they do that?'

'I'll get to that. But according to those in the know, around eighteen and a half million years ago, a group of beings from planets like Venus were brought to earth to help us get started—'

'Can I just stop you there for a moment,' I said, but as it turned out, I couldn't.

'I'm not saying I believe this, Danny, I'm just saying this is what is believed. They have lived among us for a millennium in some of the most remote areas of the world – the Himalayas, the Rocky Mountains, the Gobi Desert, the Andes, for example – and they have taken care of us from afar. But now, masters like Maitreya are said to live among us. There's a master in New York, one in Geneva, one in Darjeeling and another in Tokyo. Along with Maitreya in London, of course.'

'Right,' I said, although I wasn't really sure that it was. 'And you're saying that I've met him?'

'No,' he said. 'I am saying some would say it is possible you met him.'

'But why me?'

Brian shrugged.

'Why not? Now, again: I'm not saying I believe all this. But to show you how seriously he is taken, in 1984, it was promised that Maitreya would show himself to the world's media. Reporters from all over the world turned up to hear what the great one had to say. The *Telegraph*, the *Observer*, the *Sun*, they were all there.'

'Where?'

Brian raised his eyebrows and opened his arms.

'The New Clifton Bengali Restaurant.'

Uh?

'Here?' I said, utterly amazed. 'It was *here*?'

'Well, no. The New Clifton Bengali Restaurant used to be on Wentworth Street.'

'Oh.'

'But it's here now.'

It wasn't quite the same.

'Why did he choose to reveal himself in a Bengali restaurant in the East End of London?' I asked.

'I don't know,' said Brian, slightly testily, batting my question away like it was the first thing people *always* asked. 'Anyway, the journalists were assured that Maitreya would make his entrance and then announce his message to the world.'

'And what was his message?'

'Well … he never showed up, so no one knows.'

I was starting to wonder why Brian had insisted we meet at the New Clifton Bengali Restaurant – a restaurant that wasn't even the same New Clifton Bengali Restaurant as the one that a man *hadn't* shown up in twenty years earlier. I mean, there were *millions* of places that weren't even the same place as the one that a man hadn't shown up in twenty years earlier. There was my flat, for example, or Bristol.

'Anyway, it was announced later that despite not appearing at the New Clifton Bengali Restaurant because the time wasn't right, he would be continuing his work here on earth of overseeing the evolution of ...' he pointed at me '... lesser people.'

I didn't know whether to be grateful or annoyed. On the one hand, it was quite nice to think that, if he does indeed exist, Maitreya chose *me* to oversee that night. But on the other, I couldn't help but feel a little peeved that out of all the people living in London today, *I* was the one he decided was that little bit less evolved than all the others. But I was finding it all a little hard to believe. I decided to call Brian's bluff.

'Well ... if Maitreya lives on Brick Lane, why don't we pop round? We could go there now and say hello and I could see if it *was* the same bloke, after all.'

'I don't know where his flat is,' said Brian, shrugging and ripping a naan in two. 'I know it's above a shop, and I know it's near a temple, but that's all I know. To be honest, I'm no great expert. But ... I'd like you to meet someone who *is* ...'

At this point, it would have been *brilliant* if Brian had pointed at the door behind me, a jaunty tune had started up, and Maitreya himself had walked in waving, like we were all on some kind of very spiritual chat show. But he didn't, and I felt a little bit like how I imagine those journalists must have felt in 1984.

Instead, Brian just said, 'Pete.'

'Pete?'

'Pete. He's a sometime-Starburster and an expert on this kind of thing. What I know about Maitreya I learnt from Pete.'

'I suppose you think I should meet with Pete, then,' I said.

'Yes,' said Brian.

I left the restaurant that night rather confused. I wasn't entirely convinced that the man I'd met on the bus that night *had* been Maitreya. Fair enough; he'd had a beard, just like Maitreya. And fair enough; he was a teacher, just like Maitreya was 'the World Teacher' (which seems rather ambitious – the marking alone must be a job in itself). But there must be thousands of bearded teachers in London, so why Brian was so determined that the wisdom the bloke on the bus had passed on to me was *divine* wisdom I just didn't know.

Still, I'd given Brian the go-ahead to give my details to Pete, and I was told to expect a call within the next week or so, once Pete had 'checked me out'.

I arrived at Robert the technician's party at eight on the dot.

Amazingly, it was already in full swing. There were people in the kitchen, people on the landing, people already leaving. This just wasn't right. Whenever I've organised a party and told people to turn up at eight, the first ninety minutes have usually consisted of me and a bowl of nuts. But no. Here we all were. In quite a swanky apartment.

'Nice place, Robert,' I said, impressed. I'd always imagined Robert living on the set of *Robot Wars*. But no. He had taste. And style.

'It's my brother's pad.'

Ah.

Robert and I walked into the living room, and now there were more people, sitting in a near perfect circle, on dining-room chairs.

'Everyone, this is Danny.'

'Hello, everyone,' I said.

'Hello,' said everyone back.

Robert sat down and so did I.

'Right,' he said. 'Facts.'

Oh bollocks. I'd forgotten to bring my fact with me. What did I know? What did I know that no one else knew? How was I supposed to stump a stranger? I hadn't realised this was going to be so ... *formal*.

'Here's mine!' said a girl called Rosie. 'The call of the howler monkey can be heard at a distance of up to ten miles.'

She looked very pleased with herself, and the group made appreciative noises. One person said, 'I did *not* know that,' and shook their head. Cripes. Mine was going to have to be good to compete with that one.

'Okay, my turn,' said the man to her right.

Shit. What was I going to say? What did I know? I've got loads of great facts ... facts about lions, facts about helicopters ... but what *were* they?

'The national flag of Italy was designed by Napoleon Bonaparte.'

A couple of people said 'really?' and the man nodded enthusiastically, as if he'd discovered it through a detailed research expedition of his own.

'Who's next?' said Robert.

Oh, God, this wasn't fair. Why did we have to break the ice at the *start* of the party? Why couldn't we all just ignore each other until midnight or so and then drunkenly make friends just as the taxis were arriving?

'I'll go …' said a girl in a pink top. 'Right … if a statue of a person on a horse has its front legs in the air, then the person died in battle. If the horse has one front leg in the air, the person died as a result of wounds *received* in battle. Finally, if the horse has all four legs on the ground, then the person on top of it died of *natural* causes.'

This bloody *stormed* it. The girl was suddenly the most popular person in the room. And all through knowing a bit of otherwise useless trivia. I was amazed. And I wanted a part of it.

'Danny?' said Robert. 'What's your fact?'

Right. Quick. Come up with something. But my mind went blank. I would have to make something up. But *what*?

'Danny?'

Think!

'Since … er … since the first McDonald's restaurant opened … in, er, 1969 … in a diner just off … California Beach …' I said, adding extraneous invented details in the hope that it would give an air of confidence to wherever this was going … 'The, er … McDonald's corporation has sold … *in excess* of …' – I pointed my finger in the air to add a feeling of gravitas '… one *million* hamburgers.'

The group looked at me in stunned silence.

And then a couple of them wrinkled their noses, and someone said 'oh' with a hint of disappointment in their voice.

'A million hamburgers?' said the girl in the pink top. 'Doesn't sound like very much.'

'In *excess* of,' I said. 'Which means more than.'

There was an awkward pause. The girl in the pink top looked at me like I'd really let her down.

And then my saviour came.

'The first ready-to-eat breakfast cereal was Shredded Wheat in 1893, beating Kelloggs Corn Flakes by a full five years.'

The heat was off. The group was impressed again.

The man gave me a wink.

The man who had saved me went by the name of Gareth.

'Thanks so much for that,' I said. 'To be honest, I made that McDonald's fact up. I mean, it's *probably* true, so I wasn't *technically* lying …'

'Yes,' said Gareth. 'I imagine the fact that they've sold over one million hamburgers probably *is* true.'

'It's a lot, isn't it?' I said, still trying to make it seem more impressive than it was.

'… Yes,' Gareth said, slowly. 'Anyway, how's it going? Where have you come from tonight?'

'Bow,' I said. 'You?'

'Forest Hill. Just moved across with my girlfriend.'

Gareth worked in TV, as someone big in forward-planning for *Richard & Judy*, on Channel 4.

'Oh!' I said. 'That's a *great* show! I was *on* that once!'

And I had been. When I'd started my own cult – the cult that Hanne hadn't taken too kindly too – I'd been invited on to the *Richard & Judy* show to explain what had happened. I'd had a brilliant time, and it was one of the highlights of a very odd year.

'Yes! I saw that one!' said Gareth, which was only to be expected, seeing as he worked on it. 'I thought I recognised you. Yes … I remember Richard saying afterwards, that was such an … *odd* edition of the show.'

Let's just say that quote won't be making it on to my CV.

And then someone new had arrived at the party, and informed the room with great gusto that 'In Hartford, Connecticut, you can receive a five-dollar fine if you transport a dead body using a taxi!' He received a round of applause and an admiring glance from the girl in the pink top.

Gareth and I looked at each other and I mouthed the word 'bastard'.

My new friend and I talked about all manner of things, and I was finding out that since I'd started my Yes experiment, I'd become a fascinating human being, with new experiences to talk about and opinions on all manner of things. I told him in great detail about how men actually *can* have babies, and about how I'd hung out with peace activists and come up with both the 'War Is Bad' slogan *and* the Geese For Peace campaign that he'd probably heard about by now, and about how aliens built the pyramids, and how earlier that evening I'd had a curry just down the road from where Jesus lives.

And he nodded and took it all in and seemed to be thinking something over in his head.

'Danny, do you have a number I can contact you on?'

And I said I did, and gave it to him.

And then he said he had to be up early, but would give me a call soon about something, and he left. Maybe I wasn't as fascinating as I thought.

I decided I would never again try and tell a stranger how to cork his birth canal.

It was an hour later and I was having a great time.

Already, I'd talked to a Spanish girl who'd seen a ghost when she was four, a man who much to my amusement finished every sentence with the words 'do you know what I mean?' and a bloke who once owned a windmill. I had also attracted the attentions of a girl who was very impressed that my friend Wag was, the very next morning, to set off for Germany with Busted.

The lesson of the evening had quickly become you can never judge how a party is going to turn out just by the fact that the invitation included the words 'Bring a fact'.

Next up was Thom, a bloke who worked in the city but had the look of a traveller about him. And that was exactly what he was about to do. An unusual move, for a man who worked with stocks and shares.

'Of course, it's good money, but sometimes … you know … you just have to take a risk. Turn your back on the easy way. Which is what I'm doing. So I'm moving to New Zealand to do something else. Something new.'

'What kind of thing?'

'I don't know yet. I've just always had a thing for New Zealand. I've got enough money to see me through the first few months and get me set up and so on … but I just kind of want to see what happens.'

I admired Thom for this. He was someone who had it all, but had decided that he didn't need most of it.

'Wow,' I said. 'How long have you been planning it?'

'I've thought about it for years. But I never thought it would come to anything. And then me and my girlfriend split up, and that changed things because it was only my job tying me down after that, and I thought, sod it. I'm going to do what I want. Which means moving some-where where the quality of life is far greater than in London.'

'That's brilliant, Thom,' I said. 'Really brilliant. And quite … *inspiring*.'

And it *was* inspiring. Plus, it was a Yes. A Yes to himself. Although God knows what moving to New Zealand was, in terms of yevels. Thom looked really pleased. Like a man on the verge of something. He was excited.

'So I'm basically all packed up. I've got one more week in London and then that's it. I'm off.'

'Well. I wish you the best of luck with it.'

'Thanks, Danny. If you're ever in New Zealand, look me up.'

We clinked beer cans, and he started to walk away. What a nice bloke.

'Oh, hang on,' he said, and turned back towards me. 'I've asked everyone else, so I may as well ask you … I don't suppose you'd be interested in buying a car, would you?'

Twenty-four hours later and I had worked out that, Yes, I probably could just about afford to buy a car. It would wipe out most of my savings in one fell swoop, but with the guarantee of an overdraft (and the promise of another contract at the BBC) it was possible. Especially if I engaged in some hard-nosed haggling with Thom. The problem was, I didn't really know *how* to haggle. Not where cars were concerned, anyway; I knew nothing about them. I hadn't even asked Thom what model it was. I'd stopped when he told me it was a Nissan. I knew my limits.

I'd been in town, working out my money situation and dropping in at work, and was nearly at the bottom of Oxford Street when a bored-looking man holding a placard in one hand and a leaflet in the other said, in an accent I think was probably Spanish, 'You want?'

I mouthed a 'Yeah, okay', and took a leaflet and strode on, glancing down to see it was for an English course at University College London. I folded the leaflet and was about to stick it in my pocket when it became all too apparent that someone else had seen me take that leaflet.

'Learn English?' said the man, holding his leaflet out at arm's length. He'd made a special effort to stop me and said, again, 'Learn English?'

I half-smiled, took the leaflet and kept on walking, slightly alarmed by the look in the man's eyes. I've walked down Oxford Street plenty of times and very rarely accepted a leaflet. Mainly because no one else ever does. I'd noticed a real hunger in that man's eyes, replaced by instant relief when I'd taken one of his leaflets. I kept my head down and my speed up, but moments later another leaflet was in front of my eyes. It was for English As A Foreign Language at Premier College, London. I took it, and then, suddenly and forcefully, there was another one, from another angle. English at Academy College. Another one came at me, from over my shoulder. English at No. 1 College. Where were all these leaflets coming from? Where were all these dodgy colleges? Why did everyone think I needed to learn English?

I glanced up as I moved off, but I was instantly blocked. Two men were standing in front of me, like zombies, holding out leaflets and saying the word 'English'. I was trapped. I took a leaflet from each and tried to move around them, but a slight Italian girl hiding behind them had cleverly cornered me. I didn't want to take her leaflet, and I almost moved off, but I swear she let out a proper moan – a long, juddering zombie groan – so I did, and managed to make my way around her, but no: more foreign students, clutching placards, holding leaflets and wearing backpacks – probably full of more placards and leaflets. I was becoming overwhelmed by this never-ending group of well-meaning foreigners making their minimum wage on the streets of London, snatched a couple more fliers, and tried to make a dash for it, towards the tube, towards home, towards a world free from student zombies…

'Thinking of learning English, are you?' said a voice to my right.

I looked up. It was Hanne. Smiling. She'd just stepped out of Tottenham Court Road tube.

'Hey. Shit. Hanne. Hi,' I said.

'How's it going?' she said.

'Good. Yeah. Good.'

I glanced down at my fistful of leaflets.

'Would you like one?' I said.

'Ah … no.'

'I'll keep them, then,' I said, stuffing them into my pockets.

'Hey … er … this may be slightly awkward, but … there's someone you should probably … you know … meet.'

She beckoned someone standing by the lamppost over.

'Danny, this is Seb.'

I looked at Seb. I looked at Hanne. What were Hanne and this man called Seb doing together? And who was Seb, anyway? It was seven o'clock. Hanne should be at home by now. She should have had her tea, and be settling down to watch the news with a yoghurt. Why was she out? Why was she here? And why was she out here with Seb?

'Oh,' I said. 'Hello Seb.'

'Hello Danny,' he said, and we shook hands, limply. 'I've heard a lot about you.'

'Oh,' I said.

I didn't like Seb. There was something about him. Ah, Yes. It was that his right hand was resting gently on Hanne's back. But hang on. This was my ex-girlfriend. My *ex*-girlfriend. What did I care where some bloke's hand was? And then I realised I was staring quite a lot at where Seb's hand was. He slowly moved his hand away. Shit. Now they thought I wasn't cool with it.

'You had your hand on Hanne's back!' I said, with a big smile.

'Sorry, I—'

'No! It's good!' I said.

'Danny,' said Hanne. 'Let's not cause a scene, okay—'

'No! Hang on – I think it's *good*! I think Seb should put *both* hands on your back!'

Hanne made the face she used to make when she thought I was being sarcastic.

'I'm not even being sarcastic! I think it's fantastic! Put *both* your hands on her back, Seb!'

This was terrible. The less sarcastic I tried to sound, the more sarcastic I sounded.

Seb's mobile went off.

'Okay, I'm going to get this ...'

He walked a few feet away and started a conversation. He sounded like he was quite important. Hanne and I just stood there, awkwardly. I tried to change the subject.

'He seems nice.'

'Let's just forget it ...' said Hanne.

'You're on a date, then,' I said.

'Yes, well ...' said Hanne looking to the ground.

'Cool.'

'Cool,' she said. 'I was going to tell you, over that coffee ... you know ... about ... tonight, but you distracted me by losing £25,000. You said you're okay with things, though, yeah?'

'Yes,' I said. 'Absolutely I am. Of course.'

Hanne looked over at Seb. She was keen to go, but he was still on the phone. And I didn't feel I could leave without clearing things up with Seb. Eventually, he hung up the phone and rejoined us.

Seb smiled at me so I smiled back at him. Hanne smiled at me. Then Hanne and Seb smiled at each other and then they both looked at me and smiled, in that way that couples do. Gah. Couples! Seb and Hanne! Hanne and Seb! All of a sudden it sounded annoyingly ... *right*!

I coughed.

'So, I'll be going ...' I said, which was the right thing to say, seeing as I now wanted to be literally anywhere else on earth.

'Right,' said Hanne.

'Right,' I said, and I started to move off.

'Unless ...' said Seb, and I stopped in my tracks. 'Unless you'd like to join us?'

My stomach turned over.

That was an invitation. *An invitation.*

My stomach flipped again, and my cheeks started to burn with embarrassment.

Seb was obviously just being polite. *Obviously.* He really didn't want me there. And neither did Hanne. And the only person who wanted me there less than *them* was *me.* Shit. This was *so* Level Four.

How could I get out of this? Was there any way in the world?

Hanne smiled at me, gently, then closed her eyes and did a little nod … giving me permission to make my excuses and leave. She knew full well that the proper – the *only* – course of action would be for me to say something along the lines of, 'Oh, thanks, but I have to be somewhere else', and then leave. Seb was just being a gentleman; showing Hanne he showed no ill will and harboured no petty jealousies towards her ex-boyfriend. Bastard. Even *I* was starting to fancy him.

'Well …' I started. And then I had an idea. I could get out of this! All I'd have to say was that …

'Because you'd be welcome to join us, Danny,' he said.

Bollocks! This was becoming a cast-iron invite!

He smiled at Hanne. Hanne smiled at him.

I looked at Hanne with some degree of panic in my eyes. She smiled sympathetically as if to say she know what I'd have to say next.

How was I going to break this to her? How was I going to say Yes?

Seb took my silence to be a no.

'Hey, sure, sure …' said Seb, nodding, and holding his hand out for me to shake. 'Well, I guess we'll—'

'I'd love to,' I said, quickly, and with instant regret.

Seb's hand remained outstretched. He looked confused. Hanne's eyes widened.

'*What*?' she said, sharply.

'If you're sure. I mean, if you're actually inviting me along, Seb, then Yes. Yes, I'd love to.'

I had gone bright red. And so had Hanne. But not for the same reasons.

Seb, though, ever the gentlemen, regained his composure, took his phone back out and said, 'Right … well … let me just call the restaurant and tell them it's a table for *three* …'

It was *horrible.*

The three of us were sitting in a rather posh restaurant called Circus, in near-silence. Seb and Hanne were sitting opposite each other, and there was I, perched in the middle, sitting on a hastily added chair at a table quite clearly meant for two.

I mean, it was *really horrible*.

We'd been sitting there for ten minutes. The candlelight was doing nothing to melt the ice in the air.

It became all too apparent that this was Hanne's very first date with Seb – and here I was, gatecrashing. It is hard adequately to describe just how awkward I was feeling. But still, this was how it was to be. All I could try to do was jolly things along …

'So … how did you guys meet?' I said, in as friendly a way as I could muster.

'Danny, do we have to …' started Hanne, before Seb chipped in.

'Through a friend,' he said. 'I work with Cecilia.'

'Oh, Cecilia, Yes,' I said.

'Yep,' said Seb, picking up his menu.

'Cecilia,' I said, again, for some reason saying it in an amusing northern accent this time.

Seb didn't respond. Hanne just stared at me.

'Cecilia,' I said, normally, to prove that I could.

Seb continued to study his menu.

'It's like that song, isn't it?'

'What song?' said Hanne, sternly.

'Cecilia,' I said. 'By Simon & Garfunkel.'

'Yes,' said Hanne. 'It is.'

'Have I told you my mum's Simon & Garfunkel story?'

'Yes,' said Hanne. Seb didn't look at all interested in hearing my mum's Simon & Garfunkel story. Even though it is excellent.

At a table somewhere else in the restaurant, someone coughed.

'Yeah,' I said, taking a deep breath. 'Cecilia.'

I bit into a breadstick.

'How does that song go again?'

'*Jesus*,' I heard Hanne say under her breath, before picking up her menu.

So I picked up my menu as well and the three of us sat there, in silence, pretending to be deep in thought.

A waiter arrived.

'Would you like to order some wine?'

I don't think he'd ever heard three people say Yes with such conviction before.

* * *

I'd love to leave that particular evening there. Really, I would. But I can't. Because it didn't stop there. Plus, *I* had to suffer, and now so will you.

Twenty minutes had passed and we'd all ordered.

The waiter had recommended the fish and, though even as a child I never really ate fish, I had gone for it. Hanne had raised her eyebrows at me when I did this. Seb hadn't really said anything in about ten minutes, and so it had fallen to me to make conversation. But how?

I thought about the joke I had made three nights earlier. That'd work! Surely! At last! The perfect ice-breaker!

'I was thinking,' I said, smiling, and Seb looked up for the first time in ages. Oh, this was it. If I could give them the gift of laughter, the most precious gift of all, surely then all this embarrassment would simply evaporate?

I chuckled to myself in anticipation.

'I was walking past Pizza Hut the other day, and for a second I was sure the sign said "Pizza *Hat*". And then I thought, wouldn't it be funny if there was a shop called "Pizza Hat" that sold hats shaped like pizzas?'

I chuckled, and waited, eyebrows raised, for the rest of the laughter to start. Seb looked back down at his menu. I turned my head to see Hanne glaring at me.

'You know …' I tried, weakly. 'Because it sounds like "Pizza Hut", only it's …'

I looked to Seb.

'… a hat shop.'

Nothing.

I couldn't work it out. That joke had been an absolute *stormer* when I'd been off my tits on drugs. I guess sometimes people just don't *want* to enjoy themselves.

'Hey, I nearly got $10 million the other day,' I said, but I was interrupted almost immediately.

'Look, Danny,' said Seb. 'Why don't you just eat your fish and fuck off?'

Hanne's eyes hit the floor. Seb's remained locked on me.

And so quietly, I ate my fish, and off I fucked.

I walked out of the tube a deeply embarrassed man. I decided, quite rightly under the circumstances, that I needed a drink.

I texted Ian as I headed for the pub.

IF YOU WANT A PINT I AM IN THE ROYAL INN

He texted back instantly.

WHAT?

I checked what I'd written. Thanks to a distracted mind and predictive text messaging I hadn't quite got my message across.

HE YOU WANT A RIOT I AN GO THE ROYAL INN

I phoned him.

'Pint?'

'Yes,' he said. 'Or we *could* start a riot.'

In the pub, Ian laughed in my stupid, bespectacled face.

'You said *Yes*?! Why the hell did you say *Yes*?'

'Have you forgotten about this whole saying Yes thing, Ian? It does involve rather a lot of saying Yes to things.'

'I know, mate, but what's wrong with you? You've got to have limits!'

'*Limits*? Be consistent! You're the one who threatened to punish me if I so much as *dreamt* a no!'

'Oh, I'm not being consistent, am I?'

'No! You were the one with all the threats at the beginning – "Oh, I'll have to punish you if you don't do it properly …"'

'I don't need to punish you! You're punishing yourself!'

'Jesus, Ian, I look like a tit. I'm *happy* for Hanne; it's great that she's found someone new. I don't want her thinking I'm not cool with it.'

'Yeah, it does kind of look that way. What with you forbidding her from seeing a new man one week, and then gatecrashing their date the next. Maybe you should tell her about the Yes thing. Stop it from happening again.'

'I would rather Hanne thought I was having a mental breakdown than indulging myself in another stupid boy-project. Which this is not, by the way.'

'Sounds like one.'

'You're not being much help, Ian.'

'Not much help? Now I'm inconsistent, *and* not much help! All I do is help! Without me, you'd have been beaten up by Omar in Amsterdam!'

'Or I would have got ten million dollars.'

Ian laughed.

'Yeah right,' he said. 'Prickstick.'

Suddenly, I took great and brutal offence. It had suddenly become quite an emotional evening, and I wasn't going to sit here, in my own local pub, being called a prickstick just because I dared to have a little faith in my fellow man.

'Prickstick?! I'm *not* a prickstick!'

I was probably overreacting.

'I'm just saying, Ian … maybe Omar really *was* in danger! You can't totally discount that!'

'We talked about this! I proved it to you! The man was a scammer! You're being stupid! This whole thing is pointless and stupid!'

'It's not pointless! I'll find the point! And I'm not being stupid, either! Are you really telling me, despite all the recorded evidence, that there was absolutely no chance whatsoever – *whatsoever* – that Omar wasn't really a scammer at all? That he *wasn't* the son of a murdered Sultan? I'm being human, Ian!'

Ian simply looked at me.

'I had a *brilliant* idea for a punishment for you. But now I'm going to scrap it. I'm going to find something a hundred times worse.'

'Fine.'

'Fine.'

'Fine.'

I walked out of the pub that night, my mood not exactly enhanced by two pints with Ian and a bottle of wine with Hanne, Seb, and Humiliation. I'd been hungry so had stopped at a chip shop on Roman Road and ordered myself a packet of chips and a can of Fanta. The chips were drenched in vinegar, ketchup and chilli sauce – the three options the man had given me, the three I'd agreed to – and didn't even make it halfway to my flat before being furiously thrown in a bin.

I flicked the computer on, and started to make myself a sandwich.

Sure, I thought. The argument with Ian aside, Yes had dealt me a pretty major negative tonight. But it had also dealt me a few positives. And who knew – maybe this would eventually make me and Hanne closer friends.

My phone beep-beeped.

A message from Hanne.

TWAT

I decided she'd probably misused her predictive text too, and she'd meant to write TWAV, which was probably Norwegian for something nice, like flowers, or a tiny waving baby.

I sighed. Remember: positives. Yes had dealt me positives.

And it was about to deal me another. Another positive which would shut Ian up, once and for all. Oh, this was great. This was brilliant. *This* would show him. This would teach him to have a little faith in a project! This would force him to admit that I was neither a prickstick *nor* a twav.

Only one e-mail sat in my in-box, hopeful and alone.

It was from a Dr Molly Van Brain.

She was writing to tell me I had just won $20 million on the Spanish Lottery.

I was amazed. I hadn't even *entered* the Spanish Lottery.

And now Dr Molly Van Brain wanted to invite me to come and collect my winnings from her personally.

All I'd have to do was get on a plane.

To Holland.

8

In which Daniel lands himself in a Spot of Bother

The fact that this was a leap straight into Level Five both excited and scared me.

Clearly, this was something I simply shouldn't be doing. I can admit that now. Ian had already proved to me that 99 per cent of these unsolicited junk e-mails were scams designed to delight and entice hapless, gullible people. But surely – that still left 1 per cent. And one in a hundred isn't bad odds … think of how the odds were stacked against my *Sun* scratchcard win, after all – the one thing I still clung to as proof that Yes could work …

But I knew what Ian would say to thinking like this. He'd say that I was stupid. That Dr Molly Van Brain probably wasn't a doctor. Or a Molly. Or even a Van Brain.

But c'mon … this was worth a shot. Worth a further look. Worth a *Yes*.

It was like the world had shifted slightly. Now, I was dealing with a whole new and fascinating universe. A universe of *what-if's* …

Like …

What if the Spanish Lottery really had somehow picked me out as a winner?

And …

What if right now, somewhere in a room in Amsterdam, a lady doctor really *was* counting and recounting my $20 million out in front of her and saying, 'Well, I hope *this* one turns up, because everyone else seems to just *ignore* my e-mails …'

It was unlikely, sure. But it was *attractive*.

As the train made its way into the city, I looked once more at her e-mail.

Congratulations winner! it said. WELL DONE FROM ALL AT SKYLOW LOTTERY INTERNATIONAL!

My name, it said, had been chosen by a computer ballot system 'drawn from 91,000 names around the world!'. But I had to keep completely quiet about my win. 'Due to a mix-up of some names and addresses, it is imperative you keep this award completely personal until your claim has been processed. Do not tell anyone at all.' This was part of their efforts, it said, 'to avoid unwarranted taking advantages of the situations by other participants or improper impersonators'.

Very sensible! And of *course* I'd keep it quiet – the last thing I needed was Ian or Wag popping on a pair of glasses and impersonating me improperly. But it was the next bit that was the best.

You have therefore been approved for a payment in cash credited to file reference number: LIP/63474–444/RT6. This forms a total cash prize of US$20,756.820 (TWENTY MILLION SEVEN HUNDRED AND FIFTY SIX THOUSAND, EIGHT HUNDRED AND TWENTY DOLLAR).

And there, underneath it, the name that had brought joy to my heart. Dr Molly Van Brain. There was another name, too – someone from the legal department called Albert Heijn. I was to deal with him after processing my details with Molly, who'd told me all I had to do was come to Holland as quickly as possible, or, more conveniently and desirably, contact Albert and he would deal with all the paperwork and legal aspects for a one-off processing fee (7000 euros, which they would require before presenting me with my cheque). Well, no disrespect to Albert, but I wanted to do this myself. It would only take about £50 and forty-five minutes to fly to Amsterdam, where I could take care of business myself. Besides, 7000 euros seems a lot of money for a bit of processing.

So I'd written back to her, saying, 'Tell Albert not to worry! I will come to Amsterdam and meet with you direct! I have my ticket and will be there tomorrow!' If that didn't excite the socks off Dr Molly Van Brain, then nothing would.

I stepped off the tram as we rolled into the city centre and strolled into the Internet café.

Here we go. Bring on the riches. I logged on and went straight to my e-mails, but was a little surprised to see I had no mail. Molly hadn't replied. Not even a friendly 'hello' or a 'looking forward to seeing you!'.

No matter. Maybe she was just busy getting my money ready and buying pastries and balloons for the official handover. It was a little disappointing, that's all. You'd have thought at the very least Albert could have made the effort to write. With no processing to do, the man suddenly had loads of spare time on his hands!

So I wrote another e-mail to Molly.

> **Dear Molly,**
> **It is I, Danny Wallace – winner of the SkyLow International Lottery! I have spectacular news! I have done as you suggested and come to Holland! I hope Albert isn't annoyed that he won't get to do the processing, but I thought I'd save myself seven thousand euros!**
> **Anyway. I am just sitting around near the Magna Plaza, waiting to meet up. Please e–mail me or call me on 0044 7802 ∗∗∗ ∗∗∗ to let me know what I should do next.**
> **Danny**

My main worry was that it was already getting close to four o'clock. I wanted to get in touch with these guys before business hours were over. I was only booked into Amsterdam for one night – after all, Amsterdam's not the kind of place you want to be when you've got twenty million dollars burning a hole in your pocket – and I had an early flight home in the morning.

The one thing I found really strange about Molly's e-mail – aside from its very nature – was that it contained no phone numbers whatsoever. It was almost as if they didn't want you contacting them. And the only address on it was for the offices of Albert the legal expert – though why I'd want to see *him* I don't know.

I wandered away from the Internet café and towards the Magna Plaza, but before I'd walked even a few feet I looked up to see a man, tanned and in his thirties, slowly moving down the street, holding in his hand a small leash. He was smiling and making an odd clicking noise. And on the end of that leash was a small, fat, brown cat. I had to do a quick double take. Yes. It was a man. Walking his cat. In the middle of the day. I stood and watched.

Amsterdam is, I suppose, a city of Yeses, and one of the most liberal in the world. It is a city of freedom and acceptance; a place where new ideas are embraced, not dismissed out of hand. In the Sixties, Amsterdam's youth threw themselves into hippiedom with gusto and glee, and it's from that basic mindset that a place of outright social progressiveness grew – most notably, of course, when it comes to drugs and prostitution. Gay marriages were legalised in 2001, and the city is one of the most gay-friendly in the world; a city which, just as it should, accepts everyone equally. Street crime is rare, and friendly faces abound. It was all quite warming to the heart. I thought about that and watched, as my cat-walking friend ambled down the street, pausing every so often to allow his little friend to sniff a bollard or lick a street corner, and I thought 'good for you, sir. Go – walk your cat and hold your head up high. For you are in Amsterdam – city of acceptance. There is no shame – even for men who walk their cats in public.'

Of course, if *I* were King, walking a cat would be illegal, but then, I'm not Dutch.

I wandered past a gift shop and wondered whether I should buy a souvenir. Did one night in a foreign city warrant a souvenir? In the end I opted for a tiny windmill on a stick, and decided to write Lizzie a postcard. It had been a while, and I missed her. Plus, I feel postcards are important. They give the impression that you are a worldly and well-travelled person, with culture at their fingertips and the lifestyle of the jetset. I flicked through and found a postcard of a big clog. Yes. That was *precisely* the image I wanted to portray.

I decided to play it casual:

Dear Lizzie,
I'm in Amsterdam! No reason why, really. Sometimes you've just got to do these things, and live a little.
Hey – they walk cats here. It's brilliant.
Love,
Danny
x

I found a postbox, popped it in, and went for a walk around the huge Nieuwe Kerk, where I took in the Gothic pinnacles and soaring lines, and a couple of Neptunes blowing on a conch. But who was I kidding? On a normal day, of course, I'd have spent more time there, tried my hardest to see everything, had my photo taken with a trumpet-playing cherub. But today? Today, I wanted to be in an Internet café …

I dashed back inside, logged on, and to my delight, found an e-mail waiting.

But it wasn't from Molly. It was from something called the Standard Trust Agency of Amsterdam.

I clicked it open, and read.

Hello Mister Danny@dannywallace.com
Thank you for your e-mail to SkyLow Lottery International.
We are their agents and we will be handling your claim.
Please, we need a few things as soon as possible, as we are
running out of time on your claim.

1. Full name and address and ALL telephone, fax numbers
2. Bank account information
3. Passport number and nationality
4. 2000 euros to pay for an indemnity document which will
be used in filing process. Please, it is your responsibility to
cover this cost.

We will also require a one-off payment of 2,650 euros for
tax purposes within 24 hours to ensure the claim can be
made in time.

Immediately the process is started, you will receive all the
necessary documents to receive your money.

Robison Shaw

Hang on a second! Who was this bloke? Where was Molly? Where was Albert? And what was all this about 'time limits'?

I wrote back.

Dear Robison,
But I am already in Amsterdam at the request of Dr Molly
Van Brain! How can I collect my winnings from her? What are
these documents I need? I thought Albert Heijn was in
charge of this stuff? Where is Dr Molly Van Brain?
Danny

Something about this was deeply wrong. It was now 5 pm, and I wanted to get this sorted out as quickly as possible. But I was at the mercy of

Robison Shaw, who'd suddenly decided to take over from the much more friendly-sounding Dr Molly Van Brain. He'd given me no address, but there *was* a phone number …

I got my mobile out and dialled it. If there really was a time limit on my claim, surely this was the best way of handling things? The phone number worked … but there was no answer. I waited, and waited, hoping it would click into answerphone … but it didn't. It just rang. And no one answered. What was going on here?

I tried the number again, but still the same happened, and ten minutes later I dialled once more.

I had a bad feeling about this. I didn't like the cut of Robison Shaw's gib, either. He seemed a bit money-obsessed, unlike Molly. I needed to straighten this out with her, but I had no way of getting in touch, other than e-mail.

Or did I?

I took the printout of Molly's e-mail from my pocket, and there it was again: Albert Heijn, Westerstraat, Amsterdam. Sure, Albert was a bit out of the loop now that I'd decided to do the processing myself, but surely he wouldn't begrudge me a little visit? If I could find Albert, then I could almost certainly find Molly, and if I could find Molly, then I could find out whether I really *had* won twenty million dollars.

I needed a map. And I needed confirmation that Albert Heijn really was where he said he was. Surely if it was a scam, they'd have made an address up? So if this was real, then potentially, so was Albert.

I stopped a passer-by.

'Excuse me,' I said. 'What number do I dial to find out other numbers?'

The lady looked at me blankly.

'You mean like a database?' she said.

'Yes! Like, directory enquiries. Someone who knows the phone book.'

'Ah!' she said, and gave me the number, which was full of 0s and 8s. I dialled.

'*Naam*?'

'Hello … do you speak English?'

'Yes.'

'I need the number for Albert Heijn, Westerstraat, Amsterdam.'

'Of course.'

Moments later, I had it. Albert was real! A real man, with a real address! I could bypass Robison Shaw, and deal with the people who'd been with me since the beginning. Plus, this could work – this could be true! Why would they give out an address that exists, if they were planning to scam me? Now all I had to do was get round there. It was 5.30 now. I still had half an hour before most businesses would be shutting down for the day. And surely I could get there in less than …

My heart stopped.

The time difference.

Yeah, it was 5.30 by *my* watch, but *my* watch was a *British* watch. The Dutch watches would all say *6*.30.

I needed to get to Albert quickly. I ran to a main road, and waited, sweaty, wild and desperate, for a cab to pass. A minute or two later, I found one.

'Westerstraat,' I said. 'As quickly as you can manage!'

The taxi roared into action, and I got my phone out. I had to call Albert and tell him not to leave work yet. I had to convince him I was on my way and needed to talk to him about SkyLow, Molly Van Brain and Robison Shaw … but would he want to talk to me? I'd robbed him of 7000 euros' worth of work! I'd arrogantly thought I could do it myself!

The phone rang, and rang, but no one answered … had he gone home already? Or was this part of the scam? Was he sitting, with Robison, laughing his tits off? Or was it real? Was he sitting, with Molly, counting out my money and looking at his watch? I needed to get to him today … I needed to sort this out today…

'Here is Westerstraat,' said the driver, pulling up. 'Which number do you need?'

'I'm not sure,' I said. 'There was no number. Just this …'

I showed him my piece of paper.

'Ah! Albert Heijn,' he said, and pulled out, back into the street.

'You *know* Albert Heijn?' I said, startled.

The driver laughed.

'Sure,' he said. 'Everybody knows Albert Heijn. He is an important man!'

I was thrilled. This alone would prove to Ian that the way of Yes was the true and right way! We drove a hundred metres or so, then slowed to a halt. The driver turned to me and pointed out the window.

'Here he is.'

I looked where the driver was pointing.

And there, in big, blue letters, he was.

ALBERT HEIJN

It was the name of a supermarket.

I was distraught. And I felt stupid. So, so stupid. Of *course* it was a scam. And the worse thing was, I'd known it all along. It *had* to be. I'd never entered the Spanish Lottery. Just as I'd never met Omar's dad – the murdered Sultan so impressed by my professionalism in business.

The moment I'd seen the supermarket, I knew it: Ian had so obviously been right all along. The scammers had used a real name and address in the hope that anyone tempted to check out SkyLow would see that their 'lawyer' existed. It would be like you or I claiming we were represented in court by a Bobby Van Tesco, or the Happy Shopper twins. They just hadn't reckoned anyone would travel to Amsterdam to find out. I could see their point; Yes had been wrong to bring me here. Yes had clouded my judgement; brought optimism when it should have armed me with cynicism. I'd been suspending any disbelief in the vague hope that everything would come good. I was excited by the trip, by the possibilities, no matter *how* ludicrous. Maybe I was just looking for another hit – another injection of excitement and surprise. The kind I'd had the day I won 25 grand, but lost again all too soon. I'd tasted glory that day, and I wanted more. Maybe Yes was addictive, maybe you lived in the hope that if you just believed, it would bring you good fortune.

I found a bench and tried to find the spin I could put on today's events. How could I make it okay again? What good could I find in this?

Well, I was on a bench in Amsterdam, for one thing. I had an evening to waste in Holland that I otherwise wouldn't have had. And that, surely, beats just another night in front of the telly in London. At the very least, I had that. And that, after all, is what this was all about.

I decided not to tell Ian about how I'd ended up in Amsterdam. And if I ever did, I'd lie, and tell him I had actually won that twenty million dollars after all. I reckoned I could get away with that, even if it did mean I'd have to buy every round in the pub for the rest of my life.

So that was it: I'd decided not to be beaten. I would find fun tonight. Of course I would! I was the Yes Man!

The Yes Man could find fun in *any* city!

The National Cheese Museum of Holland features over three fascinating audiovisual displays on the history of cheese, taking in famous cheesemakers, as well as the huge array of forward-thinking cheesemaking equipment on offer to the modern cheesemaker today. Visitors to the museum in Alkmaar are able to sample more than six different cheeses, from Gouda to Edam and back again, and the whole, thrilling, cheese-based experience was kept from me only because the museum had closed two hours earlier.

I had with me a small pamphlet I'd picked up on the train into town that afternoon, full of useful suggestions and handy hints as to how I should spend my time. The problem was, nearly everything it suggested was closed, shut, or finished. I'd even missed the Holland Experience, on Jodenbreestraat, which promised 3-D glasses, a moving floor, and smellovision. That was the last straw. You know a day's gone wrong when you've missed out on smellovision.

My tummy rumbled, and at first I assumed it was a deep-seated rage borne out of a lack of 3-D windmills, before realising that as I hadn't eaten all day, it was probably hunger. I was near the Leidseplein, the heart of touristy Amsterdam, with its bright and blinking neon signs and constant flow of people and traffic and people. I wandered away from the main square, still cursing Dr Molly Van Brain under my breath (not only was I twenty million dollars down, but thanks to all the faffing around I knew virtually nothing about cheese, either), and found my way to Leidsekruisstraat, and a little restaurant called De Blonde Hollander.

The staff were friendly but the restaurant busy; so much so that they told me I may have to share a table, if many more people arrived. I shrugged and said that'd be fine, and then ordered a pancake and a beer.

All around me were happy people, from all over planet earth. I wondered how many people ended up here as a result of Dr Molly Van Brain and her evil team of scammers. Surely it couldn't be just me? When I'd first thought about her, she was a kindly figure; an elderly lady scientist who most likely worked on cures for diseases in her spare time, for free. Now, the name Dr Molly Van Brain conjured up images of an evil lady torturer, who wore a long white coat and was probably really good at cackling. My beer arrived and I tried to put her out of my mind. But then something else arrived, too. Two men. Two men who had nowhere else to sit, and had been shepherded, apologetically, to my table.

'Thank you, please,' said the waiter, pulling out their chairs. They sat down.

'Hello,' said the first man, and then the second.

'Hello,' I said back.

Now, I know the drill when it comes to things like this. The person on their own is supposed to act like they don't even notice the other people are there, and they in turn will act like the first person isn't there, either. Then those two people will gossip loudly and mercilessly, and the person on his own will pretend he's gone deaf and isn't eavesdropping. I call it the Wagamama Effect. But there was to be none of this. Because the first man extended his hand and confidently said, 'I'm Jahn.'

'Oh,' I said. 'Danny.'

'This is Sergei,' he said, and I shook Sergei's hand, too.

And from there, the conversation flowed.

Jahn and Sergei were backpackers. Or were they? They were certainly backpackers when they'd arrived, but they'd been in Amsterdam for nearly six months or so. Jahn – tall, thin, blond – had arrived after travelling through Europe from South Africa, and Sergei – shorter, squatter, bearded – was from Poland. The two had met in a hostel round the corner and been firm friends ever since.

'Amsterdam is the finest place I have visited,' said Sergei. 'Absolutely. When I am here, I feel at home. It's the way that things should be.'

'We both tend to go where the wind takes us,' said Jahn. 'If I want to see somewhere, then I go. But sometimes I just sit back and see what happens. Get a casual job, stay in a hostel, see what comes up. My dad used to say, "The only time you have no opportunities is when you decide to stop taking them." I feel that way too.'

We talked, for another hour or so, about whatever came up. About London, about Poland, about South Africa. Both Sergei and Jahn had wanted to know what I was doing in Amsterdam. I told them I was visiting my friend Albert. They asked me where Albert was tonight and I cracked under the weight of my deception, quickly explaining the whole thing. They laughed, and told me not to worry. For twenty million dollars, they thought, it was worth a fifty-quid flight.

Sergei had to leave soon after to start work, but Jahn made me an offer I couldn't refuse. Mainly because there were very few offers I *could* refuse these days.

'If you're doing nothing this evening, I will show you around,' he said. 'You can experience my Amsterdam.'

'Okay,' I said. 'That'd be great!'

This was actually really cool. I mean, it was only thanks to a precise but random chain of Yeses that I'd met Jahn in the first place. We should, by rights, never have crossed paths. But now that we had, what was the harm in allowing a stranger to dictate my evening? Particularly as we were in his city. If it'd been down to me, after all, I'd probably still be in the bloody cheese museum.

'Okay … first, we must go to Warmoestraat …' said Jahn, as we left the restaurant.

'Right. What's there?'

'Argos.'

I nodded.

Hang on.

'*Argos*?'

'It's a bar,' said Jahn, matter-of-factly. Clearly, he'd had that conversation with Brits before. 'A guy there owes me some money. We'll pop in, get the cash, and head off again. Cool?'

'Cool,' I said.

We stepped out of the cab and straight into Argos. It certainly was unlike any Argos *I'd* ever been in before. Jahn was immediately cheered by a couple of guys on a nearby table.

'Some friends,' he said.

I smiled as he moved off, and took a look about the bar. There was something … *different* about this bar. Something … missing. I couldn't quite put my finger on it. It had chairs. And lights. And drinks. And men. Black men. White men. Tall men. Short men. Lots of … men. And then I realised. Girls. Girls were what was missing from this bar. And also … oh! … normal clothes. Normal, manly clothes, like corduroy and denim … there was a lot less corduroy and denim than I was used to in this bar. And a lot more … well … there was a lot more *leather* than was normal for me.

Oh my Lord.

I was in a *leather bar.*

'Argos is Europe's oldest leather bar,' said Jahn, by my side again.

'Excellent!' I said, hoping enthusiasm would translate as some kind of urbane cool. 'The oldest leather bar in Europe. That is bloody brilliant!'

'There are these two bars, and then there is the cellar.'

'A cellar. Wicked. What's the cellar for?'

Jahn shot me a look. I knew at that moment it was probably best if I didn't know what the cellar was for.

Jahn went back to talk to his friends and get his money, while an unnerving truth gradually dawned on me – a virtual stranger had taken me to a gay leather bar in the heart of Amsterdam. Now, don't get the wrong idea about me. I've been to plenty of gay bars in my time, and each one has been a stylish and plush night out. And I've nothing against leather – I own a real leather jacket, two leather belts, and when I was at primary school it was the only material I'd even *consider* carrying a satchel made from. But I had never been to a gay bar – much less a gay *leather* bar – as *the Yes Man*.

I realised with some degree of terror that I was a man full of Yeses in a bar full of opportunity! What if someone had a suggestion to make? Or an *invitation*? Or – good God – a *favour* to ask? I'm not claiming to be a particularly attractive man who would have gay fellas flocking – I'm just saying that, from what I've seen in gay bars in the UK, some-times they're not all that fussy.

'Hi!' said a voice to my right. 'Are you a friend of Jahn's?'

The man was clean-shaven, neatly turned out and very friendly. There was no leather to be seen, though his trousers did look a bit tight. Suddenly, paranoia gripped me. Maybe he was after me! Hey – he was *after me*!

Now, I find homophobia to be a vile and despicable human trait – it is an uneducated and unevolved way of thinking, clumsily cultivated by that section of society who think singing 'Wonderwall' at pub closing time is high culture … but at the same time … I had a moral obligation to say *Yes* to this man. Whoever he was. Whatever he *wanted*!

I would have to think quick. I would have to dominate the conversa-tion. I would have to steer it into safe waters. And I would have to say something soon, because he asked me that question about fifteen seconds ago, and I've still not answered him.

'Yes,' I said, suddenly. 'Yes, I am a friend of Jahn's.'

I scanned and rescanned the sentence in my head. Was there anything in there that could be seen as a come-on? Shit! I shouldn't have said 'Yes'. And I said it *twice*! That was like *flirting*!

'Jahn's cool,' said the guy. 'Where you from? England?'

What could I say to that? What wouldn't give him the wrong idea?

'Yup.'

'London?'

I nodded.

'And is he showing you around Amsterdam?'

I nodded again.

'Yup.'

'I'm going to the bar – would you like a drink?'

He shook his empty glass. Which is neither a euphemism *nor* rhyming slang.

But bloody hell! This was going terribly! All I was saying was Yes! And now I'd just nodded and smiled and accepted a drink! This man had me right where he wanted me! I think it only fair to point out that I would have been equally uncomfortable if this had been a bar in the city's notorious red light district, and the guy had been a scantily clad girl. Well, *almost* as uncomfortable.

Suddenly Jahn was back.

'Hey … I got my money, shall we go?'

'Yes!' I said. 'Let us do that.'

The guy smiled, and said, 'Nice to meet you.'

'Hello Dieter,' said Jahn, and Dieter raised his hand and did a little wave. 'Dieter is one of the friendliest guys you can meet.'

I suddenly felt a little ashamed. I had allowed my own paranoia and preconceptions to rule me. Dieter was just a really friendly guy.

'But you have to watch him,' said Jahn. 'Because he *will* try and sleep with you.'

Dieter faked a look of shock.

'In fact, he'll sleep with *anything*.'

Dieter laughed, called Jahn a bitch, and went to get another beer. I laughed, too, until I realised that in Jahn's eyes, I pretty much constituted '*anything*'.

'So,' said Jahn, 'there's this cool bar in the red light that I should show you …'

Silently, and to no one in particular, I mouthed the word 'help'.

Before we braved the potential horrors of the red light district, though, Jahn insisted on taking me somewhere just down the road from Argos. It would be a surprise, he said. A true Amsterdam experience. So long as it didn't involve leather chaps, I said, I'd be happy to take a look.

Moments later, we were there – standing outside a place called, rather suspiciously, Conscious Dreams.

'What is this – a coffeeshop?' I said, knowing full well that the last thing people visiting coffeeshops in this town wanted was coffee.

'No, not really … it's called a smart shop. Do you smoke weed, Danny?'

'I find it best not to,' I said. 'The last time I did I became obsessed with geese.'

Jahn looked like he understood.

'Well, come in …'

We walked in, and there again I noticed the words 'smart shop'.

'What *is* a smart shop?' I asked.

'It's where you buy drugs that are good for you.'

'Like a chemist?'

'No …' said Jahn, taking a seat. 'Drugs that make your memory better, or help you concentrate, or bring you energy, you know? It's all natural alternatives to the chemicals. Why take LSD when you can have something from nature? Natural LSD. Much smaller health risks.'

'But LSD is illegal here, isn't it?'

'Sure. But all *this* stuff is *legal*. Good alternatives to speed, ecstasy, whatever you like. And really, since you're in Amsterdam, you should try a little of what goes on here …'

He was smiling, now. I got the distinct sense that this was the kind of thing Jahn loved doing to people not as familiar with Amsterdam as he is.

'You could do magic mushrooms. Psychotropic. Totally legal when fresh.'

'But they're bad for you,' I said, a little offended at the suggestion. 'When I was at school we had a whole assembly on them, because Jonathan Davies ate some in a field and then spent the whole afternoon chasing trees.'

'But they are natural, and what comes from nature can't be too bad, surely?'

I thought about it.

'Earthquakes?' I tried.

Jahn shook his head.

'Hitler, then,' I said.

Now he just looked blank.

'Well, maybe I'll buy a couple of mushrooms, Yes,' I said. 'I'll take them with me tonight when I leave. There's no need to dive straight in, you know.'

'You can't take them home with you. And you can't let them dry out. If you do, they are illegal. There was a big fuss a few years ago when this place started selling magic mushrooms, but they got away with it when they rebranded themselves as a greengrocer's.'

I looked around me.

'So, essentially, tonight, you've brought me to a greengrocer's?'

Jahn smiled.

'Come on – are you willing to give a new experience a go?'

And there it was. The sentence which would push me over the edge. I felt like Marty McFly, when someone dared to call him chicken.

'I have to say … I'm a little uncomfortable about this,' I said. And I was. I had never, ever done anything even remotely approaching Class A drugs before. I'd struggle if you asked me to even name them all. It's just not something that my circle of friends has ever really considered. That comical cigarette in Brixton with the peace protestors was as far as I'd ever gone – and yet now here I was – feeling for all the world like the Amsterdam tourist cliché – sitting with a South African who deemed the whole thing perfectly normal and decent and fine, and about to take it to the next level.

'Only do it if you want to,' he said. 'I mean, you wanted to see how I live. And *I'm* going to have something …'

He stood up and wandered over to the bar, while I sat there, wrestling with my conscience. I couldn't do this, could I? But I was in Amsterdam – the city of Yes. If I didn't say Yes here, where *would* I say Yes? Swansea? Suddenly, I felt invigorated. I felt that I was approaching a watershed moment. If I did this – something that in everyday, London, life would never even cross my mind – then surely that would mark a certain level of commitment? That would mean I was *up* for this.

And hey – like Jahn said, it wasn't even illegal. Not technically, anyway.

He was back at the table a moment later. He lit a spliff he'd bought and sat back. And then he put a small pill on the table, and slid it across to me.

'Try this,' he said. 'It'll blow your head off.'

As a recommendation, that was lacking something.

I looked at the pill.

'Jahn … when you say it'll blow my head off, well … I was more thinking I could have something a bit nicer and more gentle. Have you got anything that might stop short of actually blowing my head off, and maybe just give me a lovely headrub instead? This sounds a bit … *bigger* than I was thinking.'

Jahn tried to wave my worries away, but failed. But I thought about what he'd said earlier. *The only time you run out of opportunities is when you decide to stop taking them.* Well … this was an opportunity, of sorts. A chance to try something new. Something that, without a precise chain of Yeses, I never would've. A proper Level Five.

Suddenly, I remembered something.

'Hey … are you … y'know – stoned yet?'

'A little.'

I leaned forward and looked him in the eye.

'Imagine if there was a shop called Pizza Hat, and all it sold was hats shaped like pizzas.'

Jahn frowned, and then shook his head.

I couldn't believe it. That joke was actually getting *worse*.

'So anyway,' he said. 'Are you going to try this?'

The answer was already Yes.

'What's it called?'

'Well, the translation would be something like … Mind … bomb.'

'*Mindbomb*?' I said.

'More or less.'

'But what *is* it? I can't eat a Mindbomb unless I know what it is!'

'You don't eat them. And it's a bit like LSD. But more like a double-dipped tab.'

'I have no idea what you just said.'

'It's powerful, but safe. I'm going to do one, too. You'll be fine.'

Jahn smiled. His confidence was reassuring, but I was still nervous. I can't stress enough how unusual a thing this was for me to be doing. I've never thought I would make a particularly good drug user. When I was a kid, I remember thinking I'd had an out-of-body experience after an out-of-date Junior Dispirin. How on God's green earth would I cope with a psychotropic *Mindbomb*?

Nevertheless, in perfect unison with Jahn, I picked up the Mindbomb, and slowly, carefully, placed it in my mouth.

The following morning at 7 am precisely I sat bolt upright in a bed in the Novotel Amsterdam, confused, alone, dry-mouthed and wide-eyed.

I knew that things had happened in the last nine hours but I didn't know what things and I didn't know how. I was still feeling woozy and boozy and I appeared to have a sticker with a clog on it stuck to my face. Gradually, a few images eeked their way back into my brain. A man. A flashing light. I looked down to the floor and noticed my jeans and one trainer, and next to them a small, black disposable camera. I stretched down to pick it up. The film was full. On the floor, under the cheap coffee table, there was something else. A scroll of some sort. Oh, God. Please don't say I'd got married, or something. Please don't say I'd gone back to the leather bar and got married.

I climbed out of bed, my head thumping, and leaned down to pick it up. It felt strangely heavy, but then so did my whole body.

I unravelled the paper and saw … My God … what *was* this?

It was something which utterly horrified me. Utterly and completely. It was an unexpected and hugely confusing image.

It was an expertly crafted charcoal portrait of me and a tiny dog.

Suddenly, the memory shot back to me.

A street artist we stumbled past on the Leidseplein had asked me if I wanted my picture done. And I had giggled and shouted, 'Yes!' But only – and I remember being very specific about this – if he would draw my dog as well. What dog? he'd said. Why, the little dog on my shoulder, I'd said.

And now here it was – the physical evidence of a barely remembered drug trip which involved me wandering around Amsterdam with a tiny happy dog on my shoulder. I think in my head it could even talk.

And not only that – but Lord, it gets worse: I had photos, too! Photos! Twenty-four of them! Either Jahn or myself must have bought the camera as we moved from bar to bar and landmark to landmark, happy and laughing thanks to the explosive effects of the Amsterdam Mindbomb and some heavy-duty lager!

I looked again at the portrait, in the cold blue light of morning. What the hell was I supposed to do with this? I'd paid good money for it – I wasn't throwing it away. But I couldn't exactly take it home and give it to my mum as a lovely gift, could I? How was I supposed to explain the dog? Did I just say that I hadn't noticed it was there? Should I say it just sneaked in at the last minute? It is somewhat ironic that a portrait that came about just because I said Yes, should so effectively illustrate the sentiment Just Say No.

Much more of the night I can't tell you. I wish I could, but I can't. I have not seen or heard from Jahn since that evening, and I still do not condone the use of mind-altering illegal substances in any way (even if they're – you know – legal). I'm just telling you what happened, in the hope that maybe some young kid out there will read this and never have to have his portrait done with a miniature imaginary dog.

So here's my public service announcement: If *you're* thinking of getting into drugs, and you want help, I have two photographs in partic- ular I can show you. One is of me in downtown Amsterdam pointing at a bus that I am sure has big, pretty eyes. And the other is of me lying on my back in the middle of the road with my arms outstretched, as I tried to *tickle the moon*.

I refrain from publishing those photographs here only because no mother deserves to see she has raised a moon-tickler.

I returned home to London, satisfied that – thanks to my dealings with Albert Heijn and the world of the Mindbomb – saying Yes had at least taught me two vital lessons.

Three, if you count the fact that no man should ever walk a cat.

Selected extracts from the diary of a Yes Man: 2

July 18th

There was a most incredible question in the back of a *Metro* I found on the tube. In a little, boxed-out advert, were the words ARE YOU BRITAIN'S MOST GERMAN-LOOKING MAN? An advertising agency was casting for Britain's most German-looking man, and asking whether if you were, you'd like to be on TV. I thought about it for a few minutes as I rode the tube. Was I Britain's most German-looking man? I tried to remember what I looked like, and decided that, Yes, I could probably pass for a German. My glasses could easily sit on the face of a more European man than myself. Maybe I was exactly what they were looking for. Maybe when I walked into their production offices they would say, 'I'm terribly sorry, sir, but you appear to be an *actual* German. I think you have misunderstood our advert. We are looking for British people who only look like they're German,' and then I would smile, knowingly, and gradually it would dawn on them, and they'd say, 'Really? Could it ... are you ... Gentlemen! Call off the search! We have *found* Britain's most German-looking man!' Imagine if I got the job! What would the people at the BBC think of this? What would they think when I walked into the office, threw my keys to the floor and said, 'Keep 'em! I'm off to be Britain's most German-looking man!' I imagine some of the girls would probably swoon. God, it'd be brilliant, being Britain's most German-looking man. I have left a message and look forward to hearing back.

July 19th

I was reading the *East London Advertiser* when I noticed a colourful article, posing the following question: ARE YOU ANIMAL CRACKERS?

I read on. 'If you are,' it said, 'then your pet's mugshot could win you £100 and the coveted title of *Advertiser* Pet Personality of the Year!'

There were already some strong contenders, such as Bobbles of Mile End Road, and Pippy of Stebondale Street. Neither seemed to have much personality. One was just a dog someone had put some sunglasses on, and the other was just an overweight cat (I suppose they thought it was 'bubbly').

Well, I instantly knew one thing. Yes – I was animal crackers. Definitely. But I didn't have any pets to think of. I would have to get one if I was going to ensure neither Bobbles nor Pippy robbed me of the title.

July 20th

Today I saved £8 on a pair of 'great fit practical elasticated denim jeans!'. The ad said they were only £7.99, with free delivery. They have a drawcord-style elasticated waist – the kind that grannies or the clinically obese use – and they are fully machine-washable.

I will never, ever wear them.

July 21st

Someone has put a sign outside my block of flats saying 'INTERESTED IN SQUASH? I NEED A SQUASH PARTNER – COULD IT BE YOU?' Despite never having played squash in my life before, I buy a squash racquet and then phone the man, whose name is Bjorn. We agree to play squash at the weekend, in Bethnal Green.

July 22nd

I read in the *Standard* that the UK Trichological Association in London are giving free hair examinations to all men. I decide to have my hair examined. I arrive at the clinic and a man behind a big desk tells me what they do there, and it soon becomes clear that he is eyeing me up for a hair transplant. I'm not sure where he wants to transplant my hair, but he keeps looking at my head. He asks if he can just quickly examine me and I let him. He stands over me with a big magnifying glass and prods about a bit before saying, 'Yes, you are definitely in the early stages of male-pattern baldness.' He gives me such a fright that I can actually feel my hairline recede another millimetre. I am going bald! He made that happen! It is all part of his clever trick! He gives me some leaflets and I go home and stand in front of the mirror for an hour with a comb and a ruler. The bastard was right. It is receding a bit. Wish I hadn't said Yes, then maybe this would never have happened and I would have had the hair of a child for ever.

On the way home, I am stopped by another charity worker from Help The Aged. I think they have begun to target me.

July 23rd

Haven't been able to find a pet yet. Thought about buying a fish and sending in a picture, but this is a personality competition, and I'm not sure how much personality it's possible to garner from a photo of a fish. It's not like anyone's ever looked at a goldfish and thought 'Now *there's* a crazy character!' So in the end I took a photo of my neighbours' cat and sent that in.

Squash with Bjorn didn't go too well. I was hoping to rely on some kind of latent, natural squash talent, but it wasn't there. I don't think I'm his ideal partner. He has said he'll call me.

July 25th

My spam e-mail offers me more drugs. I am offered Propecia (for hair loss) and Prozac (for depression). I feel you can't really take the first without the second. I order them.

July 26th

I have just realised that if I win the *Advertiser* Pet Personality of the Year competition and my neighbours find out, I will have quite a hard time explaining the fact that I decided to enter their cat into a beauty pageant. Particularly as I don't know them. It would be an odd way of meeting. 'Hello. I live next door. By the way, I have entered your cat in a competition.'

So I sent another photo in which I found on the Internet. It is also of a cat, but this one is wearing a tiny hat and a wig, and will definitely beat next door's.

I have named this new cat Stuart, because hardly anyone ever names cats Stuart, and that must really upset a lot of people called Stuart.

July 28th

The Propecia arrives. The Prozac arrives with it. I read the Prozac's list of possible side-effects. Extreme fatigue. Listlessness. Constipation. Nervousness. Joint pain. Excessive sweating. Lack of concentration. Memory loss. Poor sexual performance.

I imagine you would have to be quite depressed for any of this to be an appealing alternative.

I try one pill. I feel a bit floaty for about ten minutes but that might be because I haven't eaten. My knee joint hurts a bit now but I don't think it's the Prozac.

August 1st

I have invented something new! I was in the videoshop trying to find a Jet Li film when I noticed a sign asking people to rewind their tapes before bringing them back. I realised that was a Yes Moment I'd have to remember for later, but worried that I would forget. And that was when it came to me – the Incredible Automatic Self-Rewinding Video Box! It works simply and effectively – once the box is closed, a small magnet triggers the engine, and the tape rewinds as you walk home. It is foolproof and excellent. I sent it off to the Patents and Trademarks people today.

I wonder if Su Pollard is available for the ad campaign.

August 2nd

I have begun to feel very guilty for entering a stranger's cat into a competition. No matter. The £100 cash prize will make it all worthwhile, although I will probably have to spend it on buying a cat to stop any tricky questions.

Also, today, I have begun the long and rocky road towards fulfilling an ambition I have never actually had – to be a nurse!

The University of Rochville in America is looking for new recruits for its online nursing degree. Apparently, I will not need to study, or learn anything about nursing. The degree is based on my life experience – from previous PhDs or doctorates (of which I have none), to experience of home nursing (of which I have none), right the way down to 'viewing habits'. I have set the video for tonight's episode of *Holby City*. I can't believe I am going to be a nurse! I entered my details on to the website and paid the $400 in full, using one of my new 'types' of credit card. I am nearly a doctor! Brilliant!

August 3rd

Bjorn the squash man still hasn't called. He *definitely* said he would call.
Why are men such bastards?

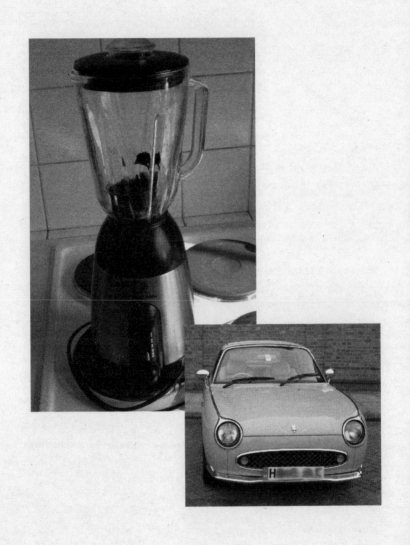

9

In which Daniel Upsets a Stranger

Now, people often talk, almost embarrassingly loudly, about the 'power of positive thinking'.

Take me: I'm usually quite a positive thinker. I tend to think things will generally work out okay. If I was stranded on a desert island and I saw a boat on the horizon, but the boat didn't see me, I wouldn't get all in a fluster and a huff about it. 'It'll probably be fine,' I'd say. 'I bet they'll probably be back in a bit.' At least then, I'd die happy.

There are others who take a more rigorous approach to positive thinking, and dedicate their entire lives to the practice. I once read an article about a lady called Jessica who'd read a self-help book about positivity and found it to be so inspiring that she bought a caravan in Cumbria and moved there immediately, so she'd be free to spend her days wandering around, thinking positive thoughts and spreading happy vibes. According to Jessica, just thinking positively could cure your illnesses, revive your love life, and get you a better job. Which is great, if you like taking career advice from a woman who lives in a caravan.

'I'll give you an example,' she said. 'If we keep repeating something good over and over then eventually it will *become* the truth. If you just keep on insisting to yourself that you are a wonderful person and that your marriage is amazing, it *will* be true.'

A handy tip for battered wives everywhere, there.

For me, I had discovered that it's not necessarily positive *thinking* that changes your life – but positive *doing*. Now, to be honest, my trip to Amsterdam hadn't been quite as successful as I'd hoped. But that didn't mean it was a failure (note the positive thinking, there). It was just another example of letting go, of going with the flow, of letting life lead the way. Sure, it had led me into a bit of a cul-de-sac, but I'd had fun. Fun I would otherwise have missed out on.

Yeah, so I'd wanted to prove Ian wrong; and no – so I hadn't returned home with $20 million despite endless positive thinking, but instead with a sore body and a portrait of me and a dog. Ian, of course, would say that this meant the whole endeavour was doomed to failure. Me, being both a positive thinker *and* a positive doer, would not. I was sure it was all for the best. And I was sure that one day, I'd find out how. One day I might even meet supermarket magnate Albert Heijn, and we'd have a good laugh about it all.

My phone rang. It was Brian, of the Starburst Group. He said that his friend Pete, who knew a lot more about Maitreya than he did, had agreed to meet with me, and when would be convenient? I told him to suggest a time. He did. I said Yes.

'Danny?'

'You must be Pete.'

'Come in.'

I did as Pete asked and stepped into his flat.

We were in Chancery Lane and I'd reasoned that as I was here for such an odd purpose, it would probably be less awkward to cut straight to the chase.

'Basically, Pete … I'm here because Brian told me that Jesus was living in Brick Lane.'

Pete rolled his eyes and let out quite a piercing laugh.

'Hah!' he said. 'Well, that's *utter* bollocks, for a start.'

I smiled, and tried a piercing laugh of my own, but it wasn't as good.

'So it's not true?' I said, relieved that this little piece of strangeness was coming to an end.

'No,' he said, shaking his head. 'No, Jesus does not live in Brick Lane.'

'Good.'

'No. Jesus lives in *Rome*.'

'Oh.'

'*Maitreya* lives in Brick Lane.'

This seemed to be getting complicated.

'Brian said that as well. But he said Maitreya *was* Jesus.'

'No. Some call him Jesus, but he is not Jesus. Jesus lives in Rome. Maitreya used to be Jesus, 2000 years ago in Palestine, but now Jesus is a Master as well. Maitreya works closely with Him, but Maitreya is Maitreya and Maitreya lives in London. So … why don't you tell me why you think you met him?'

* * *

'What you have to realise, Danny,' said Pete, as we sat in his living room sipping at our Tetley, 'is that we can never be sure where Maitreya will show up next. Or to whom. He can be anywhere, instantaneously, and can show up to people of any faith – because, you see, he is *all* faiths. He showed up last year in Paraguay in front of 200 Christians. He appeared in front of 200 Muslims in Morocco the year before. He's turned up in Japan, and Italy, and the US, and Zanzibar, and Poland, and just about everywhere else. But *never before* on *a bus* to *one man*.'

I saw what he was saying.

'Fair enough. So it can't have been him. I agree. It was just some bloke. Some bloke who said something which then struck a chord. I think Brian's just got a bit carried away with this, so—'

'Well, hang on, Danny. It absolutely *could* have been him. Because he is here to help all people. He is as likely to touch the life of *one* man as he is to touch the lives of a *thousand*. But he does so in a form which they can accept. Which is why he appears to some as Jesus, to others as Mohammed, and to others still as … well … a man on a bus.'

'But why?'

'Are you a man of faith, Danny?'

I shook my head.

'Not in the sense that I'd call myself a Christian or a Muslim or anything like that,' I said. 'I believe more in … people. The kindness of strangers. Mankind. That sort of thing.'

'And that is precisely why Maitreya would have chosen to meet you in the way that he did,' said Pete.

And that seemed to be that. It was case closed for Pete. He'd decided. I'd met Maitreya, whether I liked it or not.

'He stands for Justice, Sharing and Love – no matter what your beliefs are,' he said, offering me a biscuit.

'That sounds quite nice, actually,' I said, because it did.

'Hey – I'd love to interview you about your experiences with Maitreya if that's possible,' said Pete. 'There are plenty of newsletters that would love to hear about it. Is there a number I can contact you on?'

'Er … well … I'm not sure if I'd be able to tell you much,' I said. 'But … Yes.'

I wrote my number down on a small pad Pete appeared to have stolen from a Swallow Hotel in Chollerford and he beckoned me into another room.

'Look at this,' he said, and he showed me the same picture of a robed, bearded man that Brian had shown me that day in the restaurant.

'This was taken in Nairobi. Six thousand people saw Maitreya arrive at the Church of Bethlehem at a tiny village called Kwangware. They do miracles there. They heal people, and make mad people sane again, that sort of thing. And one day the minister told the congregation that God had spoken to her, and that a very special guest would be arriving in a few moments' time. Well, the villagers didn't know *what* to expect, but then … *then* he arrived. Maitreya. He appeared from absolutely nowhere and he appeared to be almost *shining*. He blessed them, then got in a car and drove off.'

'Goodness,' I said. 'What kind of car was it?'

I figured if he said it was a Nissan, something odd was going on.

'No idea. Now, if you want to know for certain whether that was Maitreya that you met that day, there *is* someone you can ask.'

'Who?'

'A man called Elias Brown.'

'Elias Brown?'

'Elias Brown, yes. He is in direct daily communication with Maitreya.'

'Really?'

'Oh yes. He has been "overshadowed" many times, which means that the Masters essentially got inside him; spoke through him. He is a brilliant man – kind, generous. Anyway, the Masters got friendly with him and eventually he started to have direct contact with Maitreya himself.'

'And this Brown guy definitely exists?'

Pete looked at me oddly.

'Of *course* he exists. I'll check and see if he's in the UK any time soon. And if he is, I'll call you, yeah?'

'Yeah,' I said. 'I could ask him if he got home safely that night on the bus.'

Pete nodded.

And I finished my tea and, strangely excited, I left.

It was the next morning, and I was on my way to meet Thom, the man I'd met at the party, and to take a look at the car I'd blindly agreed to buy.

He was sitting in the café outside Hendon Central tube when I arrived.

'How's it going?' I said.

'Not bad. All packed and ready to go.'

'When do you leave?'

'Not for a couple of days. But I'm off up to Liverpool tonight, to say goodbye to my family and friends. I'll stay there until I have to go, and then it's New Zealand …'

'Ace. So, what kind of car is this again, exactly?' I asked, as we walked up the road.

'It's a Nissan Figaro,' he said.

It still didn't sound particularly glamorous. But that was fine for me. In the few days that had passed since our first meeting, I'd reasoned that so long as it wasn't some kind of bright yellow turbo-charged Porsche which would both bankrupt me *and* have people pointing at me wherever I went, I'd be okay. And besides, he'd told me he'd give me 'an amazing deal'. Money wasn't important, he said. Living was.

'And … how old is it?'

'1991.'

'Oh.'

Suddenly, part of me was wishing it *was* a bright yellow turbo-charged Porsche, after all. A thirteen-year-old Nissan wasn't something that I could see helping my standing with girls very much. Not unless it was made of gold, or something.

'And what colour is it?'

'Mint green.'

Nope. This wasn't going to help my standing with girls at *all*.

That said, I'd already decided – a car could be good. And it would get me over a fear, too. I'd always vowed that as long as I lived in London, I'd never own a car. It was just too dangerous. And too much hassle. But that comes from someone who's only ever owned one car in his life – a Mini Metro I'd bought for £1,000 after saving up all summer to buy one. And I only passed my test in the first place because I'd insisted on taking it in the town of Trowbridge. Trowbridge, for the uninitiated, has more roundabouts than almost anywhere else in Britain, and I could 'do' roundabouts, so Trowbridge it was. I'd subsequently driven the Metro into the ground, until every little bit of it was groaning or screeching and had lost the will to live. I sold the car the following New Year's Eve for £50, and drank it that night. A few weeks later, I'd moved to London, and convinced myself that I just didn't need another one. For one thing, the tube network took me everywhere I needed to go. And for another, I'd been in enough taxis to know that driving in London takes a special sort of skill. And a handgun in the glove compartment.

But think of the freedom it would give me – I could go anywhere, see anything, any time. Me and my Nissan. Having adventures. Making new friends. Like Michael Knight and Kit. But in mint green. A new car would represent *freedom*.

'Nearly there,' said Thom, as we walked around a corner and into a quiet, tree-lined street. We stopped at what would turn out to be his house.

'It's in the garage,' he said.

I had been standing, looking at the car, for about two minutes, without really saying very much.

It was the oddest car I had ever seen.

'What … what on earth *is* it?' I said, eventually.

'I told you – a Nissan Figaro.'

It looked like something out of Trumpton.

'Is this a real car?' I said. 'Or did you make it yourself out of toys?'

'It's real!' said Thom. 'It's just a bit … unusual.'

'I don't see the word "Nissan" anywhere.'

Now, I don't know a lot about cars. It's not a very macho thing to admit and in front of mechanics or salesmen I would always try to at least make an effort. When I'd bought the Mini Metro I'd made a point of turning the indicator lights on and then getting out of the car to take a good, hard look at them while they blinked, just so the salesman could see I really knew what I was doing. I even squatted while I watched them. The other thing I knew for definite was that you could tell the make of the car by looking for the little sticker on the back that had the make of the car on it. There was no way of faking *that*.

'Look, Danny, I'm not being funny, but this is a collector's item. They're huge in Germany. Only 20,000 were ever made. Probably only half that still exist. They're imported from Japan.'

Which would explain why I'd never seen one before. Well, not unless you count the one I'm sure I saw in an episode of *Wacky Races*.

'So what do you think?' said Thom, sitting in the passenger seat. 'Still interested?'

'The thing is, Thom, Yes, I'm still interested, but it's not like I can go around just buying random people's cars …'

If only he knew.

'I told you,' he said, climbing out. 'I'm looking for a quick sale. I put it in the paper at four grand thinking it would get a definite sale – which it bloody should have, 'cos it cost me six – but no one bit. I'll give it to you at rock bottom. I'm off next week, and it's the last thing to go.'

He slammed the car door shut.

'Oh – unless you need a blender?'

I honk-honked outside Ian's front door.

I'd made my way through the London traffic from Hendon to Bow and I was feeling very pleased with myself. I hadn't at any point felt the need for a handgun, and the whole thirteen-mile journey had only taken three and a half hours!

I honk-honked again, and eventually, Ian came outside.

'What in God's name is that?' he said.

'It's a car!' I said.

'Did you steal it from a fairground? What the hell is it?'

'It's a Nissan Figaro. It's a bit odd.'

'Yes. Yes, it is. But, hang on – is it yours? Why? How?'

'A man asked me if I was interested in buying a car. I said Yes.'

'Jesus! Can you afford it?'

'Just. I got a good deal.'

'How good?'

'He said if I bought it he'd give me a blender.'

'Good deal!'

'And he invited me to his goodbye party tomorrow. Do you want to come?'

'Where is it?'

'Liverpool.'

'Not really.'

Ian walked around the side of the car, took it all in, kicked the tyres, and looked like a real man (although I noticed he didn't squat, like I would have done). He asked me to pop the bonnet open and, once I'd worked out how, I did. He fiddled with things, and made sure other things were securely fastened, and then he dropped the bonnet back into place.

'Looks good,' he said.

I nodded.

'All the indicators work, too,' I said. 'I checked them.'

'You know what this means, don't you, Dan?'

'What?'

'You've got a *Yesmobile*! You're like Batman!'

'It's not a Yesmobile. It's a Nissan.'

'It's a *Yesmobile*! Now where's this blender? Let's make a smoothie!'

Life was really fun.

I popped open the boot, took the blender out, and we carried it to Ian's kitchen and plugged it in.

It didn't work.

If only blenders had indicators, I would've been on it like a flash.

I think Thom had only invited me to his party out of politeness. He hadn't really been expecting me to say Yes. But that's what I'd done and now I was stepping off a train in Liverpool after a three-hour journey to attend a party which began at six. To be honest, I felt slightly awkward about travelling two hundred miles to say goodbye to a man I'd only met twice before. It smelt slightly of obsession, or, at the very least, infatuation.

As I made my way to the taxi rank outside, my phone rang.

'Hello?'

That was me answering it and speaking, by the way, not just saying hello to a ringing phone.

'Danny? It's Gareth here. We met the other night at the party.'

'Yes! Hello! And can I first of all apologise for taking you through that whole birth canal corking thing in quite so much detail?'

'Don't you worry. I mean, the diagrams were probably unnecessary, but otherwise it was a very informative nine-minute monologue.'

He was joking. I hadn't even made any diagrams. And I'd talked *way* longer than nine minutes.

'So, listen, I was wondering if you'd like to come into the office for a chat about something?'

'Yes.'

'You don't know what it is, yet.'

'Oh. Okay. So what is it?'

'Why don't you come in and I can tell you face to face?'

'Good idea.'

'Tomorrow morning?'

I looked at my watch. I have no idea why.

'Yes.'

We said goodbye and I suddenly realised that if I was going to make it to a meeting in Kennington the following morning, I was going to have to return from Liverpool tonight. What a hassle. Another three hours on a train. I wouldn't be home until the wee small hours.

So I trudged back into the station and found my way to the information booth.

'Hello,' I said. 'Can you tell me when the last train from Liverpool to London is?'

'Last direct train, 7.49,' said the man, without even looking up.

I looked at my watch. It was ten to six.

'*7.49*?' I said. 'Are you sure?'

The man looked up at me wearily. He was clearly sure.

'But isn't that a bit ... early?' I said. 'Don't last trains usually go at about midnight?'

'Not to London,' he said. 'And not from here.'

This was utterly ridiculous! The last train at 7.49? Surely there was some mistake? Unless on the way up here I'd got on some kind of special time-travelling train, and journeyed to a place where the local time was the Fifties.

'But I've got to go to a party!' I said, desperately. 'And I've got a meeting in London tomorrow!'

'7.49,' he said, again.

'Hi Thom,' I said. 'Look, I can't stay long, I'm going to have to leave in about an hour.'

'Oh,' said Thom. 'Where are you off to?'

'London.'

'But ... where have you just come from?'

'London.'

'Oh.'

I think Thom took a very small step back from me at this point.

'Well ... it's, um ... very *nice* of you to come, but you needn't have come all this way just—'

'I didn't realise the last train was at 7.49,' I said, explaining myself. 'And I've got a meeting tomorrow which I've agreed to, so—'

'Why didn't you drive up?'

'Drive up?'

'Yes. In your new car.'

He had a point. But I had an answer.

'It took me three and a half hours to drive thirteen miles yesterday. Liverpool is 215 miles away. It would have taken me over two days.'

I don't think he saw the logic, which is a pity, for someone who works with numbers.

'Well ... would you like a beer?'

'Yes.'

I was determined to make the most of my hour at the party, and I started by eating a packet of crisps. Just to let the room know I was a *proper* party animal.

We were in a bar called the Baa Bar, and only a few of Thom's friends had so far arrived. It was just after six. But there was one man, by the name of Jason, who had clearly been there for some time, waiting for the party to start. He was more than a little bit drunk.

'What do you do?' I asked him.

We'd been sitting next to each other for a few minutes now, and I'd been watching him flick ash into a pint glass.

'I'm a civil servant,' he said. 'I work in immigration. Home Office stuff.'

'Wow,' I said. 'That's a proper grown-up job.'

'Yeah.'

'Do you enjoy it?'

'No.'

'Oh. Why not?'

'Because of a lot of things. Because it's my job. It's what I do so I can eat, not what I do because I want to.'

'Right,' I said, deciding that Jason was on the point of turning from someone who seemed mild-mannered but distracted, into quite an angry drunk. 'So ... what kind of things do you have to do?'

He refilled his glass from a bottle of wine on the table and turned to me.

'Today, right, this woman comes in. She was from Nigeria and I had to interview her. She's not said how she's got into the country, and I need to know, for the forms and that. So I say to her, "How did you get into the UK?" and she looks at me like it's not her fault, and tells me a witch doctor turned her into a peanut and smuggled her into the country under his hat.'

He shook his head and smiled, and we laughed.

'Did she think that would work?' I asked, amazed.

'Yeah,' said Jason.

'So did you let her in?'

'No,' said Jason, quietly. 'Poor cow. God knows what she was running from. God knows why she wants to live in this shit of a country. God knows why she thought pretending she'd been a peanut would help.'

Usually, that's a sentence that would have made me laugh. But it didn't. There was a sadness in Jason's eyes.

'Another bloke came in last week. I said to him, "Why are you seeking residency in the UK?" He says that he'd been watching TV back home in Cameroon with his wife. It was a lovely, normal evening, he says. And then he turns round and sees a goat standing in his living room.'

'A goat?'

'A goat.'

'And what happened then?'

'No. That was it. That was his excuse. A goat had been in his living room.'

'Was he allergic?'

Jason shook his head.

'Something to do with omens. A goat is a bad one. So that's why he decided to come to Britain.'

'Well, there are less goats, I suppose. And did you let him in?'

'No,' said Jason. 'I sent him back. I end up sending most of them back.'

I didn't quite know what to say to this. This was a man clearly affected by his work. He saw suffering, and he heard tales of woe and desperation. He spent his days listening to stories of rape, or murder, or beatings. Of political pressures, and harassment. And, at the risk of sounding glib, of ladies being turned into peanuts. And all from people who just wanted a home. Jason was one of the many whose job it was to decide who was telling the truth, and who was not. It was a heavy burden, with life-changing consequences.

'I don't know,' he said, shrugging. 'Sometimes I'm happy with life, and sometimes I'm not. It's like, I know I've got a good job. It's a job with responsibility, and I'm kind of lucky in that way. I've got a good head on my shoulders, and I'm a fair man, when it could easily be some right-wing bastard doing my job and turning everyone back. And it's not a dead-end job. Not really. There are prospects. But … I dunno.'

'What would you rather be doing?'

'Anything,' said Jason. 'Pretty much anything. I mean, in an ideal world, it'd be travel. I've never really travelled. My sister, she took a year out before university and travelled round the world. She works in a call centre now, but she's happy enough, you know? Because she's *done* something. I sit in a little office with the same people every day, and I think … is this it? Surely this can't be it? My little brother finishes school in five weeks. If there's one thing I'm going to make sure he does it's travel. Don't make my mistake.'

'Why don't you go with him?' I said.

'He's asked. I can't. I've got too much on. I'm the most experienced member of the team. If I go, well … I can't. And I couldn't afford it. I've got a mortgage. Pension. No, no. I've made my choices. I've had my fun.'

There was something about the way that Jason said he'd had his fun which made me incredibly sad. He was in his twenties. And yet he thought he'd had his fun. He thought he'd made all his choices. He thought that this was it.

'Maybe this doesn't have to be it,' I said.

'It is, though.'

'All I mean is, maybe you should quit your job. Do something else. See what life brings you.'

'Oh, it's that easy, isn't it?' he said, sourly.

'Well, I dunno. Why don't you take a risk?'

'Take a risk?' he said. His anger shocked me. 'Who the hell are you to suggest taking risks? I can't take risks. I have to be measured and logical and make the right decisions. In my life and with the lives of others. I'd love to have a stupid, risk-free job where the biggest worry is whether or not you'll get down the pub before it gets crowded or not. But I don't. I have a grown-up, responsible job, with grown-up, responsible pressures.'

'I'm just saying …' I tried, before I realised that I didn't know what I was saying. I gave it one more go. 'I'm just saying that maybe sometimes it's riskier not to take a risk. Sometimes all you're guaranteeing is that things will stay the same. Sometimes it's more important to say Yes to things than it is to say no.'

Jason didn't say anything. He just stared into his glass. Maybe it was the drink inside him, but right now he felt nothing but contempt for me. I could hardly blame him. His was a tough job. The conversation had taken a darker twist somewhere along the line, and now I was a child in front of him – a stupid child with a stupid job who lived his life in a stupid way. And what was I basing my big, superficial sayings on, anyway? What did I know? I was embarrassed, and stood up to leave.

'I'm just saying that Yes is as good a word to say as no,' I said. 'When a chance comes up, I mean. When anything comes up.'

'That's the problem,' said Jason, still staring into his glass. 'I spend all my time saying no and it's depressing. I say no at work, and no at home. I tell people they can't come into the country. And why? Because of a set of rules. I tell them they can't start a new life here. I crush people's hope. Even the ones who are lying, or who don't deserve to be here, or are probably complete and utter bastards in their own countries. I even crush *their* hope. And then I take that home with me.'

I thought about leaving it there. About walking away. But I didn't. I had a sudden urge to just tell Jason the truth. Explain the real reason why I'd travelled so far to go to a party and would only be staying one hour. It didn't really compare with the kind of decisions he had to make, but it might mean *something*. I wanted to tell him about all the things I'd said Yes to … and all the things that had happened as a result. The good things *and* the bad things. I wouldn't leave the bad things out. They were just as important. I would leave Jason under no illusions, but I would show him … well … that he had a choice. He could do like Thom was doing, and walk away, and leave his job, and sell his car, and find a new life. He could do like I was doing. *He could say Yes if he wanted*. Yes to *himself*.

He could *Say Yes More*.

'Listen, you'll probably think that what I'm about to tell you is stupid. Or pointless. Or childish. But I want you to hear me out, because it's something that's become quite important to me. But at the same time, when I tell you, you can't use this against me, okay?'

'I'm not agreeing to anything, mate …'

'No, seriously. If I tell you this, you can't tell *anyone*. You could ruin my life. If Thom finds out, and he tells someone who was at the party the other night, and they tell someone else, I could be in a lot of trouble. So keep it between us, yeah?'

Jason raised his eyebrows and considered it. And then he nodded.

And so I told a complete stranger what I was up to, and what I'd done from the start, and where it had led me, and where I hoped it would lead me, in the misguided belief that it would somehow help him.

And when I finished, that complete stranger stood up, swore at me, and walked off towards the bar.

'Thom … that mate of yours,' I said. 'Jason.'

'Oh yes. Jase. Sorry about him,' said Thom. 'He's … well … he's got the weight of the world on his shoulders.'

'Why can't he give up? Do something else?'

'He feels like he's responsible for everything. And that makes him feel like there's no way out. It's no use talking to him. He won't listen. I think he's jealous that I'm in a position to leave, and he's … well … he's not.'

'I guess he's got the kind of job he can't really walk away from.'

Thom nodded. And then looked at his watch.

'Hadn't you—'

Shit. It was 7.24.

'Yes. I better had.'

The journey home was an odd one.

I'd wanted to stay at the party, make things all right again with Jason. Explain myself, and make it all much clearer. But I knew the rules. I'd said Yes to something. I had to go.

And the worse thing was, I couldn't really help but feel that Jason had a point. I was naive. And stupid. I needed to grow up. What was I doing with my life? I mean, really? What was the point in all this? To waste six hours of my day on a train? To wake up confused and bewildered in a Dutch hotel room? To severely annoy my ex-girlfriend? What was I gaining from this, really? Apart from a car and some mild abuse? Yeah, so I was keeping myself busy, and going out more, and having new experiences … but I'd learnt my lesson, now. Maybe I didn't have to be quite so religious about my Yeses. Maybe I could just calm it down a bit, come clean to Ian, accept his punishment with good grace but know that I had given it a go.

I got home to a cold and empty flat. There was no milk left to make tea. I didn't bother checking my e-mails.

I just went to bed.

The following morning I lay there, staring at the ceiling. I'd slept long and hard, and my spirits were lifted only slightly when I saw it was a very sunny day indeed. I considered, for a moment, convincing myself I was ill, and just staying in bed. But I'd agreed to go to a meeting. I didn't want to let people down.

I was at the offices of Cactus TV in Kennington not too much later. I had driven (yes, driven!) the simple six-mile journey in the Yesmobile in just ninety short minutes, meaning I was getting a lot better at this driving lark. Soon I'd be able to drive to places like Liverpool again in little under a day! Things have really come on since the horse and cart.

Gareth met me at the gate.

'Come through,' he said. 'We're going to be meeting with Dean, one of the producers here. Would you like a drink? Tea, or something?'

'Yes please,' I said, because even without this whole Yes thing, I'd never turn down a cup of tea.

We walked through a production office packed with busy young stylish people, setting up shoots, booking guests, researching subjects and looking all busy and young and stylish. The carpet was bright green and there was a cactus on every corner.

I sat down in the office and Gareth popped off to get the tea. I hadn't been told too much about why I'd been asked to come in, but that was okay, because – hey – free tea.

'Danny, I'm Dean,' said a tall man, striding into the office. I stood to shake his hand. His handshake was firmer than mine, and I tried to make up for that by squeezing harder, but I'd done it too late, and I think he thought I'd just liked holding his hand and didn't want to let go.

Gareth was next in with the teas and Dean shuffled his notes.

'Right, so …' said Gareth. 'The reason we got you in was … we're coming up with a few new features for the show, and … well … we're always on the lookout for new people to join the team, and … look … have you ever thought about being a TV presenter?'

Eh?

'Eh?' I said.

'Because we're possibly going to do a slot that may or may not be right for you.'

What? Was I being asked to … *what* was I being asked to do?

'I mean, first of all, there was that cult you started. But all the stuff you were telling me the other night, about Jesus on Brick Lane, and the pyramids stuff, and the whole – you know – corking theory … it fits in with something we've been thinking of doing for quite a while.'

Dean took over.

'Basically, we want to do a slot about enlightened thoughts and spiritualism. And when Gareth told me you believed that aliens built the pyramids—'

'Er, hang on, it's not that *I* believe—'

'And you think that men can have babies—'

'Um no, I'm just saying—'

'And that you think you met Jesus on a bus—'

'Okay, yeah, that *might* be true …'

'Well … we thought you might be right for this. We needed to find someone who already knows about that side of life, and we were stuck for presenters. So we'd like to possibly take a risk on you.'

I shook my head in disbelief. Good Lord! I was being asked if I'd ever thought about being a TV presenter! And I hadn't – I was someone who was quite happy being behind the camera, making notes and holding a clipboard and trying to look busy. I was a producer – not a presenter!

'Look, this may or may not happen,' said Gareth, 'and if it does, it won't be for a while, but what we might want to do is take you on a couple of spiritualist weekends. Get you to do some Vortex Healing, maybe hug some trees, tap into your psychic powers and try and heal a flower, that sort of thing.'

'Like E.T. does in that film.'

'Sort of,' said Dean. 'We thought we could call it "Danny's Path to Enlightenment". We've already run it past Richard and Judy, and they're going to think about it, because Richard said … what was it?'

'You were odd,' said Gareth.

'In a good way,' said Dean.

'Yes,' said Gareth. 'He said you were *odd* in a *good* way.'

'Well,' I said, 'I'm not sure I'd be any use at it, but—'

'We can work wonders in an edit, don't worry about that. But the important thing is: if we decide to go ahead with it, are you up for it?'

They were both looking at me intently, now.

I shrugged.

'Yeah.'

Blimey! I was going to be a television presenter! On a national show! A national tea-time show! A world of housewives and students awaited me!

'Great!' said Dean. 'Well … I guess we'll be in touch!'

That night, the drinks were on me.

I met up with Wag and Ian at the Yorkshire Grey and I told them my good news. I mean, fair enough – it would probably never happen. But even so, things were looking up. My recent spate of slight misfortunes seemed over. The randomness of maybe being recruited on to the *Richard & Judy* team to do a glamorous job like TV presenting – something I had never done before, and doubtless never would've had Yes not allowed it – had given me a real lift and a genuine boost.

I was enjoying the ride again.

Wag, however, looked troubled by life. He'd just returned from his trip to Germany, but he didn't seem at all relaxed or rested by it. If anything, he seemed … stressed. *Very* stressed. It didn't help that his phone kept going off.

Every time it did, Ian and I fell silent, allowing Wag to answer it. But he didn't. He just looked at the screen, cursed, and hung up on them.

'Wag …' said Ian. 'Are you in some sort of … trouble?'

'I don't want to talk about it.'

It went off again.

'Answer it, Wag …'

'I don't want to.'

'Who's calling you?'

'I said I don't want to talk about it.'

It stopped ringing, and we each took a sip of our pints. We sat in silence. We knew the next call wouldn't be far away.

We started to talk about football, before realising that none of us really knows anything about football, and it rang again, which was quite good timing, really, because it meant we preserved an air of masculinity.

'Okay … I'm going to answer it,' said Wag, and he did.

Ian and I waited in silence, pretending not to try and listen.

'No,' said Wag, with some degree of force, and hung up.

'Who was it?' asked Ian. 'What's going on?'

'I know. It won't bloody stop,' said Wag, 'I'll turn it off.'

'But who was it?' I said.

'No one. Never mind. It's nothing.'

'Come on, Wag,' said Ian. 'Who was it? Who keeps ringing you?'

The phone rang again. Wag stared at it, furious.

'It. Won't. Shut. Up,' he said, through gritted teeth. 'It just keeps ringing!'

'That means someone's calling you,' I said.

Perhaps Wag hadn't worked out this whole mobile phone thing yet. Perhaps he thought that when it rang, it meant it needed feeding.

'Hang on a second …'

Wag answered the call, said another loud and forceful 'No' to whoever was on the other end, and hung up.

'Jesus, this is terrible,' he said. 'I can't relax. It's been ringing since I got back. Every other bloody minute. It won't stop ringing. They won't stop ringing me.'

'*Who*?' said Ian.

Wag took a deep breath.

'The Germans,' he said.

I took a good hard look at Wag. It seemed he was in the early stages of some kind of paranoid attack. Ian and I made concerned eye contact.

'The Germans won't leave me alone,' he said, as if that explained all.

I made a sympathetic face and tried some slow and comforting words.

'Yes, they will, Wag. The Germans will leave you alone.'

He frowned.

'Why are you looking at me like I'm mental? Why are you stroking my arm?'

'Why don't you tell us why you think the Germans are after you?' said Ian.

'They're not *after* me. They just won't stop calling me.'

'Why?!' I said, in desperate unison with Ian.

Wag took another deep breath. He was clearly at some kind of turning point in his life. And there seemed to be something he needed to say.

'Because the Germans think I'm Busted.'

The words hung in the air. We blinked at each other a couple of times, and then we both blinked at Ian, and then we blinked at each other again.

'The Germans think you're busted? As in broken?'

'Worse.'

What could be worse than being broken?

Oh …

'No!' I said, in shock. 'Do they think you're Busted as in … the chart-topping teenage boyband?'

Wag bit his lip, rolled his eyes upwards and nodded his head silently. His phone rang again. Ian covered his mouth with both hands in horror.

'God,' he said. 'Look …'

He showed me the phone. A number was flashing up on the screen. And not a British number, either.

'Another one!' said Wag. 'Another German!'

Wag answered the phone, shouted '*Nein!*' and hung up again.

'Listen,' I said, 'we may have to backtrack here. Why are Germans phoning you up under the impression that you're a three-man teenage boyband? Because I've known you for a while, now, and you are *nothing like* a three-man teenage boyband—'

'I've been working with Busted lately, right? I've been helping out on a couple of tracks. We got on, the four of us. Or I thought we did. They're lovely lads. But they've been on tour lately, and one night...' he took a sip of his pint to steady his nerves. 'One night they were doing an interview for a German TV show, right?'

'Right,' I said.

'I was backstage setting some of the technical stuff up. And one of them decided it would be funny to give out my mobile number, live, on air.'

I tried to suppress a smile. So did Ian. We both failed.

'They said it was *their* phone number, and that their fans should feel free to phone up with their thoughts and questions at any time of day or night.'

His phone beep-beeped.

'Excuse me,' he said, picking the phone up once more, studying it, and then slamming it on the table.

'They've started bloody texting me now.'

Ian started giggling. Wag was clearly deeply affected by this.

'I try telling them I'm not in Busted, but they don't believe me. They say, "Is that Charlie?" and I say, "No, it's Wag," and they say, "Is that you, Charlie?" and I say, "No, it is Wag speaking," and they say, "Charlie? Charlie?" I *need* this phone! It's my work phone! I have to keep it on! Which means I'm being harassed by these people twenty-four hours a day!'

'Look,' I said. 'It's bound to wind up some time. How long have Busted got left in them? Five, maybe six years?'

'I can't go about being accused of being in Busted for the next six years, Dan! This is a modern-day nightmare! My phone number is all over Germany! People are even telling me they've found it on the Internet!'

I started to laugh, rather loudly.

'Shut up! This isn't funny!'

'It bloody is, Charlie!' said Ian.

'It bloody *isn't*!'

Wag's face went bright red, and he set me off again.

'See how you like it, then, Dan. What's your number?'

'Eh? You're not giving my number to random German teenagers!'

'Yes, I am. Why don't you see how *you* like it when everyone in the world thinks you're in Busted?'

I started to feel unwell. My laughter suddenly stopped. Was that a suggestion? Was that a Yes Moment? Ian's face lit up as he realised the same thing. But Wag hadn't finished.

'Why don't we give *your* number out to everyone in the world, then?' said Wag. 'See how *you* like it, eh?'

He started to type my number into his phone. He was preparing a text message.

'Wait … what are you …'

'I am about to send your number to a bunch of Germans, Dan, to tell them that your number is the new number for the International Fans of Busted Club, and that they should feel free to call you whenever the mood takes them …'

'Wait …' I said. 'Just wait a second …'

'Not so funny now, is it?' he said. 'Let's see how *you* like being at the centre of a teenage phenomenon. Let's see how *you* respond to being phoned up constantly by people you don't even know, hounding you, wanting to meet up with you, thinking you're in a boyband …'

He held the phone up in front of me, and showed me his message.

'I'll bloody do it, Danny … if you've anything to say, any apology to make …'

I went quite pale. I couldn't work out what to do. I read the message.

CALL ME. I AM NEW BUSTED NUMBER.
CALL ANY TIME. 0044 7802 *** ***

Oh, Jesus.

Should I stop him? Would that be going against my new way of life? Or should I treat it as an opportunity?

'No apology?' he said. 'Fine. Then the question we face is this: shall *I* press Send, or do *you* want to do it?'

Shit. Two Yeses. Which do I choose? What do I do now? I shrugged, helplessly.

Wag leaned forward, slightly intimidatingly.

'Dan … do you *really* want to give your number out to everyone in the world?'

Oh, God. That was it. That was the proper Yes Moment. I looked at Ian, who was smirking, and slowly nodding, and carrying in his eyes the fact that he knew *exactly* what I was going to have to do next. Wag continued to stare at me.

'Well, *do* you, Dan?'

I took the phone from Wag, and – maintaining steady eye contact – pressed Send.

He looked horrified.

'And in answer to your other question, my friend … Yes. Yes, I *do* want to give my number out to everyone in the world.'

A split second later, Ian's phone beeped. Wag had been bluffing. He'd texted my number to Ian; *not* to thousands of confused Germans.

But as for me … well, I *hadn't* been bluffing.

And I knew what I'd have to do next.

It was another Level Five job.

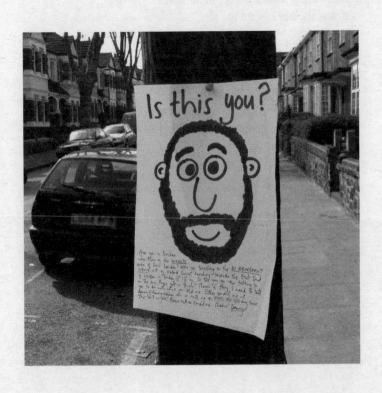

10

In which Daniel undertakes
a Most Unusual Search

Now, don't get me wrong: I know what I just said.

I know I just said I'd have to give my number out to 'everyone in the world'. But that was when I was down the pub. That was during a macho booze-fuelled face-off, when everything seemed possible and nothing seemed like too much trouble. The problem was, when I got home to consider my next move, I realised that I clearly couldn't give my number out to *everyone* in the world. That'd be crazy, and take ages, and involve rather a lot of me on the phone to people the world over saying, 'Hi, you don't know me, but this is my number in case you ever fancy a chat.' It just wasn't practical and would take the best part of a lifetime.

No, if I was going to do as Wag said and make my phone number publicly available, I was going to have to do it another way; a cleverer way. I would have to get it out there, on the streets, where it could be seen, and acted upon, and used. There was only one thing for it: a clever word-of-mouth stickering campaign. And the more I thought about it, the more I got to like the idea. What a great way to make friends. And what a great way to make human connections. They say strangers are just friends you haven't met yet. And while that can't be *entirely* true (statistically, some of them are *bound* to be muggers), I nevertheless clung to that notion as I ordered 2000 stickers bearing the legend:

CALL ME
Let's have a polite conversation!
07802 * ****

Now, I had launched a similar campaign once before, and it had worked an absolute treat. I had ended up meeting some brilliant people and having some brilliant experiences – precisely the kind of experiences I'd felt I'd been losing out on of late. But this was a more careful and considered campaign. I felt the middle line, for example, might put off the muggers and the riff-raff, but would leave room for the people like Amsterdam's Jahn; the open-minded and progressive. The people who could teach me something. And so below those two words and that one sentence was, yes – my mobile number. The number I rely on. The number, thanks to Wag's inadvertent suggestion, I would be giving out to the public at large. Starting now, with Ian, in the East End.

'When you think about it,' said Ian, walking alongside me, 'this is basic psychology.'

'What is?' I said, attaching another sticker to the side of a phonebox.

'This. You feel that there's a gap. Am I right? A Lizzie-shaped gap. And you're trying to *fill* that gap. But instead of filling it with *one* person, you're trying to fill it with *everyone*. You not having Lizzie gives you the perfect excuse to do this.'

'What do you mean, "excuse"? I wasn't looking for an excuse to do this! Do you think I've been waiting around for years, hoping desperately that one day someone would say or do something which would allow me to have thousands of stickers printed up inviting the general public to ring me up for a polite conversation? Is that how you think I live my life?'

'Pretty much, yes.'

We stickered Bow, Mile End and Bethnal Green that day. I kept a wad of stickers in my pocket, too, for whenever the mood took me.

The day flew by, but no one called.

I guess all I could do was wait.

In a large room on the Old Kent Road the following night, dozens of chairs were lined up in neat rows. A woman in a cardigan fiddled with a video-camera pointed at the table which I assumed the world-renowned Maitreya expert Elias Brown would call home for the next couple of hours.

Pete had phoned me urgently that morning, and said that he'd checked the relevant websites, and Mr Brown was apparently in town to give one of his lectures. Pete seemed to think that there could be something in all this, and, now that the people at *Richard & Judy* had decided I could well be an authority on matters of the spiritual, I thought it pertinent to attend. That, and I couldn't exactly say no.

One of the strangest things was, Pete wanted to make sure I knew he didn't believe it was possible that Maitreya, aka the World Teacher, was walking the streets, looking out for people like me ... but he'd begun to talk about him in quite reverential tones ... so much so that we were both becoming quietly excited by the prospect of learning more about the man who had apparently chosen me – *me!* – to guide and direct. Not that I believed it either, of course. No, no.

There were about forty people in the room now, and most had already taken their seats, but others were busy buying Maitreya post-cards or books, or audio tapes of previous Elias Brown lectures. A few months before I'd never even heard of Maitreya – I was surprised to see such an industry revolving around him.

'I've got a few of these books,' said Pete. 'And I subscribe to Mr Brown's newsletter, which is *surprisingly* informative.'

'He's got his own newsletter, as well?'

'Oh yes. He's quite an authority, and very nice with it. Genuinely a very nice man. All this is aimed at making the world a better—'

But that was as far as he got. Because just then, the man we'd come to see walked into the room. And the room fell silent.

'That's him!' whispered Pete, in my ear. 'That's Brown!'

He took his seat with ease, and smiled a wide and happy smile. For a man in his eighties, he was a bit of a looker. And it's not often you'll hear me say that.

'Good evening,' he said, in a soft and warm voice.

'Good evening,' replied every single person in the room, including Pete, in near-perfect unison. I was a little surprised by the choreography.

'How many of you have been to one of these lectures before?'

Pete and pretty much everyone else put their hands up.

'All I ask is that when I am speaking you keep an open mind,' said Elias. He had a kind face. 'I am not asking you to believe what you don't want to believe; merely that you keep an open mind. The truly open-minded person is not easy to find. I will give you some statistics later on, if I remember.'

This made me laugh. A woman in a pashmina frowned at me and I shut up.

'What we will do this evening,' said Elias, 'is in a few moments time I will be overshadowed by Maitreya himself. He will be here, among us.'

Pete nudged me, excitedly.

'We will play you a tape of some of his messages while this is happen-ing. After that, I will talk for a while about Maitreya and his mission here on earth, and then we will finish with a final overshadowing, which will be far more powerful than the first. It should be quite extraordinary.'

As he said this, his microphone stopped working. The woman in the pashmina whispered something to her friend about rogue energies. Elias continued to talk at a much lower level until one very exasperated man in the second row put his hand up and shouted, 'I THINK YOUR BATTERY HAS RUN OUT,' far louder than he needed to, given that he was only in the second row.

'Oh,' said Elias. 'How deeply unprofessional of us. I can promise you that this is the first time this has ever happened. Usually, we are *very* polished.'

He smiled and looked around the room and everyone laughed. He was certainly a very charming host, and I was enjoying his company. One of his helpers, however, was going bright red as she struggled to prise the microphone open to replace its batteries.

'I'm sorry,' she seemed to be stuttering. 'It's … oh … oh dear …'

A moment later a rather strapping man was by her side with a replacement battery. He took full control of the situation, clicked the battery into place, and put the microphone back on its stand, in front of Elias, who tapped it and said, 'Hello?'

It worked again.

'MAGIC!' said the man in the second row, and the terrible thing is, I think he actually thought it was.

'Now let us continue …' said Elias.

Down went the lights.

'I am going to study each of your chakras,' he said. 'I will look at each of you in turn. But don't worry if you are sitting behind someone tall and it appears that I have missed you by accident, because I won't have.'

At this, he closed his eyes, breathed very deeply and then – suddenly – he made a terribly odd noise with his throat and his eyes shot wide open again. I guessed that this must have been the moment that the spirit of Maitreya had entered into him. Either that, or we'd have to start praying that there was a doctor in the house. I found myself sitting straighter, probably subconsciously trying to make a good impression on Maitreya. Someone somewhere clicked 'play' on a tape recorder and a fuzzy, buzzy home-recording kicked in.

'PREPARE YOURSELF… TO SEE ME SOON!' said a slow, deep voice, while Elias Brown looked from person to person, a beatific smile on his face and kindness in his eyes.

'PREPARE YOURSELF … TO HEAR MY MESSAGE!'

I was. And so, it seemed, was everyone else. I appeared to be the only person in the room without their hands clasped, and their eyes closed. Instinctively, I clasped my hands together.

'I AM THE STRANGER AT THE DOOR. I AM HE WHO KNOCKS. I AM YOUR FRIEND.'

Elias continued to smile, and look from person to person. Somewhere behind me, someone sighed a sigh of pleasure.

'YOU WILL SEE ME SOON. MAYBE ... YOU HAVE SEEN ME ALREADY.'

Suddenly, it went a bit odd. I shivered. Elias Brown was looking straight at me. Straight at me, while a tape told me that maybe I had met Maitreya already.

'THOSE WHO SEARCH ME OUT ...'

Elias Brown was still looking at me.

'... ARE THOSE WHO *WILL* FIND ME ...'

I fiddled with my watch.

He was still looking at me.

I smiled, nervously.

And then he stopped looking at me, and looked at the plump woman next to me instead.

'The Masters are all around us,' said Elias Brown, a little later on. 'Now, that's a *huge* statement. And one that I can't in *any* way prove. But take it from me: it is true.'

I had started to realise, some way into this lecture, that quite a lot of what I was being told I was going to have to take on faith.

'Soon you will become aware of their presence and their wisdom. When Maitreya comes, he will appear on television, simultaneously, all around the world. The satellite systems were built purposefully for his coming. You will see a face. A face you will recognise. A face you have seen before. But he will not speak. He will not say a word. But his thoughts will take place inside us, silently. Each of us will hear him in our own language. Thousands of spontaneous miracles will then take place.'

It was half an hour in, and somewhere in front of me, an old woman took a photo of Elias. Pete had his eyes closed and was nodding, slowly.

'All those who have shaped humanity are disciples of the Master. Da Vinci ... Einstein ... Shakespeare ... Newton ... Freud ... Jung ... they have passed on their knowledge and their inspiration. The Masters know what is best for each and every one of us and they work constantly to help us. We are very lucky to have them here.'

From there, Elias talked about Maitreya's thoughts and philosophies on world hunger, the UN, war in the Middle East, nuclear power, George W. Bush, the developed nations, the G8 summit, poverty, disease and destitution. But at no point did he mention how Maitreya gets home at night, and whether on occasion he's taken the bus rather than the tube. It was all starting to get a bit disheartening. 'Deal with the issues at hand, Brown!' I felt like shouting. 'Why cover politics when we can talk bus routes!'

'One day we will all be immortal,' he said. 'I *promise* you that.'

But even that didn't help.

Mind you, it was hard to disagree with Maitreya's general principles. To save the world, he says, we need to share. There are over 30 million people in the world today who are starving to death … and yet the storehouses of the West are overflowing. It was this that I was pondering when an arm shot up in front of me. It was Pete. What was he doing?

'Yes?' said Elias Brown.

'Is the Maitreya still here tonight?' he said, and I bristled with embarrassment. 'In this room?'

Elias smiled and looked around the room for a few moments. He seemed to catch an invisible eye, and then looked back at Pete and nodded.

'Yes. He is here.'

Pete nudged me in the ribs and smiled a very wide smile.

'Probably because of you,' he whispered.

I was starting to think that Pete *did* believe in all this, after all.

'Where does Maitreya live?' asked a man on the other side of the room, and I felt rather smug, because I already knew this.

'He lives among the Asian community in Brick Lane. He doesn't sleep, he doesn't eat, he doesn't have a bed. He works 24 hours a day, tirelessly, for the benefit of planet earth. For the benefit of each and every one of you.'

And Elias Brown once again looked me right in the eye.

'I'm telling you, Ian, he looked straight at me,' I said, as we walked down the Mile End Road. 'It was a little bit spooky.'

'An old man in a cream suit looked straight at you and you think that's spooky. It's not spooky. It's just an old man in a cream suit looking straight at you.'

'But it was like he *knew* something. He kind of changed my mind when I saw the look on his face. It was like Maitreya was sitting next to him, and pointing me out, and saying "That's the one … *that's* the one I'm helping!"'

'Do you realise how arrogant that sounds?' said Ian, as I paused to stick a CALL ME sticker to a phonebox. 'Do you think you're the bloody Golden Child or something? Do you think that any minute now, Eddie Murphy's going to burst into the room looking for you?'

'Is it really so far-fetched? Why do you automatically assume I can't be some kind of Golden Child? This is precisely the kind of negative feedback that Jesus will get when he makes his second coming.'

My phone rang. I answered it. They hung up. In the past 24 hours, my CALL ME stickers seemed to have permeated London's consciousness, and this had started to happen quite a bit.

'Look, Dan,' said Ian. 'I honestly don't think the man on the bus was Jesus, or Maitreya, or *any* of those fellas. I was drunk when I suggested that. And I think it is highly unlikely that you, my friend, are the Golden Child, or the Copper Child, or a child made of virtually *any* metallic substance or element.'

'The Starburst Group think it might be possible.'

'The Starburst Group think that aliens built the pyramids,' he said, and I saw his point.

'The only way you're going to get over this, Dan …' he continued, pausing only for dramatic effect '… is if you *find* the man on the bus …'

Now, I don't know if *you've* ever walked down Brick Lane attempting to track down and meet an enlightened being from another dimension, but it's really not as easy as it sounds.

Ian had been right, of course: finding the man on the bus was the only way to confirm once and for all that he wasn't the Maitreya. That said, he hadn't been too keen to join me on the journey. I'd already tired him out with our Call Me exertions. No, this time I'd had to persuade him with the promise of a free curry.

'So what's the plan?' he said, as we stepped off the tube at Aldgate.

I smiled and opened my rucksack.

'This is …'

I pulled out a thick wodge of photocopied A4 posters, headed with the controversial and attention-grabbing question: IS THIS YOU?

It was the second great Yes Man campaign in just one week! I was deeply excited… here I was, reaching out to the world, exposing myself, not just once but twice! This was just what I'd promised myself I would do. Not only did I have my CALL ME stickers out there, circulating in society and spreading my number far and wide, but here were my Man On The Bus posters, proudly displaying the face of the bloke who'd brought me out of the depths of my depression. The only problem was, I'm not very good at drawing, and all I really remembered about my subject was that he was an Asian man with a beard. That, on its own, wouldn't be enough. So I wrote a more detailed explanation of the poster's existence underneath:

Are you a TEACHER who lives in the ALDGATE AREA of East London? Were you travelling on the BUS REPLACEMENT SERVICE out of Oxford Circus heading towards the East End on Friday the 6th? If so, I'm the man you were talking to on the bus! Please get in touch – there's a story I need to tell you! Either e-mail me at danny@dannywallace.com or call me on 07802 *** ***. This isn't a joke! Please call me! Danny

I felt sure that this would peak the man's interest and he would call – if he saw it. The best thing I could do was plaster Brick Lane – the centre of the local community – with my elaborate posters, and just hope …

And so, for the second time that week, we begun to stick things up. We stuck posters on lampposts, over club posters, in phoneboxes, and more … while also whacking the odd CALL ME sticker up alongside it. I'll be honest: we got a few strange looks that day. Perhaps it was the quality of my artwork that was causing concern, perhaps it was the fact that we were being so very thorough with our campaigning … whatever it was, I knew that at the very least, we'd caused a stir. Someone would recognise this man. They *had* to. Even if the only defining characteristic of my drawing was a beard.

And then a bell went off, and out of the mosque opposite poured hundreds of bearded men, and I realised that perhaps this was going to be a little trickier than at first I thought.

As we ate our curry, Ian and I pondered the magical possibilities of what we'd just done. Well, *I* thought they were magical. Ian still thought they were bollocks.

'It's crazy when you think about it, isn't it?' I said. 'You know … about the man on the bus possibly being a god.'

Ian laughed.

'What?' I said, offended. 'I mean, think about it: what if this whole Yes thing … what if it was *meant to be*?'

'Meant to be what? A waste of time?'

'No … you know … *destined*. What if there's a *reason* for it all?'

'If that man on the bus *was* a god, then why does he travel by bus?'

'It's like that song. *"What if god was one of us, just a slob like one of us, just a stranger on a bus, la la la la lalala."* In fact, it's *exactly* like that. Right down to the slob reference and the la la las.'

'This is a fundamentally flawed concept,' said Ian, pointing his fork at me. A small piece of chicken fell off, but we both politely ignored it. 'For a start, a god would not use the bus. Any god. Certainly not Jesus or Buddha. They make enough from statuette-based merchandising alone not to have to slum it with the likes of you. Even the *Pope's* got a special car, for crying out loud. And the slob reference – I don't think so. You'd have to make an effort if you were God. It'd be too demoralising for people when they met you at the pearly gates and realised they'd spent their whole lives essentially worshipping Worzel Gummidge. No, no. You'd wear a suit, or a nice jumper, something like that.'

I took a bite of my naan bread. My phone rang. I answered it. They hung up.

'Maybe you're right. Maybe it's all too much of a coincidence. You know … a stranger passing on his wisdom, and then me finding out the World Teacher lives locally.'

Ian nearly choked on his tikka.

'A *coincidence*? Dan … how is that a coincidence? The two things clearly have absolutely nothing to do with each other. You can't say "Oh, I sat next to a man on a bus and a month later I heard God lives in Brick Lane" and claim it's a coincidence! It's like saying, "Oh, look, there's an apple, and only yesterday I was on a boat!" How is that a coincidence? You're deluded, my friend …'

I took a sip of my beer and looked at Ian, wisely.

'You were probably destined to say that.'

When I returned home that night, I considered all the ways I could potentially find the man on the bus. He was a teacher, and the chances were he was teaching locally. Maybe I'd try and find a list of all the local schools and colleges, and send my posters there. Or perhaps I could buy a false beard and announce to the local press I would be staging my own police reconstruction. I knew Ian had been right when he said I needed to meet him. And not just to prove or disprove he was Maitreya – but to tell him what I was up to; what he'd done to my life.

I went to sleep that night, excited. But little did I know that, for a while at least, the hunt for the man on the bus would have to take a back seat. Because, as it turned out, someone was on the hunt for *me*.

My secret – the secret it was vital I kept as quiet as I could – was suddenly in real danger of being revealed.

Because someone knew.

And that someone was out to get me.

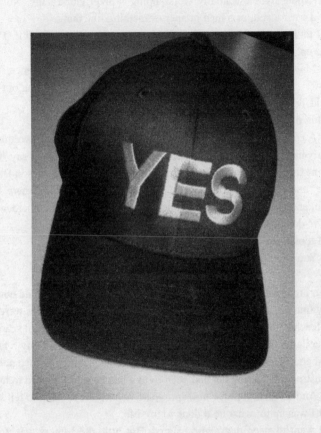

11

In which Daniel finds himself Central to a very Disturbing Predicament

I really didn't know what to make of it at first.

I really, truly didn't.

I assumed, when I first opened it, that it must be a coincidence. Or, failing that, some kind of joke.

But now … now it just seemed *sinister*.

I picked up the package once more, and carefully, quietly studied its contents.

A very short note:

If you're going to say Yes all the time, you may as well give your voice a rest.

And a dark blue baseball cap, embroidered with one word: YES.

The package had been sent from London W1. The label had been printed, as had the note. I kept on studying the hat, searching for clues, but then I realised there weren't any, and I was just a man, sitting at a table, studying a hat.

For a split second, paranoia gripped me. What if word had got out? What if Ian had let slip what I was doing? What if someone had overheard our conversations? What if someone was planning and plotting against me? Maybe I had a nemesis now! An evil, moustachioed villain, intent on my downfall! Or what if …

Hang on.

Ian.

Of course. Ian.

Simple. Mystery solved.

Ian was not only the man who knew, but the man who had something to gain from this. The man who was in on it, and who'd been in on it from the start. The man who'd already told me was going to 'punish' me. Ian bloody Collins.

I laughed, and shook my head with what I hoped looked like pity in my eyes.

Oh, he thought he was good, didn't he? He thought he could beat me. He thought that by sending me this hat – this hat-based version of a horse's head under a pillow – he could frighten me. Intimidate me. Make me think what I was doing was wrong, or bad, or pointless.

But I knew just how to handle this: I would *ignore* it. I would pretend it had never arrived. Sooner or later, he'd start probing; looking for a reaction. It was exactly the same as when he sent me that fake Valentine card – the one he pretended was from Lionel Richie. It wouldn't be long before he'd break down and say, 'Look, are you going to *wear* the bloody hat or not?' And then I would look upon him, with more weary pity in my eyes, sigh, and say, 'Yes.'

Which would be all the more frustrating for him because it would be yet another Yes in the bag.

I couldn't lose.

That said, he's never actually mentioned the Lionel Richie thing.

I was halfway down Regent Street when my phone rang. I answered it.

'Yeah, mate, who is this?' said a voice on the other end of the line.

'It's Danny,' I said. 'Who's this?'

'I found a sticker saying I should call you. Why?'

'Oh. Yes. I was wondering if you'd like a polite conversation.'

There was a pause. And a laugh. And then he hung up, but not before saying: 'Wanker.'

I sighed to myself. So far, the Call Me campaign hadn't been a great success. Sure, lots of people had called me, but none so far had wanted to indulge themselves in the 'polite conversation' side of my offer.

It was the next day, and I was desperate to meet up with Ian. I wanted to see how long it would take him to try and move the conversation on to hats.

We agreed to meet at the Yorkshire Grey in the afternoon.

I headed into town a little earlier. There was something else on my mind: I knew I should do something to try and make things all right with Hanne. It had been a while since our pleasant three-way dinner, so maybe I could find a small peace offering.

'Excuse me?' said a tall man, in what looked to be his sixties. He was standing outside Pizza Express and he was clutching a bunch of leaflets. 'I was wondering if you'd give this a read ...'

He had a kind face, and was wearing a kind of tweed hat and a blue anorak. I took a leaflet – crammed with tiny, neat print – and began to read.

> *Hello*
> *Did you know the fate of the western world lies directly in my hands?*

I looked up at the man and blinked a couple of times. If the fate of the Western world really did lie directly in this man's hands, I was about to start walking east.

> I was born in 1938, the seventh son of the sixth Duke of Portland, with a prodigious intellectual ability which developed quickly and thoroughly. Because of this, I was able to write my first book of celebrated sonnets in 1939.

I didn't quite know what to make of this. Apparently, the man in front of me had written a book of sonnets when he was one year old. I suppose that was possible. But this was a *celebrated* one. All the sonnets *I* wrote when I was one were *rubbish*.

> *I was able to quickly rise up the ranks of political power, but my influence always remained hidden due to concerns about secrecy and political espionage etc. My decisions have effectively saved the world twice, once during the Cuban Missile Crisis and again when North Korea got the bomb in 1987. I was responsible for Churchill's actions in the Second World War, and for those of many of his predecessors.*

In the words of Katherine the peace activist, this was quite literally unbelievable. This man, between the ages of 1 and 6, not only found time to write a celebrated book of sonnets, but was busy dictating military strategy to Churchill.

> *I doubt you would believe the scope and range of my political influence.*

Fair point.

> *You might also find it hard to believe that not merely have I not been paid for any of this, but the Government, in furtherance of their conspiratorial designs, has been paying me less than half of normal social security.*

Aha. And suddenly, I knew where this was going …

> *I continue to help bring stability to the world. If you believe this has helped you in your life, you may wish to make a small contribution …*

I was overawed. It was all so … *unusual.*

'So …' I said, looking him in the eye. 'Is all of this … completely accurate?'

'Yes,' he said, matter-of-factly. 'But people never believe me, which is why I had these printed up.'

He smiled, as if to show how ludicrous it was that people just wouldn't take his word, and he'd had to go to all this trouble just to prove a simple fact. I looked at the piece of paper in front of me. To be honest, it didn't really seem to be particularly conclusive proof.

'And you really dictated military strategy to Churchill when you were a toddler?'

'Around that time, yes, I did.'

I'll be honest. As I suspect you have guessed, I didn't totally believe him. My dealings with Omar, Albert Heijn and Dr Molly Van Brain had taught me not to take things at face value where money was concerned. But I wanted to give the man the chance to prove himself.

'And you *did* actually save the world?'

The man nodded.

'Effectively,' he said.

I scanned through the piece of paper one more time, trying to find some way out of this. As far as I could see, there wasn't one.

'So you're basically asking me to give you money because you saved the world and you continue to do so? *That's* your request?'

I was hoping that by repeating all this he might suddenly buckle and say, 'Ah, okay, fair enough, you caught me out there. I didn't do any of that stuff. It was actually Churchill who made all Churchill's decisions.

You're obviously a trivia buff.' But he didn't say that. He simply nodded once more, and said, 'Well, yes. But only if you think it is appropriate.'

I sighed, and got my wallet out.

'Have you got change for a tenner?' I said.

'No,' he said.

I gave him a tenner.

I guess this was one of the downsides of saying Yes to everything. You kind of make yourself vulnerable to the whims of the outside world. But, being a positive thinker, I tried to work out if I could possibly turn my encounter with the toddler politician into a present for Hanne. It had, after all, cost me ten pounds – the precise figure I reckoned I would have to have spent on her. I decided, upon careful consideration, that I couldn't. It would probably just make things worse. 'Hey Hanne – sorry about the other night. But I just gave ten pounds to a man involved in the Cuban Missile Crisis. We cool now?'

But moments later, the ideal gift would present itself … thanks to a small, laminated, A4 sign in the window of a florists: GOT SOMETHING TO SAY? SAY IT WITH FLOWERS!

I would!

So … what did I have to say?

Ian was being remarkably coy.

We'd been sitting in the Yorkshire Grey for nearly four minutes now, and not once had he mentioned hats. Or caps. Or headwear in general. The sly dog. I smiled to myself. Ian was obviously playing the long-game. I decided I wouldn't talk about hats, either. That'd show him.

'Why are you smiling like that?' said Ian.

'No reason,' I said.

'You're behaving very oddly.'

'Am I? Am I indeed?' I said, before adding, 'Of course, some would say it is *you* who is acting oddly.'

'No,' said Ian. 'Pretty much everyone would say it's you.'

'Would they?' I said, because when you're in a conversation like this, it's all about getting the last word. 'Would they indeed?'

'What the hell's wrong with you?' he said. 'Did you say Yes when someone asked you to act like a mental?'

I pitied Ian. I was on to him and he just hadn't worked it out yet. His Yes hat hadn't weakened me, as he'd no doubt thought it would. It had made me stronger.

'Listen, I invited Wag along as well,' I said, nonchalantly. 'He should be along when he gets my message.'

'Message?'

'My message saying we were in the pub and he should come along'

'Good. So. How's the project?' he said.

'Not too bad.'

'Said no to anything yet?'

I smiled.

'No. I have fully embraced every opportunity that has come my way. And I have done it without the use of even a single hat.'

I studied his face for a reaction to my subtle hint. There was none. Shit, he was good.

My phone rang. I answered it. They hung up.

'Have you brought your diary?' said Ian.

'You will have my diary in the fullness of time, my friend.'

'Well, give me details, then …'

'I have invented an automatic self-rewinding video box, and entered a competition to be Britain's most German-looking man.'

Just then, Wag walked into the pub.

'Remember: not a word to Wag,' I said, raising a finger to my lips, and Ian nodded.

'What the hell are you up to?' said Wag. He seemed angry, and he had quite a red face.

'What do you mean?' I asked. I honestly couldn't work out why he was annoyed.

Wag opened his rucksack and pointed at it. Inside was a crushed and broken bunch of flowers, with a small card attached.

'You got my message, then.'

'You could have phoned me! Why send me flowers with a little note saying "I'm down the pub"? Do you know what the lads at work thought of this? Why didn't you just text me?'

'I wanted to say it with flowers!' I said. It took Ian a second, but when he realised what must've prompted that, he nearly choked on a peanut.

'Well, don't! I'm getting a pint,' he said, and walked off.

'I wanted to say it with flowers,' I said, meekly.

My phone beep-beeped.

It was Hanne.

THANK YOU FOR THE FLOWERS BUT YOU MUST STOP THIS UNNATU-
RAL OBSESSION AND MOVE ON.

'Christ,' I said. 'This is *perfect*. I had something to say to Hanne, and I
also wanted to say *that* with flowers, and now she's beginning to think
I'm obsessed with her.'

'So you gatecrash her date, and then you send her flowers as well?'

'You should *never* send flowers to an ex. Gives out the wrong
message.'

'Let's just hope she doesn't find out about the small African boy.'

'What small African boy? You've not sent her a small African boy
now, have you?'

'No. I had an idea earlier. I gave a tenner to an old man who'd written a load of sonnets when he was a baby, and I thought about doing it
in Hanne's honour, but then I thought no, it would have to be better than
that, and I saw this thing about sponsoring kids in a copy of the *Big Issue*
I bought – my *third* this week, by the way – and so I rang up and I sponsored one for her. By way of an apology.'

'What's going on?' said Wag, arriving back at the table.

'Danny has to apologise to Hanne.'

'Oh. Why?'

'Nothing, really,' I said, hoping that would be the end of it.

'Danny forbade Hanne from seeing a new bloke,' said Ian. 'And
then, when they went out on their first date anyway, Danny gatecrashed
and stayed for the whole evening.'

Wag looked shocked.

'I *didn't* gatecrash,' I said. 'I was *invited*. Seb invited me. We seemed
to really hit it off.'

'You stayed the whole *evening*?' said Wag.

'Only until I was politely asked to leave.'

'They told him to fuck off,' said Ian, helpfully.

'Are you stalking Hanne?' said Wag, wide-eyed. 'This is brilliant –
I don't know any stalkers!'

'I am *not* stalking Hanne,' I said, and then Ian piped up with, 'Hanne
thinks he's obsessed with her. He just sent her flowers, too.'

'You're stalking Hanne!'

'I sent *you* flowers, mullet man, and I'm not stalking *you*!'

'Don't try and change the subject through mocking my hair! You
don't send your ex flowers!' said Wag. 'It sends out the wrong message!'

'And then,' said Ian, 'he sponsored a small African boy in her honour.'

Wag's jaw hit the floor.

'*You don't sponsor a small African boy for an ex*! It sends out *totally* the wrong message! *Never* do that – it's like a *rule*!'

Wag looked towards Ian and he nodded, eyes closed, in agreement.

'We've got to get you a girlfriend,' said Ian. 'You could be dangerous.'

He was winding me up. But Wag wasn't. He thought I probably *was* quite dangerous.

'Let's talk about something else,' I said, firmly.

And after ten or twenty minutes, we did.

It was a couple of days later and I'd been staying in a bit more. It wasn't that I'd stopped saying Yes. It was just that I'd stopped looking quite as hard for them. I'd annoyed Hanne, and Ian was clearly trying to scare me off with his Yes hat. Wag too had seemed annoyed with me, and I was growing tired from all the going out. Several more strangers had rung me up, and I'd nearly managed to engage one of them in a polite conversation, but then they'd lost their nerve and hung up like all the others. Plus, Hanne had clearly had a thank you letter from the *Sponsor A Child* people, because she e-mailed me to ask whether it had been me that had sponsored a small boy in her honour. I wrote back and reluctantly said Yes, and that she should let me know if I should sponsor one in honour of Seb, too. She told me that wouldn't be necessary.

I pottered about in the flat. My phone rang. I answered it. They hung up. I ran a bath.

What did Ian think his hat would achieve, anyway? Did he really think I'd crack under pressure? Was he hoping to catch me out and make me say 'no' to something, before pouncing on me from out of a bush and dealing out his as-yet-unspecified punishments? Well, I had to stay one step ahead of him – that much was certain.

I got out of the bath an hour later to find a new e-mail waiting. It was from Tom, the BBC man. He wanted to know what my plans for the Edinburgh Festival were – was I going to go up this August, and if I had no plans, did I want to help with his team? He needed an extra pair of eyes up there, seeing shows, scouting for talent, developing ideas. Did I want to pop in and have a chat about it? Too bloody right I did!

I'd been going up to the Edinburgh Festival – the world's largest arts festival – for years, but just hadn't planned on it this year. Too much had been going on of late … but now that there was an opportunity, I had to grab it. Particularly as it all stemmed from a Yes.

Edinburgh would be fun. A chance to catch up with what's going on. And it's not like it would be bad for my career. I was pleased Tom was still thinking of me. And it would be good to get out of London. I smiled. Yes was getting me out of London. Yes would take me to Edinburgh. Maybe … hang on.

I had another new e-mail.

But …

Eh?

>**To: Danny Wallace**
>**From: whoisthechallenger@hotmail.com**
>**Subject: Like the hat?**

Hello Danny....
It is me again.... hopefully you received the hat....
I have something to suggest to you....
Why...

Not....

I scrolled down.

Go....

What was going on here?

I scrolled further down.

To....

Down.

And down.

And down.

And there I saw it.

One word. One, confusing word.

Stonehenge

197

And that was that.

Stonehenge?

What? What was I supposed to do at Stonehenge? Who was this?!
The Challenger? So Ian was calling himself the Challenger now, was he?
And he was making anonymous 'suggestions', was he? Suggestions he
knew I'd have to say Yes to? Upping the stakes? Stepping over the line?
Ordering me about? Doing precisely the thing I'd told him not to do!

I read it again. *Why not go to Stonehenge*? But *why Stonehenge*?

I was filled with a sudden rage. Who the hell did he think he was,
setting up free e-mail addresses, and calling himself the Challenger? Did
he think he could beat me? Did he think I'd just roll over and stop, opening the door wide to his punishment?

The thing to do was surprise him. Shock him. Demonstrate my abilities. Demonstrate my commitment. I'd do this – I'd go to Stonehenge.
Not tomorrow. Not next week. I'd do it *now*. I could be there and back
in just over five hours, if the wind was behind me and the traffic forgiv-
ing. And then I'd find Ian, I'd show him the evidence, I'd throw him into
submission, and I'd put an end to the immature silliness of the type of
man who'd call himself 'the Challenger'.

'The Challenger,' I muttered to myself as I walked to the car. 'Who
calls himself the Challenger?'

I was right. It was a *pathetic* way for a grown man to behave.

I jumped into the Yesmobile, and started to drive.

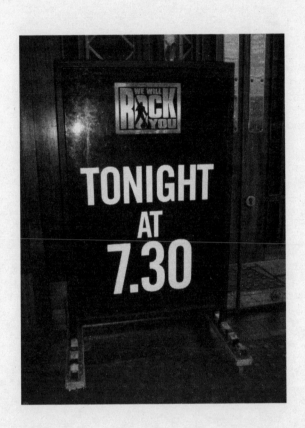

12

*In which a Friendship is brought into Doubt,
and Daniel buys some new Spectacles*

I was driving at full pelt back towards London.

I'd been to Stonehenge. I'd got out of the car. I'd had my picture taken. And now I was on my way to find Ian, confront him, show him the evidence, and tell him he was getting in the way.

His interference was actually quite annoying. He knew why I was doing this. He knew it was something for *me*. This wasn't a stupid boy-project ... this was important. Sure, it felt a little pointless from time to time ... but that's only because I hadn't worked out what the point was yet. And how was I supposed to do that when Ian was prancing about in his flat with a mask on, pretending to be the Challenger, and probably spending his time designing little 'Challenger' logos and sewing a special Lycra Challenger suit? I couldn't fathom why he thought it would be in any way useful to try and trip me up like this.

I pulled up at a service station somewhere in Wiltshire and got my phone out. I texted Ian.

WHERE WILL YOU BE IN TWO HOURS?

I'd been sitting in my small green Yes-related car for several hours and needed to stretch my legs. I stretched them as far as the mini-mart. By which I mean I walked across the forecourt; not that I have magic extendable legs.

Inside, the man behind the counter put down his paper and said hello. I said hello back.

'Is that your car?' he said, despite the fact that I was the only person for miles around and he'd just seen me get out of it.

'Yes,' I said.

'Odd, isn't it?'

'Yes,' I said.

'Where did you get it, if you don't mind me asking?'

'I bought it at a party,' I said, a little grumpily.

'Oh. A car party?'

I have no idea what a car party is.

I found a pasty, shoved it in the petrol station microwave, set it for thirty seconds and thought about what lay ahead of me. But my thoughts were instantly interrupted by the beep-beep of my phone.

I'LL BE IN STARBUCKS, CARNABY STREET. WHY?

There was no time to reply. I was on a mission. I had to get going; move fast. I was out the door and in the car before the microwave even pinged.

'Excuse me,' said a man, suddenly to my right. 'Would you have a moment to talk about Save the Whales?'

I was striding down Carnaby Street towards Starbucks and I wasn't in the mood for conversation.

'Yes, Yes I would,' I said, stopping dead in my tracks. This joker was no match for me. 'But can I go first?'

'Er … how do you mean—' he said.

'Did you know that the UK is the world's fourth richest country and yet more than two million pensioners live below the poverty line?'

'Um—'

'Did you know that there are over 11 million pensioners in this country?'

'Sorry, do—'

'Did you know that a third of pensioner households lived in poverty in the year 2000?'

'Uh, no—'

'Just a few pounds each month can keep a pensioner warm and fed all year round. Is that something you might be interested in?'

'Er … yes … I guess—'

'See that man in the green Adopt-a-Granny bib over there?'

'Yes?'

'He'll give you the appropriate forms.'

I strode on, leaving a confused and bewildered whale-saver behind me. Strode on, towards Ian. Towards vengeance.

When I arrived, he was just sitting there, all sweetness and light. He'd ordered a latte and a tiny muffin.

'Well, I'm back,' I said, standing over him. 'And I've got the evidence.'

I handed him the digital camera. He put his newspaper down and studied it.

'You appear to be showing me a picture of you with a small sign saying "Happy Now?"'.

'Yes. So are you? Are you *happy* now?'

'Is that Stonehenge?'

'Of *course* it's Stonehenge. So are you happy now?'

'Am I happy that you've been to Stonehenge?'

'Yes.'

'Why would that make me happy? Because unless you won it in a raffle, you standing in front of Stonehenge isn't at the top of my make-me-happy list.'

'Oh, so it *doesn't* make you happy? I suppose it's because I'm not wearing a hat, is it? I can wear a hat if you like. I can wear it right *now*, in fact.'

I whipped the baseball cap out of my jacket and fixed it to my head. I stared at Ian, and pointed at the hat. He took it all in.

'Now you appear to be wearing a baseball cap with the word YES on it.'

'Yes. Well done. I do. This must be a pretty great day for you. You must be over the bloody moon.'

Ian sat back in his chair.

'Danny ... I've haven't got a clue what you're on about.'

And I looked into his eyes.

And annoyingly, I believed him.

'So if *you're* not the Challenger, then who is?' I said.

We'd moved the conversation into the pub opposite Starbucks.

'Well, I don't know,' said Ian. 'I mean, why would they send you to Stonehenge? It's a bit bloody mysterious, that. Stonehenge must be a clue.'

I thought about it. Had I met any druids along the way? Maybe the Starburst Group had realised that there was more to my Yeses than I'd let on – that I wasn't just 'being more open' as I'd claimed. Or maybe they thought aliens had built Stonehenge and wanted a second opinion?

'Have you told anyone, Ian? Anyone at all?'

'No.'

'Not even Wag? You haven't told Wag, have you?'

'No. Have you?'

'Why would I ask you if you'd told Wag if I'd already told him?'

'I don't know, Dan. This is all very confusing. It's like someone's out to get you. I guess it *could* be Wag. I mean, he's *bound* to suspect *something*.'

'How come?'

'How come? Because he was out with you right at the start, when you told that bloke you were looking at his girlfriend. You always say Yes when he suggests going for a pint, when you'd done pretty much the opposite for most of the year. You sent him flowers because you saw a sign saying Why Not Say It With Flowers. He knows about all the trouble you've had by saying Yes to Hanne. It could be him, Dan. It really could.'

Oh my God.

It was *blatantly* Wag.

'So what should I do?'

'You've got two options. Confront him, or confound him.'

Ian was right. I either took a risk and told a man who may or may not be the Challenger that I was the Yes Man… or I exposed him to my steely determination. I showed him just how seriously I was taking this. I demonstrated my new-found abilities, my new-found openness, and where life could take you if you used just one little word …

'I'm going to confound him,' I said. 'I'm going to display the very essence of Yes.'

'The Yessence,' said Ian.

'I'll show him the way.'

'The Way of Yes. You can teach him a Yesson. Take him on a Yescapade!'

And then I took my phone out, dialled Wag's number, and casually asked him if he fancied a night out.

He said Yes.

We arranged to meet at 6 pm at the Pride of Spitalfields – a tiny pub just off Brick Lane packed with old men and London hipsters – and from there we would grab some food. And food wouldn't be a problem. Brick Lane is *lined* with curryhouses. It's a street in which dozens of men take to the pavements to greet you and persuade you in, with promises of free wine and discounts that they conveniently forget about when handing you the bill.

We found one such man the moment we left the pub.

'My friends, come in …' he said, making insanely welcoming gestures with his hands. 'Fantastic food here …'

Oh, this was going to be sweet. I was going to challenge the dark and brooding presence of the Challenger himself. On my terms. And my turf.

We did as he said and sat down to eat. I had the Dansak, as is right and proper. Wag had a bhuna, the mullet-haired idiot. And then, tummies full, we ordered the bill.

'This is on me, Wag,' I said, and he looked impressed when I very purposefully showed him a wallet full of new Yes-related credit cards. I paid up, and we left.

Another man was on our backs almost immediately.

'Food? You come in here, very good discount for you …'

Wag patted his stomach – the international sign of 'I've eaten, thanks …' – but I was having none of it. I bellowed a 'Yes!', dragged Wag into the curryhouse and immediately ordered some poppadoms. Wag had a beer.

'Jesus,' he said. 'How hungry *are* you?'

'I'm not hungry at all,' I said, snapping a poppadom in two and trying to look mysterious. 'I'm not hungry in the *least*.' Wag looked at me a bit oddly.

From there, we jumped into a black cab and headed into town. I had a little surprise lined up for Wag.

'What are those?' he said.

'Tickets,' I said.

'What for?'

'A musical.'

'A *musical*?' said Wag, alarmed. '*What* musical? Why?'

'I was walking through Leicester Square today, Wag. A ticket tout offered me two tickets for the price of one for tonight's performance. So that is why we are going.'

'But I don't want to go to a musical! *What* musical?'

'*We Will Rock You.*'

'The *Queen* musical? I don't want to go to the Queen musical!'

'We are going to see the Queen musical, because I have already said Yes to it, and then we are going to do whatever you want. Do you understand? *Whatever* you want …'

Three hours later we were leaving the theatre and walking towards Soho. I started to sing a medley of Queen numbers. Wag didn't. He seemed to have been stunned into silence by the raw power of tonight's theatrical experience.

'So what do you want to do, Wag?' I said, stopping to hand my *We Will Rock You* t-shirt to a tramp. 'Suggest something! Anything!'

'I dunno. Pub. Whatever.'

We found the first pub we could, and left after the first pint. I was keen to show Wag what else was out there.

We crossed over the road and through Soho Square.

'Why are you so jolly?' said Wag. 'And where are you taking me?'

I started to sing another Queen number, and we passed a man standing in the shadows saying what seemed to be the words 'Hash, coke? Hash, coke?' very quickly and very quietly.

I stopped in my tracks. Wag continued on until he noticed I'd stopped, and he turned around.

'You want hash, coke?' said the man.

'All right then!' I said, in a loud and dramatic voice, so that Wag could hear. I wanted him to know that Yes had opened my horizons, made me a man of the world. I'd already had a drag or two on a comical cigarette in Brixton, as well as a psychotropic Mindbomb. I knew what I was doing, all right!

'Dan, what are you doing?' he said, in a kind of shouted whisper, and instantly I realised I didn't really know.

'How much you want?' said the man.

'Um … I'm not sure,' I said, suddenly out of my depth. 'A pound's worth?'

'Danny!' said Wag again, and walked towards me. This made the man in the shadows a bit nervous and he started to back off.

'Wag. I am *trying* to buy a pound's worth of drugs.'

'Why?'

'Because this nice gentleman asked if I'd like any.'

'Danny. Pub. *Now.*'

Minutes later we found ourselves in a chain pub on Frith Street. We'd arrived there on a high-speed rickshaw – because a driver had asked – and our cheeks were red and our hair windswept.

'What the fuck is going on?' said Wag. 'Why are you so keen to move on? Why the *rickshaw*?'

I simply smiled, enigmatically. Now I was matching Wag drink for drink and making sure he knew it. I was showing Wag how to live. How to grab the Yeses!

At closing time, we left the pub, both with balloons, somehow, and both of us singing. Unfortunately, we were singing different songs.

'Come on, Wag … let's go to another bar … yeah?'

'No, Dan. I've had enough … "fun".'

'Come on! It'll be brilliant! We can stand in the corner and awkwardly look at girls! We can say Yes to *life*!'

'Stop bullying me! I feel a bit sick …'

'One more, Wag! Yes?'

Wag looked a broken man. I had truly taught him a lesson.

'One more,' he said.

Now we were in Madame Jo Jo's, deep in the heart of seedy Soho. We were drinking out of cans and Wag had begun to sway. I was worse. Only the adrenaline of each Yes moment was keeping me on my feet. Another novelty tequila man was here, though, and Wag and I forced a shot each before Wag grabbed my arm and said, 'Enough … enough … *please* …'

Was it a cry for help? Or – more likely – an admission of *guilt*? I knew the time was near.

Minutes later we were stumbling down the street towards a cab rank. Wag could hardly speak. I had started to be able to see properly only if I closed one eye.

'So then …' I slurred. 'That was an interesting evening. What are your conclusions? Do you have anything to say? Is there anything you wish to apologise for?'

Wag looked a little too shellshocked to apologise, if I'm honest.

And then the words we really didn't need to hear …

'Looking for fun, boys?'

I looked up to see a woman, sitting on a stool under a sign that read MODELS. I tried to focus my eyes. Her hair was elaborate, and her dress sense revealing.

'Good show on downstairs. Five pounds each.'

Shit.

I looked to Wag. He shook his head. I nodded mine. For a second, it looked like he was about to cry.

I'm not proud of this. Particularly as I can't blame it on the booze.

But I gave the woman ten pounds, and I dragged Wag in with me, through some red velvet curtains and into the seedy lair within.

It would be the final proof he would need of my commitment.

* * *

I awoke the next morning and tried my best to understand what was going on. I was lying in a position I'm not sure anyone's ever been in before; at least not by choice, or not during wrestling.

I knew I was on my own, but there seemed to be too many arms for that to be possible. I was face down on the sofa, my cheeks wet with dribble, and both the TV and the radio were on. As was my computer. As were all the lights. And I mean every single light I had. The ceiling lights, the lamps, a small anglepoise ... I'm sure if I'd checked the cupboards I'd have found all the torches and Christmas lights on, too. I had clearly come home drunk and happy and wanting to keep the night going – despite the fact that all I'd done was turn everything on, check my e-mails, and pass out on the sofa.

I was fully clothed, intensely dry-mouthed and I was aching all over. I was also boiling ... the sun was streaming in through the windows and I was half-hidden by a spare duvet. I started to wonder why on earth I was on the sofa. Perhaps I'd had a fight with myself in the night and banished myself to the living room. That seemed unfair to me. In relationships, I'd always been the one who'd ended up sleeping on the sofa. You'd think living on my own would mean I got the bed. But a vague memory reached me, clouded and slow. I began to remember that in my drunken state I'd decided it wouldn't be all that wise to try and start negotiating the stairs up to the bedroom. But worrying that I would get cold in the night, I knew I'd need to fetch a duvet. So I ran upstairs to get one and bring it down. At no point had the all-too-logical idea of just staying up there hit me. I'd even gone for the spare duvet – the one hidden away at the back of a cupboard, the one I'd have to stand on a chair to get at. Worse, I could remember feeling rather proud of myself for being so sensible, as I stumbled back down the stairs, duvet in arms, ready to pass out.

The world was still blurry, and so I reached out to grab my glasses. I grabbed a pen instead. I reached again. A remote control. I gradually worked out that in order to find my glasses, I would have to *find my glasses*. Say what you like about me, but I'm bloody good at problem-solving.

But it was proving a difficult problem to solve. I knew my specs had to be somewhere, and they had to be somewhere in here. I tried the coffee table, making huge sweeping gestures with my arms, but couldn't find them. I tried the sofa, the side table and then the floor, scuttling over to any object I could make out and sticking my face a mere inch away from it in order to see what it was. Objects that to someone with half-decent vision could never in a million years be mistaken for a pair of glasses were scrutinised, prodded and picked up. At one point I imagined a shoe could have been my glasses. It wasn't. It was a shoe. Moments later I was studying a tiny carved wooden elephant close up, just in case it had a couple of flip-out arms I could use to rest it on my face. Had a window cleaner decided that today was the day he'd buff my windows up, I hate to think what he'd have told his mates, after watching a grown man scuttling around his flat on all fours, in his pants, his face an inch from the floor, picking up random objects and holding them far too close to his eyes. Mind you, I suppose that could actually have happened. I wouldn't have bloody seen him.

I was starting to panic, now. My glasses were the one thing I needed to function in this world; the one thing I couldn't do without. They were the only thing that stopped me from having to stand a little too closely to strangers, the one thing that helped me retain my Britishness. How drunk had I been last night? Had I said Yes to someone who wanted my glasses? Could I have eaten them? Or had I lost them earlier on in the evening but not noticed? Perhaps I'd put my blurry vision down to drunkenness when in fact it was because I'd lost my specs? Had someone stolen them in the night? Perhaps a cat burglar was stealing them to order, like Nicholas Cage steals posh cars in *Gone In Sixty Seconds*? It seemed unlikely. It would have made the papers by now. Not that most of the victims would've been able to read it.

With growing desperation and a thudding head, I checked the bathroom, and the stairs, and the living room again. I tried retracing my steps from the night before but what with them being drunken steps they would have made me quite dizzy, and in my current state I could do without being dizzy. You'll know what I mean if you've ever spun a blind man.

Again I checked the bathroom, and the bedroom, and the living room again. It was a painstaking process, taking up much of the morning, and finally, with great sorrow and confusion, I was forced to admit it. I had lost my glasses. *I had lost my glasses*!

This, as the bespectacled among you will know, is a horrifying prospect for anyone low on sight. The world's a big place. It's full of … you know … *things*. Big, blurry things. It's easy for a spectacles-wearer devoid of spectacles to get lost in a world like that. To mistake buses for dragons. Short people for goblins. Men with beards for wizards. This was going to be terrifying! How would I know what I was wearing any

209

more? How would I know what I was cooking? How could I pretend to be considering an important problem, without some glasses to pop into the corner my mouth while staring into the middle distance? I had to find them!

The phone rang. I was thrown into panic again. The phone! My God, the phone! How would I ever find the phone!

And then I remembered the phone was where it always was, so I ambled over and picked it up.

'Hello?'

'Dan, it's Ian.'

'Oh, Ian, thank God!'

'What's the matter?'

'What's the *matter*? Can't you *tell*? I've lost my glasses!'

'Oh,' said Ian. 'Never mind.'

'Never mind?' I said, outraged. This was typical of the full-sighted. And of the way people with disabilities like mine are treated by society at large. 'What do you mean, never mind? I'm going to Edinburgh in a couple of days! I can't set off without my glasses! I'll never get out of London!'

'Get some new ones.'

'"Get some new ones"?' My God, this man had a cheek. How did he … well, Yes, I suppose I *could* get some new ones, actually.

'Hey – what a great opportunity to change your look!' said Ian. 'Go to an optician's and say Yes to the first pair of glasses they make you try on!'

'I don't *want* a new look!' I said. 'I just want my glasses back! They're like a part of me, Ian!'

'Where did you last have them?'

'On my face.'

'Have you checked there?'

'Have I checked my face?'

'All of it, I mean.'

'Oh, not all of it, no. Just the lips. Hang on, I'll check the *rest* of my face.'

'All right, all right … when did you last have them?'

'Well, last night, I suppose. If I took them out with me, that is. I'm very confused. Did I have them on last time you saw me?'

'I can't remember.'

'What do you mean, you can't remember? Surely you'd remember if I wasn't wearing my glasses?'

'So how come *you* don't remember?'

'That's different. I can't see me.'

'Well, do you remember seeing *me*?'

'Yes.'

'Well, you were wearing your glasses, then.'

I considered Ian's point. It was fairly watertight.

'So where are they then?' I said. 'Are *you* wearing them?'

'No.'

'Check.'

'Dan, I'm fairly sure I'm not wearing your glasses. Have you checked the whole flat?'

What did he think I'd been doing?

'Yes! Ian, this is bad. I don't want to start seeing dragons and goblins and wizards. I need my glasses. I can't see without them. I can't even be sure this is a phone I'm using. I could have picked *anything* up and started speaking into it.'

'Don't you have a spare pair?'

'No. Oh, hang on, though …'

Now, a spare pair I *didn't* have. But I did have *a* pair. A pair I used to use as a kid. Surely my eyes couldn't have changed that much in the last twenty years? They'd still work, wouldn't they? My mum had dropped them off at the flat a few years ago, along with a box full of other stuff I'd left at theirs …

'Ian, you're a genius,' I said.

I was sitting on a chair in front of the mirror, considering the problem.

I appeared to be a grown man, in his pants, wearing the spectacles of a small boy.

If there is indeed an afterlife, and our ancestors do, as is claimed, pop back every now and then to check up on us, then I hope they choose their moments carefully. The last thing I needed was word of this getting back to the afterlife. 'How was Danny?' one of them would say. 'Oh, fine,' the other would say. 'Although it appears he is now a simpleton.' And what would Maitreya make of it all, if he'd popped in to have a look-see? Surely this couldn't be part of his grand plan?

The phone rang. It was Ian again.

'So I just talked to Wag,' he said. 'What the hell did you do to him last night?'

'Nothing! I just showed him the Way of Yes.'

211

'He says you took him into a strip club where you were both robbed.'

'We were *invited* in. And it wasn't a strip club. It was a "gentleman's parlour". It was very classy.'

'Where was it?'

'In an alleyway.'

Ian made some kind of overly dramatic 'tsk' sound.

'And you were robbed?'

'We were *not* robbed. We simply walked in and, after seeking firm assurance that there was nothing illegal or immoral going on, sat down in a small room where a woman in a negligée poured us two warm beers, before a fat Moroccan in a suit walked in and told us the beers were fifty quid each and we would have to leave now because the show was over.'

'It was a clip joint! They're made for tourists! Not you!'

'I don't understand it. Why invite us in at all, if all you're going to do is take our money and kick us out again?'

'Wag thinks you're on the verge of a breakdown.'

'I'm not!'

'I know you're not, but he doesn't. He says you were ordering curries and then going into the restaurant next door and ordering even more.'

'Exaggeration! I had poppadoms.'

'He also says he thinks you might have a ... *thing* for him.'

'A *thing*?'

'He says the obsession with Hanne is a front. He says he first started to suspect something was up when you sent him the flowers. But he says you always agree with everything he says now, and you're always so eager to hang out with him.'

'That's hardly enough evidence to question my sexuality.'

'He also says you've got a new-found interest in musicals and have talked more than once about how men can have babies.'

'Oh.'

'Essentially,' he said, 'Wag thinks you may want to have a baby with him.'

'Ah.'

'I don't think Wag *is* the Challenger, after all.'

'No. I don't think he is, either.'

So Wag was off the list. Which was fair enough. He had proved himself to be no more than a confused friend in my ongoing battle with a shadowy and secretive enemy. No matter.

Two hours later I had braved my hangover and was in the optician's, trying to get new glasses, and hoping to God the woman behind the counter wouldn't try and suggest any fancy new children's frames.

'Okay,' she said. 'A few questions. First, your name please …'

'Wallace,' I said.

She typed 'Wallace' into her computer very slowly.

'Okay … Wallace … and your surname?'

'Oh. Sorry, that *was* my surname. Still is, in fact. My first name's Danny.'

She sighed, and made quite a show of having to press the delete key seven times.

'Okay. We'll start again. Name?'

'Danny.'

'Danny', she typed.

'And your surname?'

'Er … Wallace.'

I felt like I was being tested and was relieved when she nodded her head silently as she tapped my answers in. Phew. My name really *was* Danny Wallace.

'Now …' she said, obviously coming to the next prompted question on the screen. 'Is it "Mister"?'

Eh? Of *course* it was mister. Look at me, woman. I'm not exactly the most feminine-looking man in the world. Not unless you like your women unshaven. And … you know … *male*.

'Sorry?' I said.

'Is it "Mister" Wallace?'

She wasn't looking up. But she'd seen me come in. She could hear my voice. How could she not know? Was she afraid to guess? Despite myself, I considered her question carefully, before answering: 'Yes, it's "*Mister* Wallace".'

Perhaps it was the fact that I was wearing a small boy's pair of glasses that confused her. Perhaps she assumed I was going to say, 'No, it's *Master* Wallace, but I'm a big boy now because Mummy's sent me down the shops on my own.'

'Right … *Mister* Wallace. And is it spectacles you're after?'

Jesus. Did I look like someone who was happy with their current spectacles? No, I didn't. But then she wouldn't know that, because she was too busy staring at her screen.

'Yes.'

I watched her click Yes, before the screen changed and she asked her best question of the day …

'And are you a spectacles-wearer already?'

Am I a spectacles-wearer already? LOOK AT MY FACE. I am *clearly* a spectacles-wearer already! That is an entirely unmissable fact. I am a spectacles-wearer, and I am a *Mister*. You might as well call me 'Mister Four-Eyes Spectacles-Wearer, The Male Boy-Man Who Wears Glasses On His Face'.

Had this woman never seen either a human male *or* an established spectacles-wearer before? What was she used to? Monocled dogs?

'Am I a spectacles-wearer already?' I tried, just in case I'd misheard, and the image of a monocled dog had been wasted.

'It's for the system,' she said, looking up for the first time since sitting down, but still not registering that all the information she needed for 'the system' was literally staring her in the face.

'Yes, I am. I am a spectacles-wearer already.'

'Well, great!' she said, standing up. 'Let's get you sorted out, then.'

My new glasses would be ready in one or two hours, and, thanks to the power of Yes, I'd also agreed to undertake a free 30-day contact lens trial. With some free time suddenly in hand, I took the opportunity to run some errands to prepare myself fully for my trip up to Edinburgh.

I bought vitamins, and six pairs of black socks, and a pair of white ones, too, in the unlikely event of some surprise exercise being sprung on me up there. I wandered around TopMan for a while, but I kept catching glimpses of myself in the mirror and it was a little disconcerting. So I decided to head off and undertake another much-needed errand – one that would not require me to wear a pair of children's glasses. A haircut.

I found my way to a hairdresser's on Great Portland Street, but as I was about to enter, I received a most annoying text.

YOU OWE ME FIFTY QUID

It was from Wag. I hadn't really wanted to call him before now – the whole him-thinking-I-have-a-thing-for-him thing made that a little uncomfortable, as a prospect. And anyway, you're supposed to wait two days before calling someone after a first date.

But oh well. I suppose I had to give him his fifty quid – the fifty quid I'd made him spend on one warm beer in a Soho clip joint. You'd think he'd have let me off, what with the ticket to *We Will Rock You* and the bhuna, but I guess that's the risk you take when you're a Yesser. I texted him back and we arranged to meet briefly, later on in the afternoon.

* * *

'So …' said Scott, the kiwi hairdresser. 'The question I'm asking myself is, what are we going to do for you today?'

'Same basic shape,' I said, 'except I would like you to cut it so that it is a little shorter.'

'Understood,' said Scott, who I'm suddenly worried you will think is not simply a hairdresser from New Zealand (a kiwi *hairdresser*), but instead a hairdresser who cuts the hair off kiwis (a *kiwi* hairdresser). 'I can do that for you very easily indeed.'

But then Scott did something rather odd. He put both hands on my shoulders, and leant down to my level. We made eye contact in the mirror.

'Or …' he said. 'Do you want to try something *new*?'

Scott certainly seemed to be putting his back into this haircut. I'd had to remove my glasses – something I was only too pleased to do – while he did something fancy with a razor down the sides of my head, but it gave me a few precious and welcome moments of contemplation. That's the good thing about being short-sighted. When someone takes your glasses off, all you can do is think – not much good in a fight, admittedly, but *perfect* for the hairdresser's. And so that's what I did. I thought about the new cast of characters who'd come into my life of late … some of whom I knew, and some of whom I … well … didn't.

The thing was, if Wag wasn't the Challenger, then who was? Who was sending me odd things and taunting me? What was their objective? To tease me? To scare me? Had they really expected me to go to Stonehenge? Did they know I'd been? Was I too hasty in ruling Ian out of the equation? And where did the man on the bus fit into all of this? I suppose if the man on the bus was, in fact, Maitreya, as Brian and Pete and the Starburst Group had suggested, maybe *he* was the Challenger? Maybe I was merely a pawn in a very odd game of chess. Hey, 'Yes' rhymes with 'chess'. Maybe that was a clue. But who knew about my very important quest? Who had I …

'Okay, we're all done!'

Scott stood back from me, and I reached for my glasses.

'Great,' I said, putting them on. And then I didn't really say much at all. I just looked.

I now had very, very short hair at the sides. The top had a kind of mohawk effect, but it was much more spiky than it had ever been before, and there seemed to be something still tickling my neck … but, after a moment or two, I liked it. Kind of. I *kind of* liked it.

'I'll just show you the back,' he said, holding up a mirror, but then whipping it away again before I could really see what was going on round there.

'Er … could I just see the back again?'

'Sure,' said Scott, and he held it up, longer this time.

And I nearly swallowed my tongue.

Scott had given me … no, he couldn't have …

Could he?

I thought that …

Christ.

Scott had given me …

A *mullet*.

I was now a man with a mullet wearing the glasses of a boy.

I waited in the Yorkshire Grey for Wag. I'd picked up my new specs, thank heavens, and I'd tried to make my new haircut a little less manic by going to the toilets and smearing water all over my head. It just made the wax Scott had put in there go all runny, and my hair had now set in a much more unfortunate style than before. I winced. Somehow, I had found the one hairdresser's in Great Britain who shared Wag's conviction that the mullet was a somehow acceptable haircut.

Oh, God! *Wag*!

Moments later, he walked in, and just stared at me.

'What the hell's happened to you?'

'I had … a haircut.'

'Let me see,' he said, and reluctantly, I let him.

'What do you think?' I said.

There was a slightly awkward pause.

'So you decided to get a mullet.'

I nodded, a bit self-consciously.

'It appears that way,' I said.

'Right,' said Wag. 'Only … well … *I've* got a mullet.'

Bollocks. He'd noticed. He'd noticed that we'd *both got mullets*.

'Yes …' I said. 'I suppose so …'

'So now we've *both* got one. We are two men, both with mullets.'

I smiled, awkwardly. Maybe that would trick him into thinking this was a good thing. I don't know if you've ever turned up at a party wearing the same top as someone else. It's much the same when it appears you have specifically attempted to base yourself on someone else's entire look.

'Well … mine's not really a mullet,' I tried. 'I mean yours … Yes … that *is* a mullet. And a fine one. But mine isn't a mullet. Not really.'

'Well, what is it? It *looks* the same as mine.'

'It really isn't the same as yours. Believe me. It's mulletesque, certainly, but it's really only a very *small* mullet. If anything, it's a mull*ette*.'

There was a long and cavernous pause.

I cleared my throat.

Somewhere, a floorboard creaked.

I could see deep concern in Wag's eyes. I thought about what Ian had said. I thought about how this must look to a man who already suspected I had a crush on him.

'It doesn't mean I want to have babies with you,' I said.

Another substantial pause.

'I have to go now,' he said.

I walked into my flat that night and immediately found my glasses. They were on the floor next to the sofa.

Minutes later, Ian texted me.

WAG JUST PHONED. HEARD ABOUT YOUR NEW IMAGE. LOOK WHO'S STALKING!

Oh, God.

Still. Wag wouldn't have to worry about me for a while. I was off to Scotland the next morning, after all, and looking forward to it. My train was booked, my socks were packed, and I couldn't wait to get up there and begin my important BBC duties.

But I was feeling chirpy for another reason, too. I'd returned home that evening to find a small white box outside my door. A small white box that had made its way all the way from Tucson, Arizona, to my flat in London's glamorous East End. I'd ripped it open and found a world of wonder within … a video, a CD, some incense, a small laminated clip-on badge and a book of handy speeches.

At last … I was a *minister*!

The Rev. Amy E. Long from the Universal Life Church had sent me everything I needed to set up a church of my own – including a small sign which I could stick on my car which read: 'THE DRIVER OF THIS CAR IS A LICENSED MINISTER ON OFFICIAL BUSINESS'! This was great! Now I could break the law, whenever the urge took me! Thank you, God!

I even had my own certificates of marriage, commitment and baby naming to hand out to people after my special ceremonies! I could *name babies*! I don't think I've ever been so excited. But what would I name them? Was that my decision, or the parents'? Could I just walk about, naming them as I saw fit? That would be brilliant.

'I name thee "Bit of a bloater"!'

'But his name's Tim!'

'Not any more it's not. And that other one next to him – let him forever be known as … "Chao-Lee – Child of the Stars…"'

Parking wherever I wanted, naming whoever I chose … I would be a maverick minister on the edge.

I wanted to know more about the Universal Life Church, though, and so sauntered over to my computer and fired it up.

Ten minutes later, and I'd decided I was going to buy a cassock. I was feeling deeply spiritual. But this was to stop the very second I checked my e-mail.

I was pleased to see that I had one from Lizzie. But I didn't understand it.

>To: Danny
>From: Lizzie
>Subject: RE: soho ho ho ho

Danny,

Okay! I believe you! So get me a ticket then!

L
x

Eh?

What was that supposed to mean? She believes me about what? She'd clearly sent an e-mail to the wrong Danny … I hadn't asked her to believe *anything* …

I nearly deleted it, but then stopped in my tracks … I studied the subject line … Soho ho ho ho? And it had *RE:* on the front. It was a *reply*. She couldn't have hit 'reply' and mailed the wrong Danny …

But what was she replying to?

When was the last time I'd e-mailed Lizzie? And about what?

Oh, God, what had I done? My cheeks started to burn.

I knew that feeling and I hated it – the feeling that creeps up on you

218

side by side with a hangover … the feeling that you may have started sending e-mails at the worst possible time to be sending e-mails … when you were drunk. E-mails that, at nine o'clock on a Monday morning may have lost some of their Saturday-night vibe. E-mails that were hilarious or fascinating when they left your flat at four in the morning, but which had somehow lost their appeal or relevance the second they flew down the wires. What had I written? What had I said? Had I poured my heart out? Had I proclaimed undying love? Had I bored her to tears?

No. No, I couldn't have.

I found my Sent Mail folder.

Oh, shit.

Shit shit shit.

I *had*. I *had* sent her an e-mail. I had sent her an e-mail at 04.26 that morning … I'd mailed her after stumbling in from that Soho clip joint after a night of careless and determined Yeses …

I clicked my e-mail open and held my breath, readying myself for the worst. And I saw, instantly, that it was pretty bloody bad …

>To: Lizzie
>From: Danny
>Subject: Soho ho ho ho

Lizziiiiiie!

How is australia is austrlia good? Sems like it woul dbe good in australian. Have you met any australians yet hahahaha.

I am havin a great time here in london englan an have just had a night out with wag remember wag he is ok. we ended up in a place, it was a gentleman parlour in case anyone ask you and a moroccan man said get out you tossbag.s

hey listen i an going to the edinburgh festival to work for a bit you would love it their. it is big and funny and loadsa people. why don't you come, it'll be brilliant if you come there you could get a train like me. do you have trains in australia.

okay maybe see you in edinburgh its good there let me know

you are really cool an pretty an i miss you

danyy

Christ. No wonder I didn't understand the e-mail from Lizzie. I didn't bloody understand the e-mail from *me*.

My first reaction was embarrassment. Embarrassment at my drunken, pointless ramblings. My second was one of sickly realisation …

Because slowly, slowly I was piecing it together …

I had said Lizzie should come to Edinburgh.

And Lizzie had said … *Yes.*

Yes, even though she was in Australia.

But not just Yes.

She'd said, '*Okay! I believe you! So get me a ticket then!*'

Which was, in effect, a suggestion.

A jokey one, yes, and a silly one, true – but *a suggestion nevertheless* …

Let's face it – there was no way in the world that Lizzie could think I was serious. I was a drunk man, suggesting she take a train – a *train!* – from Australia, on the basis that Edinburgh was 'good' because it was 'big and funny and loadsa people'.

She was humouring me. In a sweet and gentle way. But still only humouring me.

I paced the flat.

What was I going to do about this?

Okay, okay. Let's say I did it, let's say I got her a ticket. She would never, in a million years, get on the plane. Why would she? She hardly knew me. She'd almost known me, once, but that was months ago and miles away. She was on a different continent now. She had a different life now. And anyway – with Wag and Hanne, I already had *two* people who thought I was obsessed with them – I wasn't trying to make up the *set*.

What should I do?

What if I got her a ticket and on some mad whim she *did* come? What then? Why spoil a beautiful friendship? Sure, something could have happened, once, but not now. And if she turned up and we didn't get on any more, well, what then?

It was stupid. It was stupid. It was so bloody stupid.

But it was a *suggestion*.

No. Sod that. A ticket from *Australia*, for God's sake! *And* she'd probably want a return one! I couldn't afford that. No way. They were ... *how* much were they?

I scrambled on to the Internet.

£545! Minimum!

I can't go around spending £545 minimum on girls I'm not even going out with! I can't even go around spending £545 minimum on girls I *am* going out with!

Somewhere, sometime, I would have to draw a line with this Yes thing. It was starting to cross financial and emotional barriers. And not just mine – how would Lizzie feel about this? It'd be a hell of a lot of pressure to put on her.

So it was simple.

I couldn't do it.

I sighed.

I had failed.

I would tell Ian in the morning. I would tell him that he was right. That I was afraid. That there are some things you just can't say Yes to, no matter *where* they might lead.

I zipped up my bag, put my credit card-sized Ministry ID in my wallet – just in case there were any baby-naming emergencies in Scotland – and, with a heavy heart, popped the wallet in my pocket.

And then ...

... and then I got it out again.

Something had caught my eye.

A silver, shiny, gleaming credit card.

A new *type* of credit card.

A virgin, unsullied, never-before-used type of credit card. With a substantial credit limit. And six months at 0 per cent APR.

I took it out and I looked at it.

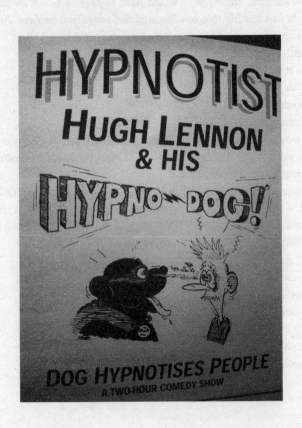

13

In which Daniel receives a Very Pleasant Piece of News

Edinburgh crept up on me outside the window of the train. I packed away my book and notes and tucked myself into my jacket.

The book, which arrived that morning, was called *EMBRACE YES: The Power of Spiritual Affirmation*, and had been sent to me anonymously – by, I guessed, 'the Challenger' – in a bid to encourage me to stop my Yes-related nonsense and come to my senses. My heart sank as I'd opened it up. There had been a note with the book, saying, simply, *Maybe you can pick up some tips.* I'd read as much of it as I could without going insane – the back cover describes it as 'a journey to the very heart of acceptance and aliveness through affirmation', and 'an opportunity to meditate and reflect on the aliveness of affirming reality and to live with the attitude of Yes'. I figured that was an attitude I was already living with rather nicely, thank you, and stopped reading to concentrate on who might have sent it to me.

I'd compiled a list, as we'd trundled through Berwick-upon-Tweed.

Suspects
Ian (he may have been cleverly bluffing)
Brian and the Starburst Group
The man on the bus/Maitreya/the Baby Jesus
Elias Brown, if he is psychic or something

People who might have it in for me
Hanne's new bloke, Seb (?)
The man I beat up in that club (sort of)
Hanne (for ruining her date)

Wag (who may think he's copyrighted the mullet)
Ian again (chance for him to punish me, if he ever comes up with something)

But try as I might, I couldn't quite see any of them fitting the bill.

It was a crisp and brisk August afternoon as I stepped off the train and into a taxi. I stared out of the window as we drove from Waverley Station to the Travelodge I'd book myself into for the next couple of weeks.

I tutted to myself. The Challenger was clever, wily. The Challenger was using psychology to intimidate. The Challenger was vindictive, and bitter, and was taking an active stand against my behaviour. The Challenger had knowledge, and was using that knowledge to gain power over me. The Challenger liked Stonehenge.

It was, all in all, a puzzling case, but one that I was determined to solve. It just didn't seem fair. I'd only been doing this about two months, and already I'd picked up a mortal enemy.

But I also had far more on my mind.

What – *what* – had I done where Lizzie was concerned?

Well … I'd bought her a ticket, of course. I had to. A ticket from Melbourne to Edinburgh, via London. It was there for her – if she wanted it. It was up to her, now. Up to Lizzie. I was taking no more responsibility for having no responsibility. I had simply forwarded her the airline confirmation e-mail, attached a short note saying, 'Here y'go, then …' locked the flat up, and headed for the train, my neck prickling with awkward British embarrassment. Another foolish foray into Level Five completed.

Yes, I'm well aware it was stupid. In fact, my trip to see Dr Molly Van Brain aside, it was perhaps the stupidest thing I'd ever done. The thing is, it would almost have been romantic, had I done it of my own volition. But I knew Lizzie and I were doomed. I knew it from the start. And now I'd spent £545 just to prove it. But a Yes is a Yes, and in some ways, by saying that one little word, I'd rid myself of a problem. By saying Yes to that ticket, I'd made it not my responsibility any more. I didn't have to think about it. Now it was *her* problem to deal with. Now *she'd* have to sit there and worry about what to do … whether to get on a plane or ignore me for ever or break it to me gently or ridicule me to her friends for the rest of her natural Australian life. Getting that credit card out wasn't as brave as I would like to think it was. If anything, it was typically male – push the problem to her side of the fence. The way inept, immature blokes one day decide to treat their girlfriends badly in the hope that they'll get dumped before they have to do the dumping.

And as well as cowardly and embarrassed, I felt slightly ... I dunno ... *creepy* about having done it. I'd definitely lost any semblance of 'cool', now. I'd bought a ticket to Britain for a girl I hardly knew. She would now either think I was some kind of misguided man of means, or an *incredibly* lazy stalker. The kind of stalker who'd say to his stalkee, 'Um, look, I'm a bit busy at the moment – any chance you could come to *me* this time?'

It was a ludicrous situation.

But the fact remained ... it was *her* situation.

The thing to do now was forget about it.

So here I was in Edinburgh, in a black cab on my way to the hotel, and for a while, at least, I could pretend my troubles were behind me. Maybe without Ian on my case, without Hanne and Seb to bump into, with no Wag to clash hairstyles with, no Elias or Pete to claim Jesus had been spotted in the Pilau bloody Palace and – fingers crossed – no Challenger to breathe down my neck, I could treat Yes just as I had in the beginning. I could start afresh in a whole new city.

'Danny! Take a seat, mate!'

I was in the courtyard of the Pleasance Theatre, and I was with Tom. There was a buzz in the air. The festival was still in early days, and all around us were theatregoers, journalists, comedy fans, actors, artists and – mainly – drunkards. The weather had lifted, slightly, and the air was warm.

'So the plan is this ... we want to find the next generation of entertainers. You know? But not the obvious ones that there's already a buzz about. People we can work with. Develop. So see as much as you can. We're looking for ... *quirky*.'

'Quirky. Right.'

'See things you wouldn't normally see. Shows that no other broadcasters will be looking for. We want to find talent in the hidden places, and then see what we can do with them. Have you got a brochure?'

'No, not yet ...'

'Here's mine ... have a look through, see what grabs you. I've got to go to a show, now, but you've got my number ...'

'Yep.'

'Okay. See you in a bit ...'

And with that, he was off. I ambled over to the bar to get myself a pint and sat down to make my way through the fringe brochure and decide how I should go about my day. My mission was to see shows – and that wasn't a bad mission, as missions go. I cheerily opened the brochure at a random page and took in a show blurb.

Death is death, but life is death – you are already dead! Or dying from so many things!! Life is a struggle, grief is a pool in which you drown. The insanity and violence of love abounds. The madness of struggle. The conquest of death.

Now, there's quirky, and there's utterly bloody terrifying. I didn't feel this show fitted with the former. I was sure, though, that I'd find something to fit the bill. I flicked to another page.

Together we are, yet together we can't be. Togetherness and the togethered – together they are as one, but Together seeks to explore not oneness, but twoness ... a play in two halves, sewn together and shown as one. A physical and metaphorical exploration.

I decided to have a baked potato instead.

But before I could even stand up, someone had slammed a leaflet down on the table in front of me.

'Are you looking for a show?'

A girl with dreads in her hair and glitter on her face looked at me with hope in her eyes.

'Yes,' I said.

'Gilded Balloon, five-thirty. We got three stars in the *Scotsman*.'

'Oh,' I said. 'Is it quirky?'

'It's a play about hope, love, betrayal, rape and death.'

'Right,' I said. 'A bit of everything, then.'

'Well ... mainly betrayal, rape and death.'

'Hmm. I'm kind of looking for ... *lighter* stuff.'

'It's very light,' she said. 'It's very funny.'

'Is it?'

'Yes ... but also ... *not*.'

I looked at my watch. Five o'clock. That would give me just enough time to go and get my food – I could pop down to the Tempting Tattie on

Jeffrey Street, and be sitting, satisifed and alert, in what she had now decided to assure me was a frankly hilarious play minutes later. I folded the flier and popped it in my pocket, thanked her, and was just about to stand up, when, from another angle, I heard the words ...

'Hello. Are you looking for a show to see?'

Oh my God.

Dear God, the leafleters.

I had managed to make it out of The Pleasance with only six new leaflets stuck in my pocket, but now, approaching the Royal Mile, I saw them.

Leafleters. Everywhere. Like a wide and rampant pack of wolves.

I had forgotten what Edinburgh was like. For one month, the entire world descends upon the city for the largest arts festival on the planet. There are literally thousands of shows to see – each one usually performing more than 25 times. That's a lot of tickets that need to be sold. And that's a lot of leafleters trying to sell them.

The desperation in the air was palpable. And for miles around, all I could see were leafleters ... leafleters with leaflets. There were leafleters dressed as dogs. Leafleters dressed as ballerinas. One leafleter who appeared to be dressed as a giant, grinning apple. And they were closing in. It was like the nightmare of the charity bib people in London – but without the oh-so-lovable excuse of 'doing it for the children. Sorry, I mean the commission.'

> 'Are you looking for a show? Ten past eight at the Assembly
>   Rooms. It's about ...'
> 'Looking for a show? Clowning and Russian dance! Six forty
>   at the ...'
> 'Would you like to hear about my play? It's a powerful one-
>   woman piece about ...'

I was striding quickly down the Mile, now, my head down and my hands out, taking every leaflet that was offered to me, stuffing them in my pockets, and watching any free time I might possibly have had disappear before my eyes. I was beginning to realise that if I wanted to get through this festival alive, I was going to have to be very, very careful about where I went and at what time of day. I could be the first person killed under the weight of a thousand leaflets. I decided I'd need to sit down with my diary and work out how to see as many of the shows I had leaflets for as possible. And then I would need to work out a system of not actually taking any more leaflets. And how was I going to explain my choice of shows to the BBC? Was this what they were paying me for?

Finally, I made it to the Tempting Tattie. I had one with cheese on. And then I went to watch a play about the lighter side of rape.

It was late. I was in the bar of the Assembly Rooms, catching up with Tom.

'Good day? What did you see?'

I took a deep breath.

'A disturbing play about betrayal and death, a powerful one-woman piece about the search for identity in an indentitiless world, a clown, and a late-night close-up magic show by an inept Dutchman. You?'

Tom counted in his head.

'Ross Noble.'

I had worked out my professional itinerary for Edinburgh fairly quickly, and I was feeling quite pleased with myself. I'd noticed in the *Scotsman* that they had a daily box-out of Five Recommended Shows You Really Must See. This, I decided, would be my system. I would see whatever they recommended, time slots permitting, while at the same time working my way through the leaflets I already had. And I'd also worked out my new system for avoiding the rampant terrorism of future leafleters. Sure, it wasn't quite in the spirit of being the Yes Man, but neither was spending 18 hours a day in tiny black rooms watching American students adapt Shakespeare to bhangra. So what was my system? I bought a pair of cheap black headphones from Argos and had them permanently in my pocket. Upon spotting a leafleter, I would pop them on, people would see me coming, realise I was immersed in a world of loud and impenetrable music, and leave me alone. It couldn't fail.

It did.

'What did you see today?' asked Tom, the next night, propping up the bar at the Assembly Rooms once more.

'A play about famine, a ninety-minute monologue about a pension book, a Canadian dance troupe who were clearly hung-over, a man who just sat there and said we should think, the Oxford Revue, and a bhangra version of Shakespeare by some guys from Nevada.'

I was tired and I looked it.

'How about you?'

Tom held a ticket up.

'Adam Hills.'

Oh.

'How about tomorrow, Danny? Anything on?'

'Yep,' I said, heavily. 'I've got my tickets already. Seven shows. Five of them *Scotsman*-recommended. First one's at ten.'

'Seven shows,' said Tom, under his breath. 'Goodness.'

'And you?' I said.

'I dunno,' he said. 'I thought I might have a night off.'

There was, of course, another reason for throwing myself into the Edinburgh Festival with such gusto. While I was sitting quietly in the back room of a pub watching Bavarian physical theatre ('Crucial' – *The Times*), I couldn't be out there, roaming around, getting myself into too much trouble. And, more importantly, I couldn't be in an Internet café, risking the wrath of the Challenger and ... well ... the rejection of Lizzie.

That, probably more than anything, was what concerned me; the Challenger I could maybe take. The fierce blunt punch of rejection, on the other hand ...

How would she have reacted? What would she think of me now? Had I spoilt things? The facts of the matter were: if Lizzie *had* written back, my heart would doubtless sink. And if she *hadn't* ... well, there was a chance it could *break*.

Suddenly, my phone rang.

'Dan? It's Ian.'

'Hello, Ian.'

'Are you enjoying Edinburgh?'

'Yes, thank you.'

'Seen any shows yet?'

'One or two.'

'Good. Well, listen. I was thinking.'

'Go on ...'

'I was trying to work it out. And I reckon I may know who the Challenger is.'

And, after a moment or two, he told me.

And it made complete and utter sense.

I said goodbye to Ian, got my diary out, and found the scrap of paper on which I'd already tried to solve the case. I added one more line.

Jason, the bloke at the party.

Jason!

Jason, the bloke at the party! A man who could *easily* have got my details from his friend Thom! A man who not only *knew* about my Yeses ... but *despised* them! A man filled with an unquenchable rage that he would be only too pleased to unleash on me! A man who said No for a living – a man who was my opposite! A Lex Luther to my Superman! A No Man to my Yes Man!

It was Jason!

I knew just what to do next. I had never replied to Jason's initial e-mail – the one sending me to Stonehenge. But I still had it. I could e-mail him back. I could e-mail Jason!

I was filled with confidence and power. It was time to strike back, before he upped the stakes. I found an Internet café just off Princes Street, and ordered myself a cup of tea. It was time to check my e-mail, and to send a couple. I reasoned that if Jason had indeed issued any more demands or instructions, I now possessed the strength to deal with them. The upper hand would soon be mine. For I was about to unmask him. There would be no more hats, no more books, and no more impromptu trips to Stonehenge. There would just be one very embarrassed man in a Lycra Challenger suit.

But this wasn't without its emotional risks. Checking my e-mail would leave me wide open to Lizzie. And if she'd written back to tell me I was a tit and I should never contact her again ... well ... I didn't know how I'd handle it.

I logged in, and instantly noticed two things: there was nothing new from the Challenger ... but there was something new from Lizzie.

My stomach turned.

I couldn't open it. Not yet. Not *first*.

So I wrote to Jason.

>To: whoisthechallenger@hotmail.com
>From: Danny
>Subject: I know who you are

Hello "Challenger",
You can stop now. The game's up. I know who you are and why you're angry with me, and I'm sorry, but this has to end.

230

Thanks,
Danny

But, just to make sure, I also wrote another e-mail to Thom – the man who'd inadvertently introduced me to my nemesis...

Thom,
It's Danny here. The bloke who bought your car.
Listen – I'm sorry to be brief, but I need you to mail me back.
I don't know if this e-mail address still works for you because you'll be in New Zealand by now, but if it does please get back to me.
I need to get a number for Jason, the bloke from your party. The civil servant. I think I did something to annoy him when I met him and I think he's punishing me for it in quite an obscure and weird way. Did you give him my details? Please get back to me asap.
Danny

Oh, Jason.

Was there really any need for this?

It was my own fault, really. I'd put my experiences with Jason to the back of my mind, hoping they might go away. I had embarrassed myself in front of him by revealing I was living life with what in his eyes was blatant immaturity. And, worse, I'd been incredibly insensitive when I'd told him to 'just say Yes more'. He couldn't, could he? He was a man of huge responsibility. He hated his job, yes, but he'd proved to me that sometimes you have to just bear it, with or without the grin. Sometimes, maybe, you'll make a decision in life that you just can't reverse. And because of that, you'll spend the rest of your days saying ... No. Sometimes, that's just the way life is. That's what Jason had taught me.

I clicked back on to my list of messages, and knew that now was the time I'd have to deal with Lizzie. What would she say? What would a girl like Lizzie say to a show of childish stupidity and apparent border-line obsession?

I clicked on her name, and flinched as I read ...

What?!

Just that.

Just that one word.

My heart sank. But at least it didn't break.

I wrote back, saying, *I know. Sorry.* And went to find a pub.

Edinburgh by night is a city of warming beauty.

The castle, lit up and towering. Parliament Square. The Balmoral – the most impressive hotel I've never stayed in, every light in the window a sign of wealth come to town. The Canongate Tollbooth, Fettes College, the Ramsay Gardens tenements …

But I wasn't bothered about any of it. It could have all been Lego for all I cared.

I was grumpy and embarrassed, and now regretting the moment I'd decided to take a shortcut through Fleshmarket Close – the only shortcut in the known world which cuts down on distance but multiplies both the time your journey takes *and* the effort it takes to get there. Finally, breathlessly, reaching the last of the million or so stupidly steep steps, I looked up to see a woman, holding out a flier.

'Interested in a show?'

I took her leaflet, just as she said …

'It's a play about betrayal, rape, and death.'

Bugger.

A short while later and I was nursing a pint in the Greyfriars Bobby, a pub named after a small dog of Scottish legend that had lain faithfully on his master's grave until he too had passed away. It seemed a fittingly melancholy place for me to drown my sorrows. I toasted the dog. By which I mean I raised my glass to it, not that I got a lighter and a spit out.

Around me were students on a pub crawl, a couple of rugby boys, a smattering of tourists, as well as a tall, tanned man, who had just looked up at me, and now approached …

'Danny?'

I jumped, slightly.

'Yes?'

There was something very familiar about this man.

'Danny Wallace?'

'Yeah. Hello.'

'It's Hugh. Hugh Lennon.'

Hugh Lennon! Hugh Lennon the Hypnotist! Hypnotist Hugh Lennon!

One of the fantastic things about the Edinburgh Festival is that it gives you the chance to catch up with people you never normally see. I hadn't seen Hugh Lennon in years – not since we'd had a drink after I'd reviewed a show of his for the *Scotsman* in …

Oh, God. I hope I gave him a good review.

'Great to see you!' he said.

Evidently, I had.

'How long's it been?' I said.

'Must be … 1996? How strange to bump into you here!'

Hugh is a hypnotist who has the distinction of owning the world's only hypnotic dog – Murphy. Together, they travel the world, hypnotising people together. Like a magic version of Shaggy and Scooby.

'Murphy's at the venue,' he said. 'So I'd better go in a minute. Just popped in for a Coke and a pee. How are you? What are you doing up here?'

'Working. Seeing shows, for the BBC. You know …'

'Seen anything good?'

Probably best to change the subject.

'So what are you doing up here? A show?'

'Not really … I mean, I'm doing a one-off tonight … just the hypnotism and stuff … Hey – do you fancy coming along? It's a kind of warm-up … I'm doing the Leeds Festival soon, you see …'

'Um …'

'We could have a drink or two after—'

'Yes. That would be great.'

I drained my pint and we left the pub. This was good. Some company. It was quite easy to spot Hugh's car. It was the one with 'HYPNODOG' written across the side in great big letters. I wondered whether I should attempt something similar with the Yesmobile.

Hugh's venue was the back room of a pub on the outskirts of town, and I sat myself down with a pint. He's in his early fifties now, Hugh, but has the personality and energy of a man thirty years younger. He travelled to Britain from Mauritius when he was 18, and his light accent and tanned skin add hugely to his on-stage mystique. I hadn't quite been in the mood for comedy hypnotism, to be honest. It's rare for me, as moods go. But as Hugh started his audience banter, and got his volunteers, and told a few jokes, I started to get into the act, and forget about whatever had been concerning me earlier.

Twelve people were now on the stage – old, young, male, female –

and all had fallen under Hugh's spell. For more than an hour, I watched as he somehow crafted a show out of them. And it was hilarious. And feelgood. And communal, somehow. I forgot all about what had been troubling me earlier, and laughed a lot, as Hugh's volunteers suddenly thought they were Madonna, or invisible, or that a tiny duck kept on stealing their drink. I can honestly say: if you're ever feeling blue, or tired, or down ... try and find a fat Scottish man who thinks he can fly. I don't know why more agony aunts don't recommend them.

But it was what Hugh did in the final few minutes of the show that truly astounded the room.

'I would ask you all to be very quiet, now,' he said, looking very serious. 'As I bring out a very special guest ...'

I knew the story behind this very special guest. One day, many years ago, Hugh came across an old and wise farmer, who talked in mysterious, awe-struck tones of a Labrador puppy not like the rest of its family. It kept itself to itself, he said, and had a remarkable ability. Hugh was intrigued, and went to visit the puppy ... the puppy that was later to become ... *The Hypnodog.*

Immediately, the music started up. The theme from *2001: A Space Odyssey.* The crowd fell silent as Hugh disappeared off stage and returned moments later with Murphy.

And ten minutes after that, the crowd cheered as twelve Scottish volunteers lay fast asleep on the stage, having stared deep into the abyss of Murphy's chocolate-brown eyes.

After the show, Hugh sat next to me with a coffee.

'Great show,' I said.

'Thanks. They loved Murphy tonight, eh?'

On cue, Murphy walked into the room, sniffed about a bit, and walked out again. When he wasn't staring people into oblivion on stage, he seemed fairly harmless.

'I lost him one year, you know,' said Hugh. 'He wandered off and I couldn't find him. It made the papers. The people in Scotland were terrified. The headlines were screaming "Do Not Approach This Dog!". Journalists genuinely thought he was going to be walking around, staring at people, convincing them they were chickens. I thought that'd be the end of it, but we started getting calls from European news agencies, and then America, and then Japan. The phone wouldn't stop ringing. It was big news in China. "Hypnotic Dog On The Loose In Scotland!" We were bigger than Nessie.'

Suddenly, we were interrupted. A lady who'd been watching the show wanted a word.

'Mr Lennon … um … I've got a fear of spiders. Is that something you can help with?'

'Yes,' said Hugh. 'You can cure pretty much anything with hypnotism. So long as it's in the mind. Which is where most problems are.'

'Really? So I should see a hypnotist?'

'If you've got a problem in your head, a hypnotist can solve it, whatever it is. Here …'

He handed her a Hypnodog flier with his number on it.

'… I'm sure Murphy and me can solve yours.'

The woman smiled, and took the flier, and walked away, satisfied.

'You'd let her come round your house?' I said.

'Yes,' he said. 'But only once I've got my spider costume out. I'll jump out at her at the train station. That'll fix it.'

I laughed.

'But no,' he said. 'It's good to be able to help people when you can.'

I was impressed.

'Christ, look at the time … I'm going to have to get going, Danny,' said Hugh. 'We've got a long drive ahead of us. But here …' he pulled out another Hypnodog flier and handed it to me '… if you're ever in Wales, look me up, okay?'

'Cool,' I said. 'And thanks, Hugh.'

Hugh smiled, and we looked at each other for slightly longer than we should have done, and for a second I was worried he was hypnotising me. I averted my eyes and looked at the dog, but he was staring at me too.

'Well, see you soon,' I said, and left, in rather a hurry.

I slept soundly, that night.

I'd bought a bag of chips on the way home and reasoned that life was pretty good, all things considered. I fell asleep with the TV on, and would have slept for days, had I not, at four in the morning, been woken by a curious beep.

I looked around and saw that my phone was lighting up the room. I had a text.

I yawned, knocked the telly off, rummaged around to find my glasses and then picked up the phone as its light began to fade.

It was probably Wag, drunk and lost in London, texting me in case I happened to be close by.

I squinted to read it. There was a message, but no name. And it was an unrecognised foreign number.

0061?

What was that?
I read the message.
And then I sat bolt upright.

RING ME. I'M COMING TO EDINBURGH

It was from Lizzie.

Four days later I was waiting in the arrivals lounge at Edinburgh International Airport, with butterflies in my stomach and a flower in my hand.
And then there she was, pulling a suitcase behind her, and smiling.
I couldn't believe it. It was *Lizzie*.
'Hi,' I said.
'Hi,' she said.
And then we hugged. And we laughed, and looked at each other.
And then she said the words that I'd been longing to hear.
'What's with the *mullet*?'

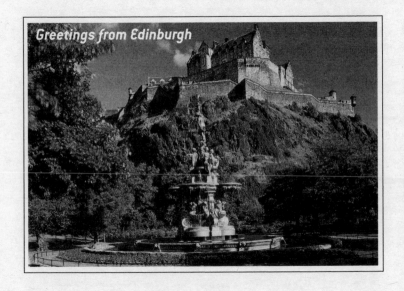
Greetings from Edinburgh

14

In which Daniel and Lizzie climb a Mountain, visit a Brass Rubbing Centre, and see a bad Play

I had been waiting, for what seemed like days, for Lizzie to wake up.

After I'd realised she was going to take me up on my offer, I'd phoned her straight away. Was she *sure*? I'd asked. Could she *really*? She told me she'd been hoping to come back for quite some time – this was the perfect excuse. Her work was sorted, she was her own person. She could do it. Especially now that she had a ticket.

I was overawed – and nervous. I mean, who does something like this? What kind of girl is that spontaneous? What kind of girl would drop everything and just think, 'Yeah, I'll do that, why not?'

'I got your postcard from Amsterdam,' she'd said, in the taxi on the way back. 'The one which said sometimes you've just got to do things like that. I thought you were right.'

So she'd travelled for 24 hours to London. And then an hour more to Edinburgh. And now here she was, asleep in front of me, in a slightly murky Travelodge in the centre of town. The power of postcards.

She'd arrived in the morning and it was now getting on for nine at night. Edinburgh was orange and phosphorous outside my window. The streetlights blushed through the condensation on the glass. I watched the news with the sound down. Eventually, I fell asleep, too.

'I can't believe you bought me a ticket,' said Lizzie, buttering her toast.

It was the next morning. We sat in front of two fry-ups in the City Café round the corner. I was unbelievably happy.

'I can't believe you came here,' I said.

Things were just as they'd been eight months earlier, in London. Nothing seemed to have changed, or shifted. It felt … natural. But exciting.

'Don't you think it's a bit … odd … though?'

'What … that I got on the plane or that you bought me the ticket?'

'Well … both.'

'Yes. It's very, very odd,' she said. 'But that's good, isn't it? Life *should* be odd.'

I thought about it. And I agreed.

'I brought you a present,' she said.

'What is it?'

She opened up her bag, and pulled out a picture. It was of a Big Prawn.

'A Big Prawn! Brilliant!' I said.

'Geek,' she said.

I suppose it must be a boy thing. I suppose in Melbourne, or Adelaide, or Canberra, these Big Things must attract boys from miles around, while the girls just sit there, in the car, wondering what on earth they're doing with their lives.

'So …' she said. 'What are we going to do today?'

'Absolutely anything you want,' I said. 'The whole festival is ours.'

We went to the zoo.

The days flew by. In the best way possible.

We did whatever came up, whenever it came up. We walked down Princes Street and accidentally ended up following a ghost tour … we walked by the shore in Leith, and down by the sea, she made me buy cod. We moved out of the Travelodge and moved into the grand old Balmoral just because the mood took us, and we wore dressing gowns and sipped whisky, and then we moved back to the Travelodge the very next night. She wanted to buy haggis, and a deep-fried Mars Bar, and looked a little green after a mouthful of both. We had fun.

I marvelled at the power of Yes.

One time, over a hot chocolate, Lizzie got the fringe brochure out. She flicked through it. She read some of it. She slammed it shut and threw it down on the table.

'You know what we should do?' she said.

'What?' I said.

'We should walk out that door and just go to the first show we get a flier for. Whatever it is. No matter how bad it sounds.'

I laughed. I'd kind of been doing that anyway, of course, but now it seemed like *fun*. Because we'd be *sharing* a Yes.

'Okay,' I said.

A couple of hours later and I had seen a show about betrayal, rape and death for the third and hopefully last time.

We took another leaflet as we strolled down Clerk Street, and booked ourselves in to see *The Ladyboys of Bangkok* in a big tent in the meadows later that night.

As the days progressed, we clambered up the 16,000 steps of the Scots Monument, and sampled the brew in all two million of Edinburgh's pubs ... on a rainy morning we bought a guidebook and Lizzie stuck a pin in the museums section. We spent an hour in the Museum of Early Keyboard Instruments on Cowgate. Later, we passed the Oxford Bar, and sat there, and drank tea, and felt like characters from an Ian Rankin novel. We ate chips on the steps of the castle, and bought things we didn't need in Kookie Hill. We swung by the Brass Rubbing Centre, play-acted fascination, and swung straight out again. We bought tickets for Hot Hot Heat and Franz Ferdinand. We read papers in the Drum & Monkey. I taught Lizzie words like Stushie, Bampot, Weejie and Youze. She taught me Barrack and Doodle.

One morning, days later, at 5 am, we were weaving our way home through a deserted city, carrying a half-full bottle of wine, when I suddenly become completely and utterly convinced that I could make this more special for Lizzie. I decided there would be snow on top of Arthur's Seat – snow on top of the extinct volcano that watches over Edinburgh. I was drunk, yes, but I was determined, too, and I told Lizzie I had a surprise for her, and she was to follow me at once. We walked and laughed for what would have been more than an hour but didn't seem half that, until we were 800 feet up, standing at the top of the hill, overlooking the Firth of Forth, and Fife, and a city so splendid in the early morning sun that I didn't know what to say. There was, of course, no snow. It was late August, for God's sake, of *course* there wasn't. But that didn't matter. Because this had surprised us *both*.

I realised that in all the years I'd been coming to Edinburgh, I'd never once walked to the top of Arthur's Seat. I'd never been to the galleries, I'd never been to the museums, I'd never been to the things that are there all year round. They were always there for me, but I'd never used them – never said Yes to the opportunities I thought would *always* be there. It was like I'd discovered a *new* Edinburgh through Lizzie. But somehow, it meant more than that.

It was like the world was full of Yeses, or something. But what I want you to understand – what I think it's *important* you understand – is that I wasn't saying Yes because I was playing the Yes game. I'd all but forgotten about that. I wasn't saying Yes to prove anything to myself any more, or to Ian, or to anyone else. I was saying Yes because I *wanted* to. I was saying Yes because all of a sudden it was coming naturally. I was saying Yes because when you're in love, the world is full of possibilities, and when you're in love, you want to take every single one of them.

And that's my roundabout, slightly awkward way of telling you that … yeah … I was … you know …

In love and that.

'In love?' said Ian, over the phone.

'Yeah,' I mumbled, shyly. 'In love and that.'

'Wow,' said Ian, thoughtfully. 'Cool.'

'I mean, I must be. I can't stop saying Yes to things.'

'Oh. Well. What a turnaround.'

'But I don't even think about it when I'm with her. I'm saying Yes because I *want* to. *Everything* seems like a good idea, so long as I'm doing it with *her*. It's like I've gone Yes mental.'

'Or … "Yental".'

'That doesn't work.'

'No, it doesn't. But all this is great, isn't it?'

'Yes,' I said. 'So maybe Yeses are meant to be shared. Maybe that's what all this is about. Maybe life's about finding opportunities to share with someone. That's all it is, when you think about it. A series of opportunities to share.'

Ian sounded like he'd take more convincing.

'Tosser.'

But maybe Lizzie felt differently. Not about me being a tosser – God knows I hoped she felt differently about that – but about the other stuff. I don't know. Maybe this was how she *always* led her life. Open to opportunity. Spontaneous. Ready to go somewhere, do something. Maybe she was *always* a Yes girl. With or without me.

I flew back down to London with Lizzie a few days later. I took her to the same terminal I'd taken her to when we'd last said goodbye. We hugged.

And then, as quickly as she'd arrived, she was gone again, and I knew, somehow, that that would be the last time I ever saw her.

Saying Yes had brought me another ten days with Lizzie. Ten days I never thought I'd have.

But it had also cost me a little bit more. I'd had to say bye to a girl I once liked but now loved. But I wouldn't truly realise that until the next day, in fact, when Lizzie would already be thousands of miles away, and I would wake up, and look around, and for the first time see just how alone I really was.

15

In which Daniel receives some Unexpected News

For a couple of weeks and a day, I did very little.

It felt like I was back at square one.

Nothing much was happening any more. The whole Lizzie thing had kind of knocked me for six. It's better to have loved and lost, they say. Yeah, maybe. But not that bloody quickly.

I'd started putting in more time at the BBC. I threw myself into my work. I wrote a detailed and comprehensive report on all the shows I'd seen while at the festival, using words like 'powerful' and 'evocative', and telling Tom who I thought it was worth him getting in for chats and so on. I said Yes to all the meetings I was asked to go to – not because of Yes – but because I wanted to do a good job for a fine company. I turned up and worked even when my contract said I could be sitting at home, larking about. Work was becoming my focus. Because as long as I was working … I was … well … *safe*. Work couldn't hurt. So I worked.

The Challenger seemed to have disappeared off the face of the earth. My e-mail to Jason had clearly worked. The e-mail I'd sent Thom hadn't bounced back but it hadn't been returned, either. And his mobile number had been disconnected, presumably to make way for a New Zealand number. Still, no matter: the Yes Man had conquered. I couldn't help but feel that should have made me happier than it did. In actual fact, I was a little disappointed that it had been so easy. Now I had neither a love life nor a nemesis – and life's exciting when you've got a nemesis.

But my work at the BBC had clearly paid off. If nothing else, a couple of months' worth of Yeses and my impressive commitment to whatever I could at the festival had marked me out as a man of dedication and positivity. Tom asked me if I'd like to come in to talk about a new position that had opened up over at TV Centre. He said he thought I could well be the man for the job, but he just wanted to have a chat first.

I said Yes.

That weekend, Ian was desperately trying to work out what I wanted to do. I was slouching, unshaven on the sofa in my boxers and a t-shirt, and he was sitting, smartly dressed and smelling of aftershave, on the chair opposite.

'So … do you want to go the pub?' he said.

I shrugged.

'Yeah,' I said.

'Or … do you want to go the cinema?'

I nodded. 'Yeah.'

'Or we *could* go and play pool.'

'Great,' I said, flatly.

'Yes to that as well,' said Ian. 'Right. Well … do you want to … I dunno … go for a bloody *jog*?'

'Yeah,' I shrugged again. 'Whatever, really.'

Ian was perturbed.

'Jesus, Dan. You don't have to keep on just saying Yes. It's me.'

'Mmm-hmm.'

'I'm just trying to find out what you want to do.'

'Cool.'

'So which is it … pub, cinema, pool or jogging?'

'Yes,' I said. 'Sounds good. Whatever. Let's go.'

However distracted I may have been, I suppose I was still at least saying Yes to things. I just wasn't enjoying it any more. The thrill had gone. It was automatic. But I couldn't see the point of it all in the way I once had; in the way I'd hoped I always would. And I didn't want to think about it.

'I suppose now would be a bad time to tell you I've come up with the perfect punishment for you if you don't do this?' said Ian.

I glared at him. He looked frightened.

'This is worse than when you always used to say no,' he said. 'At least then I didn't have to hang around with you.'

We went to play pool.

Ian had managed to pot nearly every ball on the table. I was finding it hard to muster up the energy to compete.

'Dan ... you're not going to slip back to how you were, are you?'

I looked up from my shot.

'How do you mean?'

'Well ... you're not going to give up and revert back to how you were a few months ago? Because if you are, I will be able to put the punishment into action a little sooner than I'd thought—'

'Oh piss off with your punishment talk. You blatantly haven't thought of one yet.'

Ian looked genuinely hurt.

'I have so.'

'What is it, then?'

'Okay, I haven't. But I will. And it will be excellent.'

I thought about what to say, and leaned against the table.

'When I won that £25,000 and then lost it again, it didn't really bother me. You know?'

Ian nodded.

'Because Yes had *given* me something. The fact that I lost it didn't matter. But then Yes gave me something *better* than £25,000. It gave me Lizzie. And that was a cruel thing of Yes to do, because I couldn't keep her. It gave me someone who lives on the other side of the world, and it made me fall in love with them. And then they were gone. *That's* why I'm in a foul mood. That's why I think Yes is stupid. That's why I'm playing pool, in this pub, with you, thinking life is a mess, a sad fucking mess, and I wished I'd just said No a bit more. No's all I want to say now, Ian. I don't want to be like I was, but I'm so sick of saying Yes. All it does is tire me. It was supposed to *help*. It was supposed to be *exciting*.'

Ian put his pool cue down, and nodded, sadly.

'What Yes giveth,' he said, 'Yes also taketh away.'

Ian must have told Hanne what had happened.

The next day she wanted to meet up, at a café near Old Street.

'Hey,' I said, sitting down.

I was twenty minutes late but she didn't say a thing. She was clearly in sensitive mode.

'Hey,' she said, softly. 'So I just thought we should meet up. It's been a while. I wanted to see how you are.'

'I'm fine.'

'Are you sure? You don't look fine.'

'Honestly, I'm good. I've just been a bit distracted lately.'

'Something else is wrong. I can tell.'

'No, you can't. And no, it isn't.'

'It is. I can read you, Dan. I know you better than anyone.'

'I've got a lot on my mind, that's all.'

'Look – I know things are a bit funny, because of me and Seb, but—'

'Hanne. Honestly. That's not what this is about. And you don't have to worry – I'm absolutely not obsessed with you, and I didn't want to go on your bloody date with you, and I'm sorry about the flowers and the small African child. It was odd behaviour, I know, but please – if you don't mind, let's put it behind us. I moved on ages ago. Seriously. You and Seb are fine. You're great. And you and me – well, we're friends. Great friends.'

Just then, Hanne's phone rang. She was about to turn it off, but I gestured for her to take it, pleased for the interruption. It was her mobile phone company. I could hear them, tinny and loud, from where I was sitting. They wanted to know whether Hanne had a few moments to talk about her mobile phone bill. She said not really. I smiled. It must be nice to be able to say that. But again, I gestured for her to continue. I had nowhere I needed to be except my meeting with Tom at the BBC, but that wasn't for hours yet.

'Okay …' she said, mouthing 'sorry' to me between answering questions. 'Surname is Knudsen …' she said, before giving the first line of her address, her date of birth, and her security password.

'Norway. N-O-R-W-A-Y' – she rolled her eyes – 'Yes. Like the country.'

Well, what *else* was it like? The colour?

'Sounds good,' she said. 'Okay, thanks …'

She hung up.

'They've moved me to a better call plan. Free texts, 20 per cent off line rental. Glad I took the call …'

At least saying Yes was working out for *someone*.

'So, listen …' she said.

'I'm going to be fine,' I said, cutting her off. 'Life's just a bit … strange right now.'

'Strange how?'

'Well, it *was* very uneventful. And then it *wasn't*. But now it … *is* again. But I like it that way. I'm just tired, Hanne.'

She wrinkled her nose, struggling to follow my babbling.

'I never thought I'd say this, but … it sounds like you need to get yourself another Stupid Boy Project,' she said, and I considered the irony. 'You know you're allowed to, now? You can do whatever you want now. You're free! You know … you could count all the hairs on your legs again. It's been ages since you did that. You could see if you've got any new ones. Photograph them. That kind of thing.'

I nodded. That sounded okay.

'I'll be fine, Hanne. Anyway. How's Seb?'

'He's good. He's still a little confused as to why you joined us for dinner that night.'

'He asked! I felt I *had* to say Yes!'

'Oh, sure, you *had* to. And I suppose you'd have said Yes if Seb had asked you to jump off a cliff, would you?'

I opted not to answer that one.

'There's … another reason I wanted to meet up with you,' she said.

'What's that?'

'Well … there's someone I'd like you to meet.'

'Eh?'

'A girl I know.'

Oh, no.

'Hanne, I'm fine …'

'You said you were bored!'

'I didn't say I was bored – I just said things were uneventful.'

'Look, do this for me. Just have a drink with her. What have you got to lose?'

'Hanne, ex-girlfriends aren't supposed to set their ex-boyfriends up on dates.'

'Danny, ex-boyfriends aren't supposed to sponsor small African kids for their ex-girlfriends. And yet they do. All the time. It's really very common.'

I blushed a little.

'But I don't want to.'

I sounded like a child and I knew it.

'Oh, go on. Live a little. You seemed like you'd got it back until just recently. You seemed like you were really enjoying yourself.'

'I was.'

'So have a drink with Kristen. Just a drink. I think you'll get on brilliantly. And you'll feel better for it.'

Maybe Hanne was right. I mean, obviously, I'd have to say Yes, but on another level, it might be good for me. I knew the situation I was in. And I knew the solution, too. Get over it. And how do you get over something like that? You get on with life. You don't look back. You look forward.

'Fine. I'll have a drink with Kristen. I'll give her a call.'

Hanne smiled an oddly satisfied smile, and wrote the number down on a napkin.

'That's great,' she said. 'That's really great. And listen ... tell me to get lost if you think I'm being too nosy, but ... I was talking to Ian, and ... well, don't get annoyed, but I think you should maybe see someone.'

'Well, obviously you do. That's why you're trying to set me up with your mate.'

'No. I mean, *see* someone. A psychologist. A psychiatrist. A counsellor. Just ... *someone.*'

Oh.

'What the hell did you tell Hanne?' I said to Ian.

'What?'

'Did you tell her I was saying Yes to everything?'

'Of course not! Why?'

'Because she wants me to *see* someone! A psychiatrist or something!'

'I think, to be fair, she may want you to see someone because she *doesn't* know about your Yes thing. She must just think you're mental, that's all.'

'I'm not mental!' I said, probably a bit too loudly.

'Keep your voice down,' said Ian. 'Shouting "I'm not mental!" only makes you sound more mental. And anyway, think about how it looks to *her* ... you live for months in your flat in some kind of cocooned depression, then suddenly you're out every day and night, you buy a weird car, you seem on top of the world, and then *bang!* – you're all depressed again. It's like schizophrenia! Or the beginnings of a mid-life crisis! No wonder she wants you to see someone. You've got to snap out of this. It's been weeks since you got back from Edinburgh. You're in danger of undoing all our good work.'

'*Our* good work?'

'Look ... you have to get a grip. Jesus ... think about what saying Yes has done for you. Think about all the good things that have happened, if there *are* any. And then learn from it, and put it to bed if you have to.'

'Put it to bed?'

'Yeah. I'll let you off the punishment. You can stop, right now, and that'll be that. No repercussions. Just you. Cheered up.'

I thought about what Ian had said. And I thought about what I'd achieved so far. Life *had* been more fun. I'd met some interesting people, I'd done some new things, and, all in all, Yes had been a minor success. But that had been in the early days, when the consequences hadn't seemed to matter so much. Now, I was in a lull. I wanted life to be normal again. We were only just coming up to October, for God's sake. October! If I was going to do this properly, and stick to my Yes Manifesto, there was still a long way to go. An *impossibly* long way. Could I really only be halfway through? I felt like crying. I felt like grabbing someone – *anyone* – and telling them the whole story, start to finish … but I already knew I didn't like the way the story finished. Not if it ended like this. Hanne had said she wanted me to see someone. Maybe she was right. She wouldn't have said something like that if it wasn't important.

I lay in bed that night, thinking, and thinking, and thinking. Did I stop now? Or did I see it through? In what direction should I take my life?

I needed a sign.

The next morning, my phone rang. I answered it. They didn't hang up.

And I had the sign that I so badly needed.

'I need a bottle of champagne, please. Cheapest you've got.'

'How much are you looking to spend, sir?'

'Um … a fiver?'

'We've got £2 off Dom Perignon at the moment, at £26.88, if you're interested?'

I relished the moment.

'Yes!' I said.

'Would you like to buy a cooler with that?'

'Yes!' I said. 'Yes – whatever you like!'

'What are we celebrating?' said Ian, standing at the door. 'And why are you grinning like that?'

'We are celebrating some shocking news,' I said, pushing past him. 'And a new beginning.'

'What news?'

'My promotion,' I said.

'Your *promotion*?!'

'My promotion.'

'But you're never at work!'

I ignored Ian's childish comment and found two mugs in his cupboard.

'Blimey … Dom Perignon … feeling flash, are you?'

'Not really. I wanted the cheap stuff, but the man suggested this.'

'Why have you brought a corkscrew?'

'It was on offer.'

'So …'

'Yep. "Just when I thought I was out, Yes pulled me back in." You know who first said that? Alan Pacino.'

I poured the champagne and Ian opened his packet of nuts.

'So what's the job?'

'Well … it's in a small department over at TV Centre – *tiny*, really – working up new ideas, finding new talent, developing stuff, that sort of thing.'

'What's your job title?'

I took a deep breath and told him.

'Head of Development.'

I was beaming. Absolutely *beaming*.

'*Head of Development*!?' said Ian. 'What? You? A *Head* of something? That's *ridiculous*!'

'I know. But if it makes you feel better, there's literally no one beneath me. It's like being made Head of Stationery just because I've got my own pencil.'

Ian shook his head.

'As far as I can tell,' he said, 'you've just got an executive-level promotion at the BBC, the most-respected broadcaster in the world, essentially on the basis that you say Yes a lot.'

We clinked mugs.

'Yes,' I said.

'So you're still going to say Yes?'

'Yes!'

What Ian didn't realise was what this *really* signified.

There was a reason for this. I knew it. It had come just at the right time – just when I was doubting the validity of what I was doing and considering another change in life. A change to the sensible. To the more predictable. To the more comfortable. And it had confirmed to me that that choice was *right*.

An optimist would say that Yes had given me another big chance and

I should stick with it. I would have said the same a month or two earlier. And it's true – saying Yes to that first meeting had set off a chain of events that had somehow led me to buying a bottle of champagne and toasting a new start. But a realist would see what this really meant.

I realised now, all too clearly, that you can't live life as a total optimist. I saw the underlying reason for this promotion. The secret reason. It was there to encourage me to say goodbye to my stupid, carefree ways. To say goodbye to living life like it was all about fun, and frolics, and adventure. At some point you have to grow up, move on. Hanne had always told me that. And now I'd realised it for myself. Jason had been right, that night at the party. Responsibility comes to us all. Life can't just be about fun. We have to sacrifice our freedom sometimes, so that we can progress. I would e-mail Jason once again. I would thank him for the lesson. Who'd have thought it? The Challenger won after all. No was best.

And what do I mean by 'No was best?' I mean No is power. No says 'I'm in charge.' Think about how many times you've said Yes in the past year, and how many times you would've liked to have said No instead. Maybe being able to say No is the one thing that keeps us sane. Some people go through their whole lives saying Yes over and over again – Yes to things they don't want to do but feel obliged to, Yes to things that allow other people to take advantage of them, just because that's the way things are, the way things have always been. Some people need to learn how to say No. Because every time they say Yes, they say No to *themselves*.

All those Yes moments when I'd done something I didn't necessarily want to do – all those Yes moments that hadn't led anywhere, hadn't done *anything* … what if I'd said No to those? It would've meant I could have said Yes to things I *did* want to do … Saying No gives you access to a process of elimination that can lead to a better life. If I could say No to the part of me that wasted his time doing things he knows he shouldn't – I could say Yes to the part of me that wanted to move on.

I explained all this to Ian, and he ended up agreeing with me.

'I suppose you're right. I suppose this is the first good thing that's happened to you since you started saying Yes. I mean … you won and then *lost* that money, which I've always said is *worse* than never winning it at all. You've loved and lost, which I don't think *is* better than never having loved, actually. You *thought* you were going to be a telly presenter, but that hasn't materialised, either, which is more disappointing than never thinking it. You owe thousands of pounds on credit cards you shouldn't have taken out. You are constantly phoned up by strangers who hang up as soon as you answer. You bought a car you don't need and got a haircut which was last fashionable in 1985. In Hungary. Your inventions don't work. Your—'

Suddenly, I was a little offended.

'Actually, the inventions are pretty good. Maybe not the spoon one, but the Incredible Automatic Self-Rewinding Video Box is sound.'

'Your design worked by placing a magnet on the inside of the box. It would wipe the tape as it rewound. It's basic science. Anyway, in five years videos will be obsolete and no one will even use them.'

My God ... things were even worse than I'd imagined. I'd banked on that rewinder being my nest egg. But the only way to deal with it was to treat it like a lesson. So I left Ian, that night, feeling positive about pessimism. These things happen for a reason. Thank heavens I'd seen the sign. Maybe there *is* a grand plan after all.

I thought, suddenly, of the man on the bus, and then, slowly, of Maitreya. It sounds outlandish to say it, but maybe there was something in all that. Maybe Maitreya really *was* the man on the bus; the man who'd kickstarted this whole thing. Maybe I really *was* being looked after by some higher power. A higher power who wanted me to grow up. Suddenly, *anything* seemed possible.

The thing was, Yes had started off as a way of getting back into an old, carefree life. Turns out it was a way of making me realise the *errors* of that life. It represented the end of an extended adolescence. And surely ... that was a good thing? Surely.

So I would do this. I would get this Yes thing out of the way. I would do it, and then move on. I would start the new job in January. And then I would put a stop to this chapter of my life – not just the Yes chapter ... but everything like it. But it was important to *succeed* ... I never wanted to think I'd moved on because I'd *failed*.

For now, I got on with the work at hand, knowing for sure that this would be the last stupid thing I ever did. I had a clear run ahead of me. This would be easier than ever.

But less than one week later, I received another package.

16

In which Daniel is tempted by Evil

The Challenger was back and I was a furious man.

I'd sorted this out! I'd already sorted this out!

The fact that Jason had lulled me into a false sense of security and then slapped me in the face with yet another package did nothing but infuriate me. My decision to continue the Way of Yes as a goodbye to my stupid, carefree past was a noble and pure one – and all he was doing now was sullying it. Spoiling it. Making it more about *him* than *me*. This was supposed to be self-help – a personal odyssey. This wasn't supposed to be a game of cat and mouse with me as the mouse.

I was thundering out of Oxford Circus tube towards the Yorkshire Grey, now, my face a picture of concentrated anger. I needed, once again, to speak with Ian.

'*Big Issue*, mate?' said a man standing outside Boots.

I turned to face him as I strode past.

'No!'

Yes. That's right. No.

The really infuriating thing was, once again, the Challenger had upped the stakes, and what made it all the more painful was that it was *all my fault*. I'd e-mailed Jason to tell him about my new frame of mind – that he'd been right all along. That I'd realised the true danger of Yes and the true power of No. And now … now he'd sent me *this*.

A man asked me for spare change as I walked past McDonald's. I had no time but I had the correct answer: I barked a *No!* as quickly and sharply as possible. He looked slightly shocked but I didn't care – I had to get to the Grey.

As I burst through the doors of the pub I saw Ian sitting by the fire-place in the corner. I paused by the bar to compose myself.

'What can I get you?' asked the girl behind the bar.

I maintained perfect eye contact with Ian as I said, 'Nothing, thank you. I do not want a drink.'

Ian's eyes widened. He had heard my answer. He knew something was very, very wrong.

I sat down next to him and he didn't say a thing, just stared at me.

I reached into my pocket and took out a letter. On it was one, type-written line. I put it on the table, and slid it towards him.

He leaned forward and read aloud.

I saw this and thought of you.

He looked at me again, shrugged, and did that little shake of the head people do when they don't know what's going on.

'Who sent you that?' he said.

'Guess …' I said.

But he knew. He knew *exactly* who had sent it.

'But what does it mean? What did they see?'

I unzipped my jacket and revealed a bright blue t-shirt.

On it were three simple words.

JUST SAY NO

Ian looked at me in horror.

He recognised the slogan from the old anti-drugs campaigns of the Eighties … the ones you'd usually get underneath a picture of a crack-addled teenager, or next to a beautifully crafted charcoal portrait of a man with a tiny dog on his shoulder … but he also knew what its meaning to *me* would be …

'No!'

I nodded, silently.

'You look surprised,' I said.

'I thought they'd decided to stop all that!'

'Me too.'

'So what do you think it means?' he said.

'It means I should just say No.'

'Instead of Yes?'

'Well, that's the problem. Do I say Yes to just saying No, or do I just say No to saying No? Do I make a stand and say No, or is that exactly what they want?'

'Or does it mean you should just say No to just saying Yes?'

'Yes. No. I don't know.'

'But if you just start saying No where once you would have just said Yes,' said Ian, desperately, 'you'll have failed! That goes against everything the Yes Manifesto stands for! I should know! I've got it stuck to my fridge! I can't make a cup of tea without being reminded of your plight!'

'But if I just say No to saying No, I'll still be saying *Yes* to just saying No, because I'll have just said *No*. Maybe I can just say No to just saying No, thereby cancelling it out.'

'That's a No No.'

'A double No, Yes.'

'No, a No No in that you can't just say No to saying No. You'll still just have to say Yes to just saying No, otherwise you'll have said No!'

'So I should just say No from now on, and wait until the Challenger sends me a t-shirt saying "Okay, you can just say Yes again now"? It's not going to happen!'

I was starting to wish I'd ordered a drink, and looked at Ian's beer, longingly. Ian caught me looking.

'Pint?'

I sighed.

'No.'

Twenty minutes of intense crisis talks later, we had a solution of sorts.

It was a fair and worthy solution to an unusual and tricky problem. I clearly had to do what the Challenger said ... especially now that Ian was so heavily involved. But part of me couldn't help but wonder if Ian was now in cahoots with Jason. Yes, Jason would have taught me a lesson by messing with my life – but who really stood to benefit? Whose punishment would I have to ultimately undergo? Just where was Jason getting his information? How would he know I was going through with his demands? I decided to sit on my worries for now, and see how it all panned out before making any untoward accusations.

So the solution was: I would spend *one day* just saying No. That's how this whole *Yes* thing had started – one day of utter positivity. I would do the same with negativity; I would spend today saying No to everything – *anything* and everything. And I would show the Challenger the way of the righteous.

So with confidence, I stepped out of the Yorkshire Grey with a whole new adventure to get stuck into. I knew it wouldn't make me feel as good as my Yes adventure once had, but I knew it was part of the deal. Sure, I couldn't say I'd enjoy it, and yeah, so it would grate on me, but …

'Excuse me, sir …'

It was a man with a green bib on.

'I was wondering if you'd have two minutes to talk about Help the Aged?'

I smiled.

'No.'

Hey.

That felt … *good*.

I was sitting alone at home, almost cackling.

Why had I never realised just how good it felt to say No before? Why had I thought that was a bad thing? Why hadn't I realised the power inherent in that two-letter word? The most powerful two-letter word in the world?

I'd arrived home and immediately opened the rest of that morning's mail – the mail I'd forgotten about as soon as I'd found the new package. I saw that the people at American Express wanted to offer me a new credit card. I wrote them a postcard, saying No. I specifically didn't do as the ad said by not ringing up to ask where my nearest WeightWatchers meeting was. I got the invite for Paul Lewis's stag weekend, and howled with joy as I wrote back and said I couldn't be there to watch him and his army pals destroying barges and levelling whole towns with their raucous, witless behaviour (then I scribbled that out and wrote a more polite version – I'm not an idiot). I didn't buy the Five Greatest Albums You Really Must Own, I declined the offer of a free no-obligation quote from Kitchens Direct, and I shouted a cheery 'no!' when the advert on cable TV said 'Isn't it about time you learnt to cook pasta like the professionals?'

Something was happening to me here. Something strange. I was really enjoying myself.

A text message came through from Hanne.

I HAVE AN EXTRA TICKET FOR DAMIEN RICE TONIGHT IF YOU WOULD LIKE TO COME

Damien Rice! I *love* Damien Rice! I gleefully texted back.

NO!

Minutes later, Hanne did the same.

RUDE

Rude. Yeah. But I didn't care. Because I was the No Man. And this was *just* what I needed.

It was like the Dark Side had taken over.

The Challenger had reared his Darth Vader-like head once again – but this time he had turned me. A battle between Good and Evil had started to rage inside me. Well, not *evil*, exactly. More like just-a-bit-*grumpy*. Yeah, that was it: a battle between Good and Grumpy had engulfed me. No was suddenly *good*. No was *great*. I *felt* that now. But could I let it take over? It was tempting. What if I just extended the period of No-ness? I'd done it with the Yes side of things … it'd be only fair. Did I want to go back to the good side at midnight tonight, or did I want to see where a healthy dose of negativity could take me? Sure, it was dangerous, and no, it wouldn't be much use in January, when I started the new job … but the thought was intriguing. I didn't want life to be exactly the way it had been before, obviously … but that had been when I hadn't been in control. Now, the world of No wouldn't control *me* … *I* was in charge! After all, I knew how to use the word properly now. I knew how to handle it. And I could give up any time I wanted.

Ian had thought maybe I was overreacting to the Challenger's demands. He said I was blowing it out of all proportion, letting them get the better of me and turning them into an evil genius figure when actually it was probably just someone I knew, winding me up without realising the effects.

Evil Genius, I thought. *Probably just someone I knew … Interesting choice of words, Ian. Ever been to Liverpool?*

I continued to suspect it was Jason. No – not suspect. *Know.* This was a man I'd seen as an enemy but should now treat as an ally after all he'd done for me. I'd made him furious by denying his way of life was healthy, and so now he'd made me taste it. And it was good. I would e-mail him again now … e-mail him for the third time. E-mail him to tell him that soon I would be like him. Soon I would walk among the rest of the No-bodies. Soon I would reclaim my No. Soon I would run with the Dark Side.

I was excited. I switched on the telly just in time to hear Graham Norton say, 'Join me after the break …' so I shouted, 'No, Graham Norton, I will *not!*' and switched it off again.

This was *brilliant*!

* * *

That evening, I stayed in. Nothing could tempt me out. Each option I came up with in my head was greeted with a pure and resounding No. Great. This was great. Exactly what the doctor ordered.

I stared out of the window for a while, watching the trains go by, and the people off on their nights out. When the advert for Domino's Pizza came on the radio and the voice of Tony Hawks suggested I try their new 2-for-1 combo value meal deal, I just switched it off, and tried not to think about how hungry I was.

I sat in my bedroom and found my diary. I got a pen out, and started to write down all the things I'd said Yes to Just Saying No to.

Not going to the Damien Rice gig tonight. That'd been brilliant.

Not buying randomly recommended albums that could have surprised or delighted or enriched my life, or taken my tastes in a whole new and vital direction, well, that was probably for the best, because I know what I like, and I may as well stick to it.

Not grabbing Wag and Hanne and Ian and inviting them round to watch me cook pasta like a professional, and then talking, and laughing, and eating well into the night – that had *also* been … y'know. Fun.

Hadn't it?

I sat, staring at the digital clock, from 11.37 pm … waiting … waiting for midnight.

It was taking *ages*.

I glanced down at what I'd written in my diary. I weighed up what it all meant, and realised in an instant that it meant … well … nothing. No achievement. No living. *Nothing*. I tried to feel good about it. Tried to remember that No meant freedom; choice; discretion. But I yearned for the early days. The simple days. The days when I was winning on scratchcards and enjoying an extra pint and seeing my friends. When had things started to go so wrong? When I bought the car? When I went to Liverpool? Why did this mean so much to me? Why did I have to continue? Couldn't I resign myself to the fact that a new job and a new life were only round the corner? Couldn't I just stop … and *wait*?

I made a cup of tea, and sat on my bed, and thought.

I still knew that this period of my life would have to come to an end – now more than ever. But not like *this*. Not sitting in my bedroom, on my own, trying my hardest to feel smug.

No was wrong. It didn't fit. It was a flirty, evil temptation to take me away from the real work that had to be done. And I had to *succeed* in this work. If I didn't, perhaps I would never be able to move on. But I was beginning to realise and reluctantly decide that maybe I'd need some help. And not just the kind of help that Ian brought. Professional help.

It had been Hanne's suggestion, of course. She'd meant for me to see a psychiatrist, or a counsellor, or someone who could guide me.

Well, I would get some guidance. Because I'd had an idea. A way of making this all so much easier. A way of guaranteeing I'd succeed. With this man's help, I couldn't fail. I would be rejuvenated. Enthusiastic. Ready to fight the good fight; the final fight. Full of Yes.

I opened up my diary again, and pulled out the flier on which this man had written his number. In the morning I would make a phone call and book a ticket.

I was going to see a man about a dog.

17

In which Daniel meets with Hugh the Incredible, a Tiny Soldier and a Magical Dog with a hat on

I had informed hypnotist Hugh Lennon that he was to prepare himself for the toughest case of his professional career. He was to meet me at Cardiff Central Train Station that very afternoon and immediately begin work on resolving a delicate matter of both the heart and mind. Hugh, in return, had decided this meant one thing.

'It looks like we'll be needing some takeaway.'

And so there he was, waiting for me as I stepped off the train, with a small box of won-ton he'd bought from a Chinese on the way.

'Snacks for later!' he said, enthusiastically. 'Very necessary when dealing with tricky psychological problems. Keeps the energy levels up. I find won-ton does that well. I love a bit of won-ton. Pork won-ton especially. I don't think there's much that beats it, really.'

I nodded in absolute agreement. I felt this was a matter it was vital we were unified on.

'But prawn toast is good too.'

I nodded again, even more enthusiastically this time. Basically, I'd decided that I needed this man, and I was willing to go along with *any* of his opinions on Chinese foodstuffs, no matter *how* controversial.

Hugh would simplify things for me. He was already involved in this, after all; he was part of the adventure of things. Yes had led me to him that night in Edinburgh, and now it had led me to him again. I needed him to help me focus my mind. Clarify things.

I clambered into his Renault and we began to drive out of Cardiff and towards Mountain Ash, the tiny, former mining town Hugh now calls home.

'So …' he said, as we found ourselves deeper and deeper into the blustery, bruised valleys. 'All I know so far is that you need my help. But what with?'

'Well … it's a tricky one,' I said. 'I made a decision to do something. And I think I need to keep doing it. I know I do. Just until the year is out. But I've kind of lost my willpower.'

'Aha,' he said. 'Willpower.'

He said the word 'willpower' in the way that wise old sea captains often stare into the middle distance and say the word 'wind' – like it's their old enemy or something.

'Willpower,' he said again, wistfully. 'So what is it … smoking? I can stop you smoking in five minutes.'

'No, not smoking.'

'Drink? Is it drink?'

'No. It's not drink.'

'Well … what, then?'

I thought about how to put it.

'I need to say Yes more.'

Hugh nodded.

'Fair enough.'

'Do you fancy a game of snooker, first?' said Hugh, as we approached Mountain Ash. 'It's good to reach a state of relaxation early on when approaching hypnosis. The working men's club is just over there.'

'Um … okay,' I said, although I suspected the real reason for the stop was that Hugh just quite enjoys playing snooker.

We pulled into the carpark of the working men's club, just off the high street. I'd noticed that there didn't seem to be many people out and about today. There'd been a short queue of pensioners at the bus stop, and I'd seen a man in a vest kicking a hosepipe around his front garden, but apart from that it all seemed a little … empty.

'I do a show in here every Friday night,' said Hugh. 'Usually they just have vocalists playing here, but now I do my hypnotism, and a bit of magic, and it seems to go down pretty well.'

Hugh pushed the door open and we walked down the stairs, towards the bar. I noticed the noise, first of all, and then the smell of beer … and then I realised that pretty much the entire town was sitting, pints in hand, in front of me. I looked at my watch. It was quarter to one. On a Tuesday. And everyone – *everyone* – was down the pub.

It was a happy atmosphere, based, I suspect, on a sad truth. Mountain

Ash had once been a profitable and thriving centre of industry. Men had travelled from all over Wales to work in the collieries and mine the black gold. But all that had ended in 1980, when the last main colliery shut down. The end of mining in Mountain Ash effectively meant the end of work. The end of work inevitably leads to the start of boredom. And the start of boredom had led everyone – of all ages – to the pub.

But before we'd taken even three steps into the main room, something odd happened. Something that only really happens in films. But something that seems to happen every day in Mountain Ash.

Someone, somewhere, spotted Hugh and let out a happy cheer. Then someone else cheered. Then more people. Then the applause started, and the whistling, and soon the entire room was on its feet, wildly hailing the low-key entrance of hypnotist Hugh Lennon. As we walked through a parting crowd, I watched in amazement as huge men slapped Hugh on the back, small women waved – even the copious amount of babies in the room would, I am certain, have raised their glasses to the man, had they thought to have any. I'd heard the phrase 'local hero' before, but never before had I seen one in action. It was utterly amazing.

We reached the sanctity of the snooker room and I asked Hugh if a reaction like that was normal.

'Well … you know. I suppose it's unusual having a hypnotist in town. Not many people had seen it up-close before, and so—'

A man of about thirty burst through the door.

'Hugh, will you fly for me?' he said.

He had glasses thicker than his Welsh accent – which was saying something – and he was clutching a mobile phone so small I am not entirely sure it could have been real.

'Er … not right now, Tommy, because—'

'Aw, Hugh, please, will you fly for me? I told the lads at the table there that you can fly and they don't believe me. Will you come in and fly?'

Hugh put his hand on the man's shoulders and looked him deep in the eye.

'Maybe later,' he said. 'My powers are weak now.'

Something seemed to dawn on the man and he made a face like he understood, and then backed away, bowing his head with some degree of reverence.

'You never told me you could fly!' I said, as the door closed.

'Well, I can't really. It's just that thing that David Blaine does. You know – you stand on one foot at a certain angle and it looks like you're levitating. I did it once for the poor lad and now I don't want to break his heart.'

I thought that was sweet.

Hugh put 20p in the table and out came the balls. I began to set them up.

'So … I guess this place is like the centre of the town?' I said.

'Yeah. They only ever used to have vocalists on here, or the odd bit of karaoke, so I suppose the fact that they can watch their friends be hypnotised on a Friday night is quite good. I only did it here as a way of meeting people initially. I'd moved here and I knew no one, but I got talking to a man who came round to fix my telly, and I told him I was a mindreader, mainly because I thought it would stop him from over-charging me. Well, he said I should do a mindreading show in the town. So we set something up. "A Night of Mindreading and Hypnotism." We promised all the money to charity, and we put a small banner up in the town. That night, *everyone* turned up. The whole town. And the next morning, I couldn't go anywhere because everyone knew who I was. Nowadays, it can be a bit annoying. I'll just be in the shops and every-one will be waving at me. But it's nice.'

I liked Hugh's life. And I liked the working men's club. It was cosy, and warm, and you could see its cherished place at the heart of Mountain Ash.

'It can be quite old-fashioned, though,' said Hugh, and he pointed at a door behind me. 'That room through there is the men's room.'

'The toilet?'

'No, no. The *men's* room. A room in which only *men* are allowed.'

'Wow. What happens in there?'

'Well …' said Hugh. 'Not much, really.'

'I'm amazed you can still have men-only rooms,' I said. 'What do the women say?'

'Oh, they just accept it. They know they're not going to change the club council's minds. They're very stubborn, the club council. I mean, last year, one of them resigned in absolute fury.'

'Why did they resign?'

'Because the club got a jukebox.'

'Oh.'

'It was like we'd been dragged kicking and screaming into the Sixties.'

I was starting to see what Hugh meant about 'old-fashioned'.

'Can I peek in the men's room?' I said. 'I'd like to see what all the men are doing.'

Hugh nodded. I opened the door and peered in. There were four old men, sitting silently at different tables, staring into the middle distance. One of them coughed. They didn't look particularly happy, but I suppose they'd made their stand against those pesky womenfolk and now they had to stick to it.

I closed the door again, quietly, and turned around, just as the other door was opening. It was Tommy again.

'Have you got your powers back yet, Hugh?'

'I'm using them for the snooker, Tommy,' said Hugh, and Tommy looked at me and laughed. He knew I had no chance against Hugh and his magic balls. Which is a sentence I never thought I'd write.

'You get some characters in here,' I said. And it was true; when we'd walked through the main bar, I couldn't help but notice that everyone I passed looked like they were out of a book of eccentric film extras.

'Oh, all over this town. It's incredible. But they're all lovely. Tommy, there, and Mad Harold.'

'Who's Mad Harold?' I said.

'Every Sunday Mad Harold goes to the café to have his cup of tea. And once he's done that, he stands out on the street corner, and spends the whole day waving at the cars. On weekdays, you may find him in the library, sitting at a desk reading the Bible out loud to anyone who'll listen. Last week, I drove past him and he waved to me while he cleaned the middle of the road with a vacuum cleaner. He's such a happy chap.'

I suppose happy is one word.

'Hugh,' said Tommy, back at the door for a third time. 'Arlene's here.'

And in walked Arlene, Hugh's friend.

'Arlene, this is Danny,' said Hugh.

'Hello!' I said, and shook her hand.

'You playing a bit of snooker, are you?'

Arlene had the sing-song accent of the deeply Welsh, just like Tommy, and I nodded and said, 'Do you fancy a game?'

Arlene laughed, and shook her head.

'Women aren't allowed to play snooker.'

I chuckled, and handed her a cue.

'No ... seriously,' she said, holding up her hand. 'Women aren't allowed to play snooker.'

I looked at Hugh. He shrugged and nodded.

'Women aren't allowed to play snooker?' I said, in utter disbelief. 'But … why?'

'The official wording is that "Women are not allowed to play snooker, because they might rip the cloth."'

'Women aren't allowed to play snooker because they *might rip the cloth*?' I said, perhaps a little unnecessarily. 'But that's … *ludicrous*!'

Arlene laughed.

'Why is that rule there?' I said. 'Did a woman once rip the cloth?'

'I don't think so,' said Arlene. 'But you know … one *might*.'

I was aghast.

'But so might a man!'

Arlene considered it.

'To tell you the truth, Danny, I'm not very into snooker anyway.'

'But what if it turned out you were really excellent at it, and you got invited to a big lady snooker tournament in Tokyo or somewhere, but you had nowhere to practise because people thought you might rip the cloth?'

She thought about it.

'I wouldn't mind going to Tokyo.'

Hugh and I finished our game, drank our drinks and got ready to go. I was still very keen to talk to him about how he could help me with my predicament. Was there a way of making this easier? Of wiping out nervousness, or regret, or fear, and just making Yes seem like the only sensible option? There was so much I wanted to ask him. I looked around and realised I still couldn't quite believe the timewarp I'd walked into. But I suspected that change wasn't far around the corner. In a couple of years time, there probably wouldn't be four old men in that men-only room, but three. And after that, just two. And then one. And then one day after that, maybe – just maybe – they'd turn the jukebox up, and allow women in, and they'd all dance on the snooker tables and rip the cloth up on purpose and make green baize dresses and go utterly snooker loopy. This had been a man's town, once upon a time, but with the industry gone, perhaps all some men found they had left to hang on to was their tradition … perhaps that was why it was given so much respect. Not just by the older men – but by the younger men, too. The men who'd seen their dads lose their jobs one day in 1980.

Hugh and I walked out of the working men's club the back way. We waited for Arlene by the car. She'd had to walk the long way round.

Well, rules is rules.

'I'll put the won-ton on,' said Arlene, 'and you boys can talk about whatever it is you're going to talk about.'

'Come through, Danny,' said Hugh, 'and we'll talk about this thing you're on about ...'

'Oh, and Hugh – we should probably draw the curtains ...'

Arlene gave Hugh a conspiratorial glance. Why did they have to draw the curtains? It was only about two o'clock and the weather was lovely.

'Good point,' said Hugh, and did as she said.

I decided not to ask why. Perhaps Arlene was going to get a secret snooker table out and wanted to avoid prosecution.

I made my way into the living room.

'When you were talking to Tommy in the club there,' I said, 'and you gripped him by the shoulders and told him your powers were weak ... were you hypnotising him?'

'No,' said Hugh. 'I was just speaking slowly. Sometimes that's for the best.'

'Because it looked like you were using some kind of Jedi Mind Control.'

Hugh laughed.

'I was in that, you know.'

I didn't know what he meant.

'You were in what, sorry?'

'*Star Wars*.'

My eyes widened to the size of a giant squid's.

'You were in *Star Wars*?' I said. 'No you weren't. Were you? You can't have been in *Star Wars*!'

'I was. I used to be a professional extra.'

'And you were in *Star Wars*?!'

This was too much to believe. This man in front of me had been in the defining film of my childhood! He was essentially *part of* my childhood!

'What were you in *Star Wars*?' I said.

'Oh, you know ... one of those guys in white.'

'A Stormtrooper?' I nearly shouted, my voice sounding suddenly rather pre-pubescent. 'You were a bloody *Stormtrooper*?'

271

They were only the coolest things in the film!

'A Stormtrooper, that was it. Yeah, I was one of the main ones. I've never seen it, mind you.'

My brain nearly popped.

'You've never *seen Star Wars*? And you were *in* it?'

It was unbelievable to me. It would clearly be the first thing I told people, every single time I met them! I would walk around in home-made Stormtrooper uniforms! I would have business cards made up saying 'Danny Wallace – I Was A Stormtrooper'!

'Nope, never seen it.'

I needed to sit down.

'I remember this one time,' said Hugh, 'we were filming a scene where the heroes were in this big hangar and they were trying to get away in their spaceship, and me and two other Stormtroopers arrived on this lift thing and then we were firing our laser guns at them—'

'I know exactly the scene!' I said. 'Han Solo and the others are trying to escape in the Millennium Falcon—'

'Er, yeah … probably—'

'And then Obi Wan Kenobi gets his light-sabre out!'

'Oh yeah. He got killed or something. I was there when it happened.'

Who else could say they were there when Obi Wan Kenobi was killed? Especially when you consider the fact that he was killed thousands of years ago and in a galaxy far, far away.

'Anyway, there were supposed to be a few explosions around us, but they'd been wired up wrong, and they exploded too close to our heads. One of the guys got hurt, and my ears were killing me. So they took three of us to this hospital, but we couldn't exactly walk in dressed like Stormtroopers because no one in the world had ever seen Stormtroopers before. So they took our uniforms off us and we had to walk around the hospital wearing leotards and big white wellington boots.'

'Not a good look for a Stormtrooper,' I said, still rather amazed by it all.

'Not really … hey, I should go and get Murphy …'

And with that, the man I realised I'd first seen over twenty years earlier in one of the greatest boys' films ever made left the room to fetch the world's only hypnotic dog.

The day couldn't get any stranger.

Moments later, he walked back into the room, followed by Murphy the Hypnodog.

The big, black Labrador settled in and sat himself down on the floor in front of me, sniffing my feet. I was still smiling from the *Star Wars* revelations, but I couldn't help but notice there was something a little unusual about the dog in front of me.

'Um … Hugh,' I said. 'Murphy the Hypnodog appears to be wearing … a *fez*.'

'Oh that?' said Hugh, distractedly. 'He's always wearing that old thing.'

I looked at Murphy again, who was just sitting there, staring at me, in his fez. It didn't seem entirely natural.

'You just put that fez on him a minute ago, didn't you?'

'Yes, yes, I did,' said Hugh. 'I just thought you'd like it.'

I did. And I take it back: the day had just got a little stranger.

'It's a fascinating problem,' said Hugh, munching on a won-ton. 'Usually, I get asked to help people say No more. You know … No to whatever they're addicted to. Are you sure you'd want to just blindly say Yes to things?'

I thought about it. Even without the help of hypnosis, I'd already run up an intimidating debt on credit cards I should never even have applied for let alone used, I'd found myself some kind of masked enemy figure who was out to torment and ruin me, I had the haircut of a hick, I'd bought a car, and I'd loved and lost.

'Yes,' I said, with a small shrug. 'I just need to know if there's an easy option. You know? A better way of going about things? I've still got a couple of months of this left before I move on for ever, and I thought it would get easier the more I did it. But certain … things … have happened which have made it harder.'

'What things?'

'A girl. A girl, for one thing.'

Hugh nodded, and said 'ah'.

'And a … well … a nemesis.'

'A nemesis?'

'A nemesis. Someone keeps winding me up and making me do things because they know I'll say Yes. But I don't know who they are, and I'm afraid that if I say no to them it'll ruin everything and all my hard work will have been for nothing.'

'So you want to say Yes, so that your hard work means more?'

I nodded. My phone rang. I answered it. They hung up. I was getting really bloody sick of these polite non-conversations. Whatever happened to having a good old chat?

'It's interesting,' said Hugh, leaning forward to make a roll-up. 'I suppose in some ways all this is about confronting fears. People sometimes go through their lives having fears and never realising they can be removed in just a few minutes, for ever. People are always saying No to things, aren't they? They're frightened of change, used to routine, used to doing things a certain way. Like, the people who take risks in business are the people who don't fear change and, ultimately, they're the most successful.'

'I think this started through fear,' I said. 'I was living quite negatively, and I was missing out on things. I guess I'm afraid of what you can miss out on in life. Every single day.'

'So,' said Hugh, licking the Rizla. 'It's a kind of fear of the unknown, in your case. It's a negative form of thinking. People do miss out on so much by instantly and unthinkingly saying No ... they don't realise they're putting a real limitation on their lives ... take Arlene, for example. When we were first friends, I offered her won-ton and she said "No way". And then she tried it, and she *loved* it.'

'That's true!' shouted Arlene, from somewhere else in the house. 'I *love* won-ton now!'

I didn't know how to respond to a sentence like that coming from someone in a different room. Usually a smile would have done, but she couldn't see that, so I just said, 'I like won-ton too,' quite loudly.

Hugh lit his roll-up and continued.

'It's the same with travel. People decide to stay at home. They say, what would I want to go to Spain for? What's in Spain for me? I've got everything I need right here in Pontypridd. And they miss out on a wonderful new experience. It's all they ever know. They just say No.'

I considered Hugh's words.

'Tom Jones used to live in Ponty,' shouted Arlene. 'He used to walk around the pubs, singing for pints. My granny booed him off one night.'

I smiled, and once again realised that she couldn't see me. So I said, 'Tom Jones is a good singer.'

Hugh nodded.

'*Bloody* good singer,' he said.

Murphy's fez had fallen off and he hadn't bothered to pick it up and put it back on again. That's dogs for you. Lazy.

He was sitting with his paws on my lap staring up at me with the big brown eyes that have made him the toast of the transcontinental animal variety circuit. I was on the comfy chair, ready to 'go under'. We were watching videos of Murphy and Hugh's various television appearances around the globe. Hugh wanted to show me what I'd be in for if we went ahead with the hypnotism.

We'd already watched their appearance on American tabloid shows *Hard Copy* and *Inside Edition*, and now we were watching a Discovery Channel show called *Animal X*.

'*This ... is the Hypnodog!*' bellowed an American man over some slowed-down footage of the slavering Labrador bounding towards the camera. '*Few stand a chance against his mysterious stare!*'

Some sinister music started up. And then there on the screen was Hugh, sitting on a sofa, softly lit, with his dog on his lap.

'*I must admit ... it* is *unusual,*' he said.

'*Unusual indeed!*' bellowed the American man again, who must be a nightmare to sit behind in the cinema. 'Animal X *tracked the Hypnodog down ... to Luton, England!*'

'It was actually Harrow,' said Hugh.

I suppose saying it was Luton gave it more mystique.

'*But other dogs are said to have mysterious powers too!*' said the American. '*This terrier ...*' they showed a picture of a small terrier '*... became famous in the United States for bringing a young boy out of a coma!*'

'What did he do?' I said. 'Jump on his bollocks?'

Hugh and I laughed for ages, which was fair enough, because it was a quality gag.

'*But the Hypnodog is said to have the strangest powers of all ... the power to control the human mind! Animal expert Dr Roger Mugford has come across other animals with the same skill ...*'

It cut to Dr Roger Mugford.

'*A mongoose can hypnotise a snake!*' he said, with some enthusiasm. '*And a tiger can hypnotise a monkey!*'

I made a mental note to remember these sentences for the next bring-a-fact party I attended.

'*The Hypnodog is said to have hypnotised a man into handing over his lunch. And those who fall under his spell tumble like a row of dominoes at the sight of the deep brown pools of his eyes ...*'

I looked down at Murphy. I wasn't sure I wanted to tumble like a row of dominoes. For starters, there was only one of me, so I'd have to keep getting back up and knocking myself down again. Murphy stared up at me. Suddenly, it was a little disconcerting. I had definitely caught sight of the deep brown pools of his eyes. What was going to happen to me?

Suddenly, Hugh was by my side.

'If you're still feeling nervous, have a read of these …'

He handed over a cuttings book. There were hundreds of articles, from all over the world.

Paws For Thought! screamed the *New York Post*. *Trances With Wolves!* said the *Mail*.

'It should reassure you. Murphy and I have hypnotised many, many people. You're in safe hands.'

It wasn't the hands I was worried about. It was the paws.

And what the hell was *this*?

'Hang on,' I said. 'What's this headline here about?'

I pointed it out. *Hypnotist's Spell Made Girl's Boobs Swell!*

'Ah yes,' said Hugh. 'I enlarged a German girl's breasts.'

And he left it at that.

'So you just want us to make you more open, then …' he said, his hand on my shoulder.

'Well … Yes. That, and I suppose … to give me a total and utter inability to say No. At least for a couple of months. Until December 31st.'

Hugh balked and took a step back.

'Ah. Well. Wow. That's different from just an openness to saying Yes … that's … well … you could get into a lot of trouble in two months.'

'Well … could you put a limiter on it?' I said. 'Could you perhaps make me stop short of murder and robbery?'

'You won't do anything that's against your moral code … that's not how hypnotism works. But it *will* mean that you'll lose your inhibitions … I'll have to get into your subconscious.'

'Is that dangerous?'

'Well … the subconscious is an amazing tool. People don't realise that you can literally ask your subconscious any question and when you're at your most relaxed, it will give you the answer. You literally ask it out loud, you go away, and it'll work on it.'

'Do you do that?'

'All the time. Like … last week. I was trying to come up with a title for a competition to find another Hypnodog. You know … an audition for another dog that can hypnotise people like Murphy can. But I was trying so hard to come up with a title that I just couldn't. So I asked my subconscious.'

'And?'

'Well, sometimes it takes a little time.'

'Oh.'

'Now, when I get into your subconscious, I'll remove the self-doubt you have. That fear of saying Yes.'

'It's not just fear that used to make me say no, though … sometimes I just couldn't be arsed. Someone would say, "Come and see this band tonight" and even if I was free I'd say, "Ah, I can't, I've got something on." And then I'd go home and watch *Neighbours*.'

'So you need to regain your childish enthusiasm … that's fine. We can do that. I suppose in some ways we have to find your … *reset* button.'

'Right, well … how are we going to do this?' I said, and I clapped my hands together to try and show I meant business. But I was actually becoming more and more nervous. Murphy rested his head on my lap. Was this part of it? If Hugh did the same, I was in trouble.

'I'll play some music – I generally use baroque music, because that's 60 beats a minute, like the heart, or failing that I've got a Richard Clayderman CD – and you'll relax for a little while … You'll stare into Murphy's eyes when I tell you to, and we'll take it from there … What I'd like to do is rid you of your preconceptions. Make your Yeses new and wonderful again.'

I wondered what preconceptions he thought I had, given that I had already agreed to be hypnotised by a man and his dog. I think Hugh saw that in my eyes.

'What I mean is … it's like with danger. You put a plank of wood between two buildings and no one will walk across it. You put that same plank of wood on the ground, and they won't have a problem doing it. I'm going to put all your Yeses on the ground.'

I saw what he was saying. If every option seemed secure, and every opportunity felt like a safe bet, I'd be far more likely to take them. I wanted to ask Hugh a little more about what we'd be doing, but I was a bit distracted. Murphy had started to sniff me, and it was slightly intimidating. Plus, I didn't want to wake up and discover that while I'd been asleep he'd given me a pair of huge German breasts. Although I suppose then I would at least have a chance of winning the contest held by the people looking for Britain's Most German-looking Man. Who, by the way, still hadn't phoned back.

Murphy whimpered, and suddenly I wasn't so sure about any of this. Sure, I needed a booster, and yes, this was the perfect cure-all for my particular predicament, but was it … right? Was this cheating? Would it really be me saying Yes to things, or would it be Hugh saying Yes for me? If I couldn't *help* but say Yes, that wasn't *choosing* to say Yes, was it? Or was it?

Hugh switched the video off and tried to find the right remote for the telly. He'd already found the right CD, and dimmed the lights.

What was I doing? I was about to be hypnotised by a Stormtrooper and his spacedog! I needed more time … I glanced about the room, desperate to find a distraction.

'Hugh … did you paint that picture?'

I pointed at a poster hanging on the wall.

'No …' said Hugh. 'That was Rembrandt.'

What else was there in here? What else could I use? And then I noticed something … something on the TV. Something that actually genuinely intrigued me. A strangely familiar view. When Hugh had turned the video off, the picture on the screen had turned into … well …

'Hugh … what's that?' I said.

'What's what?' said Hugh.

'That view on the telly …' I pointed at it. 'That's the view out of your front window, isn't it?'

This seemed very odd to me, whether buying time or not. Why close your curtains to block out the view but purposefully have the view piped into your TV? It seemed like something an extravagant rapper on MTV Cribs would do. Perhaps Hugh was more showbiz than I thought.

'Oh, that, yeah,' said Arlene, suddenly there. 'There's a camera on the windowsill.'

'Right … what … like a security thing?'

I was very grateful she'd arrived. She'd just bought me some time.

'No, no … nothing like that. It's very safe here.'

'Well, why then?'

'There's a little boy next door,' said Hugh, studying the back of another CD. 'Dean, his name is. He's great fun, but he wants to come in all the time. *Literally* all the time. He always knows when we're in, and so we close the curtains and put the camera on so we know if it's him at the door. Otherwise I'd end up doing magic all day, every day. Usually, we'll hear a knock, so we'll turn the telly on, and his face will be filling the whole screen. He presses his face right up to it so we can see it's him.'

'So he knows it's there?' I said. As a distraction technique, this was working wonderfully.

'Oh yes,' said Arlene. 'Doesn't stop him. He loves watching magic, and Hugh just can't turn him away.'

'I'm too polite. So that's why I had the camera installed.'

This was brilliant. They had actually installed a camera in their window so that they could avoid the little boy next door. And they'd had to do it because they were too polite to say no to him. They were trapped in their own home by a Yes.

'Can't you just tell him to come back another time?' I asked, wondering what else I could use to stall for time.

'He's crafty,' said Hugh. 'As soon as you open the door for him, he puts his foot in the hallway so you can't close it again. Sometimes we have to hide behind the sofa and keep quiet, like if we've forgotten to close the curtains, and he stands there with his face pressed up against the window for ten minutes or so, waiting for us to move.'

'Last week,' said Arlene, 'he knocked on the door and when we turned the camera on, he was holding his school report card up to the camera so we could read it. I mean, you can't really turn that away, can you?'

I loved Hugh and Arlene for this. I loved the fact that they were essentially being terrorised by a little boy who just wanted to be friends with them. I loved the fact that they wouldn't just tell him to go away, or complain to his parents, or jade him for life by rejecting him outright. And I loved the fact that when they talked about him, they smiled broadly, and with real love and enthusiasm in their voices. They loved the kid next door. They just wished he'd stay there.

'Look,' said Hugh, 'he gave me this the other day ...'

He pulled open a drawer and took out an A4 certificate. He read from it.

'It's a Best Mate Award. It says: "It's hard to find a friend like you – Lucky people have just one or two – However many, good friends are rare – And you for me are always there!"'

'But you're not!' I said. 'You're usually hiding behind the sofa!'

Suddenly, there was a knock at the door. A loud one.

'Ssh!' said Arlene, putting her fingers to her lips.

There was another knock now.

Bang.

Bang *bang*.

Hugh sat perfectly still. Arlene sat perfectly still. I sat perfectly still as well. We all stared at the TV. Suddenly, he stepped into frame. A little boy, of around eleven or twelve, with short blond hair and big blue eyes. He was staring at the camera now. He stepped closer to it, and just stared, and stared, and then tapped the window, and then stared.

No one said a thing. It was genuinely one of the most terrifying moments of my life.

And then the little boy shook his head, crossed his arms, and walked off.

'Anyway,' said Hugh. 'He's a lovely lad. But sometimes when he comes in, he'll take his jumper off, or one of his shoes, and he'll hide it in here, so he can come back later and get it. And he'll leave little presents. He gave me an ashtray he'd nicked from the pub the other day.'

'We call him "The News of the Valleys",' said Arlene. 'You tell him something and the whole valley knows before the end of the day.'

'Just before Christmas,' said Hugh, 'I told him he was doing my head in so I'd decided to move to Bosnia. The next day he turned up with a card that said "Bon Voyage" and a biscuit for the trip. I couldn't move for people coming up to me in the town and wishing me good luck in Bosnia.'

Suddenly, and with no warning whatsoever, we heard the letterbox flip open, quite violently. It was Dean. He was trying to catch us out. The letterbox remained open for ten or twenty seconds, while we all sat in our chairs, wide-eyed and silent. It started to close, but as it did so, Murphy let out a short sneeze, and the flap slowly opened up again. It was like something out of *Jurassic Park*. I held my breath. Moments later it slammed shut, and we watched the screen as a little boy who'd obviously tried to avoid the camera walked sheepishly away, and headed, grumpy-faced, back down the road.

'Anyway,' said Hugh. 'Are we going to get you hypnotised or what?'

And then, out of the blue, it hit me.

'Hugh! That show you need a title for!'

I was excited all of a sudden.

'Which show?'

'The one where you audition dogs and try and find a new Hypnodog!'

'Yes?'

'You should call it *Pup Idol*!'

Hugh's face lit up.

'*Pup Idol*! Brilliant! I told you! The subconscious! You concentrate on something else, and the answer comes to you! Right, hang on, I'm going to make a phone call ...'

An hour later, and I had just woken up.

My *Pup Idol* revelation had bought me some time ... but nowhere near enough.

I had undergone hypnosis.

I couldn't tell whether the dog had been involved at any point – which is always worrying when you wake up in a stranger's house – but he was certainly staring at me now. And so was ... a little soldier.

The tiniest soldier I had ever seen, in fact.

I recognised him more or less straight away. It was Dean. The kid from next door. He was sitting on the sofa opposite me.

'Hello,' I said.

'Hello,' he said back.

He was wearing a large black beret, full camouflage gear and shiny black boots. I wasn't sure quite what was going on, to be honest with you. It was like I'd fallen asleep and next door had invaded.

'Hey, Danny, I thought I'd let you wake up naturally,' said Hugh, walking into the room and throwing Murphy the last spare won-ton. 'Have you met Dean?'

'Yes,' I said. 'But have you hypnotised me to make children look like soldiers? Because if you have you should stop that right now.'

'Dean's on his way to ACF.'

'ACF?' I said.

'Armed Cadet Force,' said Dean.

'Oh,' I said, impressed but yawning. 'What are you armed with?'

'Nothing.'

'His wit!' said Hugh. 'Hey, he nicks all my jokes, this kid.'

'They're not yours,' said Dean, 'they're Tommy Cooper's.'

'We like watching Tommy Cooper videos, don't we?'

Dean nodded and smiled. Suddenly the fez made sense. And it was brilliant seeing the way the two boys bantered. They were clearly great mates.

But while all this was lovely, there was only one thing on my mind: had it worked? Was I now a Yes Man whether I liked it or not? I tried asking myself a question in my head. '*Shall I have a cup of tea later? ... Yes.*' It certainly *seemed* to be working.

'Danny, did you know Tommy Cooper lived down the road, in Caerphilly?' said Hugh. 'Quite a few people lived around here. Tommy Cooper, Tom Jones …'

Suddenly, Arlene poked her head around the door.

'I saw Don Estelle from the 1970s in town the other day singing karaoke and selling home-made cassettes of himself singing.' She paused. 'No one was buying any.'

There was something about her deep Welsh accent that gave that already rather melancholy image so much more poignancy. I nearly felt like crying.

'Anyway, Dean, you'd better be off to ACF …' said Arlene.

Dean nodded, gave us all a little salute, and said he'd be back round later, at which Hugh secretly rolled his eyes.

He walked towards the door, and I was about to ask Hugh how the hypnosis had gone, when he turned around.

'By the way, I came round earlier but you didn't answer,' he said, accusingly.

'I was out,' lied Hugh.

'But your car was here.'

'I … walked.'

'No. You were in.'

'How do you know?'

'Because I looked through the letterbox and your keys were in the door.'

Hugh went a bit red.

'Okay. I was in. Now get out.'

Dean shut the door behind him.

'You let him in, then?' I said.

'Arlene was putting the bins out and he ran in while her back was turned.'

'Nice kid, though.'

'The best.'

There was a slight lull in the conversation. I knew what I wanted to say, but I didn't quite know how to put it.

'So … um … I don't … y'know … feel all that different.'

'No?'

'Nope. I mean, since the … you know. Since you …'

'Since you fell asleep?'

'Yes. Well, no. I mean, since you put that Richard Clayderman CD on and … *hypnotised* me.'

Hugh sat down.

'Danny … listen … don't be annoyed, but … I decided not to hypnotise you. Not properly, anyway.'

'Eh? Why? I thought that's what you did? You and Murphy?'

'Well, it's mainly me. Murphy's a dog, after all. And I decided not to.'

'But why?'

'I talked to you when you were under and … well … you don't need it. From everything you've told me, you're doing this because you want to, and because you need to. It takes a certain amount of dedication, and that's what you've done … and it means more if you can fail. Because if you can fail, then you can also *win*. The way I see it, it means more if you do it yourself. As humans, we seem to go to more effort to avoid trouble and pain than we do to make things better. Avoiding, rather than *doing*. Am I anywhere near the mark?'

'I think so,' I said, knowing he was. If I was going to do this, if I was going to survive until the end of December, I was going to have to do this myself. What good is sorting out your own life, if it's not you that's sorting it? Where's the achievement in being *programmed* to do something? What's the lesson? That someone will always be there to help? If I was going to act irresponsibly, the least I could do was be *responsible* for it.

Hugh dropped me off at the station half an hour later. We sat in the car as rain began to spatter the windscreen. Hugh offered me a carton of Ribena as we waited for my train to arrive.

'When you think about it,' he said, 'probably some of the best things that have ever happened to you in life, happened because you said Yes to something. Otherwise, things just sort of stay the same.'

We let the thought hang in the air.

'I mean, just ask Arlene. She can't get enough of bloody won-ton now. She wants me to pick some more up on the way home.'

I smiled. I'd never realised that won-ton could be a real symbol of hope in this world.

'But some things we have to do for ourselves,' said Hugh. 'I mean, take me … *I* had a fear once. A terrible one. But I conquered that fear. Through hard work and self-belief. Not hypnotism.'

'Oh. What were you afraid of?'

Hugh blushed.

'Dogs.'

'*Dogs*?!'

He nodded.

'Dogs.'

I rode home to London, and braced myself for the final push.

Selected extracts from the

diary of a Yes Man: 3

September 28th

On the way home from Wales the other day, I noticed an advert in the paper saying, do you want to be a writer? and then dutifully sent off for the information pack. They asked, by return of post, for a 300-word sample of my writing in any genre. I chose science fiction and wrote the following this morning. I have called it, rather ominously, 'Future War'.

Tex McBellamy cast his eyes to the skies, and smiled the smile of victory. He had done it. He had single-handedly taken on the entire Kraxxon race with only his trusty friend and robot, Figgy5000, for back-up.

'I don't think they'll be coming back for more,' said Tex, which was true, because they were all dead.

'MEEP I think that MEEP we should both go to the MEEP,' said Figgy5000, but he was stopped from saying any more by the sudden sound of an explosion on the horizon.

'What the ...' said Tex, never intending to finish the sentence and actually leaving it at that.

'MEEP,' said Figgy5000, 'MEEP.'

It was a Heli-chopper, a futuristic cross between a helicopter and a chopper. It was the vehicle of choice for Senator Greenglove, the evil Senator who had first imprisoned Tex all those years ago in that cell he was in at the start.

'Greenglove,' said Tex. 'So he's come back to finish the job himself ...'

'McBellamy!' screamed Greenglove from out of the big

tannoy on the front of the Heli-chopper, and shaking his trade-mark green begloved fist at Tex. 'So we meet again! Well, prepare for your doom! You know that it's a crime now that we're in the twentymillionth century for you to have your own thoughts and ideas! Well, you've had far too many of them, and you've had your last! So it's back to the big prison made out of ice that I made for you!'

Tex groaned. He hated that big ice prison.

'You dumb bastard!' he shouted. 'Why don't you and your frozen cell just melt off! I will not return there!'

'Yes you will!' retorted Senator Greenglove.

'Figgy5000,' Tex whispered. 'On my order, reverse the polarity on your positron deactivators.'

'MEEP okay,' said Figgy5000, who by the way was shaped like a beautiful woman.

'Well, Senator Greenglove, I suppose I'll have to come quietly then ...' said Tex, but Greenglove couldn't hear him because he was still miles away and Tex didn't have a tannoy on his front like he did.

I enclosed a note with the words 'To Be Continued ...' and I told them that this was merely a small part of an epic Tex McBellamy trilogy I have in the pipeline. Hopefully they will like it and we can publish sometime early next year.

October 5th
Paul Lewis was the boy at my school who used to bully people. He has just found me on Friends Reunited and said we should go for a pint sometime. I had to say Yes.

My most vivid memory of Paul Lewis is from the end of every school day, when he used to give Anil Patel, a boy in a wheelchair, a dead arm – just because he liked 'watching him go round in circles'.

We are meeting next Thursday in Bath.

October 7th
Saw something in the *Standard*. 'WOULD YOU BE INTERESTED IN PARTICIPATING IN A CLINICAL TRIAL INVESTIGATING WOMEN'S SEXUAL LIBIDO AFTER MENOPAUSE?'

I rang the number, but it turned out I was ineligible.

Sometimes it surprises me how deep the discrimination in this country runs.

October 8th

My mum has sent me an article she thinks I might be interested in. A girl called Laura, who I knew when I was 12, is now 26 and has opened a dried flower shop in Trowbridge. When I unfold the article, I see that the bottom half of the paper says, in very bold type, DISCOVER MIDSOMER NORTON!

It is an advert paid for by three local businesses – Docky's Delicatessen ('As well as selling a wide range of continental cheeses, Docky's also sell baguettes!'); The Barber Shop ('After 16 years in the business, Emma, the inspiration behind The Barber Shop, noticed a gap in the market and decided to open a men's hair stylists in Midsomer Norton!'); and Katona Cast Stone Ltd ('Come to Katona Cast Stone Ltd – Pots, Garden Ornaments, Bird Baths, Urns etc.').

Midsomer Norton is a small town quite near Bath. I will discover its three shops on Thursday before meeting Paul.

October 13th

Paul Lewis thinks we should stay in touch and become great friends. He is in the Territorial Army now. He says it gave him targets and focus and changed his life. He thinks I should apply too – that way we could be comrades as well as great friends. He has invited me to his stag weekend which will take place on a barge with his army pals. I think Paul Lewis may be planning to abduct and kill me.

I discovered Midsomer Norton. It was all right, but Docky's were out of baguettes.

October 14th

A reminder e-mail from celebrated bully Paul Lewis about my joining the Territorial Army. He says I should fill in their online application form to get more details. I go to the site and fill in the boxes. At one point it asks me if I would like to offer any particular skills to the TA. I click Yes and it presents me with a huge list of options. I choose 'receptionist'.

October 15th

I have three hairs on my chest – but not for much longer. Today I accepted a no risk, 30-day, money-back-guarantee trial pack from the people at HairBeGone – an 'amazing new product that says goodbye to shaving, tweezing and waxing!'. I will receive my two tubes of hair removal cream and a hair growth inhibitor spray very soon. However, I noticed no recommendations from doctors and no safety notices, either, so who knows what it will do to my hair. It is at times like this that I wish Stuart the cat was real. I know animal experimentation is wrong, but something that hairy has to get self-conscious every now and again.

Plus: *result!* If I say Yes to upgrading my mobile phone to a new, fancy Siemens one, my phone company will give me a free, return flight to any major European city! What a cracking Yes!

Also sent off for an information pack on learning Flemish within 28 days. I guess I could have chosen a different language, but I had a waffle yesterday and I suppose the feeling just stuck.

October 16th
Paul Lewis has e-mailed again. Just to say hello.

October 17th
Another e-mail from Paul Lewis. He wants to know if I want to meet up again soon. I am a bit scared of Paul Lewis.

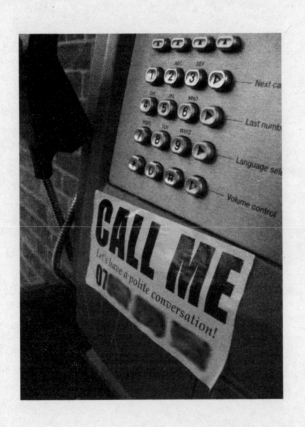

18

In which Daniel finally
has a Polite Conversation

It was 7 am and my phone was ringing. What kind of society do we live in, where someone can make your phone ring at 7 am? There should be rules.

'Hello?' I said, my voice gruff and my eyes bleary.

But no one spoke.

'Hello?' I said, again.

I could hear what sounded like trains in the background, and the bing-bong of a tannoy.

'Who's that?' I said, but there was no answer. I was about to hang up, when …

'It's Paul,' said a man. He had a northern accent and what sounded like caution in his voice. 'Why? Who's that?'

'It's Danny.'

'Right …' said Paul. 'And what do you want?'

I was confused. What did I want? I thought about it. I didn't know. Why was I speaking to Paul? What *did* I want?

'I don't know,' I said. 'I thought you called *me*.'

'I did,' said Paul. 'I wanted to find out what you wanted.'

This isn't the kind of conversation I'm used to having at seven in the morning.

'I'm afraid I am very confused,' I said. 'I'm afraid I don't know what I want. Why? What do *you* want?'

'Er … well, I found this sticker, saying "Call Me" and then this number, and it was playing on my mind, so—'

'Oh!' I said, sitting up, suddenly on top of the situation. The mere mention of my sticker was like a slap round the face. 'Yes! That's mine! Don't hang up!'

Amazing! It was someone who genuinely wanted to have a polite conversation!

'Right … so … what's it all about?'

And I told him.

It turned out that Paul didn't want to have a polite conversation. At least, not right then. He'd love to have one at some stage, but it'd have to be a bit later. He had to get on his train to go to work, he said, and he had a meeting first thing which was about European strategies and business integration and he had to go to it because he was going to be taking the next meeting and he wanted to make sure he knew the form because they had a very different approach at his last company, but he did wonder whether I'd like to have a polite conversation after work, when his train got back in, which should be about a quarter past six but could just as easily be a quarter past who-knows-when these days, what with one thing and another but he's been putting the hours in after work a lot recently so he should be able to get away without any problems, really, oh look, there's his train, he should be on his way.

To be honest, I somehow felt like I'd had about six polite conversations with Paul already, but he sounded like a nice man who just wanted a chat, and I was excited to have finally had some success with the scheme. So we quietly and politely arranged to meet.

I was happy. That was precisely the kind of thing I should be doing with my life. Throwing open the doors. Seeing who walks in. Saying Yes to a new friend.

I'd been doing a lot of thinking about things like this, these past few days.

And much of it had been to do with what Hugh had told me.

When you think about it, probably some of the best things that have ever happened to you in life, happened because you said Yes to something. Otherwise, things just sort of stay the same.

It was true. The more I thought about it, the easier it was to trace almost any of the best things that have ever happened to me back to one, single moment of Yes. Maybe you can, too. I mean, think about the best thing that ever happened to *you*. And now think about *how* that thing happened.

I tried it one night with Wag, over a pint.

'Wag, mate … what's the best thing ever to have happened to you?'

'1998. Newbury. The hour was late. Domino's brought the wrong order round. We got four pizzas instead of—'

'Apart from that?'

He thought about it.

'My girlfriend.'

'Your girlfriend. And how did you meet your girlfriend?'

'A stroke of good luck. I happened to be at a gig, and so was she, and that was that.'

'Why did you go to the gig?'

'Someone asked me to cover for them. I was playing bass.'

'Okay. And you said Yes?'

'Yeah.'

'And did you really want to do it?'

'No. But it was a favour.'

'Yevel Three. Right. And who asked you?'

'Ben.'

'Who's Ben?'

'A guy I met at a party.'

'Who invited you to that party?'

'Neil.'

'How did you meet Neil?'

'University.'

'You nearly didn't go to university, though, eh?'

'Well … yeah … but …'

'So by saying Yes to going to university, you ended up meeting Neil, and he, in turn, helped you end up with, in your words, the best thing that's ever happened to you.'

Wag looked a bit affected by it.

'Do you think I should get him a card?'

The thing I realised instantly was that at first, Wag had blamed all this on luck. But *he'd* made that luck happen. He just hadn't realised it. He'd made a series of 'correct' choices, which led him, bass in hand, to his girl. Maybe we can *all* do that. Maybe we can all change our fortunes. Maybe there's no such thing as destiny – there's just a series of choices we create ourselves. I guess it's only when we look at how a No could have changed our lives for the worse that we realise the value of the tiny Yeses that fly at us each day.

It was a revelatory moment – maybe we really did all have the power to change our lives for the better using this one simple word. Yes had made me fall for Lizzie, true – but rather than mope around, pining after a dream, maybe a Yes could help. Maybe it could at least help me get over her. Maybe it could even work again. There was now a hole where she'd been and somehow I felt I needed to fill it. It was down to me to say Yes.

I found the number Hanne had given me for her friend Kristen, I took a deep breath, and I gave her a call.

I found it difficult to sleep that night. I was anxious. There were a few things to be anxious about. I'd had a slightly stilted conversation with Kristen, and she'd suggested a time and a place, and I'd said, 'Yes, great, that'd be nice.' But was it the right thing to be doing? It was something I would never, ever have done before – a blind date, essentially. Hanne seemed to think it was for the best. But then Hanne used to think it was okay to make smoothies at five in the morning with the loudest blender in the world. But what would Lizzie think? Fair enough, we had no future, but wasn't it all a bit … soon? Something else was on my mind, too. I couldn't help but wonder what the Challenger had up his sleeve next. The need to unmask him was pressing. Every couple of weeks there was something else – something worse – and I was due for another some time soon. Plus, it was clear that Jason – if it was, indeed, Jason – was slowly upping the pace of his challenges. From 'wear this', to 'drive there', to 'change your rules' … I had to find him quickly and efficiently and before he reached the next level of mischief and intrigue. And what would that be? '*Fly* there'? '*Run* here?' '*Kill* that'? It was time to be pro-active. To *stop* him, rather than just react to his whims.

I got up and switched on my Mac. First, I e-mailed his hotmail address again.

>To: whoisthechallenger@hotmail.com
>From: Danny
>Subject: Stop

Look here,
Why aren't you writing back to me? I know exactly who you are, and what you're up to. I've done everything you've asked so far, but once I've unmasked you, you will have no

**choice but to stop. So you may as well stop now and avoid
my wrath, which can be quite considerable once I'm riled.
So there.
Danny**

And then, to make sure I was covering all the angles, I e-mailed Thom
again.

**Thom,
It's Danny again. I'm sorry to bother you, but could you let
me know if you get this e-mail. Did you get my last one? I
think your mate Jason is still playing pranks on me. I need to
get in touch with him but I don't know how.
Please – get back to me!
Danny**

I pressed Send, then sat back in my chair with a sigh.

This was a mystery I needed to solve.

It was two evenings later and I was sitting in a pub just off Oxford Street
with Paul, the man who'd phoned me up for a polite conversation.

He was a pleasant chap, in his forties, with neat hair and a blue suit.
He wore a chunky watch and slightly raised shoes. Our polite conversation had started well, but somewhere along the line had taken an
odd turn.

'There's a lot of shit talked about Border terriers,' he said.

And that's where I have to interrupt. Border terriers was pretty much
all Paul and I had talked about tonight … well, pretty much all Paul had
talked about. The phrase 'let's have a polite conversation' does, I hope
you'll agree, imply two people exchanging opinions and viewpoints …
Paul had clearly misread that, and taken it to mean, 'please deliver some
lengthy monologues on subjects only you have an opinion on'. It just
went on and on and on.

'The number one thing people say about Border terriers,' he said,
which had instantly terrified me, because I knew I was in for a list. 'Is
this: "Border terriers do not shed their hair." Well, that is a total fallacy.
They *do* shed, and some of them shed very heavily. Contrary to popular
belief, they are *not* a non-shedding breed.'

'Okay,' I said. 'Got you.'

But Paul clearly wasn't finished. He pointed his finger in the air and continued.

'Also … the number two thing people say: "Border terriers are easy to train." Well, how exactly are we defining "easy"?'

He laughed like this was the most common and ridiculous mistake a rookie in the Border terrier field could make, and he laughed as he carried on.

'Do you know what I mean, Danny? How does one define "easy"?'

'That's right,' I said. 'There are probably a lot of variables.'

'Precisely, Danny. That's right. There are a lot of variables.'

Saying 'there are probably a lot of variables' is my number one tip for appearing to be on top of a conversation when, really, you are six miles out of your depth. Consider it a gift from me to you.

'"Number three: Border terriers are good around small children". Well, to a certain extent that *is* true. But Danny … no dog should *ever* be left with a child unsupervised. That is a definite no-no.'

'Definitely.'

'Do you know why?'

I didn't even know what my name was any more.

'Er … lots of variables?'

Paul just looked at me. I never said the variables thing would work twice in a row.

'Well … I suppose so.'

Oh. It does.

'Another pint, Danny?'

Inwardly, I collapsed.

'Sure,' I said.

'Your round, then, maestro!'

And I went to get them in.

I liked Paul – he was a nice and gentle man – but after another ten minutes I do have to admit that I did wish he would stop talking about Border terriers.

We agreed to meet again, in a week or two. He said he'd call me. I didn't doubt it. I was now the world's second foremost authority on Border terriers. Who *wouldn't* want to hang around with me?

There was huge and explosive excitement upon my return home that night. For two reasons.

The first was a message on my home phone. It was from Gareth, at

Richard & Judy. He was apologising for the delay, but they'd finally decided to go ahead with what he called *'Danny's Path to Enlightenment'*! He wanted to know if I was free this coming Saturday to go up to Yorkshire to film a report with a load of Buddhist monks! Of *course* I bloody was! Although, as I'd decided to play it cool, the e-mail I sent him read 'Should be fine, yeah, talk soon.'

But how cool was that? My Yes had come good! I was going to meet some monks! On *telly*!

The second exciting event was that Thom had finally replied to my e-mails.

> **Danny!**
> **How's the car?! Got your e-mails about Jason, sorry, things been manic here with the move and all. Tried e-mailing him but he's not there at the moment apparently. Annoying! Have another couple of avenues to chase up, think his sister works at Lancaster Uni, will get back to you. What's your address, by the way? And what's Jason been doing? Sounds naughty!**
> **Thom**

This was fantastic news. I mean, fair enough, I was no closer to catching Jason out, but at least now I had an ally. Thom was aware of the situation and would help me bring Jason to justice. The Challenger was nearing his end.

I went to bed, happy. Things were on the up again.

I think Kristen had been looking forward to our intimate tête-à-tête. And so, I think, had all her friends.

'I'm Kristen,' said a tall, attractive, Sloaney girl, when I walked in. 'And this is Dan, Michael, Bri, Jane, Rudi and Nick.'

'Hello … everyone,' I said.

'Hello,' they all said back.

Kristen had suggested the time and the place. A slightly grubby pub in Islington. During the Arsenal versus Tottenham match. With just about everyone she knew. It wasn't classic date material.

'When Hanne suggested I met up with you for a drink,' she said, 'I was, like, *oh, you fucking wankers*!'

Kristen was on her feet now, shouting at the telly. As were Dan, Michael, Bri, Jane, Rudi and Nick. Arsenal had just scored.

'… but then I thought about it,' sitting back down, 'and, you know, I thought, sometimes …'

'*Get a fucking grip ref you blind bloody bastard*!' shouted Nick, next to her, and she patted his knee.

There is little I find more terrifying than girls in pubs who are really, really into football. For one thing, they are the loudest, angriest women in the world. They're up and out of their seats quicker than my eye can move. Many's the time I've thought the girl in the seat next to me had evaporated, when in fact they were now on their feet screaming obscenities I didn't even know existed. As you can probably guess, I'm not really very big on football. International games I love, but your normal, run-of-the-mill pub-based Arsenal-versus-Tottenhams I tend to leave well alone. Maybe it comes from having a dad who supports Carlisle United, a team who scored once, sometime in the '80s. It somehow wasn't enough to enthuse me to the merits of league games, although I remember the occasion well because Dad bought some biscuits to celebrate. You can still see him to this day, in empty, windswept stadiums up and down the country, standing wet and silent with half a dozen or so other retired men also old enough to remember the glory days – though old enough to know better, too.

I sat in near-silence as the group stared intently at the screen, but I couldn't shake my feeling of awkwardness. It felt like I was … cheating, somehow. But hey – this was only a drink. And it was only a Yes. I remembered something. I could *choose* to be okay. So I turned to Kristen, and I started to talk to her.

'So is it reds versus whites?' I asked, only partly in jest.

Kristen looked at me.

'You're not into football, then?'

'Not exactly. Who's the guy in the black? One of their dads?'

She smiled. A nice smile. All of a sudden this wasn't so bad.

'The referee,' she said. 'But I think you knew that. To tell you the truth, I'm not all that into football either … force of habit from my dad.'

'Ah. Me too. What does your dad do?'

'He's retiring next year.'

'Oh. Are you going to get a new one?'

She laughed. I'd scored a point.

'Oh, come on you *utter wankers*!' she suddenly shouted. I guess if she's not all that into football, she must just really love swearing in public.

'This is bollocks,' she said. 'Do you want to get out of here?'

* * *

Kristen and I sat in a bar on Upper Street.

My phone rang. I answered it. They hung up.

Kristen leaned forward.

'Don't you find it a bit weird that Hanne's set you up on a kind of date?' she said.

'Yes,' I said, turning my phone off. 'Do you?'

She sipped at her wine.

'Pretty much. So why have you come?'

'You could call it … open-mindedness.'

'That's a good thing,' she said. 'It's good to be open-minded.'

There was a pause, but not an awkward one. I took a breadstick.

'Relationships are tricky,' she suddenly said. 'Sometimes you know where you are with them, or you think you do, and then one day you realise that you just don't. All of a sudden. Like it happened in an instant. Don't you find that, sometimes?'

'Yeah,' I said. 'Sometimes.'

'My last boyfriend, Ben. Everything was cool. We'd been seeing each other since university. And then one day he met someone else. And that was that. Four years, over in an evening.'

'Oh,' I said. 'I'm sorry. That must have been—'

'It was. It was shit. But … probably for the best. Better now, than when we had kids, or something.'

I nodded.

'It just makes me … I don't know … now that I'm single, I'm worried that I'm always missing out on something … I felt more *content* before. I guess it's just because I don't—'

'Is it like you're not grabbing opportunities? Ones that could lead somewhere? But you're not sure where?'

'Exactly!' she said. 'Yeah … like I could be missing out on the important things.'

I didn't quite know what to say next. I knew exactly what she meant, but saying I did would cheapen it, somehow. Make it seem less unique to her. Because until now, I'd thought it was unique to me.

'How about you?' she said. 'Last relationship? Or was that Hanne?'

'Well … kind of. There was a girl. But it couldn't work. Long-distance. I mean, it *could've* worked … but …'

'Sure,' she said. 'That's tough in its own way. The *not knowing*. Worse than the knowing, in a sense. No matter how many friends you have, sometimes you just want to be with one person.'

I liked Kristen. And I felt sorry for her. Things were still raw for her. And me? Well, I'm sure she felt sorry for me, too. I took another breadstick and realised that my heart just wasn't in this. The meeting, I mean, not the breadstick. Kristen was right – sometimes you *do* just want to be with one person.

And then she smiled.

'Do you want to get some food?'

I felt like I'd made a new friend in Kristen. It was good to meet someone who … *understood*. I was glad I'd said Yes to this.

We bought ourselves a fine meal of pasta and wine, and chatted, and laughed, and the time didn't seem to matter any more. We hit another bar, and soon we'd forgotten our woes and our pasts and absolutely everything else, and, as the bar shut and we prepared to go our separate ways, she suddenly said, 'Coffee?'

Christ. What did she mean by that? But it was a Yes moment. A moment to be grabbed, just like Kristen had said. But all I could say was 'Um …' before Kristen jumped in, with, 'Come on. I *actually* mean coffee. I live round the corner. You can have a coffee and call a cab. You can also have a biscuit if you're lucky.'

I smiled, and said, 'Cool,' and we made our way to her place.

I heard her open a bottle of wine in the kitchen, and I laughed when she brought it through, and we talked some more, about holidays, and childhoods, and families. She told me she was going to try and get tickets to a gig in Camden soon, and should she get one for me, and even though I'd never heard of the band, I smiled and said Yes.

And then, when I was putting my coat on, getting ready to go downstairs and find my way home, she tilted her head, and said, 'look, I don't normally do this' and my heart leapt and my shoulders tensed as I realised what was coming next.

'Would you like to stay with *me* tonight?'

19

In which the reader is required

to read between the lines

I probably shouldn't talk about it.
  And I'm not sure I really want to, either.
  For now.
  Just for now.
  Sorry.

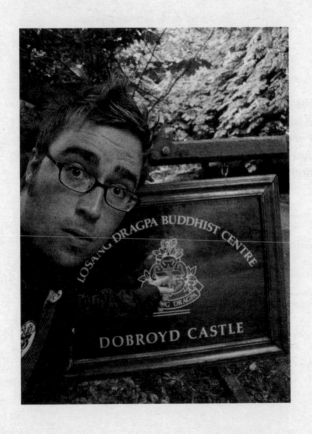

20

In which Daniel travels to the
goodly Castle of Dobroyd, and chances
upon more of the Wisdom of Maitreya

Now, if there's one thing that we all learnt at school, it's that the towns and villages of England's West Yorkshire region make up the global centre of international Buddhist activity.

Which is why I was now on my way there to meet some monks.

My new and unexpected employers at *Richard & Judy* had charged me with an exciting mission – go to West Yorkshire, hang out with some Buddhists, and film a short report. It sounded easy enough. And exciting enough. I still couldn't really believe that I'd been asked to do this. I mean, there were *plenty* of people far more qualified than I was. Su Pollard was advertising *steam cleaners*, for God's sake – surely *she'd* have been free? I can only imagine that, after meeting me, Gareth and Dean had decided that out of everyone who could possibly benefit from a series of enlightenment courses, I was probably the one who needed it most.

The journey from London to Yorkshire is a long one. I was driving up with Robin, the researcher, and Jeff, the sound recordist, and we'd been on the road for several hours already. We'd spent much of that time stuck on a narrow road behind a blue estate car with a sign in the window that said 'Baby on Board'. It had taken me nearly forty minutes to realise that, unless that baby was *steering*, I really didn't need to know it was on board at all. Eventually, we managed to overtake, and to our joy saw a sign marked 'Todmorden'.

I'd be meeting the director and cameraman from *Richard & Judy* at a secluded castle in this small town. But this made me a little nervous. After all, as I slowly worked out, Todmorden is made up of two basic words:

'tod' and 'mord'. Tod means Death in German. And mord means Murder. I'm not sure about you, but spending the day in a secluded castle in a town called Deathmurder doesn't sound like the ideal weekend break to me. I decided very quickly that if I was approached by any monk named either Professor Plum or Colonel Mustard, I'd be out the door, in the car, with a five-iron. Which is a scenario Cluedo never seemed to cover.

'So you're the man looking for enlightenment, eh?' said Jim, the director.

'Well, I suppose so,' I said, shaking his hand. 'If there's any enlightenment going. So this is the place, eh?'

We were standing outside Dobroyd Castle – an imposing but friendly castle surrounded by trees and woodland. It was built in 1865 as a symbol of love from husband to wife, but things hadn't quite worked out. He'd been the rich mill owner's son; she a poor mill worker. He'd fallen deeply in love with her, and she'd said she would only marry him if he built her a castle as a present. In a grand gesture of love, he did just that. She didn't like it very much. She moved into a little chalet on the grounds instead. The man was heartbroken, the woman died an alcoholic. It can be no coincidence that soon after, someone invented gift vouchers.

'So,' said Jim. 'Here's what we're going to do …'

He took me to one side.

'I've had a look about the place. There are some great locations. This should be easy. So what we'll do is this: we'll film you arriving, and then we'll film you meeting a couple of the monks, and then we'll film you leaving.'

'Right. Sounds easy enough.'

'Yes. The whole thing shouldn't take more than six or seven hours.'

'Oh.'

'Have you presented much TV before?'

'No. This is my first time.'

Jim went a bit pale.

'Right. Well, the whole thing shouldn't take more than nine or ten hours. Robin will brief you on what else we'll be doing, and Jeff will put a mic on you.'

'Basically,' said Robin, who was wearing a baseball cap and had the chin of a superhero, 'we want you to get *under the skin* of the Buddhist monk. Find out if Buddhism is the way for you. What makes a monk tick? And we need to work in the stuff they do here; the courses, the things you can learn, the people you'll meet. Sound good?'

'Yep. Just point me at a monk and let's do this.'

Jeff the sound man sprang into action. He pulled my jumper down and attached a microphone to my chest with a piece of tape.

'Good. Smooth chest,' he said. 'I won't be ripping any hairs out, then.'

'It's all thanks to HairBeGone,' I said, and he laughed, because I don't think he believed me.

'Right,' said Robin. 'We've arranged a meeting for you with …' he paused '… Samten.'

'Who's Samten?'

'Samten's the man. He's the big monk on campus. He's in charge. And he's agreed to let you talk to him.'

'Great.'

'But first, why don't you take a bit of a walk around? Get to know the place?'

Dobroyd Castle was bought by the monks in 1995, for a few hundred thousand pounds. It was in total disrepair. The monks decided to use it to start up a centre – the Losang Dragpa Centre – which would offer cheap courses, teachings and meditations to anyone who decided they needed it. It's a remarkably giving attitude, seeing as all they want in return is some help with rebuilding the castle. Anyone is welcome, at any time of year. If you're stuck for something to do, I'd genuinely recommend it.

'Oh,' said a man, suddenly in front of me. He had a shaved head, and was wearing a long red robe. I guessed he was probably a monk. 'Hello.'

'Hello,' I said. 'Nice place.'

'Thank you. Are you with the TV people?'

'Yes,' I said.

'Welcome,' he said.

And he started to walk with me.

His name was Liam and he loved it here.

'This is a place to nurture inner peace,' he said. 'Anyone can get refuge here. They don't even have to be Buddhist. You can just come along and free your mind from the negative. We just want to help increase peace and happiness in the world.'

Liam and I talked more as we walked around the castle. Eventually, we found a bench and sat on it.

'We learn things here like … you know … we should value all our moments,' said Liam. 'And live each day as if it were our last on earth.

Well, actually, that's a bit strong. Let me rephrase that. What I mean is, we should constantly be aware that we may die today.'

I raised my eyebrows. Liam thought about it.

'Actually, that's even *stronger*, isn't it? All I mean is: we must be aware that there is a distinct possibility that you and I may die today.'

Bloody hell. I was in a secluded castle in a town called Deathmurder with a man who was repeatedly telling me there was a distinct possibility that I may die today.

'I mean, we may *not* die today,' he said, raising his finger. 'But … we *may*.'

He wasn't making me feel much better, to be honest, but there was no stopping him now. We were on a path to existentialism.

'Both statements – that we *may* die today, and that we may *not* die today – are ultimately true. But it's more meaningful to say we *may* die today because we then value every moment.'

'It's also a bit more frightening,' I said. And it was. Fair enough, I'd be valuing every moment. But I'd probably be valuing them from under my bed.

'Well, maybe. But the thing is, Danny, it's very easy to become complacent. Samten says that being aware of our mortality makes us more open, and, ironically, makes us feel more alive. Now, let's take a walk over here …'

For the next hour and a half, the *Richard & Judy* crew filmed me chopping celery with monks, cleaning toilets with monks, wandering around the gardens with monks, and generally just getting up to all sorts of monk-based mischief. And I was having fun. The monks had welcomed me with open arms and shaven heads, and I was slowly falling in love with their way of life. It's hard to explain, but everyone had a certain … glow. They were happy. And rested. I was taught how to meditate, and I was given a slap-up lunch, and I learnt about their teachings.

Eventually, the director called a break.

'Are you getting what you need?' I asked.

'It's fine,' said Jim. 'But we need something … *else*.'

I nodded, enthusiastically.

'What else do you need?'

'I'm not sure … it's just that … at the moment, it's all quite … *nice*.'

'But monks *are* nice. That's one of the things about monks. Especially *Buddhist* monks. They're *renowned* for their niceness.'

Which is true. Very rarely will you hear that a Buddhist monk has attempted a kidnapping, for example, or tried to carjack a pensioner. That's one of the main things about Buddhist monks – they possess a total and utter inability to carjack a pensioner. I call it a weakness.

'Monks are nice, yes,' said Jim. 'But I just wonder … well … you already seem pretty sold on Buddhism …'

'It's lovely!'

'Yes, but … you see, if you decide that Buddhism is the way ahead for you, then there probably isn't any point in doing any further films with you. Because you'll already have decided. So you need to take a deeper look at their way of life, I think … show them from another angle.'

'Right,' I said, determined to come up with a solution. Yes had given me a chance. I wasn't about to stuff it up.

'I'll leave that with you,' said Jim, and he went off to do something important.

I was having a biscuit with Jeff. He said he'd known I was hungry, because even at a distance of thirty feet he could hear my tummy rumbling through his headphones.

'I have to try and show them from another angle,' I said. 'Look at them in a deeper way. How am I going to do that?'

Jeff took a bite of his biscuit and thought about the situation.

'You could mess with them a bit,' he said.

'Mess with the monks?'

'Mess with their zen. They're supposed to be the calmest people on earth. See if you can get one riled. It'll make great telly.'

'You think I should anger a monk?' I said, in disbelief. 'It'll never work! They're too laid-back!'

'Well … you could give it a go. It'd just give them some options in the edit. You know … you could spice it up a bit. You could show the darker side of monks.'

'But monks don't *have* a darker side. Do they?'

I can honestly say that if there was one thing I wasn't comfortable with, it was this. After all, Robin had said I'd be getting under their skin – not getting on their tits. But it was a *suggestion* – from a television professional! Plus, I knew why I was there, and I didn't want to be a prima donna, and so I nodded, and said that was a good idea. Well. It was the *only* idea.

Rather reluctantly, I set about finding a way of severely vexing a Buddhist.

* * *

I wandered around the grounds, looking for potential ways and means.

I'd be meeting Samten later on and I didn't really want him to think I was some kind of maverick monk-baiter. But suddenly, I noticed a pond. If all else failed, I could always push a monk into the pond. But that seemed too harsh, somehow. It seemed to me that it would be a shame if, at some point in the distant future, when scores of young people take up the Lessons of Yes, all they did was get drunk and push a couple of monks into a pond.

Inspiration just wasn't coming. I walked on, with lead in my shoes.

'So you're going to be meeting with Samten later on?' said a monk on the bench.

I'd sat myself down for a moment to compose myself.

'Yes,' I said. 'I think so.'

'Oh, that's great. You're lucky. He's amazing. You'll love him. He's amazing.'

'Is he?'

'Yes. He's amazing.'

'Why?'

'Why? Because he's *amazing*. He makes you feel like the only person in the world when he talks to you. He's the most spiritual man you'll ever meet. He just *knows* things. You can ask him anything, and he *just knows things*. And he's patient, and he sets a pure example to all he meets.'

'He sounds brilliant,' I said, genuinely convinced.

'He is. He's brilliant,' he said. 'He's *amazing*.'

Suddenly there was a voice from one of the windows behind me. It was Jim.

'Danny! You ready?'

I signalled that I was and began to collect my thoughts.

'So …' I said, to the monk on the bench. 'I was just wondering … not that this has anything to do with anything, really … but what *annoys* someone like you?'

The monk breathed in, through his nose, and thought long and hard.

'War,' he said.

'War?' I said.

'War,' he said, and he turned to face me, and nodded, grim-faced.

Jesus. If I was going to have to start a bloody war before I could vex a monk, this was going to be a very long day indeed.

* * *

'Okay, Danny,' said Robin. 'Samten is ready for you now. We'll just do a general interview with him, okay?'

'Okay,' I said. 'I'm ready.'

Jeff winked at me and gave me a little thumbs-up. And then the tallest monk in the world walked into the room. He smiled, and shook my hand.

'I'm Samten,' he said.

'Wow!' I said, genuinely impressed. 'You're the tallest monk in the world! You should be *King* of the Monks!'

'Well … thank you,' said Samten, who had taken it as a compliment, when I'd actually meant it as a fact. 'Why don't we sit down in the lounge and have a chat?'

Samten had the kind of voice that made *anything* sound peaceful and appealing. He could have said, 'Why don't I tie some bacon to your face and bring a wolf round your flat?' and I'd have said, 'Definitely! Let's go!'

So I did as Samten asked and, while the crew set up cameras and microphones, we sat in the lounge of Dobroyd Castle and had a bit of a chat. I instantly warmed to Samten. He had a kind face, with round glasses and short, neat hair. His smile never seemed too far away.

'I should warn you,' I said, 'I've never done this before. So I might be a bit rubbish.'

'You're going to be fine,' said Samten, and I believed him.

'Have you ever seen the *Richard & Judy* show?' I asked.

'No,' said Samten. 'We don't have televisions here. But this will be very good for us. We rely on donations, and on people coming to visit us and lending us their skills. So rather than giving us money for staying here, people can help out. If they're an electrician, they can help make sure our wiring is safe. Maybe they're good at gardening, in which case they can help maintain the garden for a bit. Or, like, in your case …'

Samten looked at me, but then stopped. It was clear he was struggling to come up with a way of someone like me being of any use whatsoever to a castle full of monks. I tried to help him.

'I usually make radio shows,' I said. 'Maybe I could … you know … come up with a half-hour radio light entertainment programme about monks and monk-based issues.'

'Mmm,' said Samten.

'A programme *by* monks, *for* monks.'

'Maybe.'

'We could call it "Monky Business".'

He nodded.

'Yeah. Or … are you any good at cleaning?'

The interview began minutes later.

The Venerable and very tall Samten Kelsang, I found out, has been a Buddhist since 1983.

'I first met Buddhism while I was at college,' he told me.

'What were you studying?'

'Well … I started out doing maths and statistics … and then I realised that wasn't quite right for me, so I moved towards zoology.'

'So you did zoology?' I said, impressed. It seemed quite a leap from maths.

'Well, yes. I did zoology. But then I decided that wasn't quite right for me, so I moved on to psychology.'

'Psychology? Wow. So you're a psychologist?'

'Well, I didn't do that for too long. In the end, I moved from that as well.'

'Oh. To what?'

'Um …'

He coughed.

'Pottery.'

I was amazed.

'You went from maths to *pottery*?'

'Via zoology and psychology.'

Which, of course, is the *classic* route.

'The good thing about this was that after all that I didn't get the chance to apply for university, because it was so obvious I just wasn't going to make it. So I got out of the machine. Usually, you're pushed straight into university, and then you're pushed straight into a job … but I wasn't. I had time. I could figure out what I wanted to do with my life. I think everyone should take a year out between school and university. It's important to have time to figure out what you want to do. Because there are key points in life … key times where one decision will affect the next twenty years of your life. And only then will you have the freedom to make another choice, which could affect the *next* twenty years.'

The words struck a chord. My decision to take the new BBC job was one such moment. It represented the end of jobs … but the start of a *career*. A career which could very well affect the next twenty years of my life. Instinctively, I thought of Jason, and the bitterness that that reality had brought him. I had to make sure I didn't fall into the same trap.

'Yes,' said Samten. 'You have to be very careful with your decisions in life.'

'Well ... there's always the *next* life,' I said, which was quite a good joke about reincarnation.

My Buddhist friend thought about it.

'Yeah. I suppose so.'

'Okay,' said Jim, 'And cut there for a second. Danny ... could you ask Samten what usually brings people to a place like this?'

'Yes,' I said, still quite pleased with myself for the reincarnation joke. Jim started the camera rolling again.

'Samten – what usually brings people to a place like this?'

'It can be anything. I often talk to people about what led them here; what milestone in their life it was that brought them to us. Sometimes it's a feeling. Sometimes it seems pure chance. Sometimes it's a passing comment made by a stranger. Sometimes an encounter with an inanimate object or animal.'

My heart leapt for a second.

'Hang on – go back. What was that about strangers and passing comments?'

I could sense Jim looking at me oddly here from beside the camera, but suddenly I wasn't doing this for *Richard & Judy* – I was doing this for me.

'You'd be surprised,' said Samten. 'Sometimes people end up here because of something someone happened to say. Something that clicked with them, or just seemed to make sense to them. Something that struck a chord. Often, the person who said it has no idea of the resonance of their words. But sometimes it can be the work of ... well ... an *enlightened being* ...'

I was shocked. *What* had he just said?

'An *enlightened being*?' I said.

'Yes,' he said.

'Like ... *Maitreya*?'

Samten nodded.

'Yes. You *know* about Maitreya?' he said.

Did I know about *Maitreya*? I couldn't quite believe what was going on here. When you think about it, *I* was here because of a passing comment made by a stranger. A stranger who some people thought

313

might be … an *enlightened being*. This couldn't be possible. My head was spinning.

'Yeah, I know about Maitreya! I know *all about* Maitr—'

'And cut there,' said Jim. 'Um … I've a feeling that might be a bit obscure for our audience, guys. Let's ask the same question again, but let's keep it more general … and, action …'

I was confused. And frustrated. Suddenly, these days, it seemed Maitreya was everywhere. Which is handy, I suppose, when your business is in omnipresence. All I wanted to talk about right now was Maitreya, and the stranger on the bus, and what all this could mean. All the things that had seemingly randomly led me here, to Samten. But Jim was right: there was work to be done, and so Samten and I continued to chat about the courses on offer as we wandered around the grounds of Dobroyd Castle. It was great here, and I was beginning to really like my lanky pal. He showed me round the different rooms, told me a few stories, introduced me to more monks, and it was only when he explained that he needed to change a bandage on his thumb that filming came to a halt.

'What did you do to your thumb?' I asked.

'I fell down some stairs the other day. Stupid, really. I'll be back in a little while …'

The crew went off to scout for some new locations. I realised I was rather enjoying myself. TV was quite easy. It was just talking to people.

'Remember, Danny,' said Jim, as they wandered off. 'Try and challenge him, soon. Get a reaction out of him. Dig deep into Buddhism. TV's not easy. It's not just talking to people.'

Jeff smiled. Clearly, he was looking forward to the bit where I tried to annoy them. I nodded at Jim, ruefully, and just stood there, wondering how I was going to achieve my unlikely mission.

Seconds later, I spied Liam coming round the corner.

'Hey Liam,' I said.

'Hello. How are you enjoying it?'

'It's great,' I said, and we started to walk through the gardens.

'Have you ever thought about being a monk, Danny?'

I smiled.

'Well … when I was a kid, I had a few martial arts videos,' I said. 'There were all these Shaolin monks that spent half their time meditating, and the other half jumping over tables and smashing bricks over

314

their heads. It looked brilliant fun. I suppose that's as close as I ever came to joining up.'

'That's not what it's like in real life,' said Liam, but to be honest, I'd guessed that.

Liam stooped to look at a flower, and I continued.

'I had this one video called *Shaolin Monks Versus the Ninja*,' I said. 'In it, all these Shaolin monks took on a mighty warrior ninja.'

Liam stopped looking at the flower and looked at me.

'Really? What happened?'

I shrugged.

'There was some fighting and stuff. Someone jumped over a table and smashed a brick on their head.'

'Who won?'

'I don't remember. Either the ninja or the monks. But I think that by the end of it all, they at least had a new-found respect for one another.'

Liam looked pleased at this.

'That's good. A good moral.'

I turned to face him.

'Liam … have *you* ever fought a ninja?

He shook his head, with some degree of sadness.

'No.'

I was back with Samten, and keen to finish the interview so I could ask him about the vital issues now dominating my mind. We were in the World Peace Café, in the grounds of the castle, and we were waiting for the team to finish setting up for the final interview.

I wasn't really saying much. I was nervous. This was my last chance to do what I had, in my head, decided the *Richard & Judy* people *wanted* me to do. To vex a Buddhist.

But then Jim said, 'Okay, we're rolling', and Samten sat up, and I had to get on with it instead … I had one idea, and now was the time to make it happen.

'So … Samten … would you say that since you got in Buddhism,' I said, 'you've become a much calmer person?'

'Well, yes, I would—'

'Good, good. Because that's the thing about Buddhists, right? You're very calm people, aren't you?'

'Yes, I suppose that's true—'

'So does anything annoy you?'

'Well, as a Buddhist, one learns to cope with situations, and realise that what goes on around us is—'

And then I did it.

I don't know why I thought this would work, but it was all I had.

I started poking Samten.

Tap-tap-tap-tap-tap on his arm …

He looked slightly startled, and stopped, mid-sentence.

'Er … I mean … does *this* annoy you?' I said. 'If I poke you?'

Samten looked at me, confused. I didn't stop poking.

'Because that *is* quite annoying, isn't it?' I said.

I'd gone red. I could tell. I was poking a monk.

'Well,' said Samten, finding his composure, somehow, 'no, it's—'

'It's *quite* annoying, isn't it? How about if I up the pace?'

Tap-tap-tap-tap-tap-tap-tap …

Samten's eyes widened. I looked up. Jim's eyes were even wider. Robin's jaw had dropped.

I was tapping him very quickly indeed now.

'Are you annoyed? Come on – say you're annoyed!'

I was virtually pleading with him. I really, really wanted him to be annoyed, but I couldn't tell whether it was working. I couldn't tell whether I was messing with his zen. I couldn't tell whether he was getting annoyed or not. All I knew was, I felt dreadful.

I looked up, hoping Jim would shout 'cut'. But he didn't. He was just staring. Even the cameraman had stopped looking through his lens, and was peeking round the side, instead, his eyebrows arched. There was perfect silence, save for the sound of the *tap-tap-tap* of a man poking a monk on the arm.

'Danny,' said Samten, eventually. 'There's something I think you should know.'

My poking slowed.

He looked me deep in the eye.

'I am a very violent man, Danny … and I have a very short fuse.'

I stopped poking him.

'So …' I said. 'Tell me a little more about the centre …'

'Was that okay for you, Jim?' I said. 'I think I got him a *bit* annoyed.'

'Well, I suppose so, Danny, but to be honest, what I meant for you to do was challenge him intellectually. You know? Probe him on his beliefs. Not … *poke* him.'

'Oh.'

* * *

Samten had been joking, of course, when he'd said that he was a very violent man. It was his way of dealing with a very odd situation.

We'd finished filming for the day now, and the crew started packing up the gear. I'd be travelling back down to London with Jeff and Robin, and wanted to talk to Samten about certain things quite urgently. I found him, facing the pond, and resisted the urge to tap him on the shoulder. I reasoned he'd probably had enough of that.

'Samten,' I said. 'Could I have a word about something? In private?'

I don't know why I said that last bit. We were totally alone already. Samten eyed me with some degree of suspicion.

'You're not going to start poking me again, are you?'

'No, the poking is over. And I'm sorry about that. I promise not to poke you or any other monks. I realise now that poking a monk is highly irresponsible behaviour.'

Samten nodded, slowly, and then beckoned me to follow him inside. Eventually, we came to a door, and he pushed it open to reveal a room full of sunlight.

'I'll put the kettle on,' he said, as he hitched his robes up and started to take off his shoes. I was slightly surprised. They were huge hiking boots. But I'm not actually sure if this is unusual or not. Perhaps hiking boots are standard monk issue. I think I'd probably been expecting a pair of flimsy moccasins, or a couple of brown sacks, maybe, but no. Hiking boots. Under his robes. It struck me that perhaps Samten was a fan of Extreme Monking. Perhaps he kept a hang glider under there, too.

He flicked the kettle on and opened up the fridge.

'Do you take your tea white?'

'Yes, please.'

'Right. Well … oh. You can either have it black, or with yoghurt.'

'Um … what flavour yoghurt?'

Samten bent down to take another look, and stood up again.

'Strawberry.'

I thought about it.

'Black, please.'

Samten brought the tea through and sat down on the chair next to mine. He settled into his seat, fixed me with a friendly grin, and nodded to me, letting me know I should say whatever it was I wanted to say.

I didn't really know where to begin. But I began anyway.

'Samten, when I was downstairs, we almost started talking about … Maitreya.'

Samten nodded gently.

'Well … I mean … who *is* he? Because I've … heard of him.'

'Maitreya is the Buddha of love. He's the next World Teacher.'

'Right … well … what I'd like to know is … is it possible that I met him on a bus recently?'

I cringed. Maybe I'd got to the point a little too quickly. But Samten didn't seem to mind.

'Well … I suppose it's *possible*. Why?'

'Because, in a roundabout way, that's why I'm here, talking to you. This is the first bit of presenting I've ever done. I'm not a TV presenter. But someone offered me an opportunity, and instead of saying no, I can't do that, or no, I've never done it before … I said Yes. And I only had the chance to say Yes to that because I'd ended up at a party I probably wouldn't have gone to six months earlier. I took a chance. *Lots* of chances. And if some of the people I've met along the way are to be believed it's because I met Maitreya on a bus.'

Samten nodded as if he understood. But I listened to the exchange back in my head and decided that he probably didn't.

And then Samten said, 'I'm not sure I fully understand.'

And so I let it all pour out. I explained everything. I explained about how earlier in the year I'd been living my life in a more negative way. About how I'd been saying no to the little opportunities in everyday life, and how I'd become scared that that was all I'd ever do. About how I'd started to regret not knowing how much I'd missed out on. And about how one night, on a bus in the East End, a stranger uttered a sentence that would change all that. A sentence so stark and simple and a sentiment so obvious that I'd overlooked it as a viable course of action. *Say Yes more.* And I told him that that's just what I'd been trying to do – to say Yes more. And I'd been learning from it. And having more fun. And … well … *living*.

Samten thought about what I'd said. In his presence, the silence felt heavy, but when it was there, it was like it was *supposed* to be there. And eventually, he smiled, and a moment later he spoke.

'It sounds like you've found your path to enlightenment.'

The crew had finished packing up and were grabbing some food before the long trip home. Jeff was chewing on some celery, and Robin was trying to find the toilets.

Samten and I walked around the grounds of the castle, and talked more about Yes. It was still sunny and, save for the odd monk cycling to or from the town, we were alone.

'What I think is interesting,' said Samten, 'is this idea about giving up control. Letting what you call your Yes Moments lead the way. Because actually, we don't even have control in the first place. It's a myth. In life, absolutely *anything* can happen.'

'Like you hurting your thumb.'

'Exactly. I didn't know that was going to happen.'

'No. Neither did I.'

I probably didn't need to say that.

'But I *did* hurt my thumb, and I had to accept it, and adapt. If we have faith that some higher powers, some enlightened beings, are helping us to develop spiritually, then you begin to relate to life completely differently. And I suppose life starts to become a little more magical. Every opportunity must be seen as a chance to learn. We have to be open to whatever happens, good or bad. Because anything that happens is a chance to increase our wisdom, and to walk further down the path to enlightenment. So if you miss the bus, that's an opportunity to learn. If you become ill, that's an opportunity to learn something new, like compassion, maybe.'

'What did you learn from hurting your thumb?'

'Not to trip down the stairs, mainly.'

I laughed.

'But in reality ... hurting my thumb limited what I could do physically, and so it gave me plenty of time for meditation. It presented me with a valuable opportunity.'

'Nice spin.'

'Thank you.'

'You should hurt your thumb more often.'

'I don't think that would help.'

We found a bench and took a seat.

'I suppose it's like you discovering you were rubbish at maths,' I said, 'and ending up doing pottery instead. It may have meant you couldn't go to university, but that was for the best, wasn't it? It meant you could do something you really cared about.'

'Exactly.'

'And I imagine you can also make your own mugs now, too.'

'Well ... I wasn't much good at pottery, either.'

'Oh.'

A breeze picked up. We both took a moment to listen to it.

'So tell me about some of the things that have happened to you, then. As a result of saying Yes.'

I thought about what to tell him. And then it seemed obvious. Something bad that had happened, which was also something *good*.

'There was this scratchcard, right? And I never normally play scratchcards. But the card told me I should, and so I did. And I won £25,000.'

'Wow,' said Samten.

'But then I lost it again.'

'Ah,' said Samten.

'But the thing is, that just proved to me that what I was doing was right. It didn't matter that I'd lost the money – the important thing was that I'd won it in the first place. I didn't have £25,000 when I found the card, and I didn't have £25,000 when I'd finished with it. I hadn't actually lost anything. But I *did* feel like I'd *gained* something.'

Samten thought about it.

'Nice spin,' he said.

'Thank you.'

'You should lose large sums of money more often.'

'I don't think that would help.'

I waited for Samten to say something else. I was keen to hear what his reaction to my scratchcard tale would be. But he was far away, lost in thought. When he did finally speak, it was to say a sentence that, under any other circumstance, would probably have lead to a brief scuffle and a broken nose.

'You're a peacock.'

Uh?

'I'm a what?'

'You're a peacock. You see, if you're open to a situation, you can transform it. You can be like a peacock. Apparently, they can thrive on poisonous berries, when other animals would get sick. If you have the mentality where you can't open up to things, you can get into situations where you feel down, or depressed. If you have this ability of openness you can actually thrive on difficult situations.'

'Like hurting your thumb?'

'Or losing that money. What have you learnt so far? As a result of saying Yes?'

'Well … lots, really. Men can have babies. Aliens built the pyramids. No man should walk a cat. And that I'm a peacock.'

Samten looked a little uncertain about the valuable lessons I'd learnt along the way. And to be fair, I could see what he meant. If this were an episode of *Quantum Leap* or *Highway to Heaven*, you'd be a little upset if those were the only morals to the story. The fact was, I wasn't *sure* what I'd learnt yet. Not exactly. Not quite yet.

'Well ... whatever,' he said. 'What I'm saying is, there's so much we can learn from just accepting the way we are rather than being attached to the way we'd *like* to be.'

Samten was right. His words made sense. He was a wise man. While I'm not a religious person, if I ever do decide to be, I think it might be alongside people like him. Plus, I'd save a fortune on conditioner.

'Can I ask ...' said Samten, as we headed back to the crew. 'Did you find that more coincidences happened when you let go of controlled life and opened up a bit more?'

'Well ... I suppose so,' I said. 'I mean, the very fact that everyone's been talking to me about this Maitreya fella, and then thanks to Yes, I end up here, and you know all about him ...'

'Yes, we should talk about Maitreya.'

We stopped walking, and I asked him my question.

'Samten ... do you *really* think it's possible that the man on the bus – the one I met that night – was Maitreya?'

'Your guess is as good as mine. But yes. It *is* possible.'

I was shocked. As of right now, it wasn't just Brian telling me this was possible. Or his friend Pete. Or even Elias Brown. It was someone else; someone *new*. There were now four of them. That's more or less a *group*!

'The thing you must be asking yourself,' said Samten, as we reached the front of the castle, 'is what on earth inspired that man to say that to you? What made him utter the words "say Yes more" to a man who needed to say Yes more?'

I nodded, wide-eyed. I heard Jeff call my name. They were ready to go now, and I waved to say I'd be there in a second. Samten continued.

'From a Buddhist point of view, we talk about inspiration coming from the enlightened source. Sometimes we can feel inspired to say something, and then think – where did *that* come from? In reality it came through the inspiration of enlightened beings.'

'Enlightened beings like—'

'Maitreya, yes. Any enlightened being, like Maitreya, is constantly working for all human beings. He walks among us. He's ever present in this world, working to help all human beings.'

'Like Superman?'

'Yes. Kind of. But he helps us, whether we know he's there or not, just as the sun shines equally on all human beings. Now, a blind person won't necessarily *see* the sunshine … but that doesn't mean the sun doesn't shine on them …'

Robin tooted the car horn.

'If that *was* Maitreya on the bus,' said Samten, 'then to be honest he's a bit early. He's not supposed to turn up for another few thousand years … but maybe this is a sneak preview. It could have been him. And you may find, as you progress down your own path to enlightenment, that you receive more help from enlightened beings. Or maybe more help from the people around you. People you wouldn't expect it from. Listen to what they tell you. Sometimes, inspiration comes in the strangest places. Even the ordinary can be magical. Be open to it.'

I said 'okay', and I meant it. I would.

'I think you're going to be all right, Danny. You seem to be quite a free spirit in many ways. There is a lot to be said for childish innocence.'

I smiled, warmly. And then I realised that, in effect, Samten was calling me a simpleton. I nearly said something, but then I remembered what he'd said about being quite a violent man, and I bit my tongue, just in case.

Somewhere, on the motorway home, we stopped the van, and made our way into a faceless, peeling service station. Jeff wanted a milkshake and Robin needed a pee. It was his third pee in as many hours. The man appeared to have the bladder of a moth.

I sat down at a table and Jeff joined me moments later.

'So that was fun,' he said. 'I'm quite into all that Buddhist stuff, now. Peace and joy, you know. Did you like it?'

'Yeah, definitely,' I said. 'And thanks for your tip, by the way. I think the poking went down really well.'

'No problemo,' said Jeff, stirring his milkshake. 'So this was your first go at presenting? How did you get into it?'

'I just said Yes. I met Gareth at a party, and we got talking about this and that, and then there was a meeting, and they asked me if I wanted to have a go, and I just said Yes again.'

'Simple as that.'

'Yup. I just said Yes.'

Jeff smiled, and muttered something under his breath.

'What was that?' I said, and he repeated it, louder.

'*Si!*' he said. '*Si a Todo!*'

I blinked a couple of times.

'Eh?'

'*Si a Todo*. It means … oh, what does it mean again? "Yes To Everything". It's Spanish.'

'It means "Yes To Everything"?'

'Yes. *Si.*'

He sucked at his milkshake. It made a horrible noise.

'But where does Yes To Everything come from? I mean, is it a phrase, or something? Or a proverb?'

'I dunno. A couple of years ago, I was helping make this holiday show for BBC2. We were in Barcelona, and we met this guy, called Marc, or Marco, or something. And that was his motto. Yes To Everything! *Si a Todo!*'

'*Si a Todo*,' I said, again.

'Yeah. He was running this tapas bar, or something, and he lives his whole life by that maxim.'

'He's … a *Si* Man …' I said.

Jeff looked confused.

'What, like … a sailor?'

'No, no … a *Yes* Man. He's a bloody *Yes Man*!'

I couldn't believe it. I thought I was the only one. Out there, somewhere … there was someone just like me!

Jeff smiled, and said, 'Yeah, I s'pose so.'

'And is this bloke … *happy*?'

'The happiest man I've ever met.'

I sat back and looked around me. The cleaners had started to wash the floors of the service station. A fat man was eating a burger. I glanced back at Jeff, who was scooping out the last of his milkshake with his fingers, and I shook my head. Sometimes, inspiration comes in the strangest places. Sometimes, even the ordinary can be magical.

'Have you ever been to Barcelona?' he said, licking his fingers.

'No,' I said. 'Never.'

'You'd love it. It's great this time of year.'

He stood up as Robin arrived back at the table.

'You should go there sometime.'

And I nodded.

Because Yes, I should.

21

In which Daniel meets his Match

I was on the bus and my phone was ringing.

'Hello?'

'Danny? Hello … it's Gareth from *Richard & Judy* here.'

'Hiya Gareth!'

'Just thought I'd keep you updated on things …'

'Okay.'

'We had … well … an *unusual* reaction to your piece after it went out on Monday …'

'Unusual?'

'Yes … we had … er … well … an *abnormal* number of complaints.'

'What? Really?'

'We think it might be because you spent a large portion of the main interview poking a monk.'

'Ah.'

'Where are you now?'

'I'm on a bus.'

'Give me a ring when you get home. We'd like to start planning the next VT to film.'

'Oh. Ah. I won't actually be home until tomorrow night.'

'Okay, well … give us a call then.'

'Will do. And listen – can you tell Jeff something?'

'Sure. What?'

'Tell him I'm on my way to Barcelona …'

It was three days since I'd poked a monk and such a lot had happened.

I had found it quite incredible that somewhere out there, there was someone else, like me, saying Yes not as an option – but as a way of life.

But from what Jeff had told me, this man wasn't an amateur like me. He wasn't just doing it until the new year, or because he felt he needed to, or because he couldn't get out of it … he was doing it, it seemed, because that's just what he did. He said Yes. To everything.

Even if Jeff hadn't suggested going to Barcelona, I would've wanted to meet this man. But now that I'd said Yes, I couldn't *not* meet him. And so Jeff had given me an e-mail address he thought might work, and I had tried it.

I told Marc the truth. That I wanted to speak to him about *Si a Todo*. That I knew I was a complete stranger, and that this must seem a bit odd, but a man I'd only just met through a Yes had told me about him … he was the Yes Man of Barcelona, I was the Yes Man of London … It seemed only right that we should compare notes.

He wrote back the same day.

It was, of course, to say *Si*!

querido danny,

in this moments i'm in la riviera (italy), over a mountain surrounded of a fullpower nature; clear days you can see corsica from here, and the cinghiale come into the garden to eat fruits...

after two thunder trips it is now possible for me to be in barcelona this thursday — we could have a shock proteico de gambas and seafood in taller de tapas and burn a part of Barcelona ...

si a encontrarnos, si al shock proteico y SI A TODO !!!

it would be very elegant to meet with you ... are you free to come on thursday??

saludos cordiales, me parece atomico el encuentro,

marc

Thursday! Was I free to come on Thursday?

What kind of Yes Man would I be if I said no?

So here I was, on Thursday morning, on a bus to the airport, and excited.

Everything was sorted. One night in Barcelona – the flights courtesy of the good people at Siemens, who, because they offered me a new handset all those weeks ago, had also come good on their offer of a free return flight to anywhere in Europe. I couldn't believe my luck. It was like Yes was looking after me, all of a sudden.

I didn't know what to expect from my trip to Barcelona. I didn't know what to expect from life any more. I got to the airport, got on the plane, and flew to another country.

I was standing, as agreed, in the square at Plaza Del Juamo, waiting for Marc. I had no idea what he looked like, no idea what we'd be doing tonight, no idea what to expect. I didn't know how old he was, how he dressed – all I knew was his name, and that he worked in PR. I didn't know what Marc would be like. Whether other than a predisposal to say Yes to things, we'd have anything in common. But it was too late to worry about that now. I cast my eyes about the place … an old man in a hat, with his hands in his pockets. Could be him, I guess. Over there – a middle-aged man with a pipe. Maybe. But none of them seemed to be looking for anyone. None of them seemed to be looking for me.

Another five minutes passed. Then another.

And then, on the other side of the square, a taxi furiously revved its way through the streets and came to an abrupt halt. A tanned and handsome man in his thirties wearing a suit jacket and t-shirt jumped out of the back and gave the driver a high-five through the open window, before leaning down to give him a little hug. He waved him goodbye and then looked up, across the square. He was searching for someone. He was searching for me.

It was Marc.

'Come on, we go first to a friend of mine,' said Marc, 'and then we do full power Barcelona! Atomico, Danny – come, we walk through here …'

Marc was marching me through the back streets of the Gothic Old Town, through narrow, dark streets, and he was a friendly ball of energy. He was also whistling. Not a normal whistle, either. A kind of … *chirp*. The noise a small, happy bird makes, in bursts of one or two seconds, and like no noise any other human being has ever made in my presence. It was happening a lot. Between every few sentences, or whenever we rounded a corner … a short, sharp *chirp*. It was a pleasant noise – but not one that you could ever really say you'd been expecting.

'Come, it is not much further …' *chirp* '… we find my friend in his shop …'

I was struggling to keep up with Marc's pace … he was moving quickly, striding through the alleyways and streets, as if there just wasn't enough time for everything we had to do tonight.

'Hola Marc!' came a shout from high above, quite suddenly. I looked up to see a large bald man leaning out of his window, waving at Marc.

'Hola Emilio!' shouted Marc, and we continued on, just as quickly.

We pounded through a square, where teenagers were playing experimental music with keyboards and smoking cigarettes. The walls were pockmarked with bullet holes that Marc – pausing for only the quickest of split seconds – explained remained from the Civil War.

'Barcelona is the finest city, I think,' he said. 'I have lived here always, until recently. Now I live in Italy, in the quietest village, but Barcelona is always my home … it is a special place … a Mediterranean city in Europe—'

'Hey Marc!' shouted another voice from high above, and Marc raised his hand, and continued on, and chirped his chirp by way of an answer.

'You have been here before?' he asked.

'Never,' I said. 'But I like it—'

Then it happened *again* – someone else leaning out of a window, three or four floors up, and shouting his name … and then I realised. Marc was only chirping when we walked through residential areas… places where people would have their windows open and the sound could drift in. He was chirping for his friends. People here knew his chirp, and this was his way of saying he was back in town.

I tried a chirp of my own. It was rubbish. Marc laughed, and was about to say something, when we heard a voice coming from the end of the alleyway. We looked up to see yet another someone waving at Marc. He'd heard the chirp but he'd been late to react. He'd nearly missed us. Marc said 'back in one minute', ran back down the alleyway and in just three or four swift and impressive movements, scaled the front of the building and pulled himself through the appropriate window. A minute later, he appeared at the front door of a building opposite and walked casually towards me. It was a little confusing.

'So,' he said. 'Now we continue—'

'Marc,' I said. 'You just scaled the front of a building and appeared from somewhere totally different ...'

'Yes,' he said, as if nothing odd had happened at all. 'I had to say hello to my friend.'

The next friend we had to drop in on owned an antiques shop, hidden away in another tiny street. His name was Oleos, and he didn't speak any English, but he looked delighted when he heard Marc chirping. Oleos shook my hand with vigour, and I can only assume Marc then told him why I was there, because suddenly, he started saying '*Si a Todo!*' over and over again, before running off to fetch three antique glasses and a bottle of whisky. He dusted the glasses off, filled them, and handed them round.

'*Si a Todo!*' he said.

'*Si a Todo!*' said Marc.

'*Si a Todo!*' I said.

I was enjoying myself.

An hour later and we were in a cramped but friendly bar in the Old Town. Amazingly, everyone – customers and bar staff alike – had cheered when Marc the Barcelona Yes Man had walked in. Perhaps he was secretly a hypnotist.

Since our whisky in the antiques shop, we had been joined by Oleos and his little dog Mervyn, a German photographer called Jonas, and a Spanish actress called Isabel, who had come straight from filming another episode of the slightly depressing-sounding TV drama, *The Town of My Life, It Hurts!*.

Marc had once again explained what I was doing in Spain, and everyone had seemed delighted.

'So you just thought, yes, I will go to Barcelona?' asked Isabel. 'Just like that?'

'Pretty much, yeah.'

'Just because a man you met had met Marc?'

'Yup.'

'And you just said, Marc, I will come to meet you?'

'That's right. And Marc said Yes.'

'And then you just got on a plane and came? All the way to Spain? To meet a stranger?'

I shrugged.

'Yes. It was an odd coincidence. A man I only met because I said Yes to a job had met Marc a couple of years ago, and it turns out that he only says Yes too!'

'*La casualidad no existe, Danny!*' said Marc. 'There is no such thing as coincidence! *Si a Todo!* It is the only way!'

'*Si a Todo*,' said Oleos, and everyone raised their glasses.

'It is good to say Yes!' said Isabel. 'Yes to everything!'

We were a small and happy group, and I felt incredibly welcome. There was such warmth in the air. Warmth towards me, but also an overwhelming warmth towards Marc. It seemed to me that he was one of those people you meet in life who have an almost magnetic optimism. Nothing ever seemed like too much trouble for Marc. He loved life, and life seemed to love him right back. Maybe he seemed so comfortable in his own skin because he knew what was important to him – and right up there at the top of the list was friends.

But I wanted to know more about what saying Yes meant to him.

'Marc … could I ask you something about … you know … *Si a Todo*?' I said. 'How has it affected …'

But Marc wasn't listening.

'Danny!' he said. 'An egg!'

Eh?

'Here – take this …'

Marc suddenly produced an egg. By which I mean he took one out of his pocket – not that he sat down and laid one.

'An egg?' I said.

'Here! For you!'

And then he slammed it onto the table, rolled it, and peeled off its shell in one elaborate movement.

'An egg for you!'

I didn't quite know what to say. It's not often men I've just met take eggs out of their pockets and peel them for me.

'*Si a Todo*,' he said. 'Take the egg!'

'Take the egg?'

'Take the egg!'

I could only imagine that this was some kind of proud Spanish tradition, and to refuse a boiled egg when it is both peeled and offered would be a major racial slur. I took the egg and raised it at the girl behind the bar.

'I am taking the egg!' I said, and then popped it in my mouth.

'So is this a Spanish tradition?' I asked Jonas, the German, between chews.

'No,' he said. 'Sometimes Marc just likes to eat an egg.'

* * *

'Come on!' said Marc. 'We continue on … *Si a Todo*, Danny, we go some-where else, now … a party for a new club, I have invitations for us both.'

'Great!' I said. A party! An exclusive, nightclub opening, in a hip and slick city! I was filled with a new hope. Surely, this was what being a Yes Man was all about. Marc knew it, and now so did I.

'Come on, we go now.'

And so Marc and I left the others at the bar and set off in search of this brand new party. For once, it wasn't *me* chasing a Yes … I was saying a Yes to someone *else's* Yes. It was like Yes squared!

'Hey, Marc,' I said, as we walked through a precinct and around a man on rollerblades who appeared to be doing tai-chi, 'could I talk to you a bit now about saying Yes … because I've been saying it for some months now, and while it's been great, there have also been downsides … I've done things I should never have done, and—'

'Like what?'

'Well … saying Yes has been great. But certain things have happened. And …' I thought of Lizzie, and then of Kristen, but pushed the thought aside again '… I just want to make sure I'm doing this prop-erly. I mean, did you ever—'

'Here we are! The club!'

Marc approached a bouncer, and pointed at me, and said something, and the bouncer nodded, and we were ushered straight in.

I had been desperate to talk to Marc and seek his advice. But almost as soon as we'd entered the club, I'd ended up speaking to a friend-of-a-friend of his friend, who seemed determined to tell me every last detail of her life.

'My ex-boyfriend,' she said, as my eyes darted around the room, trying to find Marc again. 'He went to London in the summer.'

'Oh, did he?' I said.

I couldn't see Marc anywhere. Just acres of suited, booted, ultra smart and trendy Spaniards, in Barcelona's newest – and most velvety – club.

'Yes. He liked London very much.'

'Good,' I said.

A man in a black suit with his shirt unbuttoned to the waist walked past me. He stopped at a mirror to check himself out. I think he was wearing foundation.

'My ex, he is a liar,' said the girl, and my ears pricked up.

'A liar?' I said.

'Yes. A liar,' she said.

She didn't seem at all sad about it, but I felt bad for her.

'God,' I said. 'I'm sorry about that.'

The man was still checking himself out in the mirror. He seemed to be really enjoying the view.

'Why you say you are sorry?' said the girl.

'Well … it's not good to be a liar.'

'It's good!' she said, a little offended. 'He was liar, famous Spanish liar!'

'He was a famous Spanish liar?'

'Yes. A criminal liar.'

The man in the mirror had been joined by his friend, this one with the most elaborately crafted facial hair I have ever seen, and who had now *also* locked eyes with himself in the mirror.

'He was a famous Spanish criminal liar? Are you sure that's good?'

Both men nodded at themselves, then at each other, and wandered off, probably to find another mirror.

'My ex was a liar in the best court in Spain!'

'Oh,' I said, realising what she'd meant. 'A *lawyer*?'

'Yes. Liar. What did you say?'

'I said "lawyer". I thought *you* said "liar".'

'What is different?'

A more cynical man than I would say she probably had a point.

'Danny! *Si a Todo!*' shouted Marc, when he was back by my side. He had two glasses of champagne in his hand and he now appeared to be wearing a cravat. He handed me a glass and then slapped me on the back. I laughed. I really, really liked Marc. I found it hard to explain. After all, we'd only just met. But it seemed like he had a passion for life that up until now I'd been trying to force … it just seemed to come naturally to him.

'Come, sit up there,' he said, pointing to a raised area near the dance floor. A few people sat there, sipping drinks and looking like the Barcelona elite. The man with the elaborate facial hair was staring into his glass, probably trying to catch a glimpse of himself in an ice cube.

'I will,' I said. 'And perhaps then you could talk to me about being a Yes Man …'

I was keen to bond with Marc. Not just as friends – but as Yes Men.

'Sure, sure, we will,' he said. 'But remember – this is only the beginning! We have plenty of time!'

It didn't feel like the right moment to remind Marc that I'd be returning home to London the very next day, so I took my drink over to the raised area, and took a seat. Marc made it halfway, but was whisked away by a glamorous woman who seemed to want to speak to him. A moment after I sat down, I was joined by a gentleman in a shiny, sequinned suit.

'Hola,' he said.

'Hola,' I said, and then there we sat, neither of us speaking, both of us staring at the dance floor, which was slowly filling up.

I decided I shouldn't be too fixated on asking Marc about his experiences of Yes. After all, I was seeing it first-hand, right now, and here, in Barcelona. For Marc, saying Yes wasn't as technical and regimented as I'd made it. It was just a general attitude of positivity and freedom – of going with the flow, and of seeing what happens.

Some kind of announcement came over the speaker system, but as it was in Spanish, I couldn't make it out. Whatever it was, it must have been encouraging people to get down onto the dance floor and have a bit of a dance, because as soon as it finished, the five or six people sitting on the raised area with me got up and headed towards it. Only myself and the man in the shiny suit remained, and we looked at each other and smiled. I felt bad, though – what was I missing out on? Had I ignored a direct instruction? Had I missed a Yes moment? Where was Marc to translate? I looked out over the dance floor, but couldn't see him. It was suddenly crammed. No one was dancing, though – they were all just standing there, chatting. I stood up to get a better view, and so did the man in the shiny suit next to me. He leaned over and said something to me in Spanish, and I masked the fact that I didn't understand it by just smiling. He said it again, and I shrugged, and smiled. And then, suddenly, and quite without warning, I lit up.

A spotlight had swung around and was trained on the raised area. Some music kicked in. It got louder, and there was a cheer. What the hell was going on here? I went to tap the man in the shiny suit on the shoulder but to my horror noticed he had just whipped out a microphone. Oh, good God. This man was a singer. A singer in a shiny suit. A singer, standing on a raised area, in front of a dance floor packed with specially invited guests. A singer, who had just started to sing a Spanish pop song while I – a hugely embarrassed-looking bystander – shared a stage with him.

I immediately tried to get off the raised area and into the crowd in front of me, but the man in the shiny suit had moved forwards, effectively blocking off the stairs. Unless I physically tried to move him aside, I was stuck. I looked behind me. There was just a wall. I had no way out. *I had no way out!*

So I did the only thing I could. I sheepishly sat back down on my chair and pretended I hadn't noticed a thing. I stared at my feet and prayed that the song would be over soon. Once, I managed to look up, only to see a vast sea of people staring at me like I was some kind of freak of nature, or part of the show that they just didn't understand. Soon, people started taking photographs. In the corner of my eye, I noticed a news crew. I had no idea who this man singing this song was, but he was clearly someone a little more famous in Spain than he is in Britain. I realised, with mounting horror, that any and all footage of this bloke's opening song would feature a bright red man with glasses sitting quietly in the background wishing to God he spoke Spanish and could have understood what can only have been a request for anyone who wasn't a Spanish pop star to leave the stage!

The song went on for an absolute age. It was longer than any song I have ever heard in my entire life. But it was probably the instrumental section that was worst. At least the singer could do a little dance while that was on – but me? I could only sit there. I glanced up once again, and noticed that most of the people in the front row were fixated not on the celebrity gyrating in front of them – but on his backing group. Me.

I tried to affect a casual air now, tapping along in time with the music, like in some bizarre and very wrong way I was *supposed* to be there, and finally, thankfully, the song came to an abrupt and welcome end. The crowd went mad. The flashbulbs flashed all over the place thus ensuring my embarrassing bit part in the history of this club was recorded for ever, someone somewhere screamed, and one man shouted *encore.* The man in the shiny suit took a bow, raised his hand to the crowd, and backed away, casting me a suspicious look as he exited stage right. The spotlight faded, some different music started up, and I slowly and carefully stood up and tried to walk off the stage with as much dignity as a man who'd accidentally gatecrashed an important gig could muster.

'Danny!' said Marc, suddenly behind me. 'Come on! I have just received a phone call … a friend has invited us for a drink! A beautiful house! High on the hills! You will see all of Barcelona! Come, now, we go!'

Half an hour later I was standing on the balcony of a renowned Spanish architect called Gaspar, surveying all of Barcelona beneath me. I knew

Gaspar was renowned, because there was a shiny leaflet on his couch which said as much, and I knew he was Spanish because he had a huge glass of wine in each hand.

Marc and I looked out over a beautiful city, while Gaspar fixed us some olives. It was an altogether quite random moment. Another example of where Yes had taken me, when I had just let it.

'Danny ...' said Gaspar, a bearded and important-looking man. 'I feel I have met you before ...'

'Do you?' I said. 'I've never actually been to Barcelona before.'

'Maybe in London? I was in London very recently. But we did not meet, I think ...'

'I don't think so,' I said.

Somewhere in the house – a grand, airy, house – a phone rang, and Gaspar excused himself.

'Marc ...' I said, and he made his little chirping sound in response. 'I find it incredible that I'm here. You know? I mean, I know that on paper, I'm just at some bloke's house in Spain. But at the same time, I feel like it's fate that brought me here. Because all I did was let things happen ... and here I am.'

'You *have* to let things happen,' said Marc. 'The world knows what it is doing. *Si a Todo* is a very powerful expression—'

'But what does it mean to you? Because I think that although we both say Yes a lot, you do it slightly differently.'

'For me, it is an attitude. People look at me strangely when I say *Si a Todo* ... they say, you would say Yes to war as well? To *terrorismo*? To bad things? Well, no. I like to live by a more positive way ... I don't say no to war. I say Yes to peace.'

The words were familiar. Very familiar.

'That's exactly what some other people said to me recently,' I said. 'I met some peace protestors in London, by chance. They wanted me to help them Chalk for Peace ... and when I did, that's what they said. "Yes to Peace", instead of "No to War".'

'*La casualidad no existe, Danny!*' said Marc. 'The world knows what it is doing.'

Just then, Gaspar walked back onto the balcony.

'My apologies,' he said. 'I am preparing for a big exhibition. New ideas. No one has seen them before, and I am getting things ready. That was a friend of mine calling. A Portuguese artist, who lives in England.'

'Oh,' I said. 'Whereabouts?'

'He lives in Bath.'

I was shocked.

'That's where I grew up,' I said. 'My parents live there.'

Marc made his little chirping noise.

'Coincidence does not exist! *La casualidad no existe!*'

'How strange!' said Gaspar. 'But also… *this* is strange, too. After I talked to him about my trip to England, I remembered where I know you from.'

He stood a little bit closer to me.

'I saw you on television.'

Oh. God. I knew exactly where, as well. In the background of the nine o'clock news, as I sat behind a man in a shiny suit, as he sang a Spanish pop song. But then he looked concerned, like he was straining to remember something…

'You were doing… ah, what was it? Like this…'

Gaspar started making a poking motion.

Oh my God.

Gaspar had seen me on *Richard & Judy*!

'But… *how*?'

'I was in London. I had a TV in my hotel.'

'But that was only the other day!'

'Yes!'

Holy bloody Mary.

Marc started to laugh, and laugh, and laugh.

'*La casualidad no existe!*' he said. 'There are connections everywhere! Sometimes we are brought to certain points and we do not know why…'

I was amazed, and I thought of Samten. This was a *ridiculous* coincidence. And this wasn't some bloke off the street in London who'd seen me do my first-ever piece of TV presenting… this was a renowned architect – in *Spain*! A man whose house I was in only because of another man who I would never have met had a sound recordist on a show I should never have been on (were it not for a party I probably never should have gone to) had told me about … I mean, *what* were the *odds*?

'It is incredible what can happen,' said Marc, 'when you allow it to …'

I stood there, on a balcony under a million stars.

The following morning I had a few hours to kill and I started by killing one of them in an Internet café, on Las Ramblas – the most touristy of all Barcelona's roads. I wanted to tell someone – *anyone* – about the events of the night before. I wanted to e-mail Jeff and thank him for telling me about Marc.

I had been genuinely inspired by my short time with Marc. He was someone brave enough to just let things happen. To roll with the punches. To go where the wind took him. And he'd changed my attitude, somewhat. I realised, slowly, that I had been treating Yeses like they were against me. That they were challenges to be overcome. That they were things I could *fail*. In actual fact, they were just part of life. And if I treated them like Marc did, they would *become* life.

It seemed to me that perhaps Maitreya was a red herring. It seemed to me that we could meet enlightened beings every day – if we just looked out for them. The ordinary could be magical.

There was another reason for coming to the Internet café. There was something I needed to check out. Something I'd seen in a magazine. Something I had decided to let happen …

I'd found the magazine in the lobby of the hotel that morning. It was a general lifestyle magazine, with all that that entails – fashion, music, sport, travel … the usual. I'd flicked through it, taking no real interest, but there'd been one thing in it that really struck me. One sentence that I'd needed to translate, and then check out. And once I'd checked it out, needed to act upon …

I'd be meeting Marc to say goodbye and thank him at a restaurant just down the road – and to give him a gift, as well. A special one.

I bought a can of Coke and sat down at a screen, logged in, and headed for my e-mail. I had a few waiting for me, but one name leapt out at me straight away.

Lizzie.

Hey, you…

Guess what? I'm coming to London. I'll be there on December 2nd, for nine days, for work … this might be a little cheeky, but … can I stay at yours? Tell me to get lost if not. But it would be great to see you …

L

xx

It was the best news I could have hoped for. December 2nd. Ten days away. Amazing. Just look at what life does when you let it.

* * *

I was understandably buoyant when I met up with Marc. Isabel, the soap-opera lady, had come, too.

'*Hola, hombre,*' he said, and we walked through the streets at pace again. 'Come, I show you some of the city that you didn't see …'

And even though it didn't seem like we had time, we squeezed it in. Marc bumped into more friends, of course, and said *Si* every time they told him about another event he had to come to …

'They have a party next week,' he said, after meeting one. 'He has a house to paint, I help him,' after meeting another.

What struck me about this wasn't the way his diary was filling up. It was the connections he had made. The friendships. The time he had for people. *That* was what it was all about.

At a café someone had seen fit to call Colon, I ordered a sandwich from the waiter and looked Marc in the eye.

'Marc … I want to thank you.'

'Why?'

'For letting me hang out with you. I had a lot of fun.'

'Hey – we are not stopping being friends … this is only the beginning.'

'No, but … you didn't have to agree to meet with me. I was a complete stranger, after all.'

'*Si a Todo*, Danny. *Si a Todo.*'

'Well, thanks, anyway. And I brought you something…'

I delved into my bag and pulled it out. I'd brought it with me for God knows what reason – evidence, to show Marc? Inspiration? A reminder of what I'd done, and what I still had to come?

It was my blue, embroidered YES cap.

I figured Marc deserved it more than me. Marc was a man who lived his life with positivity and verve. Marc was a *real* Yes Man.

He was delighted.

'Atomico!' he said. 'Thank you, Danny!'

And then, to prove just how delighted he was, he popped it on his head and did a little chirp.

'So … what is next for you? You go home today to London, and then you see what life brings you?'

'Well … not exactly. I mean … I wanted to ask your advice on this, but … what does this mean?'

I reached into my pocket and unfolded a piece of paper. It was an advert. An advert I'd ripped out of the magazine in the hotel lobby.

I pointed at the sentence I meant. It was big, and bold, and colourful. It was next to a picture of a plane, and a smiling air stewardess, and some palm trees and sunshine.

'It means, *Fly Away, Towards Singapore*,' said Marc, before looking up, and smiling.

'What do you think?' I said.

'*Si a Todo*,' he said.

22

In which Daniel goes far beyond the Call of Duty

I felt as free as a bird.

What I was doing was utterly unheard of – at least for me. This was blatantly a dive straight into Level Six. A once only-mythical level. A level I had never been in before.

I was going to Singapore … *because I could.*

That was it. That was all.

I had seen an advert, said Yes to it, and now here I was … recovering from a lengthy flight to a whole new place for no reason whatsoever other than life had dictated that I should. Life had conspired to show me that advert. Yes had conspired to make me obey it. Marc had inspired me to simply sit back and enjoy it.

I was at the airport when my phone rang.

'Dan? It's Wag.'

'Hey, Wag, how's it going?'

'Not bad. Where are you?'

'On my way to Singapore.'

'Singapore? *Why?*'

I shrugged.

'No reason.'

Thirteen hours later and I jumped into a cab outside Changi airport and chucked my small bag onto the back seat.

I was happy. Living in total acceptance of my decision. I would be in Singapore for a little over 48 hours – 48 hours in *Singapore*! A weekend! Who has a *weekend* in Singapore? Who comes back from a trip to Barcelona, finds a credit card he should never have taken out, and books himself on the next available flight to South East Asia?

'Hello! How are you!' said the driver, more as a statement than as a question.

'I'm incredibly fine!' I said. 'How are you?'

'I'm fine,' he said, putting the car in gear. 'An' how are you?'

I balked. I was pretty sure I'd just answered that, but couldn't be entirely certain. Singapore is many thousands of miles away, and I'd been in the air for many hours.

'I'm fine!' I said, again rather cheerily. And that should have taken care of that, really. But despite the fact that I already knew the answer, I felt rude not then asking him how *he* was. It's force of habit, and I'm British.

'And … how are you?'

He looked at me, happily.

'I am fine.'

Good. End of story. We're all fine.

'And …'

Oh no.

'… how are you?'

He turned towards me and raised his eyebrows expectantly. Well, what did I do now? I'd *definitely* already told him how I was, and I'd *definitely* already asked him how *he* was, but he was looking at me, waiting for me to say something. I could hardly change the subject – we were locked in a battle of etiquette. Mine ingrained in me from childhood; his learnt word for word from some kind of 1950s textbook.

'I'm fine,' I mumbled, before, awkwardly, barely audibly and towards the window, 'you?'

'Fine,' said the driver, quickly, now evidently satisfied. 'Very fine, thank you.'

There followed a minute of silence, for which I thanked my lucky stars. I switched my phone on, and it beep-beeped, welcoming me to Singapore. It beep-beeped again a moment later. A text message from Hanne.

IT'S BEEN A WHILE! HOW ARE YOU?

I texted back.

I'M IN SINGAPORE!

I waited for the reply. Within thirty seconds, it was mine.

WHAT? WHY?!

I laughed.

NO REASON!

It was hotter than I think I've ever known. The car's air-conditioning system wasn't the greatest in the world, and it blew hot, sickly air towards our faces. We were driving through downtown Singapore now, past giant shopping malls and wide, tree-lined streets. I looked out of the window, drinking it all in, noting Serangoon road and Little India, and gleefully revelling in what I was doing. Why was I here? Because I happened to see an advert when I was in Spain meeting a man who says Yes a lot and been so inspired that I'd almost been looking for a Level Six. I had made this happen. Samten the monk had effectively told me that in life anything can happen. I took that to mean there was no such thing as destiny. And if there's no such thing as destiny ... then I can make *life* happen!

'Where are you from?' asked the driver, all of a sudden.

'London,' I said.

'Ah,' he said. 'Nice. London.'

Another pause.

'And how far is London from England?'

'Oh. Er ... London is *in* England. It's a city.'

'England or London is a city? Which is capital city of London?'

He looked at me with eager puppy-eyes. I explained that *London* was the capital of *England*, and he said he felt silly, but I reassured him. After all, you can barely find a minicab driver in London itself who would've known that for sure. He – Ong Chee Kieng – had been driving a cab for sixteen years, as it turned out, and he'd moved to Singapore from China to marry his sweetheart.

'We very happy,' he said. 'Two children, also very happy. Singapore is a good place for children. Very clean. Very nice.'

Singapore certainly is very clean. And very nice. Mainly because it'll fine anyone for anything, and fine them heavily. Gone are the days when tourists with long hair would be turned away as they arrived at the airport, or offered a short back and sides by a burly customs official with a pair of blunt scissors, but it's still a place that looks down on a scruff. There's little else you can get away with, either; you'll be fined for jaywalking, for smoking in a public place, for dropping litter. Eating a sandwich on the subway will considerably lighten your wallet, too. According to Ong, radicals used to urinate in lifts by way of making a statement against the system, until they started putting cameras in lifts. Either that or the radicals ran out of urine. And, perhaps most famously: chewing gum is expressly, forcefully forbidden. It seemed to me that Singapore was a little like a nation of rather religious aunties: you love them for their affable strictness and sense of fair play, but you just wish they'd overdo it on the sherry and try and get off with the vicar once in a while. Funny, how a life of Yes had led me to a place of No. Their chewing gum fury is particularly harsh. Those found selling it, importing it, or even using it, face a $1000 fine. It was as Ong was explaining this to me that I suddenly realised with some degree of horror that somewhere at the bottom of my bag was a half-full bumper pack of Wrigleys that Wag had given me one night. There were at least twenty sticks left. Twenty! Essentially, in the eyes of the law, I was now some kind of drugs mule! There are some things you know are going to happen when you decide to say Yes to everything, but being arrested for smuggling isn't one of them.

'So why you come to Singapore?' said Ong, before repeating a phrase he'd obviously learnt off the telly. 'Business or pleasure?'

I smiled.

'Neither, really,' I said. 'I'm just … here.'

Ong looked confused.

'Pleasure,' I said. 'Just pleasure.'

I thought about it. It actually really was. Even my other trips abroad had had a vague point – whether to win the Spanish Lottery or meet a Yes Man. The travel was just a by-product of a Yes. But this … this was a Yes in itself.

Ong dropped me at my hotel, Traders, and gave me a small yellowing business card, saying that should I need driving anywhere I should give him a call. I promised him that Yes, I would, then checked into my room, flushed my Wrigleys down the toilet, and slept for a very, very long time indeed.

Later, I wandered out of my hotel and into the kind of heat that quite instantly robs sweat from every inch of your body. I had no idea what I was doing or where I was going, and neither did I need to. I had nowhere to be, nothing I needed to do, and so instinctively I walked down the very stylish, very long Orange Road; a shameful celebration of capitalism, and really nothing more than dozens of vast shopping centres linked together by underground tunnels and air-conditioned walkways.

I found a McDonald's, and bought myself breakfast. I was slightly surprised to see that this month's specially featured dish of choice was called the Chicken Singaporridge. Porridge doesn't appeal to me at the best of times, and less so when it appeared to be chicken-flavoured porridge in a bap. I wasn't convinced by their slogan, either: 'For that breakfast taste'. Yeah, in *prison*, maybe. Still, Singaporridge was, at least, a catchy name. Presumably, over in Little India, you'd be able to buy a BK Whoppadom.

Relieved that I was under no direct orders to buy Singaporridge, I bought a Big Mac, said Yes, you *could* SuperSize me (some Yeses are the same the world over) and studied my map. But it was just words, and drawings, to me. What should I do? How do you let the wind take you, when there's no wind? *Literally* no wind, in the case of Singapore. I sat there for a moment, and then realised the solution. I would have to *create* the wind. Ong. I would call Ong.

'So what you want to see? Tourist place, or real Singapore?' he said. He had an apple, and he'd brought one for me, too.

'Well …' I said. 'What do *you* recommend? What should I do?'

'I drive you round some places first,' he said.

I had booked Ong and his car for a couple of hours, for an almost embarrassingly small fee. He'd drive me round, show me the sights, act as a guide. And so he took me round the classic tourist spots – the CBD, the statue of Raffles, the proud alabaster-white Merlion, a Chinese temple – and stopped at a supermarket to buy us both water. We wondered what to do next. But I had an idea. Yes was all about experiences. New experiences, at that.

'How about things I would never normally see?' I asked him. 'Can you show me that?'

Ong thought about it.

'I show you paradise!'

I was glad Ong was married, or I might have got the wrong idea.

'Paradise?' I said. 'What's paradise?'

'Paradise is *kampong* – Pulau Ubin.'

There were two words I understood in that sentence.

'Sorry?'

'*Kampong* is paradise for people. Pulau Ubin is island of paradise. For me.'

'But what's a *kampong*?'

'Traditional village. Very quiet. Lot of nature. No hurry, no hurry. Pulau Ubin is best island.'

I scrutinised my map of Singapore to find Pulau Ubin. And there it was, north of the airport. It turns out that Ong, like 90 per cent of Singaporeans, lives in a high-rise block. There's little space in Singapore.

Nowhere to relax around nature. Rapid urbanisation and a relentless onslaught of shopping malls put paid to that. And while much of rural Malaysia still has that traditional *kampong* feel, Singaporeans fear they've lost it for ever. Pulau Ubin is their last chance. Their last glimpse of local paradise. The one place they've got that remains untouched.

'Business want it already,' said Ong. 'Not long now before it goes. Two year, maybe. Maybe one. So sad.'

I put my map down, and Ong said, 'So you want to see?'

'Yeah,' I said. 'I'd like to see.'

Ong dropped me off by the harbour and told me to give him a call when I got back. No hurry, no hurry, he said. I sat on the hard wooden bench by what Singaporeans charmingly call the bumboats. I sat there, and I sat there, and I sat there. And nothing happened. But it didn't matter to me. I was perfectly relaxed. Perfectly happy just to *be*. I was there with four other people, and we sat, in silence, staring into the middle distance, just waiting for the captain to finally invite us on board. But after thirty minutes, I'd had enough of just *be*-ing, and turned to the girl next to me.

'Excuse me,' I said, slightly startling her. 'This is the queue for the boat to Pulau Ubin, isn't it?'

'Yes,' she said. 'But we have to wait.'

'What for?'

'We have to wait until there are enough people. There are only five of us. It must be twelve before we can go.'

I'm glad that the British bus system operates in a far different way. Imagine a coach bound for Swindon that needed twelve people before it could set off. It'd be sat there for months.

We continued to wait in silence.

Finally, thankfully, from around a corner, we were joined by two elderly men. Presumably even the captain of the bumboat was bored off his tits by this stage, as he decided that he'd cut his losses and take just the seven of us.

We set off for paradise.

Twenty-five minutes later and we were there.

I stepped off the bumboat and onto a long, wooden pier. Ong had been right about the island's natural beauty. On first sight, the place was virtually untouched. A sandy beach, with lush green trees and bushes, and just a few rickety wooden piers leading from small, neat houses to tiny, barely seaworthy fishing boats. I walked towards the island with the others, until we passed a carved wooden sign, saying WELCOME TO PULAU UBIN. I stopped to look at it while the others overtook me, and then they were gone, and I was left, deserted, with no one around me, and no idea of where to go. It felt good. It felt random, and … *free*. Where would I be if I hadn't said Yes all those months ago? Would I be at home now, sitting in a dark flat watching *Trisha* as the winter evenings drew in? Wherever I'd be, I'd never have been *here*.

I considered just setting off, but noticed a sign saying VISIT THE TOURIST INFORMATION KIOSK and a big pointing hand, so I obeyed. It was a large wooden building that I imagined contained all sorts of useful information and handy hints on where to go and what to do. I walked through the door, however, to find one vast, virtually empty room. There was a desk to one side, with a door behind it, but apart from that – nothing. I decided I'd probably found the wrong kiosk, but just as I was leaving, a man walked through the door. Wordlessly, he tossed a leaflet onto the desk, looked at me, then turned around and walked back through the door. I picked up the leaflet. '*Pulau Ubin: An Island Getaway, Just a Bumboat Away*'. There were a couple of pictures, but it was rather sparse, as leaflets go.

'Er … excuse me?' I called out, rather pathetically.

Nothing. I tried again, louder.

'*Excuse* me?'

The man popped his head back round the door.

'Yes?'

'Um … do you have any other information on Pulau Ubin? Any more leaflets?'

The man looked at me as if I were asking him to sing a little song for me.

'No.'

'What – nothing whatsoever?'

'No. This is all we have. Everything you need is there.'

I looked at the leaflet. There was virtually nothing on it. Just a few pictures, a tiny map and a couple of poetic paragraphs.

'Oh. Okay. Thanks,' I said, and walked out. I decided it was slightly strange that in order to house one set of rather rubbish pink photocopied leaflets, they'd not only built an unnecessarily huge building, but also employed a man to sit there all day on the off chance that a tourist might arrive and fancy one. It was like buying a bus, just to use it as a pram.

Nevertheless, I was grateful for what I'd been given, and set about reading it.

LIFE ON PULAU UBIN

No need for alarm clocks here – the early morning crowing of roosters sets the day off. A chorus of birds descend on the fruiting trees for the first meal of the day. The jetty rouses itself and the revving of motorcycles fills the streets. All is set for an easy and relaxed start to the day for the islanders.

Oh, yes. What an easy and relaxed start to the day. Woken at 5 am by roosters, and then tormented by motorcycle revving until breakfast or suicide. To be honest, the *end* of the day didn't sound much better, either:

As night settles upon the island and people come to rest, the sound of diesel generators floats through the air. The insect-eating Tomb Bats emerge suddenly from their roosts and may be seen as flitting, silent shadows. And while you are gazing upwards, keep your eyes open for the lime-green Oriental Whip Snake reptile, as it slides through the grass underfoot.

Jesus! Woken unnaturally early and harassed by motorcycle gangs, then killed by bats and snakes by lights out. No wonder Pulau Ubin's remained untouched for so many years. So long as the tourist office kept doing such a sterling job of selling the place, I had no doubt it would remain untouched for many years to come.

I wanted to see the island, and decided that the best thing to do would be to rent a bike. So I did, from a thrilled-looking bike rental man who appeared never to have rented out a bike before, and set off for a cycle around what Ong had described to me as the Singaporean idea of Utopia. I felt cool. I felt like an explorer, pushing bravely into the unknown. On a small bike.

Even though it's just 1.5 kilometres wide and 8 km long, Ubin is Singapore's second largest island, and, as Ong told me, it remains the only true *kampong* left in existence; the only one not replaced by shopping malls and Singaporridge shops.

I cycled down a small incline and around a winding road until I faced rather a large hill in front of me. But I had the energy and the willpower and set about pumping away at the pedals until I was about halfway up and about to pass out. It was maybe 35 degrees and I was sweaty, and my boxer shorts already appeared to be trying to attempt an expedition of their own, exploring areas of my body usually reserved for someone with a qualification. I stopped to straighten myself out, hopped back on the bike, and continued on for a good few kilometres.

Two hundred people live on Ubin, relying on the land to support them, or the odd tourist renting a bike. I didn't see one of them. I passed abandoned farms, and dogs playing around derelict shacks, but not one, single, solitary person. Maybe this was why Ong liked it so much. In a place where you are never more than a few feet from someone else, an island like this must mean so much.

That said, it became creepy after a while. Particularly when I started to cycle up roads surrounded by high hedges and lush, overhanging trees, where my only possible route was forwards or backwards, and the ambient noise suddenly and surprisingly became absolutely deafening.

It's no more than a buzz at first … then it sounds like someone's left a few whistling kettles on the boil … then it becomes as loud as, or louder than, a car alarm. And you just can't tell where it's coming from.

I began to feel paranoid. Here I was, totally on my own, far away from anyone, in the middle of nowhere, for virtually no reason whatsoever, surrounded by screaming, unseen kettles. What on earth would the authorities think if they found my body out here? How in God's name would they piece together my final movements? What kind of motives would they come up with?

Suddenly, I felt slightly panicky. I cycled on as quickly as I could, but started to realise that, in the bushes to the right of me, something was noisily running along with me. I couldn't see it, but it was causing enough of a disturbance in the long grasses for me to know it was big, and it was fast. Oh, Christ, what *was* it? I couldn't stop now … I pedalled on, faster and faster, and now I could definitely hear it thundering alongside me … what was it? Was it after me? I felt more like a character in a Stephen King book than I ever have before, and despite the fact that I was going deeper into what was now essentially a jungle, I couldn't turn around and go back for fear of coming face to face with it – if it had a face – and whatever it was was still there, still pounding the ground, mere feet away …

I rounded a bend at speed, but so did my potential captor. I was panicking properly now. Was I being hunted? What if whatever it was decided to eat me? What did they have over here again? Did the leaflet mention crocodiles? Or rhinos? Snakes can't run, can they?

I cycled on, and furiously on, not once looking behind me, and thankfully, the noise from the long grass started to fade, until it wasn't there at all. I was knackered, but determined to continue, and when I was far enough away, I stopped and got my leaflet out. I scoured those hundred or so words for any mention of killer kettles or things that might run alongside an innocent British cyclist, but there was nothing. Which, if I'm honest, just added to the sense of foreboding. Was Yes trying to get me killed? It was supposed to help me live! The other noises around me still hadn't settled down, and I was now on a road surrounded by huge trees that blocked out the sunlight and gave everything a musty, evening feel.

And then I heard a scuffling sound behind me and the sound of leaves being thrashed about and I whacked my shins against the pedals as I tried to get the bike going again, desperate fear taking over – but my balance was off and my feet suddenly too big and the noise got louder and louder and then a lizard the size of a tank rushed past me and thundered, low and muscular, through a gap in the bushes where it stopped moving completely. My heart raced. I was being stalked by a lizard. A bloody *lizard*! This wasn't right. *This* wasn't paradise!

And, in fact, if this *was* paradise, how come so few people seemed keen to live here? I was still to pass even one person. Where *was* everyone? Was everyone lizards? Maybe David Icke had been right!

I pressed on, sticking to the road and without once looking back for fear of seeing anything else that freaked me out. The lizard decided the prey wasn't worth it, and left me soon after. I was knackered and red and in the mood for sitting down, which is when I spotted something. A signpost. It told me that a place called Nualong beach wasn't far away, and that sounded perfect for me. A beach. Safety.

Before too long I found it. It was becoming slightly overcast now, but it was still warm, and I parked my bike up and sat down on the beach. I was exhausted.

The water was calm, and the sun warm. Despite my lizard-based shenanigans, I was suddenly inordinately pleased to be here. I felt further away from London than I'd ever been – and further away from anyone else. It was just me. Thousands of miles away from another life. I thought about what had brought me here. The chain of Yeses that had led to me to be sitting on a beach on Pulau Ubin. Of course, it began with the man on the bus, but my Singapore weekend was all thanks to saying Yes to a dull, bring-a-fact party. To Gareth. Then Jeff. And Marc. Who knew how many other chains I'd started, who knew what else I'd set in motion? Where else could this lead me? What did a Yes I'd said last week, or last month, have in store for me *next* week, or *next* month?

It was late November now. Soon it would be December. That left just one more month of Yes, before a whole new way of life started. A more responsible life, with nine to fives, and spreadsheets, and overhead projectors. No more jetting off to Singapore on a credit card and a whim. No more ruthless spontaneity. Just calm. Like the calm around me now. But there were still treats in store. Lizzie, for one.

I sat there, in the sun, and smiled. It was drawing to a close. Just another few weeks. I was looking forward to them.

An hour later, at the end of the pier, a large group of people – who seemed to have come from nowhere – were sitting down, in near silence, waiting patiently for the next bumboat to arrive and take them off to the mainland. I floated serenely towards them, and recognised one or two of them from the journey over. There were maybe fourteen of them in all. But the strange thing was, they were all sitting on the one bench. There were four benches, forming one big square, and yet these people had all chosen to sit on just the one side. This one group of disparate people had chosen to sit *alongside* one another rather than *away from*, and stare in the same direction, at me, the approaching tourist. But I didn't feel intimidated, or embarrassed. Because *they* didn't. They thought it was completely normal to all sit, wordlessly, on the one bench. This would never have happened in London. We would all have sat on separate benches, always chosen the one with less people on it, always kept ourselves to ourselves.

I was heartened by this simple sight. I raised my hand as I approached, and smiled. I had to decide where to sit. Well, I couldn't very well be the only person to sit on a bench of his own, could I? That would mark me out as a typically aloof, unfriendly Westerner. So I conquered my awkwardness and did what I would never normally do. I strode up to them, and sat myself down right in the middle of them. I was suddenly feeling very philosophical. Yes had done that to me. Opened me up a bit more. I was just another stranger, after all. A white stranger, maybe, with unusual trainers, but really, I was just another person to have sat myself down on that bench, to share a view and wait for a boat. No one said anything at all. A few people glanced at me, and I glanced back and smiled. There was a feeling of deep mutual respect on that bench. Silent, wordless respect. Me, from a land far away, and they –

simple Malay folk, calm and serene, regarding me with quiet wonder. I breathed deeply and thought about this unexpected sense of community. How we could come from places so far apart and still share this sense of unspoken, unthreatening togetherness. Maybe *this* was what paradise was all about, I thought. Maybe it wasn't Pulau Ubin itself … but the attitude of those on it. Maybe paradise wasn't *around* us. Maybe it was *inside* us.

And then they all started talking about me, and it became clear that they were one big family group, and *that* was why they were sitting together, and now they were wondering who on earth *I* was and why the hell I was sitting right in the middle of them, and not on a bench of my own like any *normal* person. And I went a bit red.

I pretended I needed to stretch my legs, and stood up and yawned, strutted about, pretended to find something fascinating about one of the other benches and then sat down on it and studied my feet. A year or so later, the bumboat arrived, and I made sure I was the first one on it. I didn't want that lot getting there first and then taking bets on where I would sit.

Back at the hotel, I sipped on a cocktail and sent Marc a text.

I AM IN SINGAPORE. I WAS CHASED BY A LIZARD

I received one back, ten minutes later.

ATOMICO, DANNY!

I laughed. I really hoped I'd see Marc again.

It was getting late and I would be returning to London the next day and so I studied my map and thought about how I should spend the remainder of my time in Singapore.

I needn't have bothered.

Because I was to spend the rest of my time in Singapore worrying.

Fretting, stressing, and worrying.

I had made my way into the hotel's Business Centre and checked my e-mails. I'd planned to send one to Lizzie, telling her where I was and what I was doing, and how much I was looking forward to seeing her again.

I hadn't reckoned that someone might have e-mailed me.

> **To: Danny**
> **From: whoisthechallenger@hotmail.com**
> **Subject: Next…**

Hello Danny,

Enjoying yourself? Still saying Yes?

Well, that's nice.

So why don't you...

Go to Stonehenge... 2...?

My heart sank. I was thousands of miles away, and yet the Challenger was still like a shadow. Who was this? Everything was worthless while they were still controlling me. I was supposed to be in control! Master of my *own* destiny! If it was Jason, he was being remarkably persistent for a man who should have got bored and moved on weeks ago ... so *was* it Jason?

But Stonehenge 2? What was Stonehenge *2*? *Was* Stonehenge 2 anything? Or did they mean I should go to Stonehenge again?

Quickly, I opened up google.com and typed in 'Stonehenge 2'.

A second later, I had my result.

Stonehenge 2 existed.

They intended to send me to Stonehenge 2!

But what *was* it?

The original Stonehenge, an ancient Druid monument located in England, is shrouded in mystery. But Stonehenge 2: The Sequel is more of an oddity than a mystery. This 92-foot diameter creation is made of hollow plaster and is accompanied by two ...

My eyes darted around the site. Stonehenge 2 is a monument to a monument ... but where?

And then I saw it.

Shit.

Texas. Stonehenge 2 was in *Texas*!

Shit.

Suddenly, my world seemed to collapse.

Just when I'd accepted that in order to survive the world of Yes it was necessary to just sit back and enjoy the ride, someone else had reached in and grabbed the steering wheel ...

23

In which Daniel faces a Terrible Crisis

I returned home to London knowing one thing.

There was no way I could go to Texas. Enough was enough. The Challenger had pushed me far enough when he'd sent me to *England's* Stonehenge ... he had another think coming if he thought I was about to let him send me to a *Texan* one, too.

This was it. It was time to take a stand. But by not going to Texas, or ignoring his cryptic words, I'd be failing. Breaking the rules. Saying no to something I'd sworn I'd say Yes to. And I couldn't do that.

I knew that by the time Lizzie got to London, this was something I would have to have dealt with. A battle I'd have to have won. She'd be here in little over a week ... I'd said Yes to her and couldn't now break that Yes, meaning if I obeyed the Challenger's whims, I would have to organise and make the return journey incredibly soon, and incredibly quickly.

But how would I explain it to Lizzie? How would I tell her what I'd been up to? That I was, in effect, living a double life? Maybe she'd take it well (because Yes, I would have to tell her). Sure, I was still the mild-mannered, bespectacled Clark Kent-style radio producer of old ... but now I was something else, too. A man with more going on in his life. A man with more confidence, more openness. A man who'd recaptured his spontaneity. Maybe she'd take a shine to that. She'd seemed to in Edinburgh, when she was to blame for it.

Or ... would she *hate* it? Would she, like Hanne, find it immature, and unnecessary, and *stupid*? And would she feel it devalued our relationship, when I told her that I had bought her a ticket from Melbourne to Edinburgh not out of some grand romantic gesture ... but just because she *asked*? Because some bearded bloke on a bus said it'd be *good* for me?

Either way, I was going to have to tell her.

But no matter how she reacted, everything could still go wrong. Even if I went to Texas, and got back well before Lizzie arrived, it would solve absolutely nothing. The Challenger would still be in the picture, meaning the threat of considerable trouble and awkwardness would always be a moment away …

Desperately, I e-mailed Thom once again … and he wrote back the same day …

Danny,
Really, really sorry – not been able to get in touch with
Jason. To be honest, we're not all that close as friends, but I
have left a message with his sister asking her to get him to
e-mail me asap. I do have these details, though...

And below that, Jason's place of work and mobile number.

Excellent! Now I *really* had him! All this man's power lay in the fact that I couldn't prove it was him. While he was an anonymous threat, he was able to make me do things against my will. But once I'd unmasked him, he'd be another Ian; another person who knew – and who I *knew* knew. By exposing him, I would rob him of all authority. By exposing him, I would be able to *ignore* him.

I launched an immediate and forceful three-pronged attack …

First, a strongly worded e-mail.

Jason,
I have your mobile number and I know where you work. And
I'm not doing it. I'm not going to Texas. I know who you are,
which means I know that you know, which means you can no
longer do this to me. I want to speak to you to make sure
you understand, though. YOU ARE NO LONGER ELIGIBLE TO
MAKE ME DO THINGS BECAUSE I KNOW YOU KNOW THAT I KNOW
YOU KNOW.
I'm going to phone you now.

Danny

I picked up my phone, and dialled his mobile.

Frustratingly, it went straight to voicemail.

*This is the Vodaphone VoiceMail Service for 07*** *** ***, please leave a message after the—*

'Jason, it's Danny,' I virtually shouted. 'The jig's up. I have your number now. Read your e-mail, and never get in touch with me again. We've all had a lot of fun with it, and I'm sure you've had a great laugh with your mates down the pub, but the party's over. Goodnight and go to hell …'

I hung up, and looked at my watch. It was four o'clock – well within office hours. I dialled the work number that Thom had given me. I was pumped up, ready for a showdown, ready to tell this bloke to piss right off.

'Welcome to the Immigration and Nationality Bureau,' said a recorded voice. 'Please note that all calls are recorded …'

There was a click, while the call transferred to an operator, and then …

'Good morning, Home Office, how can I help?'

'I need to speak to a man called Jason, please.'

'What's the surname?'

'I don't have a surname. I've only met him once. He works in immigration, making decisions about people …'

'I'm afraid I can't place your call without knowing a surname.'

'I need to speak to him. Urgently.'

'All appeals must be in writing …'

'I don't want to make an appeal … I want to speak to Jason …'

'Did you receive an RFRL?'

'I don't know what an RFRL is … I just need to speak to a bloke called Jason, it's a personal call, it won't take a minute … please, just put me through to someone in the department who makes decisions about things like that …'

'Hold the line …'

My heart started to race. I was getting closer. My three-pronged attack was about to climax. I was closing in on the man who had been mocking me from afar.

'SEO?'

It was a girl's voice.

'Hi … is Jason there, please?'

'Jason who?' she said.

'I'm not sure. He works there. Making decisions about people. Saying no a lot. I *have* to speak to him—'

'Hang on …'

The phone is muffled as she asks someone about something.

'He doesn't work here any more,' she said. 'There was a Jason here, but he's gone. I'm new here. Sorry.'

Curses!

'Well … where's he gone? Do you have a number? I tried his phone but it's switched off. I need to speak to him. I need to speak to him *right now* …'

'Hang on …'

Another muffled conversation.

'No, I'm sorry. We're not allowed to give out personal details.'

'But honestly – I'm not a stalker or a lunatic. This man, he's been—'

'I'm sorry.'

I sighed, and rubbed my eyes.

'Well … if you see him … can you get him to call Danny?'

'Sure. I'll tell the others too.'

'Thanks.'

I put the phone down, slightly dejected. I'd thought that was going to be it.

What would happen if I didn't get him? Never got him? What would happen if I could never track him down, and grab him, and shout, 'I know who you are!' at him? Then the Challenger would live on. And I'd have to go to Texas after all.

It wasn't just that I was tired. It wasn't just that I'd had enough of travelling, and wanted to stay at home, and see Lizzie, and finish the last month of Yes in relative comfort. It was that I'd been all but ignoring another aspect of my journey up until now.

The cost.

Texas wouldn't be cheap to get to. I knew I'd have to fly to New York, then probably change and get a flight to Austin, and then a cab or a bus or a train to Hunt. And I'd have to do it in the way I'd been doing everything else: on credit.

I now had far too many credit cards, thanks to the various offers, suggestions and invitations of the kindly people at Visa, Barclaycard, American Express and everywhere else, and I'd used each of them. I'd used them only for smaller things, early on, sure; things like a curry with Wag. Or maybe a round of beers with Nathan, or Jon, or Ben, or Rich, or any of the other friends who'd suddenly found me all too easy to coax out of the flat or tap for a pint. But later, well … the bills had *grown*.

Buying the Yesmobile had eaten up my savings, and I hadn't exactly been working very much lately – I'd been putting it off, knowing that a new job was just around the corner, hoping that everything would sort itself out. Then there'd been Lizzie's flight to pay for. And the insurance, and road tax, for the new car. The train tickets to Liverpool. And Cardiff. The thousands of stickers I'd had printed up. Up until a week ago, I could bear all that … but the next bill would feature a hotel in Barcelona. Meals. Hasty withdrawals for taxis and trains. Flights to Singapore and back. And maybe, now, even a series of flights and hotels to get me to Hunt, Texas, to look at a smaller version of a monument that was already pretty small, and which anyway I'd seen just a month or two before.

And what would I have to show for it all? What would I have to show for all the effort, and expense, and debt? A *feeling*. Try telling *that* to the bailiffs. Was this all worth so much money?

The problem, early on, was winning that £25,000. It had made me feel like a very rich man indeed. It had made me think everything was going to be okay; like Yes was going to look after me. But now, sitting at my desk, studying my bills, I suddenly didn't feel like it was. Yes just wasn't living up to its end of the bargain.

So I did what any man sinking slowly into debt would do. I shoved the bills into a drawer and went out instead. In January I'd be turning a corner. Starting again. I'd pay it all off when I chained myself to that desk, where I'd stay for the rest of my life. I only had a month to go. *I only had a month to go.*

So tonight I would drink. Drink to forget.

The problem was, I'd have to do it with Paul.

I was on my way to meet the man who'd called me for a polite conversation for a second time. So far, he remained the only person who had taken me up on the offer. I was not in a good mood. And I was not in the mood (and I hope he will forgive me for this) for meeting Paul. I needed to be with someone who understood; not with someone who understood Border terriers.

We met at the Yorkshire Grey. The polite conversation was stilted, at best, but I don't think Paul had noticed. He was off on another mono-logue, while I just sat there, scowling.

'Musically,' he said, apropos of virtually nothing, 'my interests are varied. I'm probably *most* into Sarah Brightman. Do you like Sarah Brightman?'

'She is a very talented entertainer,' I said, downbeat and down-trodden, when what I really wanted to say was, 'I can't *stand* Sarah Brightman.' But this was a polite conversation. That was the deal.

'I think she's touring early next year if you're interested?' said Paul.

Nope. I am not interested at all.

'That is excellent news,' I said.

'I've loved her stuff ever since *Phantom of the Opera*. That's what brought her to my attention first of all. And then some friends in Brazil sent me an album of hers, called *The Songs That Got Away*, and I was so glad that they *hadn't* got away, because that was me hooked!'

I made a polite ha-ha noise.

'I'll let you borrow that CD if you like?'

'Oh, Yes please.'

'Since then I've been to see her in concert a few times. I saw her in Edinburgh in '97. I had tickets for the seventh row, on the right of centre, and that was fantastic, even though Sarah was standing to the left of centre, but it was still good, you know.'

'Right,' I said, as if I'd been making mental floorplans in my head. I had finished my pint and was waiting for Paul to finish his. I didn't want to add yet another round to my Yes bill.

'And then I saw her again on that same tour in Norwich, and it was a bigger crowd this time ...'

And please, *God*, make this *end*. Make him talk about Border terriers again. Anything.

'... and basically I started the standing ovation at the end of that gig, so if you ever meet her walking around the BBC, you should say, "I met the man who started the standing ovation in Norwich in 1997" and see what she says!'

'I will certainly do that,' I said, playing with my glass. My very *empty* glass.

'Do! Do that! She'll love that. Yes, as I say, I think she's touring again next year ...'

I put both my thumbs up.

'Hey – if you work for the BBC, Danny, you could probably get me an autograph.'

I looked at him, blankly.

'Couldn't you?' he said.

'If I bump into her,' I said.

'You could fax her and ask for one.'

What did he want me to fax? *'Dear Sarah, the BBC would like an autograph'*?

'Would you do that for me?'

Sigh.

'Yes.'

Paul looked at his watch.

'Oh. I should probably get going ... going to the cinema tonight.'

'The cinema?' I said, partly out of relief that the subject was chang-ing, and partly because, despite all this, I now wanted to extend the conversation. I didn't want to be alone right now.

'Yeah,' he said. 'Oh, God, I would invite you, but someone else got the tickets. It's kind of a date.'

I nodded, a little relieved that my days of gatecrashing dates were at an end.

'Is she nice?' I said.

'I hope so,' he said. 'Friend of a friend.'

I nearly told him about Kristen, but caught myself. I still didn't want to talk about that. And with Lizzie getting ready to come back to London, it just didn't feel ... right, somehow.

'Well, good luck,' I said.

'Cheers. My friend Simon set this up. He knows I'd never say no to a redhead. My own personal weakness. That's the thing, eh? Your mates know your vulnerabilities.'

I was pleased for Paul. And I felt slightly guilty, too. Why had I been so grumpy about meeting with him? I suppose at the back of my mind I'd thought I was doing him a favour. He seemed lonely. But look at him; a successful man, with friends who thought highly enough of him to set him up on dates; an active social life. We'll brush over the Sarah Brightman fixation, but the fact was, he was fine. Life was sorted. If anything, he must've thought he was doing *me* a favour. Me, who never seemed to have anything to talk about. Me, who'd put stickers all over town, essentially saying, 'Please call me! I am a sad and lonely oddball who craves the polite conversation of strangers.'

Paul put his jacket on, and, as he shook my hand, said, 'I meant to ask ... I'm in town again tomorrow night. I could bring you that CD. Do you fancy a quick drink then? Save you sitting here all on your own.'

I felt wretched. Paul obviously saw me as a somewhat pathetic loner.

I put my thumbs up again, and said, quite gratefully, 'Yes.'

* * *

And that, I'm afraid, was my big night out. Those were my efforts to drown my sorrows. Don't get me wrong; I rang around. I rang Wag, and I rang Ian, and I rang Nathan, Jonesy, Ben and Rich. I even rang Cobbett. But each had an excuse. Each had somewhere else they had to be, or something else they had to do. Each had the power of No. I found myself growing jealous of those freedom-loving bastards.

I trudged to the tube, and walked heavily down the steps of Oxford Circus station. Two stops later, at Holborn, I was forced to get out. There was trouble on the line. Some kind of power failure. We were instructed to find other means of getting home, or to hang around and wait for the bus replacement service.

It was a common enough occurrence, but it had real resonance with me. Maybe, I thought, this was a sign of hope. This was how it had all begun, after all. Perhaps it was a sign. Maybe Maitreya would come to me. Maybe I'd bump into the man on the bus. Maybe all this meant something. Maybe it *wasn't* all pointless.

The buses arrived soon after. With genuine hope in my eyes, I looked around me. Scoured the faces of the other affected, moody commuters and travellers, but I didn't see him. I moved upstairs, but to no avail. There were no men with beards. No men who looked like they might be enlightened. Plenty of men on a bus … but *no man on the bus*.

The journey was long and the stops many. By the time the bus was running parallel with the Roman Road, minutes from my flat, I was completely on my own. A lone figure, on a top deck, on a dark night, staring out of the window.

As the bus slowed at a junction, I walked downstairs and jumped off. I would walk the rest of the way home. The last half an hour had confirmed a lot of things for me. I knew, once and for all, that I was on my own. That Maitreya did not exist. That the man on the bus had just been a man on the bus. That I'd done all this myself. That there was *no* grand plan. That I alone was responsible for my actions.

And so I stopped at an off-licence, bought a bottle of wine, and went home, the pit of my stomach churning as I realised that at some point this evening I'd have to investigate how much a flight to Texas was.

Oh. And fax Sarah Brightman's agent.

That night, I had a bath. A long, long bath. I didn't want to get out. As long as I was in the bath, I felt protected. I wasn't near my phone, or the Internet. No opportunities or favours or requests could sneak in through the locked door. It was a steamy, warm cocoon. Things really had changed since my Yes heydays ... I'd only had time for showers, then. I'd always wanted to be out there, on the other side of the door, searching for Yeses and grabbing them with both hands.

I'd brought my diary in with me. I wanted to see what I'd been through. Analyse my actions. Understand them. See whether, with a month to go, it had been worth it. Whether it could inspire me to want to travel to the other side of the world just one more time. I flicked idly through, from page to page, through July, and August, and September, wondering what Ian would make of it all at the end of the month, when it would be me and him, on New Year's Eve, in the same pub we'd been in when I'd told him about the man on the bus. What would he think when I explained what October had done ... what November had taught me ...

There were things he knew about, sure – the scratchcard, Amsterdam, the undeserved promotion, my new-found status as both respected minister and (failed) inventor – but there was so much more he *didn't* know about. So many experiences I'd had – people I'd met or places I'd seen. Things I'd done. Little changes in habit. Little efforts I wouldn't normally have made. No matter how well Ian knew me, much of this would surprise him. A lot of it surprised *me*. I suddenly felt rather proud of Ian. He'd been a constant support. A constant friend. Someone who *could* have used his special knowledge to teach me a lesson I'd never forget, but who *hadn't*. He'd seen the worth of this project. I guess it was like Paul had said. The people who know you well are the people who know your vulnerabilities. They know your weaknesses. But you trust them not to pounce on them; not to take advantage. And they don't, because they care. It's the strangers you've got to watch out for. The people like Jason. The people who sense weakness and for whatever reason, feel they have to crush you. Strangers were bad. But why were some strangers *so* bad?

And as I flicked through the diary some more, and I thought about that, I nodded at myself, impressed by my own wisdom ... until I was struck by one aspect of the diary in particular. One set of Yeses ... one single chain of events ... one idea that turned into a feeling that wouldn't go away ...

The people who know you well are the people who know your vulnerabilities ...

But I pressed on. Reading through the diary. Taking it all in. Seeing who I'd met and when, and what had happened before and after, and then I just couldn't help it … I started to feel less and less well, and more and more nervous. I couldn't put my finger on why, exactly … but it had something to do with the thought that was slowly creeping up on me, slowly forming somewhere …

It was an uncomfortable thought – one that made the back of my neck prickle and my heart start to beat a little faster. I pushed it to one side, knowing that it just couldn't be possible, that there could be no truth in it, that I was just being silly …

But the more of the diary I read, the more I started to understand …

I got out of the bath and started to whistle. I hoped that would be enough to distract me. But it wasn't.

Suddenly, I had to make sure of something. I had to make sure that this was all down to just mild, unshifting jetlag and ground-in paranoia.

I pulled my shirt and boxers on, walked into the living room, and turned the computer on. There was an e-mail I had to check. One I'd received a little while ago, from Thom … it had been a throwaway sentence and had not really struck me as odd until now … but now it struck me as *very* odd indeed …

I uncorked my bottle of wine while the Mac started up … this was stupid. What was I doing? But I had to check …

Finally, it was ready. I clicked into my Mail, and there it was … the sentence …

What's your address?

My heart leapt. Shit. Thom didn't have my address. *He didn't have my address.* So if Thom didn't have my address … how did Jason find it with such ease?

Oh, God, it was true.

Maybe Jason had nothing to do with this at all. Meaning that there was a chance it *could* be …

I picked up my phone and started to dial … but then I put it down again.

I couldn't just phone someone up and accuse them of having a hidden identity. Of being the Challenger.

Could I?

I poured a glass of wine and paced the living room … this was stupid. A stupid idea. It couldn't be true. But the more I tried to force it out of my head, the more control the thought seemed to gain.

The people who know you well are the people who know your vulnerabilities ...

Was I being paranoid? Was I going mad? I mean, I already *knew* who the Challenger was, didn't I? It was Jason ... the man who'd taken an active stand against the way of Yes. The man who'd sworn at me, and made me feel like a little boy with a stupid hobby. The grown man who said No for a living.

But ... *what if? What if it wasn't Jason? What if it wasn't a near stranger? What if it was ... a friend? A friend who knew what I was up to, and where I lived, and exactly what I'd been doing with my life?*

Maybe there was a way of finding out. Or maybe not finding out exactly ... but at least setting my mind at rest. It was a long shot, sure, but at least I could take that long shot and be done with it.

I walked to my computer and headed for the Internet.

It couldn't be a friend ... the hat ... the book ... the t-shirt ... the trip ... it couldn't be a friend ...

I went to hotmail.com.

Would this work? Could it?

In the log-in box, I typed an e-mail address. One that had become rather familiar to me.

whoisthechallenger@hotmail.com

Below that, it asked me for a password.

What was the password? What would the Challenger's password be?

Slowly, and with two fingers, I typed in one, familiar, six-letter word, and then looked at it.

If this works ... I thought.

My finger hovered over the mouse.

I pressed it.

The screen went white. The computer whirred. And there, in the blink of an eye, it appeared.

An in-box.

I stared, and stared, and I still couldn't believe it. I was looking at an in-box. The password *worked*.

There was one e-mail. It was unread. It was from me. The angry e-mail I'd sent only a day before telling Jason that the game was up, that I was making a stand, that he could go to hell. But the very fact that I could see it meant that it never got to Jason.

I was stunned. The only reason I'd been able to guess the password was that it was a password I knew all too well.

Which meant that it was a *Challenger* I knew all too well.

My head spinning, I picked up the phone, and I dialled.

Eighteen hours later, I pulled the car up a few moments away from the Horse and Groom. I tried to make it screech to a halt, but the braking system of the Nissan Figaro is annoyingly well designed.

I got out and slammed the door shut.

'I wouldn't park there, mate,' said a street cleaner. 'There's traffic wardens all over the place. They'll have you fined within five minutes.'

Oh *would* they? I wasn't in the mood to be messed with today.

I opened the door of the car again, leaned over to open the glovebox, brought out a small laminated sign, and fixed it to the window.

MINISTER ON OFFICIAL BUSINESS.

Sod 'em.

It had been my suggestion where we would meet, and I wanted to do it on *my* turf. The Challenger, of course, hadn't realised they'd been found out yet. They assumed this was a social call – a normal day in a normal place, just as we'd done thousands of times before. I was calm on the outside. But on the inside I was full of adrenaline.

We sat down, and I spoke first.

'Well … it's nice to see you again,' I said, making sure to pause dramatically before saying, 'it's always nice to see … *the Challenger.*'

There was a silence. I remained like that on purpose, trying to force a statement from someone who was now looking very embarrassed indeed.

'How did you find out it was me?'

How did I find out it was them? I found out for the same reason they knew I was the Yes Man. Because those who know you best, know your vulnerabilities.

I took a deep breath, and said one word.

'Norway.'

'Sorry?'

'N-O-R-W-A-Y. Like the country.'

Something dawned on Hanne.

'You used the same password on your fake hotmail account as you've used for everything else for the past five years,' I said. 'Including your mobile phone account.'

I imagine that after she reads this book, she probably won't be using the word 'Norway' for passwords quite so much. But it serves her right.

Her pin number, by the way, is 4626.

'Oh … well. Right. I should probably apologise,' she said.

'Yes, you probably bloody should! When did you first know, Hanne?'

She drummed her fingers on the table as she thought about it.

'Early on. I mean, I *assume* it was early on. God knows how long you'd been doing it by then. But at that restaurant, you ordered fish. You never ordered fish before. You never even *ate* fish before. You said they were too creepy. You said you were sure they were looking at you funny, even when they didn't have heads. But as soon as the waiter recommended it, you just said "Yes". *That's* how I first knew something was up.'

I suppose the lesson here is that you should never underestimate an ex-girlfriend's intuition.

'And then there was the fact that you came to dinner at *all*,' she said. 'I mean, that was *odd*, Danny. You'd done some odd things before, but that was *really* odd. I was fuming. I was fuming for days. I knew you were up to something, and every time I met you or heard from you you did something to confirm it. *Yes*, you minded if I started seeing someone new. *Yes*, you were going to help the murdered son of a sultan. *I've* had those e-mails, Danny. And *then* … sponsoring a small African child for me, Dan … do you think I haven't seen those leaflets, too? And the flowers? At first I thought you were just being easily influenced by advertising, but then I put two and two together and got … well … an idiot. An idiot who says Yes a lot.'

'But why not just *tell* me you were on to me? Why all this Challenger business?'

'You'd never have stopped if I just told you! And this way, it was like … a prank, or something.'

'A *prank*? You were going to send me to bloody *Texas*!'

'Texas? No I wasn't!'

'You said "Go To Stonehenge 2!" That's in Texas!'

'No – I wanted you to go to Stonehenge – for the *second time*! I wanted you to go to Stonehenge, *twice*! When I texted you and you were in Singapore, I thought right, well, for some reason he obviously wants to bloody travel. So I was going to keep sending you to Stonehenge until you'd had enough! It was going to end up like Groundhog Day! It would've been "*Go To Stonehenge 3*" in another few weeks!'

'But why *Stonehenge*?'

'Because you hate theme parks. You always have.'

I put my head in my hands.

'Stonehenge is *not* a theme park! Shelf Adventure – *that's* a theme park! Stonehenge is a … you know … a … *thing*. A monument. An *attraction*. But it's not a *theme park*! I could understand if you thought I hated *druids*! Or *big stone circles*! But …'

Something else flashed into my head.

'You set me up on a *date*, Hanne!'

'And again, I didn't expect you to actually say Yes! It was a blind date, Danny! Set up by your ex! How much more creepy did you want me to be? Or did you expect me to gatecrash *your* date, like you'd gatecrashed mine? You should have just said no!'

I didn't say anything. I was still reeling slightly from my lucky escape. I didn't want to think about how close I'd come to booking a ticket to Texas; about sinking even deeper into debt. And all because I'd got carried away with this evil Challenger figure. The evil Challenger figure sitting before me now, looking not particularly evil at all. I had invented a motivation for them. My mind had exaggerated their intent … but why? As another way of making life more exciting? I had become a fantasist. I had *made this happen*.

'I thought you were a bloke called Jason,' I told her, for what I really must assure you was the first time in our relationship. 'I thought *he* was "the Challenger".'

'I didn't want to call myself that,' she said. 'That wasn't my idea.'

Hang on.

'Well, whose idea was it, then? Seb's?'

She started to backtrack.

'No, what I mean is—'

Something started to dawn on me.

'You had *help*, didn't you? You weren't doing this alone, were you?'

'No, no, I—'

'You didn't get all this from fish at all! That *wasn't* the starting point! You made that up!'

'I was worried about you! I thought I was helping!'

'And the t-shirt – the *Just Say No* t-shirt … it's a little convenient that that arrived just when I was thinking how much I missed the word "No"…'

'We were trying to help – we were both trying to help—'

'Who's "both"? Where were you getting your information from?'

But she didn't have to tell me. Because instantly, I knew.

'It was … my God, it was *Ian*, wasn't it?'

Hanne looked at the table, and nodded, silently.

Treachery!

Ian had *betrayed* me!

'He said he just wanted you to stop,' said Hanne. 'We felt it was our fault. You were going mental, Danny. Ian told me. He said we had to break your new habit. He said it was important that we got you to say no.'

My eyes nearly popped.

'He thought it was important I said no? Well, of *course* he did! He wanted me to say no so he could punish me! He's wanted that all along!'

'Punish you? No … *help* you.'

My head was spinning. All this time I thought I'd been battling a dark, brutish presence … a Challenger intent on my demise. I'd blamed it on a man I hardly knew – when in reality the enemy walked alongside me. Two mates. Playing a trick on me. A trick they thought would *help* me! I needed to calm down. Maybe she was right, maybe I'd been taking this far too seriously; attaching too much importance to it all. Maybe I'd been doing that all along, right from the start. Maybe all this was the greatest waste of time ever committed in the name of self-help …

'I'm sorry, Danny … it was just supposed to be a bit of fun—'

'But it's … *devalued* everything somehow …' I said. 'All my efforts!'

'It was only supposed to be a bit of revenge for all the stupid boy-projects you put me through when we were going out … but you know what? I got quite *into* it … it was like a stupid *girl*-project. I used to go to sleep at night giggling about all the things I could make you do! I'm sorry, Dan. I can kind of see what you saw in those projects now.'

I looked Hanne straight in the eye.

'That is highly immature,' I said. 'I am glad I am past all that, and I hope that one day you grow up, as I have.'

Hanne watched me as I started to stand up.

'Where are you going?' she said.

'Don't tell Ian about our meeting, okay?' I said. 'I have to go and think of a suitable punishment for him. I am sure that he must have contravened the rules set out by the Yes Manifesto in *some* way …'

Suddenly, there was a none-too-subtle cough from my right, and I remembered something I'd completely forgotten to do.

'Oh, God, I'm so sorry. Hanne, this is Paul. He's a new friend of mine. I gave him a lift here. We have polite conversations.'

Paul had been sitting there in confused silence for the last fifteen minutes. In the rush to expose Hanne, I'd forgotten to introduce him, and as I'd already said Yes I'd have a drink with him, I'd had to bring him along.

'Hello Paul,' said Hanne.

'Hello Hanne,' said Paul.

'Hey … *Hanne's* got a dog,' I said, a thought suddenly coming to me. 'Don't you, Hanne?'

'Er, yes …' she said. 'A poodle.'

'A *poodle*?' said Paul, and he let out a little laugh. 'I can tell you a thing or two about *poodles* …'

And, much to Hanne's horror, I left them to it.

As I drove through London, I laughed. I was relieved. There was no one after me any more. There was nothing anyone could do to stop me. The Challenger had challenged. And the Yes Man had prevailed. Hanne had received an appropriate punishment: I had unleashed Paul on her. And I would get Ian back for this – make no mistake about it. But that would come later. Later, when I'd thought of something suitable. Something that would *really* make up for the deceit and the pranks … but not today.

Because today I had to get home, and clean the flat for Lizzie – happy in the knowledge that life was now a good deal simpler.

December was going to be *easy.*

an invitation to

Tim Miller's
GAY MEN'S PERFORMANCE WORKSHOP

This workshop is for gay men and queer boys to gather together and explore some performance stuff. Jumping off from a warm up, we'll tell stories and share some from what goes on in our lives: sex, growing up, our bodies, love, fears & more. We'll try different ways to bring the life and stories inside us into performance. No experien~~ce~~

Bring your hea~~rts~~

24

In which Daniel is Content

I was content.

Lizzie was asleep in my flat.

I'd picked her up a few mornings after my victory over the Challenger, sleepy and fragile, a little the worse for wear after 24 hours on a plane. I was in the kitchen, making a cup of tea, when I heard her wake. Moments later, I turned around and there she was: a brunette ball of hair and sleep.

'Hello, you,' she said.

For a second we just smiled.

'Tea?'

'Be rude not to,' she said. 'You can't go turning tea down the minute you arrive in England.'

I flicked the kettle on again, and her eyes scanned the flat.

'Nice to see the place again,' she said. 'You've tidied up for me, haven't you?'

'No. It's always like this. It is always very tidy indeed.'

'Mm-hmm, I'm sure it is. And you always have fresh flowers on the table, do you?'

'I walked past a stall on the Roman Road. The man was shouting out loud about how it was a bargain not to be missed, so I—'

'Sure, sure.'

She smiled, and started to slowly walk around the flat, looking at my shelves, studying my books. I made the tea while she peered out of the windows at the trains going by outside. It felt good to have her around again.

'What's that thing?' she said, pointing at something odd and plastic in the corner.

'That,' I said, proudly, 'is the new Light 'n' Easy Steam Cleaner. It is both brilliantly simple *and* simply brilliant.'

'Have you used it?'

'Twice. The first time I nearly scorched myself. And the second time, too, as it happens.'

She raised her eyebrows, and continued her casual meander. She picked up a book that was face down on the table, and studied it.

'You're learning Flemish?'

'*Ja.*'

'Why *Flemish*?'

I shrugged.

'*Spreekt du Engels!*' I said, with some degree of jollity.

She looked impressed.

'What does that mean?'

'It means "Flemish is a complex and enigmatic language."'

It doesn't mean that at all. I don't know *what* it means.

She smiled, and said, 'Is it okay if I have a shower?'

'I'll get you a towel.'

Twenty minutes later, her shower over, she walked back into the living room, drying her hair and smelling of mint. She looked lovely. And she was carrying something.

'What on earth is *this*?' she said.

It was a neatly framed certificate. One of three I'd hung up in my bathroom.

'That's my nursing degree from the University of Rochville,' I said.

'Rochville? Where's *Rochville*?'

Good point. I had no idea.

'It doesn't matter where Rochville is,' I said, with all the authority of a man who'd bought his degree off the Internet. 'All that matters is that I am now a fully qualified nurse. Based on my life experience and television viewing habits.'

'Full of surprises. What are the other ones on the wall in there?'

'One is my *Certificate of Excellence*, the other is my *Certificate of Distinction*. I did very well. I imagine I was probably top of my class.'

'Why didn't you tell me you had a nursing degree?'

'I am not a boaster.'

She started to walk backwards. I assumed she was going to put the certificate back, but she stopped, and pointed down the hallway.

'There was something else I noticed. In the hallway?'

I wasn't sure what she meant.

'You appear to own a large portrait of you with a dog.'

'Oh. Yeah.'

'So … ?'

'Um … well, y'see …'

I didn't really want to tell her about my psychotropic Mindbomb. It might give her the wrong idea about me. But how else to explain it?

I know!

'I entered my local newspaper's Pet Personality Contest, and the prize was a lovely portrait of me and my dog.'

'But you haven't got a dog.'

'That's right. I actually entered Stuart, my cat, but the artist got it wrong.'

'But you haven't got a cat, either.'

'No. Correct. Look … it's probably best if we don't discuss that portrait.'

This was all getting too weird for her. I could tell. I took a step closer to her.

'But it's probably best if we *do* discuss something else …'

She looked concerned. So did I.

'Sounds a bit serious,' she said. 'If you don't want me staying here, then it's cool, I can—'

'No! No, it's not that. It's something else. Something about me. And I think I need to tell you sooner rather than later because I've made that mistake before, and I'd not rather not make it again. Maybe you should sit down …'

It was time to tell her. To get it out in the open and out of the way. To reveal my hidden identity.

And so down she sat. And I told her. I told her what I'd done. I told her everything, right from the start, the whole story. The man on the bus, the Yes Manifesto, Ian's threats of punishment, my determination to succeed. I told her about Jason, and about Hanne and Seb, and about hanging out in Wales with a hypnotic dog that I thought could cure all my worries. And she nodded, and she smiled, and frowned, and nodded some more, and she looked like, despite it all, she understood. So I told her more; I told her about how sometimes it had all got too much for me, that sometimes I thought what I was doing was pointless and worthless and stupid, and how for a moment I'd looked for meaning in the arms of Maitreya until I realised that *I* was to blame for all this, and how just when I thought I'd had enough, something else would happen to pull me back in. And then I held my breath as I told her about Edinburgh – about how buying her a ticket was something I never would have had the confidence to do, but how by blaming it on Yes I'd made it okay somehow. And she nodded quietly again, but I couldn't gauge her reaction this time, so I just pressed on, and told her about Ian and Hanne conspiring against me, and how I'd defeated them, and how now, here she was, in London, in front of me, and maybe if I'd never said Yes to a ticket, and she'd never said Yes to that ticket too, we wouldn't be where we were now … in short, I told her everything. Or *nearly* everything. The only thing I left out, in fact, was my time with Kristen.

It was a lot for her to take in.

Eventually, she collected her thoughts, and exhaled, heavily.

'Well, thank *God*,' she said.

It wasn't quite the reaction I'd been expecting.

'Eh?'

'Well, I'm hoping that you saying Yes explains the *Amazing Penis Patch* I found in your bathroom.'

I went a bit red. Shit.

'No,' I said. 'That's Ian's.'

I was pretty pleased that I'd told her about the whole Yes thing, as it turns out.

We were in the Royal Inn, now, on a cold and dark winter afternoon, and I was telling her more about what I'd done. She loved the sound of Marc, and said she too wanted to be stalked by lizards on Pulau Ubin, and expressed amazement that I'd dropped the Geese For Peace campaign so early in its development. Part of her was humouring me, sure. But another part of her seemed genuinely intrigued by the idea. The Yes idea, I mean – not the geese one.

'There's one thing I need to know, though …' she said, tracing a short line on the table with her finger. 'Me coming here, and staying with you—'

'No. That's not part of it. That's a Yes I would *always* have said.'

'Because I understand the Edinburgh ticket … things were different then, but now, if I felt that you—'

'No. Lizzie. Honestly.'

'Cool.'

But I didn't want her to think I was just being polite.

'Seriously,' I said, 'I never—'

'Ssh. I believe you.'

And from the way she looked at me, I think she really did.

* * *

The next few days flew by, just as they'd done in Edinburgh. Lizzie attended her meetings, and I picked her up afterwards, and we ran around town together. We met Ian for lunch – he had never before met the mystical Lizzie – and she said all the right things and made all the right noises.

Ian had come clean and admitted his part in the whole Challenger debacle the moment I'd confronted him about it. He'd tried to persuade me that it was for my own good; that he'd been worried I'd get bored; that anyway, he thought it best if I said no; that as I hadn't technically said No yet I was still winning. I was stern with him, but the truth was, it was fair enough – there was nothing in the Yes Manifesto which expressly forbade him from confirming Hanne's suspicions. So I told him I forgave him. But only – and this is between you and me – because I had something rather special planned for him.

Anyway, Lizzie had treated the two of us to an ice cream afterwards, and laughed graciously at all of Ian's jokes. I think she felt sorry for him because of the whole Amazing Penis Patch thing.

'She's fantastic,' he said, when she'd popped to the bathroom, and I nodded, because she was.

We piled in my little car and drove to the cinema near Canary Wharf that night, the three of us, and despite Ian's protests we agreed to go to the first film the man behind the counter recommended. Afterwards, we sat in a Docklands pub and Lizzie chastised Ian for taking such pleasure in my trials and tribulations, for encouraging Hanne, and for keeping his mysterious punishment a mystery.

'The punishment still stands, by the way,' he said. 'You may have won the battle, but you haven't won the war. You can still fail. And I can still unleash my punishment.'

'So what *is* "the punishment"?' asked Lizzie, for probably the third time that night. 'You can't just keep it a secret. You have to tell him. It'll be good motivation for him.'

'I am not at liberty to divulge it,' said Ian. 'But rest assured, it's a good one.'

'What *is* it?' she said. 'You haven't got one, have you? There *is* no punishment. You thought by helping the Challenger, he'd never succeed!'

'No. There is. But I am not telling. That's how good it is.'

She had an idea.

'It's only fair to punish Danny if *you* experience life as a Yes Man …' she said. 'So you know what you're talking about and can tailor the punishment accordingly …'

I smiled. I knew what she was up to.

'That way you can come up with a really *suitable* punishment.'

'*I'm* not bloody saying Yes to everything!' said Ian. 'Talk to the Yes Man over there! I'm not the one spending all my money on degrees and potions from the Internet.'

Lizzie and I exchanged a conspiratorial glance. We knew *exactly* what he was buying from the Internet.

But she charmed him, and charmed him, and eventually he agreed to say Yes – if only for the rest of tonight. He ended up buying drinks for the three guys behind the bar, texting Yes to an eminently dull colleague who wanted to have dinner the following night, and having a lovely conversation with a blonde girl on the next table. At one point, we had to rescue him from the arcade machine in the corner. Every time he finished a game, it said PLAY AGAIN?, and it was forty minutes before we noticed.

The next morning Lizzie drove back to Bath with me to see the city and meet my parents and Sammy the cat. And back in London one rainy Saturday afternoon, I took her for a Chicken Dansak at the Madras Valley, and then on to spend a few hours on Great Portland Street, where she sat and laughed with me and a few hundred of my very closest friends.

We were … *becoming* something, her and me. No. Scratch that. We *were* something. And that was great.

But it was sad, too.

One afternoon, she came to back to the flat with a small gift.

'I found this on the tube. I thought you might like it.'

It was a flier. I read the top line.

'*An Invitation To Tim Miller's Gay Men's Performance Workshop.*'

'It's a chance for gay men to express their personal stories through performance and dance,' she said. 'I know you're not gay, but that's an invitation, and anyway, I imagine you like dancing, don't you?'

I laughed. She was into this. She didn't think it was stupid.

'Also,' she said. 'I thought *I* might try it.'

'Try what? Expressing your personal stories through dance?'

'No. Saying Yes. So I went into a travel agent's. I asked them where would be a good place to spend Friday night. They said Prague. So I got us two tickets.'

'You did *what*?'

'I got us two tickets to Prague. So what d'you say? Do you want to go to Prague with me on Friday night?'

'You … *wow* …' It was the first time a girl had done something like that for me. I didn't know they *could*. I'd found a Yes Girl! I wanted to tell her she was brilliant, that *this* was brilliant, that *Prague* would be brilliant … but all I could manage was '… Yes!'

It was an incredible trip. Spontaneous, carefree, fast and fun. We'd flown out for one night in the late afternoon, and by nine o'clock we were walking through the Old Town Square. It was a bitterly cold December night, but crisp and fresh, and we bought hot chocolates to keep our hands warm. We walked to St Nicholas Cathedral, and we kissed on Charles Bridge. And just after ten o'clock, we looked up at the sky, because instinctively we knew that something was changing. I couldn't tell exactly what at first, but then, slowly and gently, it started to snow. We laughed, but there was something different about Lizzie's laugh. And then I realised – this was the first time Lizzie had ever even *seen* snow. Here. Now. This. I was amazed. Saying Yes had done this for her; given her a present. In the prettiest city in the world.

You'll have to forgive me when I tell you that it was *perfect*.

The day that Lizzie had to go, neither of us wanted to talk about the future.

We skirted around it. We'd had two great weeks together. One in Edinburgh. And now one in London. That's what I tried to focus on.

I'd woken early, and watched her sleep, and although I felt calm, I felt uneasy, too. I knew she was going. And I knew something inside me was going to have to change.

I cooked breakfast while Lizzie ordered her cab to the airport. When she'd finished packing, she came into the living room, where I was sitting, quietly, with a carton of juice.

'I've got a Yes for you,' she said, quietly.

'How do you mean?'

'Something for you to say Yes to.'

'What is it?'

She smiled.

'How about you come out to Australia for Christmas? Meet everyone? You could spend New Year's there. With me.'

I didn't know what to say. It was a lovely idea. But my head felt heavy. I mean, technically, Yes, I could clear it with my parents, and sort out a flight, and spend Christmas in a country I'd never even come close to before. But was it the right thing to do? This wasn't a normal Yes. This was a *big* Yes. Because it was a Yes that could and probably would end up hurting me.

'Look … let's say I did come out. What would happen afterwards?'

'Afterwards? Well … I guess we'd see.'

Yeah. We'd see. But I could already see it. Afterwards, I'd come home, to London. And I'd be here, alone. On my own again. Back in precisely the same situation that I'd been in exactly one year before, effectively throwing all my good work away. If I got any closer to Lizzie than I was already, I'd be setting myself up for the biggest fall of my life. And I was scared.

'Well, if you can't make it out at Christmas,' she said, 'how about January? Or February?'

'I'm starting that new job in January,' I said, slightly more coldly than I'd meant. 'I'm not going to be able to do the things I did any more. I've got to move on from all that. Get responsible. Make sensible choices. And anyway, I don't think they'd give me time off so soon just so I could fly out to Australia and see you.'

'Oh. Right. So … it's kind of now or never, then?'

I shrugged, and looked at my feet, feeling terrible.

Don't get me wrong: I wanted to go. I really, truly did. But I just couldn't.

If I allowed myself to hope that this could work, that we had a future, that somehow distance didn't matter … then I'd be making the inevitable far worse. The fact was, this *couldn't* work, and the longer this went on, the deeper it would cut me. It was a part of my Yes life, and my Yes life was almost over. To drag it into the *next* life would be unfair. Sometimes you have to make a decision to protect yourself. Sometimes it's better to lose a foot than risk a leg.

'I can't …' I said, before realising that there was something else I could say. Something that might make all this so much easier. 'The other thing is … I kind of met someone, recently. And… I don't know, maybe it'll lead nowhere, but you know … at least she's in England, and—'

Lizzie looked hurt, and I hated myself, but she nodded. I avoided her eye.

'So thank you, Lizzie,' I said. 'But it's a No.'

She touched my arm, and said she understood.

'A pity your first No had to be to me,' she said, and I smiled, sadly.

And an hour later I carried her bags to the cab, and she left.

25

In which Daniel makes a Terrible Admission,

searches his Soul, and finally accepts

that he must be Punished

Two nights later, in the Yorkshire Grey, Ian seemed nearly as upset as I was that Lizzie had gone. Far more upset than when I'd told him the grand Yes adventure was over. I was stopping. That was it. I'd said No.

'I just can't believe she's gone,' he said, shaking his head. 'Why does it have to be like this?'

I nodded, but the truth was, I was getting a little annoyed by Ian's outpourings of grief. I wanted sympathy – not empathy.

'She really livened up the place, didn't she?' he said. 'Such a *special* girl. And funny, too. And down-to-earth. And with a really cool accent.'

He really wasn't helping matters. But I nodded along.

'Well … here's to Lizzie…'

He raised his pint and took a sip. We sat for a few moments, in silence.

'I did the right thing, didn't I?' I said.

'Oh, absolutely. Definitely. You did the right thing, yes.'

'In saying No to Australia, I mean.'

'Yes. You did. No doubt about that. Remind me why you said No again?'

'Because sooner or later, we'd have to say goodbye again. And if it's sooner, I'll be less hurt than if it's later. Sometimes it's better to lose a foot than risk a leg. And she lives in *Australia*, for Christ's sake. Australia! That's, like, twice as far as *Singapore*!'

'Ah. Yes. You did the right thing. You can't be going over to Australia every weekend just because your girlfriend lives there.'

Girlfriend. It was the first time anyone had called her my girlfriend.

'But you know … it's not too late,' he said. 'I mean, technically, you *could* still go. It wouldn't be a No, then. It would be a Yes. Which would mean you were still in the game.'

'Ian—'

'No, you're right. About that whole foot thing in particular. Taking a risk is definitely overrated. I remember thinking that when you said "sometimes the biggest risk is never taking one". I remember thinking, "No. What about kayaking?" You're *right* not to take the risk. It *is* better to be safe than sorry.'

'Yes. Because I wasn't just saying Yes to a trip to Australia, was I? I was saying Yes to letting myself get possibly very hurt. That must be, like, a Level 7, or something. Totally unacceptable.'

'*Totally* unacceptable, yes. But you know … still *possible*. All I'm saying is, you haven't definitely said no until you definitely haven't done something. And you haven't definitely not gone to Australia yet. Your No to Lizzie is still in the Maybe stages. It could still be a Yes, it depends how it evolves. You've still said Yes to everything *else* so far …'

And as if on cue, the barmaid was suddenly by our table.

'Hello lads,' she said, picking up our empty glasses. 'Another pint?'

Ian smiled, but then saw the look on my face. He stared at me, wide-eyed.

I stared back at him. He knew what was going to happen next. I opened my mouth to speak, and Ian raised his hand, trying to stop me … trying to stop me from saying…

'No. Thank you.'

The barmaid walked off and Ian looked furious.

'You fucking *idiot*!' he said. 'You *threw it away*! You threw the whole thing *away*! You could have done it! You could have still gone to Australia! But oh, no, Danny doesn't want another pint, and what Danny doesn't want, Danny doesn't get. All that work, Dan! All for *nothing*!'

'That's not true,' I said. 'Not true at all. Yeah, okay, so I failed. But look at what else happened to me. Look at the difference in me now. I'm alive. I'm having fun again.'

'Fun? You're back where you started. In the pub, with me. You don't have Lizzie any more, you're seriously in debt, and you're about to start a job I'm not certain you truly want.'

'I *do* want it. Yes has been good to me. I'm moving on.'

'And Kristen? Where does Kristen fit into all of this? You can't just transfer what you feel for Lizzie to some girl you happen to have slept with along the way …'

I looked Ian in the eye, and held his gaze.

Gradually, it dawned on him.

'Oh, my God … you didn't sleep with her, did you?'

I couldn't look at him, now.

'You didn't, did you? You said no! You *already* said no! This is a travesty! This has been a sham! You said no to a girl, and then no to a pint! You haven't just broken the Yes Manifesto! You've virtually broken the *law*!'

He threw his hands up in the air and sat back in his seat with a jolt. He said nothing for maybe ten or fifteen minutes. He went and got himself a pint – but for the first time in our lives, not one for me (I had, after all, said No). Maybe this was his punishment.

Turns out it wasn't.

'Be here on Tuesday night,' he said. 'For … *the punishment.*'

And he drained his pint and left.

I know. I'm sorry. I should have told you. But I was worried you wouldn't like me as much. I was worried you'd think I was a failure. I hadn't done anything I shouldn't have done with Kristen. And that's precisely why I didn't want to talk about it. Had I said Yes, of course, I'd have been discreet, sparing you the gory details – but I would at least have ticked it off as another fantastic Yes in a very odd period of my life.

But I couldn't do that. It wasn't a tick. It was a big, red cross over my head.

I'd thought if I ignored it, it would go away. It wouldn't count. I'd never have to think about the fact that I'd failed. And so I'd kept schtumm, kept it out of my diary, said nothing – not even to myself. Saying Yes to Kristen would have been a Yes too far. I didn't want to do something like that. I couldn't. It wouldn't have just affected me, but Kristen too, and – if I ever stood a chance of seeing her again – maybe even Lizzie.

But ironically, my No had just made me Yes even harder. It was only then that I truly threw myself into the fight, determined as I was to make up for lost ground. So I jetted off to Barcelona, and then, just when I was starting to remember again, I found a way to push myself further, and I booked a flight for Singapore. Subconsciously, I can't have just *stumbled* upon that advert … on some level, I must have been *looking* for it …

So that was that. Ian was right. I'd said No to a girl, and No to a pint. Two things that if as a teenager I'd known I would one day do, would have utterly horrified me.

My Yes adventure was over. I had failed, and Ian knew all about it. I'd never before imagined the moment would be like this. Failure just hadn't seemed an option. It was only saying Yes, after all. I'd wanted to make it all the way to New Year's Eve, and be standing underneath a sky full of fireworks, with my friends by my side, as I reclaimed my right to say No.

But tonight the sky was dark and dull. Nothing was lighting it up. Just a clouded moon and the odd passenger jet, flying off to who knew where.

Ian was right, of course. Sometimes you *do* have to say No. I knew that now, and I knew it more than anyone. It's part of the human experience, and I'd been wrong to deny myself. But it had been fun, and I'd learnt a lot. And it wasn't as if I was alone, was it? Not *really*. All over the world, right now, people were making their decisions. Millions were saying Yes to their friends, to new experiences, Yes to themselves. And millions more were saying No, too. No to opportunity, to chance, to life.

Maybe that's what I needed to do for a while. Just for a while. Start saying No again. Stay in. Rest. Maybe that would be good for me. I was exhausted, physically and emotionally.

I got home to the flat and found my diary. I hadn't bothered to update it since Lizzie had left. Maybe now was the time. It's funny, writing a diary. We assume that all the experiences are our own. That we're unique, and they're unique to us. But every thought we've ever had, everything we've ever said, every time we've surprised ourselves with a new experience or idea, every memory we've made, every story we've heard, or told, or been part of ... it's already happened before. Somewhere, and somehow, and sometime, someone has shared our experience, without us even knowing.

Maybe there were other diaries out there, just like mine. People who'd been through things like I'd been through.

I was online, now, but rather than check my e-mails, or read up on the news, I headed for Google. I'm not sure why I did it, but I typed the phrase "I wish I had said No" into the box, and clicked "Search".

I expected to get a million results. But I didn't. There were very few corporate sites, very few business pages coming back at me. I suppose regret doesn't sell. But what did come back to me was an Internet we only see when we look for it. The personal side of the Web. The people's side. The side I suppose I wanted.

There were blogs, and diaries, and entries in guestbooks, and the odd celebrity interview. But the blogs were the most revealing. The innermost thoughts. The diaries tapped away in Tulsa, or Peckham, or Moscow, by people who have something personal to say and want to say it to an unseen world. A diary to be read by people they'll never meet. A way of being brave and sharing every aspect of their daily lives ... the dull, the meaningless and the meaningful.

I read my way through dozens of different pages that night, searching for God knows what. Advice? Guidance? Instead, I found just what you'd expect. People who'd said Yes when perhaps they ought to have said No.

A girl in Oklahoma wished she'd said No when a guy called Ryan asked her out, because he ended up taking Stacey to the party instead.

A man in France wished he'd said No to playing basketball that night, because he'd sprained his wrist and now couldn't type prolpery.

A guy called Ken wished he'd said No to bringing inexperienced bird-handlers to a summer falconry event, because it was 'just plain embarrassing'.

And there were many, many others …

*Today, Saturday, I'm at my aunt's. **I wish I had said no**, because she'll want to play rummy all night and I'll miss Pop Idol.*

*Have said I'll look after Jon and Carol's dog this weekend. **I wish I had said no.** It stinks of s**t.*

***I wish I had said no.** He turned up and he was wearing his nan's tea cosy cos he said it made him look like an admiral.*

But oddly, it all seemed quite trivial. Apart from the crack users, or the drink-drivers, or the people who'd done something so obviously bad and wrong that it should never have been an option in the first place. But what I found next was different. What I did next seemed important. What I did next was type in 'I wish I had said Yes.'

There were 85 results.

I read through them.

At first, things seemed to be just as trivial.

***I wish I had said Yes** when he offered to go halves. It was forty bloody quid and it wasn't even cooked properly.*

***I wish i had said Yes** because at least then i wouldn't have had to walk most of the way in the rain.*

But slowly, I started to find themes developing. Sure, there were people out there who wished they'd said Yes to certain things and it had been no more than a casual annoyance. There were people who'd kicked themselves once or twice over the years, and probably uttered the odd 'tsk' when the memory shot back to them and disrupted a lazy afternoon. People who'd probably lost a few hours sleep over a careless no …

But there were also people who knew … *pain*.

The pain of missing something … the pain of not knowing what *could* have happened … the pain of discovering that sometimes, opportunity really will only knock once … the pain of knowing where a No had brought them, and realising too late where a Yes in its place could have led them.

The pain not necessarily of having said No … but of not having grabbed a Yes.

We gave the PlayMobil away today. I wish I had a penny for every time Harry had asked me to sit with him and play. **I wish I had said Yes** *and sat with him every single time he asked. Now he is older, and he never asks his dad to play. I miss that so much.*

"Yes, oh Yes!" would have been the easiest answer. And why I did not say those words, I do not know, and even today, **I wish I had said Yes***.*

I will never be able to explain just how much **I wish I had said Yes***, because then at least we could have stayed where we were, and we could have held him in our arms until he was gone.* **I wish I had said Yes.**

i miss her, i miss her. **i wish i had said Yes** *to her, because i miss her so much now.*

I wish I had said Yes *every time he wanted a hug. But I was always too busy, and now I just can't …*

I didn't know these people. I didn't know their lives, or their back stories, and I'd never know why not having said Yes to one moment in time meant quite so much. They were just voices in the dark. But I could see their sadness.

Maybe I was reading all this wrong, but suddenly, not having said Yes to something that would have been great seemed *worse* than having said Yes to something that could have been bad.

Sure, it's a case by case thing, but I was starting to realise that regret could always be with you. And maybe there's a real difference between doing something we regret, and regretting not having done something. And it seemed that difference could be … well … *sadness*.

Take the stupidest thing you've ever done … at least it's done. It's over. It's gone. We can all learn from our mistakes, and heal, and move on. But it's harder to learn, or heal, or move on from something that *hasn't* happened; something we don't know and is therefore indefinable; something which could very easily have been the best thing in our lives, if only we'd taken the plunge, if only we'd held our breath and stood up and done it, if only we'd said 'Yes'.

If only.

If I went to see Lizzie and it didn't work out, would I regret it as much as I would regret never having done it? Would knowing be better than not knowing?

But suddenly, I snapped out of it. I switched the computer off. I was being stupid. I had done the right thing. The only thing I could. This wasn't a film. This was my life. A part of me – and maybe even you – had hoped that by reading those random people's experiences, and seeing their grief, something would snap inside me … and I'd realise that I wouldn't want to be like them, wouldn't want to regret like them, realise that it wasn't too late, that I could still take a chance …

But it didn't.

It just made me feel like there were other people out there who would understand; who would know exactly how I felt. And, right now, that was enough for me, somehow.

The following morning, I would cut up my credit cards. I would book an appointment to get a haircut, during which I would lose my mullet and regain my old self. I would look into the best ways and means of selling my car. I would go back to how I was, in preparation for how I *would* be.

Soon it would be Friday. I still had a couple of days to brace myself for whatever punishment Ian lined up, and I would undertake his wishes with a smile and good humour. *You want me to dance around the pub in little blue pants?* Fine. *You want me to dress like a pirate and call myself Mister Shitler for three weeks?* Done. I'd do whatever he wanted. Once again, and for one night only, I'd be a boy who just couldn't say No.

And so I got on with life. I went to the supermarket. I rented some DVDs. I started thinking about what I was going to do in January at the BBC. I played a few videogames, replaced the batteries in all my remote controls, and fixed a broken pen. I stayed in and watched telly. Lizzie left a message, saying she'd got back safely, and wishing me a happy Christmas. I didn't phone back.

And just when I thought that any hope had gone, and that the course of my life was now more or less set, I received a postcard.

And that postcard, my friend, changed *everything*.

Phi Phi Islands Krabi

26

In which something remarkable happens

It was Tuesday afternoon and time to face my punishment.

I drove through central London on my way to Langham Street and the Yorkshire Grey, where Ian would already be waiting for me.

I parked my car outside the Yorkshire Grey, popped my MINISTER ON OFFICIAL BUSINESS sign on the dashboard, and walked through the doors. He was sitting at a small table by the fireplace. He smiled when he saw me. Of course he did. The bastard. He'd been looking forward to this since the summer, and the fact that I'd lied to him about Kristen had only doubled his venom.

I had my diary in my hand – the result of nearly six months of intensive Yes-saying, the proof of my decision to live my life religiously by the power of Yes – and yet the very document that also confirmed I had failed. I set it down on the table, and saw that Ian too had brought something. A long, red envelope, with the words 'The Punishment' written across the front.

'Is that the punishment?' I said, slightly unnecessarily.

'It certainly is. It's a good one. I think you'll like it. I have put a lot of thought into it, Danny. A *lot*.'

Ian smiled.

'You did far better than I thought you would,' he said. 'I'm sorry it had to be this way. But a deal's a deal. As we have established, you have failed on three counts, averaging out to roughly one failure per two months. Not an impressive record.'

The fact that all three Nos had happened in the last six weeks apparently meant nothing to Ian. And he'd conveniently forgotten about his role in the dastardly plot to make it all so much harder, too.

Luckily, I hadn't.

I would still have my revenge on Ian. But not today.

'So … let us count the ways in which you have said no.'

'Well, hang on. What about the ways in which I said Yes?' I said.

Ian considered the point, and with a theatrical wave of his hand, signalled for me to explain. I felt like a serf being granted an audience with the King.

'Well … what I mean is … I've tried really hard at saying Yes to things. Yes to everything. And what I've learnt is that Yes is a powerful word. It's a word that can set us free, and let us open our hearts, and fly like the wind. It's a word—'

'Oh, Jesus, shut up, mate. Yes. It's a word. But the point is, it's a word you failed to say three times. To a pint. To a girl. To Australia. And now, by the power vested in me by the Yes Manifesto, I—'

'There's something else I haven't told you.'

Ian put his head in his hands.

'If I've got to rewrite the bloody punishment …' he said. 'What is it? What haven't you told me?'

'Well, what you're saying isn't strictly true. I mean, Yes, I did say no to those things, and so *technically* I failed, but—'

'Oh, here we go,' said Ian, throwing his hands up in the air. 'You're going to find a loophole, now, aren't you? Or some kind of last-minute twist. Well, that isn't fair. You said no. That's the end of it. You failed.'

'That's just it,' I said. 'I *did* fail. I *didn't* say Yes to everything. But I only said No to two of those things. I only failed on *two* counts.'

Ian looked at me, suspiciously.

'Have you been round Kristen's house? I *thought* you were looking a little tired—'

'No. I'm tired because I've been up half the night packing.'

'*Packing*?'

'I'm going to Australia. To see Lizzie. See how things go. Take a risk. I'm saying Yes.'

'*What*!?'

'I'm flying out tonight. I'll be there Christmas Eve. I'm afraid your elaborate and well-thought-out punishment will have to wait until I get back.'

'But the punishment is *brilliant*!' he said, holding up his little red envelope, with some degree of desperation in his eyes. 'You can't do this to me! I worked long and hard on this!'

'I'd better go.'

I started to stand up. Ian looked at me pleadingly.

'But … what changed your mind?'

I picked up my diary and flicked to the last page.

I found the postcard – the glorious, glorious postcard – that had arrived two mornings before. I put it on the table and slid it towards him.

'Read this,' I said, and I watched him while he did.

'Oh …' he said. 'Wow.'

And then he handed it over, I put it back in my diary, and got back in the car. I was driving to the airport. But there was one thing left to do.

I got my phone out, and dialled Wag's number.

'Wag?'

'Hiya, Dan.'

'Where are you?'

'I'm in Italy.'

'Right. Well. This'll sound a bit odd … but there's a big favour I need …'

Many thousands of feet up in the air, I thought about what I was doing. It was a risk, yeah, but it was a risk I was glad I was taking. Lizzie had been delighted when I'd phoned her up to ask if the offer still stood, and to explain my behaviour the last time I'd seen her. And like Ian, she'd wanted to know why I'd changed my mind; what could possibly have happened to make me decide to find the one credit card I hadn't cut up – the one credit card I'd saved 'for emergencies' – and book myself on the first available flight to Melbourne.

I opened up my diary and took out the postcard. It was battered, and bruised, and smudged, and it was all the way from Thailand.

Danny,
How's it going? It's Jason here, I met you a while back at Thom's party in Liverpool. Sorry for being a bit of a dick that night – one too many methinks. Well, a few days later I realised that I really did want to go with my brother travelling. Work was getting me down anyway, dunno if you could tell! So here we are in Thailand, dunno where next. We're having an amazing time. Thom gave me your address and said you wanted to chat to me. I'm back home in a few months, how about then? My new e-mail address is *******@hotmail.com or call me on 07*** *** ***. Gotta go, the beach is calling …
Jase

I smiled. Jason had said Yes.

I had no idea whether his decision to give up his job and do something that made him happy had anything to do with me. I suspect that on the whole it didn't. But a part of me still hopes that it did.

It's incredible how a few words from someone you hardly know can have an impact on your life. Of course, some would call this divine intervention. That maybe Maitreya *did* exist, and it had been him that had done this. But I knew something. A stranger can affect your life in a thousand different ways – with a new thought, or idea … or suggestion. I had my Man On The Bus – perhaps Jason had his Stranger At The Party. And maybe right now, he was on some beach in Thailand, telling a local girl (who one day, I like to think, he might marry), all about the night he met The Stranger At The Party, and all about those few words he'd said that had made him change his ways.

It was actually more likely that he was on some beach in Thailand getting drunk, but it's a nice thought all the same.

The fact is, saying Yes hadn't been a pointless exercise at all. It had been point*ful*. It had the power to change lives, and set people free. People like me, or Jason. Maybe even you. It had the power of adventure. Sometimes the little opportunities that fly at us each day can have the biggest impact.

And now, as I sat, cramped and sleepy, in a passenger jet high above the ocean, I would see what else Yes had in store for me.

This was it. This was *life*.

I leaned against the window, and fell asleep in an instant.

Selected extracts from the

diary of a Yes Man: 4

December 26th

I have been in Australia for a full three days.

Everything is ...

Great.

Lizzie met me at the airport with a kiss and a smile.

On Christmas Day, we had a barbecue with the family, and drank beer with all the various cousins and brothers, and stood around and baked in a 30 degree heat. I feel it is important to stick to as many international cultural clichés as is possible in life, so as well as the barbie, I also had someone lend me a hat with some corks in it. Plus, despite my lack of tan and muscle, I really fit in here. Australia is the land of the mullet! I feel that at last I am among my own people.

Lizzie's just made me a cup of tea. She's looking after me. I am pretending to be more jetlagged than I am. I get a lot more tea that way.

December 28th

This morning, Lizzie woke me up to tell me we were going on a journey in her little red Nissan. We set off in the direction of a place called Glenrowan. She wouldn't tell me why. It took a full three hours to get there, and when we arrived, there didn't seem to be much of it. A dirt track, a few dusty wooden buildings, and an old man in dungarees and a beard he must have been growing since the 1800s.

Lizzie got out the car and asked the old man, 'Where's Ned?'

He poked a thumb to his right and said, in a gruff and husky accent, 'Round the corner.'

I tried to ask Lizzie who Ned was, but she put her finger to her mouth and then beckoned me to follow her.

And then I saw it. Towering high into the sky, with a gun in one hand and a bucket on his head ... a Giant Ned Kelly! A Big Thing! My first-ever Big Thing! It must have been a hundred feet if it was an inch! A true Australian hero, lovingly recreated in concrete and fading plaster. Okay ... so it was no Big Prawn ... but it was brilliant nonetheless.

We stood there, for what seemed like an age, just staring quietly at the silent majesty of Ned. There was reverence in the air. I loved Lizzie for that.

When we got home, I sat down with a map and enthusiastically attempted to plot the most efficient route around Australia with a pen. A grand, epic journey that would take in The Big Rock, The Big Lobster, The Big Cow and The Big Oyster. Me and Lizzie. On the road, in a tiny red car. For months and months and months.

December 29th

It appears that the map has mysteriously disappeared.

How curious. Lizzie seemed just as shocked as I was, and gave me a look that some would have mistaken for guilt, but which I know was genuine disappointment.

December 31st

It's New Year's Eve.

Exactly one year since the last one.

And the night I was supposed to have finished being the Yes Man, in a pub, with Ian – either triumphing as the Yes Man, or receiving my punishment with humility. But here I am instead, on the other side of the world, having said the biggest and most unexpected Yes of my life ... and happy. Happier than I've been in ages. So happy that I came here.

Melbourne is ablaze with fireworks. We've been standing in Federation Square, watching live bands and drinking bottles of water, counting down to midnight – all around us happy Australians, who are hugging and shaking hands and ooh-ing at the fireworks that bang and burst above our heads.

Lizzie and I hug. And at one point she looks at me, and she says something along the lines of 'we can make this all work out, can't we?', and I look at my watch, and I see that it's 12.04 in a brand new year. And I realise that for the first time in months, I feel like I can say whatever I want, with no restriction, and no regrets. Anything I want.

And so I turn to her.

And I say 'Yes.'

Epilogue 1

In which Ian gets his just desserts

>To: Danny
>From: Ian
>Subject: Help me!

Dear Danny,

In the last 48 hours I have received over one hundred calls on my home telephone. Each one of these has been from a confused Italian looking for someone named Charlie. One of the more persistent callers is a teenage girl who, as soon as I pick up, spends upwards of a minute simply screaming at me.

I did the sensible thing, of course, and switched my answer-phone on. However, I forgot that my outgoing message contains my mobile number and consequently I woke up this morning to find 32 texts and 40 voicemails – one of which was just a minute and a half of screaming.

I take it that all this is not just coincidence.
You bastard.

Your former friend, who wishes he had helped the Challenger even more now,

Ian.

PS. Enjoy Australia.

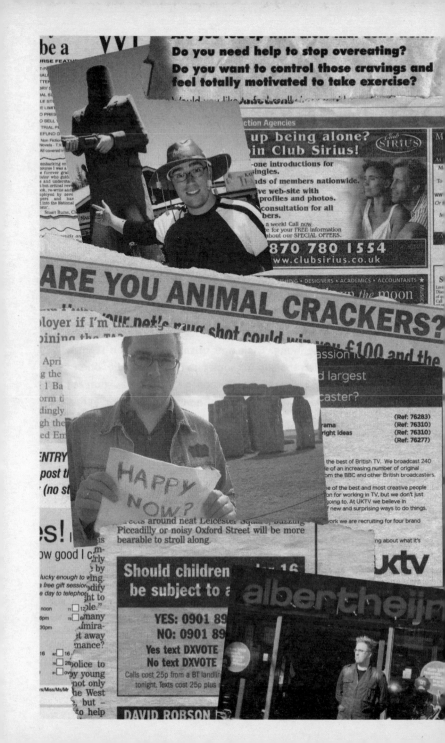

Epilogue 2

In which we must finally say goodbye

Well, then, there you have it.

The very strange story of a very small word.

Now, I am fully aware that technically, I failed at being the Yes Man. I'm sorry about that, and I hope you don't feel too cheated. But I hope you'll agree that, in the end, I probably gained something a little more important. And I hope that maybe at some point today, or tomorrow, or next week, even, *you* might say Yes to something you'd normally say No to.

Not necessarily to psychotropic Mindbombs, mind you, or big blokes in pubs who think you're looking at their girlfriends, or random trips to tiny islands in South East Asia. But little things. Yes to a friend. Yes to a drink after work. Yes to a stranger. Yes to yourself. You'd be amazed at where it can lead.

In other news, there are a few things I should probably fill you in on, if you've time.

I never did track down the man on the bus. But I kind of like it that way. Because that way, perhaps Maitreya really *is* walking the streets, looking after each and every one of us. It's quite good not knowing for sure. Although it does mean I can never look at a bearded stranger without a quick double take, which one day could potentially land me in some trouble.

Jason returned from Thailand a few months after I got back from Australia, and we met up in Liverpool for a pint. He seemed far happier this time. By complete coincidence, it turned out that he'd been in Melbourne on New Year's Eve, too – though neither of us had known that at the time. It's strange to think that if a tube train hadn't broken down one night in London, it's possible neither of us would have been there, under the fireworks at Federation Square, welcoming in a new year and a fresh start. Samten the monk might say it was an inevitable coincidence. Marc would say there's no such thing. Who knows what the Hypnodog would say, so I'll leave the deciding vote with you.

Ian's punishment, it turned out, was an old-fashioned one. He handed me the prized red envelope on my return. I opened it to see the words 'Go to Australia'. It seems he was determined that if I didn't do it myself, he would send me to Lizzie anyway. I thought that was incredibly sweet, though when I told him that, he blushed, and called me a tosser, and said he was only sending me there because 'that's how they used to punish the criminals in the olden days'. And then his phone rang and he had to go off and answer it.

And since you're probably wondering, yes, me and Lizzie are still together. Though I should tell you that Lizzie isn't her real name. She chose it when I decided to write down everything that had happened, because she said she'd always wanted to be called Lizzie, and even though it's her middle name no one ever calls her that, and if she was going to be in a book, then that's the name she'd like to have. Which is a very Lizzie thing to do.

Anyway, a few months after New Year's Eve, Lizzie got a job offer in London. She moved over shortly afterwards, and she's behind me right now, watching as I type this. She says hello.

She also thinks you should know that, a few months after she moved in, I decided it was *my* turn to ask *her* a question. A *big* question.

She said Yes.

Epilogue 3
Yes Man, The Movie

Hello once again!

And *welcome* to the specially extended version of *Yes Man*. Mind you, it's a bit late to welcome you. You've already read the book. But welcome, at least, to the specially extended part of this specially extended version. A version – and I hope I'm not speaking out of turn here – which you probably only really picked up because it's got Jim Carrey's face on the cover.

Or because you've seen the film and you liked the bit with the motorbike and you've been faintly disappointed ever since you started reading and realised I am rarely seen doing wheelies on motorbikes down the streets of East London at 90 miles per hour. Also, how come Wallace never ended up in a telephone museum in Nebraska? Why didn't he fall over more?

Well, for that – and all those things – I apologise. Saying Yes does different things to and for different people. The first Yes you say is a little like pushing over that first random domino that sets you off on your own personal adventure, in your own personal direction, with your own personal set of Yeses, all unique to you. Jim, for example, ended up in that telephone museum, whereas I ended up in the Museum of Early Keyboard Instruments. You see how exciting things can get when you just let go?

But it can also lead to bigger things. To *fun*. And, for me, it led to a series of phone calls one week from my agent, Jago. A series of phone calls which were exciting. And unbelievable. And really just a little surreal. Phone calls involving Big Hollywood Stars and Big Hollywood Producers and Big Hollywood Promises. Phone calls at nine or ten at night. Phone calls which were sometimes one on one, sometimes *nine* on one. Phone calls which Lizzie and I couldn't quite believe were happening, each and every time they happened.

And when I put the phone down every night I'd switch the news on and try not to think about it … but then call Wag or Ian and head down the pub.

CUT TO:

INT. THE PUB. NIGHT.

DANNY, IAN and WAG are standing in front of a
dartboard, holding pints. None of them looks as
if he is particularly good at darts.

IAN takes a step forward and eyes his target.

                    IAN
          I think it is only natural that
          Hollywood would come calling. I
          imagine they are *fascinated* by me.

He throws the dart but misses the board. DANNY
and WAG look impressed.

                  IAN (CONT'D)
          A supporting character I may be,
          Dan, but *what* support I lend. I
          hope for your sake, the Ian char-
          acter doesn't steal this movie.
          Because that would be embarrassing
          for *all* of us.

He throws another dart. It lands on the floor.

Wag, on the other hand, was slightly more excited.

'Who'll play me? Who'll play me?'

'Who do you *think* should play you?' I said, throwing my dart and *also* missing the board. This was weird. This was like a pub conversation we'd have been having *anyway*. But this was *real*.

'De Niro would be good, obviously. Or Baxendale.'

'Baxendale?' I said, confused.

'Helen Baxendale. From *Cold Feet*. And season five of *Friends*.'

'Helen *Baxendale*?' said Ian and I, in unison, and staring at him.

'There's just something *about* her,' shrugged Wag.

But while we were talking about this happening, it never really felt real. It felt like it couldn't happen. Because these things just don't. And even if they do, films take *ages* to get made. Hundreds of *years*, in some cases. I think *ET* was first pitched sometime in the 1700s.

And yet … things kept moving forward. Jago kept talking to people. He gave them a deadline. And then, one night, we found ourselves choosing someone. Someone to *make the film*.

'This is *amazing*,' said Lizzie, and we hugged.

'This is *ridiculous*,' I said. 'But *amazing*.'

A company named Heyday Films – who make the Harry Potter films – had gotten together with Warner Bros. and said they'd like to make it. I liked them instantly. They seemed … nice. But *genuinely* nice, not let's-make-a-deal nice. Granted, I hadn't actually met them yet, but they seemed to want what *I* wanted – a film that was good, and warm, and funny. A film with the right *spirit*.

And so it was decided. We would be friends with them.

                                                    CUT TO:

INT. THE WOLSELEY RESTAURANT, LONDON. DAY.

DANNY is sitting with two film execs - ROSIE and
DAVID. He has ordered the steak. This is because
he always orders the steak. When he gets home, he
will notice he has accidentally spilled some
mustard down his front. But he has not noticed
this yet. ROSIE and DAVID have.

A month or two later and I'm in an incredibly posh restaurant in London, sitting opposite David Heyman and Rosie Alison.

Rosie was softly spoken, with a very kind face. David looked like he probably dives with sharks, and owns a number of ski chalets across Europe.

And it was exciting. Of *course* it was. Plus, it seemed the wheels were already rolling. Names were mentioned. Of writers. And directors. And stars.

'How would you feel if things were reset in America?' asked Rosie at one point.

'I think that would be great,' I said. And I did. The world of films was new to me. But one thing I could work out on my own was that a story about a former BBC radio producer living in a flat in Bow who ends up on *Richard & Judy* and has a picture on his wall of him and a small dog *might* not be the specific key ingredients for a blockbuster comedy.

Call it a hunch.

What was important to me was the *feel* of the film. The book was one thing. It's in your hands now. It'll never change. It's done. But here was a chance to create something entirely *new*, for an entirely new audience. Something that still held onto its key message, but did so in a different way.

Because surely it's better to have two new things in the world than two things the *same*?

That was what excited me.

And eight or nine weeks later, an e-mail arrived, marked 'YES MAN – First Draft'.

I printed it out immediately, and read it. And it made me laugh. And I put it down, went to make a cup of tea, and then sat back down and read it all again.

CUT TO:

EXT. LOS ANGELES AIRPORT. DAY.

```
It is two years later.  Our hero, DANNY -
scruffy, unshaven, squinting in the bright
sunshine of LA - stands outside the airport,
clutching a copy of the script he's been reading
on the plane.


A long sleek limo pulls up alongside him. The
DRIVER gets out and opens the door for DANNY.


Pretending this is normal, he clambers in.
```

The final version of the script has been signed off. Everyone is happy with it. Several versions have fallen by the wayside, or been adapted or developed or moved on somehow. Some kept my favourite moments from the book; others lost them and took the story elsewhere.

But this one – *this* is the one they're going with.

I've been out to LA once or twice in the meantime, to meet with Tiffany, one of the glamorous and powerful producers. She is cool. The first time we met, she took me to a strange but hip restaurant where everyone ordered a different dish but all the meals looked precisely the same. We met writers, and producers, and then I went back to my hotel and ordered a hamburger.

But this time I'm here for another reason entirely. To watch *Yes Man* being *filmed*. And also … to meet its *star*.

I'd been in New Zealand with Lizzie when I'd had the call. Jim Carrey had had the book. He'd had the script. He'd had the meetings. And now … he was *in*.

'Jim Carrey!' I'd said, to Lizzie, as we walked along a beach on a blustery Great Barrier Island. 'Jim *Carrey*!'

'I know,' she'd said, delighted, and shaking her head. 'Jim Carrey!'

I'd stopped walking, and made her stop walking too, and I'd looked at her.

'Jim *Carrey*!' I'd said.

And now, just six months later, and on the other side of the world, here I was in LA, in a sleek and slick black limo, jetlagged but happy, and about to go on set.

Warner Bros. had been good to me. I was an associate producer on the film, given ready access to scripts, asked interesting questions (like 'Do you mind if we change your name in the movie to Carl? It just sounds more believable'), flown first class, picked up by Town Cars, and staying in fine hotels.

In the past couple of months, things had been moving forward apace. Tiffany would call up, and update me on who else had signed up to be in the film. Zooey Deschanel. Terence Stamp. Bradley Cooper. But more than that … suddenly there were *editors*. And *set decorators*. And *first assistant directors*.

There was an art department. A stunt department! An animal trainer! A *Korean* coach! In fact … there were *hundreds* of people.

Including a great director.

Peyton Reed was probably the first person I saw on set. Not that I realised it was a set at first …

EXT. WARNER BROS. STUDIOS, HOLLYWOOD. MORNING.

DANNY and TIFFANY walk across the lot, passing a parking space marked 'G. CLOONEY'. It is mid-morning and they've just witnessed several dozen striking writers and a man with both arms in plaster who is either very unlucky or working on *ER*.

They enter a huge brown building with STAGE 23 written on its side.

INT. STAGE 23. MORNING.

Immediately, they find themselves in a log-cabin-
style bar. Cameramen are moving around, and some
people sit at tables, drinking beers. PEYTON REED
stands at one end of the bar, pointing at things.
Danny looks around in awe and wonder.

>   **DANNY**
>   *That's* nice.

>   **TIFFANY**
>   What's nice?

>   **DANNY**
>   The way there's a lovely bar here
>   for the actors to relax in.

>   **TIFFANY**
>   This … uh, this is a set.

>   **DANNY**
>   Sorry?

>   **TIFFANY**
>   A *set*. This is a specially built
>   set. This isn't a bar. We *made*
>   this.

TIFFANY looks appalled by DANNY. DANNY realises
his mistake, and attempts to play it off.

>   **DANNY**
>   Yes. That's what I meant. When I
>   said that. That's what I was
>   saying about.

What was?

DANNY

[changing the subject] I like
films, do you like films?

'Danny, this is Peyton Reed,' said Tiffany, and I shook the hand of the man in front of me, firmly.

'Hi, Danny!' he said. 'I hope you like what we're doing with your book!'

'I'm in a bar!' I said. 'So far, you seem to have *nailed* it.'

And there, over his shoulder, I saw an incredibly familiar figure. He was tall, and casually dressed, and he was reading some pieces of paper. It was Jim Carrey. Jim Carrey! From the films! Jim Carrey who I'd loved ever since seeing him in *In Living Color* on pirated videos my friends in America had sent me! Jim Carrey from *The Mask*! Jim Carrey who was so great in *The Truman Show*, and *Liar Liar*, and *Dumb and Dumber* and *Eternal Sunshine of the Spotless Mind* and the hugely underrated *The Majestic*! It was *Jim Carrey*!

I looked away, not wanting to bother him, but a second later, he was right in front of me.

'Hey, man,' he said. 'I'm Jim!'

And we started to talk.

When I get back to the hotel, I switch on the TV. The entertainment news is on. Someone has managed to record Jim out and about, filming a scene.

'And it's all in aid of his new movie, *Yes Man*,' says the reporter.

It's an incredibly strange moment.

'What if I'd called it something different?' I think to myself. 'What if I'd called it *Leg Horn*? Or *Table Manners for Children*? Or *Yes Yes Yes Man Man*? Then that reporter would have had to have said something *different...*'

It is like my own rubbish version of the Butterfly Effect.

The producers had given me a trailer as big as my old flat, with a plasma screen and its own bedroom and bathroom. More exciting even than that, was the day I arrived to find my own director's-style chair, with YES MAN on one side, and DANNY WALLACE on the other. I was suddenly a Hollywood bigshot with literally no experience or useful purpose.

But it was *great*.

I sat and watched, as Jim and Peyton worked out the scenes, and the thing that stunned me most of all was that *it looked like a proper film*. It sounds insane saying that, seeing as that's precisely why everyone was there, but that's how surprising and surreal it felt. Soon, I got to know the people working there. Jim's burly Israeli security guard, Dotan, who'd refer to me simply as Wallace. Jim's Oscar-winning make-up artist, Billy. The people in wardrobe. The blokes operating the cameras. Everyone was just so … *nice*.

                                                    CUT TO:

EXT. STAGE 23, WARNER BROS. STUDIOS, LA. DAY.

A group of bored-looking tourists are on a small
electric train. A desperate tour guide is trying
to find things to show them.

                    TOUR GUIDE
        So … um … the writers' strike has
        obviously had quite an effect on
        activity here … I'm afraid there's
        not much going on …

                    TOURIST (INTERNAL VOICE)
        This is the worst trip I have ever
        been on.

                    TOUR GUIDE
        Um … that's Stage 23, there. Films
        shot there include the 1999 Will
        Smith classic *Wild, Wild West* …

                    TOURIST 2 (INTERNAL VOICE)
        All these buildings look exactly
        the same. I am going to commit
        suicide. But first, I would like a
        full refund.

Suddenly, from nowhere, American film actor JIM
CARREY appears. He sees the boredom on the
tourists' faces. He leaps into action, running at
the electric train, rocking it with his hands,
high-fiving the strangers as they try and snap
photos of him. He stays with them for ten
minutes, answering their questions, making them
laugh, taking photos. The electric train slowly
moves off. The tourists get their phones out and
start texting their friends and family. Within
minutes, thousands of people worldwide know of
this event.

Later on that day – a particularly hot one – an ice-cream truck turns up
out of the blue, handing out limitless free ice creams to cast and crew. Jim
has bought it for the day, and given it to the production. On other days,
I'd walk around the lot with Richard Zanuck – legendary producer of
Jaws and *Butch Cassidy* – listening to stories and laughing. I'd eat lunch
with Tiffany or mess about with Rhys Darby, or share a joke with Zooey
Deschanel – who I suddenly realised was the same size, wearing the same
kind of clothes and had the *same haircut* as Lizzie. I recorded some backstage interviews for the DVD, and messed around with the crew, and then,
one day, it was time for my very own feature film debut …

INT. THE BIGFOOT LODGE, LA. NIGHT.

ROONEY and TILLIE are at the bar, getting ready
for their scene. Next to them is a man who looks
fairly out of place. He is the only man drinking
from an English pint glass. This is DANNY,
preparing for his role as MAN AT BAR. He looks a
bit odd. American film actor JIM CARREY
approaches Danny and rests his hand on his shoulder, staring soulfully into his eyes.

                    JIM CARREY
          You ready?

                    DANNY
          I am. Prepare yourself. You are
          about to witness something very
          powerful indeed.

                 JIM CARREY
          First time's free, my man. You'll
          get the *taste*. This is just the
          beginning.

                    DANNY
          Try and keep your eyes off my
          performance. It will be tricky.

                 JIM CARREY
          Break a leg, dude.

I take my place on set where I am about to make my *second* much-anticipated cameo appearance as Man At Bar. I have decided it must be very easy being an extra. All you do is stand there and pretend to talk. But I am taking no chances. I have given myself a convincing back story (failed chiropractor, no kids, possibly gay) so as to fully intensify what I have already hinted to Jim is likely to be a very dramatic performance. I am placed opposite a small and nervous Japanese girl and pick up my pint of non-alcoholic beer. Why is she so nervous? This must be easy.

And then someone has an idea.

'Can we put a microphone on you?' says a kindly-looking man named Jonathan. 'For more behind-the-scenes stuff for the DVD … If we mike you up we can hear what you're saying between takes.'

I say absolutely, and I'm miked up. And then I smile. I have thought of a brilliant joke.

'Right,' I whisper quickly to the girl. 'Those fellas just put a microphone on me, so what I'm going to do is, I'm going to pretend to be really arrogant and self-important and actorly between takes, so that it looks like me being in the background of a scene in a bar makes me think this is the start of a glittering Hollywood career, okay? But don't take me seriously!'

I smile again, and the girl nods, slightly confused. I look up and get the okay from Jonathan.

'Basically,' I say, loudly, while Peyton sets up the shot, 'this is a very big moment for me. It may look like I'm just in the background of this scene, but actually, this scene is all about me. I'm going to have to power down my performance because I don't want to distract from the other stars in this bit. These eyes are basically radioactive. People are very excited by my acting. Word's spread. There's a queue of agents outside already.'

The girl looks over my shoulder, concerned. This is good. She's acting too. And we haven't even begun the scene! I continue.

'The writers' strike has been good for me,' I say. 'I don't need writers. They slow me down. They bring boundaries. I work outside those boundaries. I've actually shot two writers.'

And then Peyton shouts, 'Okay, getting ready …'

It is time for me to stop talking. I look up at Jonathan, and he smiles and gives me the thumbs-up. He enjoyed my brilliant joke. Now all I have to do is pretend to have a silent conversation with the girl, while the real actors do their thing. But the girl is now looking at me very oddly indeed.

'You … are … very …' She struggles to find the right word. 'Confident …'

I laugh, but she doesn't. And then I realise. She doesn't speak much English. She clearly hadn't understood my explanation at the start. She now believes that I truly think I am the star of the film.

'Oh, hang on,' I say, trying to show her my microphone.

'And action!' yells Peyton.

The scene begins. And I have to sit opposite a girl who now thinks I am America's most deluded extra. Still. I must concentrate. I cannot allow this to put me off. And so I begin to mouth various words. But I don't know what to say. I can't think. I end up spouting nonsense.

'There was a child with the face of a clam … I once followed a duck to court because I thought it had stolen one of my pencils … I wonder if a man will ever be born who can swim …'

This is terrible! What am I saying? But I can't stop.

'Once, I fired a cannon … An egg cup makes a handy bin for a hamster …'

'And … cut!' shouts Peyton. 'Print that one!'

Everyone seems very pleased with how the scene went. I am not. Mainly because I am now very concerned that anyone who watches the film and can lip-read may assume I am mentally ill.

'You were very … good …' says the girl, getting up to go.

But I was wearing a microphone! I want to shout.

'You weren't that good,' says the extra who was sitting behind me.

'But I was wearing a microphone!' I say, a little too loudly.
I am stared at.

INT. BIGFOOT LODGE. LATER.

TIFFANY wanders up to DANNY, a confused look on
her face.

> **TIFFANY**
> What the hell was all that about
> *hamsters*?

DANNY remains silent.

Next morning, I am walking through a suburb of LA towards a building to which filming has moved. But before I can get there, I notice fire trucks. And police cars. And some kind of huge *cordon*. I start to think something *serious* must have happened. But then I look closer, and I realise that, no, this is all for the *film*. They've shut down *whole streets*. I am amazed. This was never something we were allowed to do when recording BBC radio comedies.

I flash my pass at someone and walk towards the building. I look up, and there, five floors above me, standing on a ledge and holding an acoustic guitar while singing a beautiful love song, is Jim Carrey. It is the scene in which he convinces a depressed Hispanic man not to jump.

Again: apologies this did not happen in the book.

My phone rings.

I answer it.

'Hi!' says the person on the other end of the phone. 'Where *are* you?'

'I'm in LA!' I say, happily. 'I'm looking at Jim Carrey, five floors up, holding an acoustic guitar and singing a beautiful song to a depressed Hispanic man who's about to jump.'

'Oh…' they say, and there is a pause. 'Is that … for the *film*?'

I don't quite know what to say.

'No,' I say. 'It is just a very odd coincidence.'

Later, as the sun sets on another evening, I take a picture of Rooney – played by Danny Masterson – and text it to Wag. 'This is you!' reads the text. Wag phones up and just laughs excitedly for two minutes.

And then I turn around and am introduced to a striking-looking woman who smiles, broadly.

'This is Molly,' says Tiffany. 'She's playing Jim's ex.'

'Hello!' I say, and then I realise – blimey! It's Molly *Sims*! Actor! Model! Star of the *Sports Illustrated* Swimsuit edition 2000, 2001, 2002, 2004 and 2006! (I had to look that up – I promise you.) We start to chat, but really I am thinking, 'I wonder what Hanne's going to make of this?' And so I text her.

'Molly Sims is playing the character based on you,' I write. 'Please let me know if this is all right as if it is not I will have her sent home before she's had her tea.'

Moments later, her reply is in.

'I have considered it, and supermodel Molly Sims is fine with me.'

I am relieved.

Then I watch as Jim, Molly and everyone else shoot a scene. It's the scene in which Carl bumps into his ex for the first time in a long while … and she's with a new man. In the book, it ends in a three-way date – something which had made it through every draft of the script except the last. In the film, it ends with Carl's incredibly awkward exit through a bar.

Jim and Peyton film it three or four times but it's clear they think it needs a little more energy somewhere. On the fifth take, Jim tries something new … which ends up with him launching himself several feet into the air and landing flat on his back. It looks incredibly painful. But it's very funny.

When I next see him, he approaches with a huge bag of ice clutched to his ribs.

'Man … I'm in a liiiittle bit of pain,' he says.

'It looked ace,' I said. 'Although it also looked *painful* …'

'Sometimes you gotta just go for it,' he said. 'In every movie I've done, there's a moment where a little voice says, "Try it" … and so I do.'

And a little under a minute later, for reasons I'm still not sure about, we're talking about *American Idol* and *Celebrity Mastermind*.

Jim limps off to be told by his doctor that he's cracked several ribs.

I really hope they were recording.

It is my birthday, and Lizzie comes to LA. We head for the set. But Jim's ribs have proven too painful. There'll be little filming today. I introduce Lizzie around, and we chat to Bradley Cooper and to Molly Sims, and then we raid Kraft Services and steal bagels, but then I remember it's my birthday. We decide to head into town. Tiffany books us into the Chateau

Marmont, pretending we are major Hollywood powerplayers, and we order a bottle of champagne, and watch Terence Stamp wander by, and Dawn from *The Office* talk to a flamboyant Australian man. John Mayer is nearby, Anna Friel saunters around, and some of the guys from *Superbad* order a beer.

We start giggling, but then we remember that we are major Hollywood powerplayers, and so we stop giggling and put our sunglasses on and look cool.

Soon, my first trip is at an end. I feel as if I've made some great new friends. I'll be returning in a matter of weeks to witness more filming, and I'll be back for the wrap party, too ... but it still feels sad to go. It seems so strange that a little adventure I've had has led to such a big thing.

I say goodbye to Tiffany, and to Katterli, and to Marty, and to everyone else I've met, and I start to leave.

On the way to the car, I bump into Jim.

'So, you're off?'

'I am,' I say. 'Thanks for everything.'

We shake hands, and say goodbye, and then Jim gets into his big SUV, and Dotan drives him away.

As I get to the gates, I notice a group of tourists around me fall quiet. I decide to ignore it, but I can't, so I look up, and they're looking past me, in shock. One of them points. Another takes a picture. Another says, 'Is that ...?'

I look around, and Jim Carrey is looking at me from out of his SUV's window.

'And remember, Danny!' he shouts, a little *too* loudly. 'ANYTHING YOU NEED! YOU JUST *CALL* ME!'

He makes a little phone sign with his fingers, his window shoots up, and he's gone.

I laugh, but when I turn around, the group of tourists is looking at me, mouths agape. I smile, and begin to move off, and I realise Jim has done that just to embarrass me, and I smile again, but bright red and a little sweaty.

'Who *is* that guy?' says one of the tourists, and I break into a small jog.

A number of weeks later, I am sitting in my study in London, surrounded by props from the film. Shooting has finished, but Tiffany has sent me many souvenirs. I now have a *Yes Man* bag. A *Yes Man* diary. A *Yes Man* bottle opener. Jim has donated a *Yes Man* dressing gown. I look like I am starting a course.

And then I take the dressing gown off, because the cab is here, and today is a big day.

CUT TO:

INT. WARNER BROS. HQ, LONDON. DAY.

DANNY sits in a darkened cinema, alongside ROSIE
from Heyday. She has noticed he has no mustard
down his top, and she secretly approves. The
curtains on the screen begin to draw across it.
The lights come up. They've just finished watching the first cut of the new Warner Bros.
comedy, *Yes Man.*

ROSIE

So … what did you think?

CUT TO:

EXT. LONDON. DAY.

DANNY is pacing quickly down the street. He gets
his phone out. He dials LIZZIE. She answers.

DANNY

You there! Meet me at the pub!

CUT TO:

INT. THE PUB, NORTH LONDON. EVENING.

DANNY, LIZZIE, WAG and IAN are deep in conversation. They're laughing. DANNY is describing the
film in a little too much detail. He is pretending he is doing a wheelie on a motorbike.

Suddenly, his phone goes off. It's TIFFANY. She's
on the line with PEYTON.

                    TIFFANY (OOV)
          Hey, Yes Man … so … did you like it?

DANNY takes a deep breath. And then he smiles.

                       DANNY
          Yes.

So there you go. Another small Yes-based adventure, and another thing
that proves what can happen when you take the plunge, and you decide
to say *Yes*.

I hope you enjoyed this book. And I hope you enjoyed the film, if
you've seen it. I am sorry if the MAN AT BAR spoiled it for you, either
through being rubbish, or through being so totally watchable that you left
the cinema or put the DVD away thinking, 'Yes, that's all well and good
… but what happened to the MAN AT BAR? What's *that* guy's story?'

It is inevitable, and I think that Carrey knows that.

But the good thing is, you *know* that guy's story.

And here is where it ends.

For now, at least.

Si a Todo.

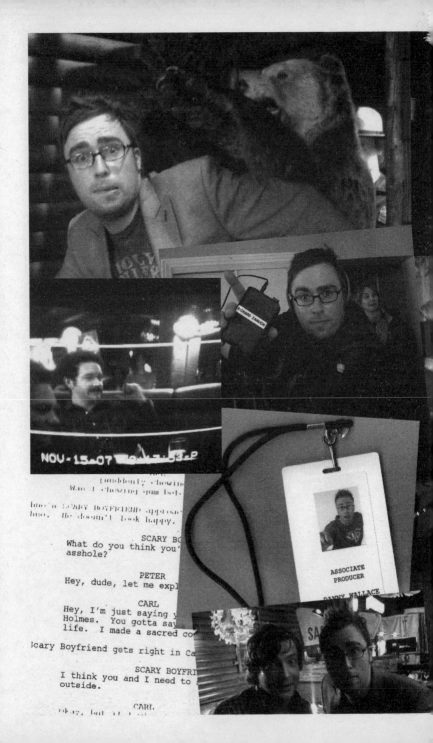